America
in the
Twentieth
Century

America
in the
Twentieth
Century
fourth edition

Frank Freidel
Harvard University

New York · Alfred A. Knopf

To the Memory of

WILLIAM BEST HESSELTINE

1902–1963

THIS IS A BORZOI BOOK
PUBLISHED BY ALFRED A. KNOPF, INC.

Fourth Edition
987654321
Copyright © 1960, 1964, 1965, 1970, 1976 by Frank Freidel

Library of Congress Cataloging in Publication Data

Freidel, Frank.
 America in the twentieth century.
 1. United States—History—20th century.   I. Title.
E714.F7   1976   973.9   75–23443
ISBN 0–394–31995–8

Manufactured in the United States of America

Preface

Both the rapid course of events and the equally swift flow of new contributions to historical scholarship have necessitated the thorough recasting of *America in the Twentieth Century* in this fourth edition. Not only does this new edition follow developments into the bicentennial years, but, in keeping with recent research and interests, it further explores demography; the role of the electorate; and especially the contributions of women, blacks, Indians, and Spanish-speaking Americans. To fit changing classroom requirements, the text is much more concise. There are a number of new illustrations. Theodore R. Miller has redesigned several maps, and charts and graphs have been brought up to date. Some two hundred fifty new books are cited in the bibliographies.

I am grateful to Richard N. Current and T. Harry Williams for their very substantial aid and to the scholars who have generously read and criticized parts of the manuscript of this and earlier editions. I also wish to thank users of the text—students as well as instructors—who have sent us corrections and suggestions. I appreciate the creative and careful editorial work of the staff of Alfred A. Knopf, Inc., particularly that of David Follmer, History Editor; Anna Marie Muskelly, Manuscript Editor; and Barbara Beidler, Editorial Assistant. My greatest debt, as always, is to my wife, Madeleine Freidel.

Frank Freidel

Cambridge, Massachusetts
July 1975

Contents

ILLUSTRATIONS

CHARTS

MAPS

Designed by Theodore R. Miller

America in the Twentieth Century

one

America Enters the Twentieth Century

The American people, proud of the rapid growth and modernization of their nation, entered the twentieth century with optimistic enthusiasm. They were proud of their achievements, confident they could quickly remedy the social ills that had accompanied recent changes. The future seemed to hold almost limitless potential for good. As yet there was no indication of the two world conflicts to come, nor of the threat of global destruction. So too, there was little hint that population increase or expansion and development within the United States represented anything but progress. A few conservationists and Malthusians might have had qualms, but to most Americans there seemed to be practically unlimited resources to provide endless growth and increase in living standards. Americans lived in a relatively untroubled era, an age of self-confident optimism.

Pride in past achievements and anticipation of the prosperous future did not blind the reform-minded to the problems the nation faced. Those who came to participate in the progressive movement were well aware that the years beginning with the Civil War, along with the rapid growth of industry, transportation, and cities, had brought maladjustments. Women, blacks, Indians, and Spanish-speaking Americans suffered discrimination inherited from an earlier, traditional way of life; immigrant minorities in urban ghettos also bore handicaps within the new order. The question was whether the progressive leaders, predominantly middle class, themselves limited in their viewpoints, could revitalize American institutions decisively enough to remedy these injustices, yet increase the material abundance from factories and fields. Could they nurture the best of both the old and the new Americas?

In 1900 the solutions to the problems of industrialization seemed relatively simple. Reformers believed that relatively minor readjustments could right the wrongs without losing the benefits of the machine age. As rapid industrial growth continued to bring basic changes, it was only a matter of time before the full complexities of the corporate, technical order would become apparent.

3

TOWARD A TECHNICAL MILLENNIUM

The growth of industry was not a phenomenon limited to America. It was a great shift in Western civilization, a cycle of change that, with all its accompanying blessings and evils, had swept England and Belgium decades earlier and that in the last third of the nineteenth century was remolding Imperial Germany and the United States. In other nations, as in this country, it raised questions concerning the relationships between the new industrialists and government, among capital and agriculture and labor; it brought the unprecedented growth of cities at home and stimulated the quest for areas for investment and markets overseas. Through the mass exploitation of mineral resources and stimulation of agricultural production, it made possible high living standards in the United States, helped spur population increases in other parts of the world—and by the second half of the century was creating new critical problems. Then limited resources and farm productivity began to make themselves felt. The arms race was born, and out of the new technology came quantities of the deadliest weapons ever known. Mankind had never before been confronted by such a potential for good or ill; and the United States played the key role in realizing this potential.

The modernization of the United States came with startling speed. Between 1860 and 1900 the country jumped from fourth to first place among the manufacturing nations of the world. There were scores of significant inventions or innovations that wrought remarkable changes: steel rails, bridges, skyscrapers, elevators, electric lights, electric street railways, gasoline engines, telephones, and new industrial and agricultural machines of every kind.

Technics promised even more change in the future. In 1904 Henry Adams, a detached sexagenarian, looked back over his own lifetime and recalled the development of the ocean steamer, the railway, and the telegraph. Might not the next nine or ten decades bring still more change? Adams wrote in his famous autobiography, *The Education of Henry Adams:*

> He could see that the new American—the child of incalculable coal-power, chemical power, electric power, and radiating energy, as well as of new forces yet undetermined—must be a sort of God compared with any former creation of nature. At the rate of progress since 1800, every American who lived into the year 2000 would know how to control unlimited power. He would think in complexities unimaginable to an earlier mind. He would deal with problems altogether beyond the range of earlier society.*

Whether the American would be able to control the power, to think in the requisite complexities, or to cope with the new problems seemed far from certain generations later. To well-educated men of the early 1900s,

* Henry Adams, *The Education of Henry Adams* (Boston: Houghton Mifflin, 1918) pp. 496–497.

State and Madison Streets, looking northeast, Chicago about 1905 (COURTESY CHICAGO HISTORICAL SOCIETY)

however, the complexities seemed less overwhelming. With a simple faith they regarded the scientific approach as the key to the ready solution of the manifold problems marring American civilization. They were hopeful that the nation was rushing toward a technical millennium. Most reformers still believed in Social Darwinism—the idea of the survival of the fittest applied to human society—and almost all of them considered this an optimistic faith. It meant in part that, through the application of science and technology, what was new and superior would drive out what was old and inferior. The scientists, engineers, and inventors would lead the way.

American technical achievements by the beginning of the twentieth century were impressive. The steel furnaces of Pittsburgh outproduced those of England and Germany and functioned with such efficiency and low cost that Carnegie could have sold steel rails at a profit in Birmingham, England. New manufacturing marvels of every kind were giving Americans their high living standard.

In the factories the new era meant acceleration of the introduction of labor-saving machinery. There was, for example, a bottle-making machine patented in 1903 that virtually eliminated the hand blowing of glass bottles and another machine that ended the manual production of window glass. The invention of a rotating kiln in 1899 made possible the cheap, standardized production of Portland cement at about the same time when a

The Wright Brothers making their first flight (OFFICIAL U.S. AIR FORCE PHOTO)

demand for paved highways was gaining momentum. A shift toward electric power was already well advanced. The first 5,000-horsepower alternating-current generator had been installed at Niagara Falls in 1895; within a few years steam generators of 100,000 horsepower were commonplace. Electricity was entering the home, but even more important it was becoming a great new source of efficient industrial motive power. In 1899 it ran only 5 percent of the machinery; by 1919, 55 percent; by 1925, 73 percent. Large-scale electric power also made possible electrolytic processes in the rapidly developing heavy chemical industry.

In the automobile and other industries new principles of scientific management found spectacular application. Scientific management began with the work of an engineer, Frederick Winslow Taylor, who helped revolutionize the machine-tool industry with carbon steel high-speed cutting edges. As soon as Taylor learned how to manufacture tools that could cut efficiently while running white hot, he began to insist that machinists operate their lathes at correspondingly fast speeds. Taylor was beginning to apply the same kind of scientific techniques to management as to machinery. At first he regarded workmen much as he did machines. Fewer and fewer men could perform simpler tasks at infinitely greater speed; if not, Taylor would discard them as unhesitatingly as he had discarded the poorer cutting steel.

The new system, "Taylorism," meant less need for skills among workmen and more monotonous tasks for them. At first organized labor rebelled

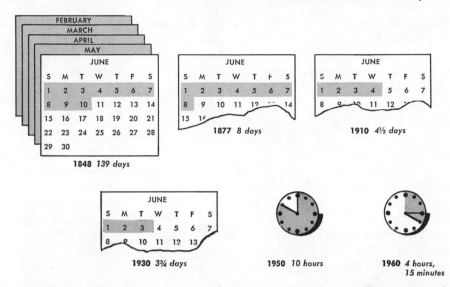

New York to San Francisco, 1848–1960 (Commercial or Regular Transportation)

and won at least a minor victory when it persuaded Congress in 1915 to forbid the introduction of efficiency systems into government arsenals or navy yards. But Taylor and his followers regarded themselves as scientific seekers after higher production and thus a higher living standard. He talked of the greatest good for the greatest number, including the workers. Indeed, if Taylorism was used to eliminate the intolerable inefficiencies in many industries, it could mean not only lower prices for consumers but also higher wages for employees. By the 1920s some unions recognized this and were cooperative.

American industrialists, usually ready to try new techniques, increasingly undertook Taylor scientific-management studies of workers' motions. They also brought scientists and engineers into their plants to engage in research for new tools and products. A few years earlier, any industrialist

Motor Vehicles, and Horses on Farms, 1900–1959

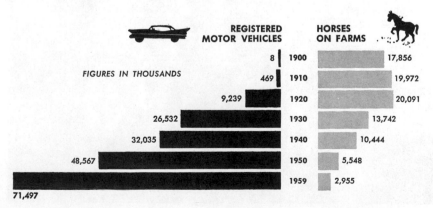

who established a laboratory would have been regarded as a crackpot. Now laboratories became accepted, partly because of the phenomenal success of some of the pioneering ones. There was, as every schoolboy could proudly cite, the industrial laboratory of Thomas A. Edison at Menlo Park, New Jersey, out of which had come the incandescent lamp, the phonograph, the motion picture, and scores of other devices. By 1913 Bell Telephone, Du Pont, General Electric, Eastman Kodak, and about fifty other companies had established laboratories with budgets totaling hundreds of thousands of dollars per year.

Out of these new methods and machines came mass production. It required the technology, raw materials, transportation, and markets that the United States could supply in the twentieth century. Precision manufacturing made possible the interchangeability of parts, even in assembling a machine as complicated as the automobile. Henry Ford began with stationary assembly, used earlier in manufacturing guns, clocks, and the like, then gradually changed by 1914 to the moving assembly line. This revolutionary technique cut the time for assembling a chassis from twelve-and-a-half hours to an hour and a half. While Ford raised the wages and lowered the hours of his workers, he cut the base price of his Model T car from $950 to $290. Other industrialists, following his example, soon adopted the assembly line and mass production in their plants also.

By 1914 American manufacturers were producing 76 percent more goods than in 1899. They were doing so with only 36 percent more workers and 13 percent more establishments. The greater output of goods reflected the rising living standards and the growth of population at home and increased markets abroad. The lower increase in the number of workers demonstrated the greater efficiency of the new technical age; the very low

The Ford Assembly Line (FORD ARCHIVES)

increase in the number of manufacturing establishments pointed to the rapid growth of industrial concentration.

THE PERILS OF MONOPOLY

Americans at the beginning of the twentieth century were ambivalent about industrialism. President Woodrow Wilson summed up their thinking when he remarked, "I am for big business and I am against the trusts." This meant that he was proud of the size and efficiency of the new corporations, but he was also fearful that if they could create monopolies, they would overcharge consumers. If corporations could stamp out competition, they could charge higher prices and make larger profits, factors that were often the basic reasons for the creation of trusts. (Their promoters, meanwhile, argued the reverse, that combinations led to greater efficiency, lower prices, and a higher living standard. Several recent economists have also agreed that the combinations were essentially beneficial.) Furthermore, the monopolists could use their great economic strength to wield great political power.

Despite all the agitation against trusts, American industry moved toward greater consolidation and monopoly. From 1887 to 1897 there had been only 86 industrial combinations, and the capitalization of all of these combined had been less than $1.5 billion. By 1904 there were 318 so-called trusts with a capitalization of over $7 billion. These combinations included basic industries such as copper, oil, and steel and industries directly affecting the consumer such as sugar and tobacco. Six financial groups controlled 95 percent of the nation's railway mileage. In the highly competitive steel industry twenty-one significant mergers between 1898 and 1901 prepared the way for a large-scale struggle between Andrew Carnegie and John Pierpont Morgan. When Carnegie announced plans for plants that might be ruinous to Morgan and his associates, they chose to buy him out at his own inflated figure of $447 million, and then they established the nation's first billion-dollar corporation, United States Steel. It was able to set standard prices for steel everywhere in the United States—prices from which none of the smaller steel companies dared to deviate.

Whatever pride Americans might have felt over the emergence of these industrial giants was mingled with serious misgivings. The United States Industrial Commission reported in 1902:

> In most cases the combination has exerted an appreciable power over prices, and in practically all cases it has increased the margin between raw materials and finished products. Since there is reason to believe that the cost of production over a period of years has lessened, the conclusion is inevitable that the combinations have been able to increase their profits.

Whether or not monopolies were to blame, prices were rising so rapidly between 1897 and 1913 that the cost of living went up about 35 percent.

The Rich and the Poor

For millions of Americans the economic system meant personal poverty and misery. There was a vast disparity between the incomes of the wealthy few and those of the poor multitudes. One percent of the families owned nearly seven-eighths of the wealth; seven-eighths of the families owned only one-eighth of the wealth. While a fifth of the families were comfortable or even rich, four-fifths lived precariously. A careful estimate in 1904 indicated that about one-eighth of the people, or a total of 10 million, lived in poverty.

At the top Carnegie had earned an estimated $23 million from his steel company alone in the year 1900. It had paid him an average of $10 million a year during the previous five years. On none of this did he pay a cent of income tax. Carnegie lived comparatively modestly and devoted his millions to worthy causes, but many of the very rich created sensational headlines through their ostentatious living. The Vanderbilts, like a clan of feudal barons, maintained, in addition to their many country estates, seven mansions in seven blocks on Fifth Avenue in New York City.

These wealthy few often spent incredible sums on parties, accounts of which fascinated but also angered readers of popular newspapers. The most notorious was the ball upon which Mrs. Martin Bradley spent $250,000; it created such a furor that she and her husband fled to exile in England. A less exceptional dinner, served on gold plates at the old Waldorf-Astoria in 1899, cost $10,000 for forty people, or $250 apiece. At this time $250 was six months' wages for the average workingman. In part, the millionaires were able to get their huge incomes because of the low cost of labor in

Andrew Carnegie about 1890

their factories, and they could afford their immense estates and townhouses because of the low cost of servants. Middle-class families also benefited from cheap labor. While they did not enjoy the great variety of household appliances of later generations, they were able with the aid of servants to maintain large homes.

Servants at least were entitled to meals and garret rooms. Working girls could not count upon even these. One woman in five worked, and often for wages as low as $6 or $8 per week. Unless a girl lived at home, it was almost impossible for her to exist upon these wages. The magazine writer O. Henry (William Sidney Porter) was reflecting the widespread indignation of contemporary Americans when he described in his short stories how strong the temptation was for these nearly starving girls to succumb to predatory men. Advocates of a minimum wage law to protect women created a sensation in Chicago by bringing several women to a hearing to testify that low pay and poverty had driven them to prostitution. Nevertheless, the Illinois legislature failed to enact the desired law.

Child labor, which had always existed in the United States, was becoming an increasingly serious problem by the early 1900s. At least 1.7 million children under sixteen were employed in factories and fields. Ten percent of the girls between ten and fifteen, and 20 percent of the boys, were gainfully employed. At least thirty-eight states had laws to protect children, but these typically applied only to children employed in factories, and they set a minimum age of twelve years and a maximum workday of ten hours. Sixty percent of the child workers were employed in agriculture, which could mean a twelve-hour day picking or hoeing in the fields. In the cotton mills of the South children working at the looms all night were kept awake by having cold water thrown in their faces. In canneries little girls cut fruits and vegetables sixteen hours a day. Some children worked at dangerous machines without safety devices. As these young workers became exhausted at the end of a long day, or night, they might become careless as they leaned over a loom to retie broken threads, have their hair caught in machinery, and be scalped as it suddenly started up again.

Industrial accidents were commonplace. For most laborers, whether children, women, or men, working conditions were far from ideal. Many women labored in dark, cold, dirty factories or sweatshops without restrooms or fire escapes. For men working conditions were even worse. As early as 1877 Massachusetts had required safety devices on elevators and machinery; some states also required mine inspection. But there was little effective enforcement of the laws, if indeed personnel for enforcement existed. In American factories and mines, and on the railroads, the accident rate was higher than in any other industrial nation in the world. As late as 1907 an average of twelve railroad men a week were killed. In factories not much had been done to prevent occupational diseases such as phosphorus and lead poisoning.

Nor was there economic incentive for employers to improve working conditions. Under the common law if an accident was caused, even in part, by the negligence of an employee himself or a fellow employee, the

Child at spindles in a Carolina textile mill, 1909 (PHOTOGRAPH BY LEWIS HINE; COLLECTION OF THE INTERNATIONAL MUSEUM OF PHOTOGRAPHY AT GEORGE EASTMAN HOUSE, ROCHESTER, N.Y.)

employer bore no responsibility. Even if the employer was liable under the common law, the courts were slow and often too expensive for the maimed worker or his widow. Until 1911 there were almost no state workmen's compensation laws.

Cheap labor was one of the reasons for high profits; unrestricted immigration was one of the reasons for cheap labor. At the same time that the big industrialists fought against a lowering of the tariff bars, they welcomed and even recruited the low-paid workers of Europe. While the flow of immigrants from northern and western Europe continued, a new flood, comprising about 72 percent of the total immigration betweeen 1900 and 1910, poured in from southern and eastern Europe. For the most part they were Italians, Slavs, and Jews. In the year 1905 over 1.2 million arrived. In most big cities of the North, immigrants and their children outnumbered the native-born. Bewildered at being thrust into an alien culture, living under conditions far below the level of native Americans (except blacks), they filled most of the backbreaking unskilled jobs in the new heavy industries, on the railroads, and around the cities. The Jews, many of who brought their skill with the needle, went into the garment trade, but under similarly wretched circumstances.

The American Federation of Labor (whose president, Samuel Gompers, was himself an immigrant) fought to cut off this flood of cheap, unskilled foreign labor, which was said to keep wages down and hamper

"The Steerage" by Alfred Stieglitz (COURTESY MISS GEORGIA O'KEEFFE FOR THE ALFRED STIEGLITZ ESTATE; COLLECTION MUSEUM OF MODERN ART)

unionization. Many Americans, both conservative and progressive, were susceptible to the popular dogma of Anglo-Saxon superiority and joined in the anti-immigration movement. They feared the high birth rate among immigrants as compared with the low birth rate among natives in the higher-income groups; Theodore Roosevelt warned darkly against "race suicide." They blamed the squalor of the slums and the power of the political bosses largely upon the immigrants and felt that immigration restriction could bring improvement. In 1907 they succeeded in stopping the immigration of Japanese to the agricultural lands of the Pacific Coast through the gentleman's agreement that Roosevelt negotiated with the

Japanese government. A series of restrictive laws prohibited various undesirables, ranging from ex-convicts to alcoholics, from entering the United States. In 1917, over the veto of President Wilson, Congress passed a law setting up a literacy test as a means of reducing the number of immigrants.

For all those, immigrant or native, who were crowded into city tenements, life was far from enviable. Jacob Riis, the crusading journalist, thought that by 1900 the worst of the New York slums were gone. In their place were a scattering of parks and playgrounds; in some of the worst remaining areas there were privately financed settlement houses to aid the poor. Nevertheless, for millions of city dwellers housing was barely tolerable. In New York City, two-thirds of the 3.5 million people lived in tenement houses. Most of these had direct light and air in only four rooms of the fourteen on each floor.

Submerged Minorities

Even less conspicuous and more helpless were the submerged minorities, the American Indians, Mexican Americans, and blacks. They were the objects of the solicitude of some social workers, but the years of progressive reform largely passed them by.

For Indians it was the era when a considerable part of their remaining reservation lands was being wrested away from them and they were being forced into pauperism. The purpose of white reformers was quite the opposite, to transform Indians into middle class people like themselves. Therefore (with the enthusiastic cooperation of land speculators), they had backed the Dawes Act of 1887, which authorized distributing tribal lands in 160-acre parcels to individual Indians. Since Indians often did not know how to farm, nor wished to learn, white ranchers often leased these holdings. Speculators frequently gained title to the reservation lands left over after distribution. Further legislation in the early 1900s hastened the process of breaking down tribal landholdings and tribal authority in the expectation that these acts would hasten the integration of Indians into White America. The outcome, concludes one historian of the Indians, Wilcomb E. Washburn, was quite different:

> The blow was less economic than psychological and even spiritual. A way of life had been smashed; a value system destroyed. Indian poverty, ignorance and ill health were the results. The admired order and sense of community . . . were replaced by the easily caricatured features of rootless, shiftless, drunken outcasts, so familiar to the reader of the early twentieth-century newspapers.*

The lot of the Spanish-speaking minority in the Southwest continued to be as difficult as it had been, except for a privileged few, since American annexation a half-century earlier. By 1900 the demand for cheap labor in the Southwest was leading to the importation of numbers of Mexican-

* Wilcomb E. Washburn, *Red Man's Land—White Man's Law* (New York: Scribner, 1971), pp. 75–76.

Mulberry Street, New York City (LIBRARY OF CONGRESS)

Sioux Indian children from the Dakotas arriving at Hampton Institute, Virginia, for training (CARPENTER CENTER FOR THE VISUAL ARTS, HARVARD UNIVERSITY)

American workers. They found it difficult to support large families on their dollar-a-day wages, crowded into slums as wretched as those in Eastern cities. A social worker reported, "When the heavy rains come in winter, imagine those shacks and tents that have no floors! Sick women lie on damp mattresses which are embedded in mud. . . . And the household stays wet till the sun shines again. Fortunately the sun is usually shining in Los Angeles."

Blacks by the turn of the century had lost almost all of the civil rights they had gained during Reconstruction. Reformers in the Southern states, ostensibly to end political corruption in the competition for black votes, disenfranchised remaining groups of black voters. Through one or another device they circumvented the Fifteenth Amendment. One of the most frequently used tactics was the grandfather clause, a proviso that one could not vote if one's grandfather had been ineligible to vote; another was the exaction of a poll tax, which served also to keep numbers of poor whites from voting. The number of registered black voters in Louisiana fell from 130,000 in 1896 to 1,300 in 1904. States also passed numerous new Jim Crow laws to enforce segregation. In *Plessy* v. *Ferguson* in 1896 the Supreme Court sanctioned these laws as not being in violation of the Fourteenth Amendment provided the facilities for blacks were separate but equal.

There were few indications of black advancement under these severe legal handicaps. Lynchings had declined from a high point of 235 in 1892 to 50 or 60 a year in the early 1900s, but neither Theodore Roosevelt nor his successors sought federal antilynching legislation. Black literacy rose from 65 percent to 70 percent in the first decade of the century, but schools for black children, while separate, continued to be gravely inferior. As late as 1910, few more than 8,000 black youths attended high school.

While the great majority of blacks continued to live in the South under conditions that had changed little since Reconstruction, a trickle of migration to the Northern cities was beginning. By 1900, there were 70,000 blacks in New York, 35,000 in Chicago, and enough in Washington, D.C., to make it the world's largest black city. "The great majority of the Negroes of New York live in poverty," a social worker pointed out, "Negroes pay more and get less for their money than any other tenants."

THE HUMAN COST

Even middle-class Americans felt that they had to pay some of the human cost of the established order of things. Consumers did not receive any protection from insanitary or harmful foods and drugs. The advance of science brought, along with the marvels, many harmful preservatives and adulterants. Much meat and milk was processed or sold under revoltingly dirty conditions. Medicines, purportedly cures for almost any disease from tuberculosis to cancer, contained little but bright coloring, a bitter flavor, and a copious lacing of alcohol. Syrups did, as they advertised, soothe babies because of the narcotics they contained.

Along with these immediate dangers to the American public were the long-range threats implicit in the reckless exploitation of natural resources, the wasteful and destructive cutting of timber, the pouring of industrial poisons into streams, and the overgrazing or improper cultivation of fields. Hillsides eroded to clog rivers and increase the threat of alternating drought and flood.

"Our life contains every great thing, and contains it in rich abundance," the new progressive President, Wilson, pointed out in his first inaugural in 1913. The irony was that with the good had come unnecessary evil:

> With riches has come inexcusable waste. We . . . have not stopped to conserve the exceeding bounty of nature. . . . We have been proud of our industrial achievements, but we have not hitherto stopped thoughtfully enough to count the human cost. . . . The great Government we love has too often been made use of for private and selfish purposes, and those who used it had forgotten the people.

two

The Progressive
Movement

In the early years of the twentieth century a political movement called progressivism grew rapidly in size and force. It became the rallying point of a number of Americans of differing backgrounds and views who united in believing that the wrongs that had come with rapid modernization must be righted. Progressives differed among themselves in both their aims and their methods. To some the main evil was monopoly; to others it was corruption and a lack of democracy in government; to still others it was the inequalities forced upon women, minorities, and the poor; and so on. Depending upon the issue, various groups combined and cooperated or divided and worked against one another. For example, while some favored imperialism, others opposed it. Progressivism was an aggregate of causes rather than a single movement. Nevertheless, most progressives shared two important convictions. They believed that the people ought to have more influence in government and the special interests less. They also thought that the government ought to be stronger, more active, and more efficient in serving the public welfare.

In many respects progressivism was a continuation and coalescing of the many reform movements that had been active in the last decades of the nineteenth century. There were those who had sought clean government as Liberal Republicans, Mugwumps, or Cleveland Democrats; there were the followers of Henry George in the single-tax movement; there were those who had been striving to bring better living conditions in the slums, who formed the social-justice movement; and there were advocates of women's rights, temperance, and the social gospel.

There were similarities, too, between much that the Populists had advocated and the progressive program, so much so that William Allen White, a Kansas newspaper editor and ardent progressive, once commented that the progressive leaders had "caught the Populists in swimming and stole all of their clothing except the frayed underdrawers of free silver." But progressivism and Populism differed in important respects. The People's party members had been mostly distressed farmers of the Southern and Great Plains states and miners in the Rocky Mountain states. Their leaders were quite separate from the subsequent leadership of the progressive movement; White had been a vigorous foe of Populism. Some former Populists voted for progressivism, but progressive ranks included men and women from all parts of the country, especially the Northeast and Midwest. Prominent among the progressives were persons of the urban middle class. The progressives had a broader concept of both the electorate and the public welfare than that of the Populists.

Both Republicans and Democrats were active in the progressive movement. It spread across party lines, and in 1912 a third party, splitting away from the Republicans, called itself the Progressive party. Each party had its own special brand of progressivism. Those in the Democratic party continued to favor a states'-rights approach and were more willing to place limitations upon the role of government. Republicans continued, in the Hamiltonian tradition, to be more receptive to strengthening of the federal government and its regulatory powers.

Within each of the major parties the progressives struggled for control against traditional conservative leaders. The split in the Republican party in 1912 was an indication of how serious that struggle could become. Yet to some degree the progressives succeeded in making each party a vehicle for reform, as they carried the fight from the city halls to the statehouses to the houses of Congress and to the White House.

Progressivism became a new factor in the two major parties. Already in the late nineteenth century they were split along regional, urban, ethnic, and religious lines. Through quantification techniques historians have delineated these divisions in some states and regions. Thus, in general, the Republican party in the North and West included most voters of white, English-speaking Protestant heritage, together with small numbers of urban blacks. In the 1890s the Republicans became the majority party when voters came to prefer the more positive Republican response to the depression of the 1890s to either the conservative measures of the Democratic President Grover Cleveland or the silver panacea that William Jennings Bryan offered in 1896. Among the Republicans there were some Protestants of immigrant background; in Wisconsin it was the Scandinavians within the party who made it progressive despite the stalwart leanings of the Yankees. Robert M. La Follette took advantage of the upsurge of progressivism in Wisconsin to become its leader and a national progressive Republican figure. It was a New York Republican, whose family had been many generations in the United States, Theodore Roosevelt, who brought progressivism to the White House.

The Democratic party, strong in the South and in some Northern cities, combined Protestant agrarianism with an appeal to Catholics of immigrant origins. Progressive leadership in the party most often came, as among Republicans, from young lawyers and businessmen, who in many states, such as Alabama, were quite different from the earlier Populist leaders. Yet in Colorado the Democratic party absorbed the former Popu-

Robert M. La Follette campaigning in Wisconsin (STATE HISTORICAL SOCIETY
OF WISCONSIN)

lists to become the dominant party in the state. Bryan, who in 1896 had
stolen the rhetoric of the Populists, became in the early 1900s the great
national progressive leader among the Democrats until, in 1912, Wilson
outshadowed him. Another source of Democratic progressivism was the
cities, where in some instances members of city organizations, such as Alfred E. Smith and Robert Wagner of New York, became effective fighters
for reform.

The Urban Progressives

Progressive leaders in the cities were largely members of the urban middle
class and were to a remarkable extent college-educated and self-employed
professional men or small businessmen, of native-born Protestant background. For the most part they were about forty years old, financially
secure civic leaders who had earlier been McKinley Republicans.

Following these leaders was a middle class, like them still clinging to
the traditional agrarian values, but caught up in the social whirlpool of
the new industrial age. The older segment of the middle class—the independent professional and businessmen from which such a high proportion
of progressive leaders came—somewhat more than doubled between 1870
and 1910. This meant it grew as rapidly as the population as a whole,
which increased about two-and-a-third times. The working class (including
farm laborers) trebled; farmers and farm tenants doubled. But there was
another group, a new middle class of white-collar workers—the clerks, sales-
people, and technicians who worked for corporations or service enterprises.

William Jennings Bryan in action, 1908 (LIBRARY OF CONGRESS)

This group increased almost eight times, from 756,000 to 5,609,000 people, thus reaching a number almost double the size of the older middle class.

While members of this new white-collar class did not provide leadership for the progressive movement, they did help to provide it with voting strength. Political action was their only outlet for economic protest, since they did not belong to unions or trade associations. Often it was they, on their fixed salaries, who were worst caught by rising prices. And basically, like the older middle class, they were urbanites who still expressed the emotions of their rural backgrounds. These two groups, the white-collar class and the older middle class, combined to form the respectable element of the towns and cities and, along with many of the more successful farmers and some of the laborers, were ready to accept the new progressive creed.

Middle-class people were frightened by urban political bosses, not only because of the latters' corrupt ties with the industrial moguls but also because of their hold over the ignorant laboring masses (often largely immigrants) of the cities. Moreover, these middle-class people had some fear of the new rising labor unions. Populist farmers had shared these suspicions of the moguls and the masses. One of the Populist papers had said the purpose of the party was to serve as a "bulwark against the anarchy of the upper and lower scums of society." Progressives continued to espouse the same prejudices.

Theodore Roosevelt in his *Autobiography* has stated clearly the reasoning that led him, a conservative young plutocrat of the upper middle-class gentry, to enter politics. The men Roosevelt knew best, cultivated clubmen, warned him that politics was a cheap affair of saloon keepers and horsecar conductors, which gentlemen should shun. "I answered," Roosevelt wrote, "that if this were so it merely meant that the people I knew did not belong to the governing class, and that the other people did—and that I intended to be one of the governing class."

If Roosevelt and others like him, with intelligence and social position, were to win a wide following (as the Mugwumps had not), they would have to modify their conservatism. And so they did. They still clung fundamentally to laissez-faire economics as their guiding star, but as a means of returning to it they came to advocate government intervention of varying kinds and degrees. They had aristocratic tendencies and certainly had shown no love for the masses, but they became the advocates of more popular government. Above all, they made an appeal not on economic grounds but on those of morality. Most progressives had a simple faith in returning to the old law or in passing new laws. In greater democratization they saw the way back to the old American utopia, which of course had never been realized. "The way to have a Golden Age," one progressive novelist wrote, "is to elect it by a . . . [secret] ballot."

By contrast with these views, the business titans and the political bosses, not the progressives, were the realists of the era. It was they who had seen the opportunities implicit in a nation of growing cities still governed by agrarian laws. George Washington Plunkett, the sage of Tammany Hall, was in many respects more pragmatic than many a progressive who had listened to lectures of William James. Plunkett asserted that the political machines were all agreed on "the main proposition that when a man works in politics, he should get something out of it." And so the members of the machines dispensed recreation, coal, shoes, and jobs to the immigrant masses in return for their loyalty at the polls; and they dispensed large privileges—most often franchises—to the business interests in return for huge gifts. Boss Charles Murphy of Tammany was quite ready to accept these gifts, but he was also realist enough to allow Tammany legislators to vote for social reforms when these became popular among the constituents. Murphy, who was personally puritanical, would not knowingly let his supporters fatten themselves on graft from saloons and prostitutes, but he made the Pennsylvania Railroad pay dearly for the privilege of coming into New York City.

To progressives graft was graft and immoral. They, as God-fearing people, felt a personal responsibility to attack it and to legislate into existence a new moral order. It was the cult of the hour, White explained, to "believe in the essential nobility of man and the wisdom of God." Frederic C. Howe wrote:

> Early assumptions as to virtue and vice, goodness and evil remained in my mind long after I had tried to discard them. . . . It explains the nature of our reforms, the regulatory legislation in morals and economics. . . . Missionaries and battleships, anti-saloon leagues and Ku Klux Klans, Wilson and Santo Domingo are all part of that evangelistic psychology that makes America what she is.

Howe was correct; each of these was a part of progressivism. Yet scarcely any progressive would have accepted them all. Out of all these varying drives there emerged two great streams of progressivism: the demand for political reform and the movement for social justice.

THE CRUSADE FOR SOCIAL JUSTICE

The social-justice movement was already well advanced by the turn of the century. It had its roots in European, especially English, reform movements. Almost every prominent English reformer visited the United States, and conversely almost every American progressive leader fell under the influence of the British. Jane Addams had worked at the newly established Toynbee Hall in the Limehouse section of London; in 1889 she returned to the United States to establish Hull House in Chicago. Settlement houses, slum clearance agitation, and a great variety of other English reforms quickly had their counterparts in the United States.

The Salvation Army, which had recently come to the United States from England, by 1900 boasted a corps of 3,000 officers and 20,000 privates. It offered aid as well as religion to the dregs of the cities. So did ministers, priests, and rabbis who by the nineties were working in the slums. These men were united in their determination to improve the existence of the miserable people around them. "One could hear human virtue cracking and crushing all around," Walter Rauschenbusch wrote of Hell's Kitchen in New York City. To him the way of salvation for these human souls seemed to be a Christian reform of the social and economic system. Darwinism to Rauschenbusch meant working for a better order on earth. "Translate the evolutionary themes into religious faith," he asserted, "and you have the doctrine of the Kingdom of God." Thus many an American Protestant minister arrived at the social gospel. Catholics such as Father John Augustine Ryan joined in the fight for social justice under the authority they found in Pope Leo XIII's encyclical *Rerum Novarum*. It declared that "a small number of very rich men have been able to lay upon the masses of the poor a yoke little better than slavery itself. . . . No practical solution of this question will ever be found without the assistance of religion and the church."

Close behind the ministry were middle-class and upper-class women. In the nineties many of them had seemed restless and discontented, reading more widely than their husbands or brothers, joining literary circles and women's clubs. By the early 1900s these clubs were beginning to display a remarkable growth. The membership of the General Federation of Women's Clubs increased from 50,000 in 1898 to over 1 million by 1914. In the new era the clubwomen agitated for the ballot and legal equality for themselves and for a wide array of reforms on behalf of children and workingwomen. They took an especially keen interest in improving standards of public health and safety. At the 1904 convention of the General Federation, the president-elect proclaimed to her fellow members, "I have an important piece of news to give you. Dante is dead. He has been dead for several centuries, and I think it is time we dropped the study of his *Inferno* and turned our attention to our own." The clubwomen heeded her words. On the local level in particular they provided a strong impetus toward social justice. One president of the National Association of Manufacturers urged businessmen to forbid their wives and daughters to join women's clubs in which they might be converted to reforms that endangered profits. He would have been even more alarmed had he known how often these upper- and middle-class women combined with women of the working class in organizations such as the Women's Trade Union League to fight for better working conditions for women. Numerous women also became skilled lobbyists persuading legislators to enact social-justice legislation.

A small but significant segment of the social-justice movement was a group of experts, both men and women, who gathered data and statistics on the need for reform. Some of these were social-welfare workers who wrote for *Survey* magazine. Others were frustrated crusaders working for federal or state agencies. In many states before 1900 there were bureaus of labor that could and did, as in the case of Illinois, compile great quantities of data on deplorable working and living conditions. They could not act directly to ameliorate the conditions, but they could present evidence that dramatized the need for reform. On the federal level the Industrial Commission undertook a searching investigation of the trusts as they had operated up to 1902; subsequently the Bureau of Corporations carried on similar studies; and because of its investigative powers the new Department of Commerce and Labor seemed to Theodore Roosevelt to be a virtual Department of Sociology. In conservation the same technique was used. It was a scientific age in which progressives felt that through research they could arrive at the correct answers. But research alone could not gather a great force of public opinion behind the progressive movement. That was the task of the muckrakers and the politicians.

The Muckrakers Publicize Injustices

The muckrakers were the many journalists who dramatized the need for reform by writing exposures of what was unsavory in business and government. They began to attract attention toward the end of 1902 and were at their peak of popularity in 1906. The literature of exposure had a long history, from the *Harper's Weekly* crusade against the Tweed Ring through Henry Demarest Lloyd's denunciation of Standard Oil in *Wealth Against Commonwealth* (1894). What was new was the scale of the revelations and the rapid attraction of a wide audience. It began almost by accident in about ten of the new popular magazines, selling for ten or fifteen cents, which were then building mass circulation. *McClure's*, already a magazine of broad appeal, began publishing Ida Tarbell's series on Standard Oil, which McClure had not commissioned as an exposure and which the authoress did not write to start a crusade. Coincidentally, McClure sent a new editor, Lincoln Steffens, out to see the country firsthand; this experience led Steffens to begin a series on municipal corruption.

At the height of the muckraking movement ten journals with a combined circulation of about 3 million were devoting considerable space to the literature of exposure. In addition, some books such as Upton Sinclair's *The Jungle* (1906), an exposure of the meat-packing industry, sold over 100,000 copies. Many newspapers, most notably the New York *World* and the Kansas City *Star*, printed articles by muckrakers. It was exciting for a while, but by 1912 it was over. This was partly because of the hostility of business, which at times withheld credit and advertising from the muckraking magazines, but probably it was more because the public had become fatigued. After nine years of sensationalism, there was little new to whet the public appetite. In fact, it is rather surprising that the excitement continued as long as it did.

The Crusade Against City Bosses

Steffens entitled his series on municipal corruption *The Shame of the Cities*, and indeed shame was what civic-minded progressives felt. They tried to wrest control of their city governments away from the machines, reorganize the governments scientifically, and use them as instruments of economic and social reform.

Arrayed in opposition were the bosses, and behind them were those interests so abhorrent to the progressives, the saloons, brothels, and various businesses that could gain more from the bosses than from clean government. Allied with the bosses were some newspapers that ridiculed the progressives as either kill-joys or scoundrels. Finally, there was the great constituency of city working people, mostly of immigrant origins. To them the bosses were friends who could be counted upon to help them when they violated the law in some minor way or were in need of jobs or food. Progressives, on the other hand, seemed to be do-gooders who were trying to take away the saloon—the poor man's club—and to deprive him of his amusements from prize fighting to Sunday baseball.

Many progressives, finding it difficult to grasp the relationship between the bosses and their constituents, saw the problem in simple moral and legal terms. Bad government, they thought, came from bad charters. Reformers should seize the municipal governments and, by remaking the charters, usher in the urban millennium.

Municipal reform began in response to a tragedy in Galveston, Texas, where the old, ineffective government broke down in the wake of a tidal wave. The citizens replaced it with a commission of five, whose members were jointly enacting ordinances and singly running the main city departments by 1908. In 1907 Des Moines, Iowa, adopted the commission plan with modifications to make it more democratic, and other cities followed. Another variation was the city-manager plan, which placed a trained expert, similar to the manager of a business, in charge of the city, and made him responsible to the commission or the mayor and council. Staunton, Virginia, hired a city manager in 1908, and the new device attracted national attention when Dayton, Ohio, adopted it in 1913 to speed rehabilitation after a serious flood. By the end of the progressive era approximately 400 cities were operating under commissions, and another 45 under city managers.

Whether through old or new city machinery, progressives fought to destroy economic privilege on the municipal level. This meant primarily trying to prevent the sale of streetcar franchises or to force exorbitantly high fares downward. The most notable of the reform mayors was Tom Johnson of Cleveland, who had invented the streetcar fare box. He was a traction magnate converted to the ideas of Henry George. As mayor, Johnson fought to raise the ridiculously low assessments upon railroad and utility property, introduce city planning, and above all, lower streetcar fares to three cents. After his defeat and death his brilliant aide, Newton D. Baker, was elected mayor and helped maintain Cleveland's position as the best-governed American city.

Many of the urban gains of progressivism were permanent, but in some cities, as soon as progressives relaxed their efforts, the old forces recaptured the city halls. In other municipalities state control over city government made reform almost impossible. Cities derived all of their powers from the state, and many state legislatures granted new charters only reluctantly or controlled a large city within the state through special legislation. In the state of New York, which functioned this way, the reform mayor of Schenectady complained: "Whenever we try to do anything, we run up against the charter. It is an oak charter, fixed and immovable." Consequently, a municipal home-rule movement spread, to try to obtain state laws allowing cities to write their own charters. Much of the difficulty with state legislatures was even more serious. Many a reformer, such as Johnson in Cleveland or Joseph W. Folk in St. Louis, found himself helpless in the cities because the trail of corruption led back to the legislature.

IN THE STATEHOUSE

Hiram Johnson in California, Folk in Missouri, and other progressives moved on from the cities, where they had been crusading district attorneys, to become progressive governors. Only by taking this step could Folk, for example, break the bosses. Johnson's avowed purpose as governor of California was to end the political hold of the Southern Pacific Railroad upon the state.

At the state level progressives enacted a wide array of legislation to increase the power of crusading governors, give the people more direct control over the government, and decrease the functions of legislators. These ill-paid, relatively inconspicuous men were being exposed by muckrakers as the villains in many states. White wrote about Missouri in *McClure's* in December 1905: "The legislature met biennially, and enacted such laws as the corporations paid for, and such others as were necessary to fool the people, and only such laws were enforced as party expediency demanded." This view of the legislatures led progressives to circumscribe and circumvent them in almost every conceivable way. The most important of the devices, the initiative and the referendum, were first enacted in Oregon in 1902 as a result of the quiet but persistent advocacy of the secretary of several voters' organizations, William S. U'Ren. The initiative enabled voters to short-circuit the legislature and vote upon measures at general elections; the referendum forced the return of laws from the legislature to the electorate. By 1918 twenty states had adopted these schemes.

Progressives also tried to obtain better officials. By means of the direct primary they tried to eliminate machine choice of candidates; it was first instituted in Mississippi in 1902 and adopted in some form by every state by 1915. Unfortunately, machines often dominated the primaries.

Another way in which many progressives hoped to thwart the machines was by giving the vote to women, who presumably would bring purity to politics. For decades the suffrage had been the main objective of the women's rights movement, since women felt that once they had obtained this right, they could vote in their other rights. As early as 1897 Colorado women obtained the right to vote, at a time when those of Kentucky still could not legally even make wills. By 1914 women could vote in twelve states, all west of the Mississippi; in 1916 Montana elected the first woman to the House of Representatives. During World War I, Congress finally gave in to the suffragists, and in 1919 the Nineteenth Amendment was added to the Constitution. It seemed to make no spectacular change in voting patterns.

A more controversial and less often used device for improving officials was the recall, which made possible their removal at a special election to be called after sufficient numbers of the electorate had signed petitions. This became a national issue when President William Howard Taft vetoed a

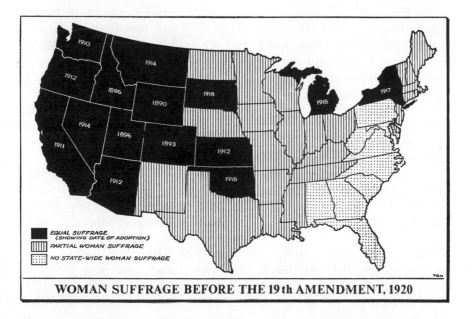

WOMAN SUFFRAGE BEFORE THE 19th AMENDMENT, 1920

Suffragette being arrested for picketing the White House, July 4, 1917
(NATIONAL ARCHIVES)

bill admitting Arizona as a state because its constitution authorized the recall of judges. Horrified conservatives approved of the veto, but soon after Arizona entered the Union without the offensive provision, the state's voters restored it.

Undoubtedly, all these devices did bring about a greater degree of democratization. Progressives used them to obtain control of states and then eradicated corruption and passed reform legislation. La Follette in Wisconsin obtained firm regulation of railroads, compensation for workmen injured in industrial accidents, and graduated taxation of inheritances. Charles Evans Hughes in New York obtained a commission to regulate public utilities. In New Jersey, when Wilson, fresh from the presidency of Princeton University, became governor in 1911, he obtained from the legislature a substantial array of measures to transform the state from the backward "mother of trusts" into a model of progressivism.

Much of the sorely needed legislation came only late and after a difficult struggle. New York, for example, adopted factory safety laws only when shocked into action by the Triangle Shirtwaist Factory fire (1911), which trapped and killed 148 persons, most of them young women, in New York City.

Progressive legislators in the states ran the risk that the Supreme Court would invalidate their handiwork. The Court made one great, although temporary, shift toward progressivism. This came in 1908 when Louis D. Brandeis argued in support of an Oregon law to limit women workers to a

Governor Charles Evans Hughes
(HARVARD COLLEGE LIBRARY)

ten-hour day. He presented a brief in which he devoted only 2 of 104 pages to the legal precedents and the remainder to proofs that Oregon's police power was necessary to protect the health and general welfare of the mothers and thus of all mankind. The Supreme Court accepted this argument and thus moved toward the sociological jurisprudence that Dean Roscoe Pound of the Harvard Law School had been deevloping. This, Pound explained, was intended to adjust "principles and doctrines to human conditions they are to govern rather than to assumed first principles."

Progressives seeking state reforms looked not only to the Supreme Court but also to Congress and the White House. Here obviously rested the ultimate power for the control of the many problems that crossed state lines. Reformers obtained from Congress in 1910 several laws to reinforce state legislation. The Webb-Kenyon Act, passed over Taft's veto, prohibited the interstate shipment of liquor into dry areas. The Mann Act outlawed the interstate transportation of "white slaves" and thus helped in the fight to break up prostitution syndicates, one of the main sources of underworld income.

At the state level progressives fought to liberalize the United States Senate through the direct election of senators. State legislatures were occasionally open to bribery, and much too often they elected conservatives who did not represent the public choice. David Graham Phillips in his senatorial articles, "The Treason of the Senate," scourged the body as a rich men's club; a California senator replied that there were only ten millionaires in the Senate.

Twins when they began to take modified milk (CARPENTER CENTER FOR THE VISUAL ARTS, HARVARD UNIVERSITY)

By 1902 the House of Representatives had already passed resolutions five times for a constitutional amendment for the direct election of senators; each time the Senate had blocked the amendment. Impatient progressives in various states provided in effect for direct election by means of preferential votes for senators; the legislatures were obligated to choose the candidate whom the voters preferred. By 1912 twenty-nine states had adopted these devices. In 1911 Governor Wilson of New Jersey gained renown by blocking the legislative election of a party boss. At the same time, in New York, Franklin D. Roosevelt, just twenty-nine, won his political spurs by leading legislative insurgents against Tammany's hand-picked candidate, a Buffalo traction magnate. That same year, the Senate ousted one of its members, Boss William E. Lorimer of Chicago, for vote buying. In the wake of the public indignation that followed, the Senate in 1912 passed the Seventeenth Amendment, for the direct election of senators, and by 1913 the requisite number of states had ratified it. The new amendment did not startlingly modify the nature of the Senate, since most progressive states had already elected senators of a new mettle.

Nor did another progressive reform measure, the preferential presidential primary, have much consequence. This was begun in Oregon in 1910 and spread to twenty states by 1920, but it by no means eliminated the maneuvering in conventions. Its main effect was to provide a series of statewide popularity contests among leading candidates in the months before the convention.

PROGRESSIVES AND BLACKS

The blacks were the forgotten people of the progressive era. In some respects the plight of black Americans worsened, and in the Southern states, progressives were in part to blame. Progressive leaders there concluded that political reform was hopeless as long as blacks remained potential voters, and they joined in the popular demand to remove blacks finally and completely from politics.

In the North some white progressives and black leaders combined into two enterprises, one to obtain better working and living conditions and the other to fight for civil rights. The Urban League, founded in 1910, was acceptable to those whites who felt, as Booker T. Washington had suggested, that first blacks must obtain education for the trades, as he had at Hampton Institute. Others, although ready to work also for civil rights, wanted to improve the appalling conditions in black ghettos. Within the Urban League both blacks and whites worked to help blacks obtain better housing, recreational facilities, and employment. They tried to break down the color line in labor unions.

A number of well-educated young blacks, under the leadership of William E. B. Du Bois, a black historian and sociologist with a Harvard Ph.D., openly challenged Washington as the spokesman for blacks. They

Booker T. Washington (HARVARD COLLEGE LIBRARY)

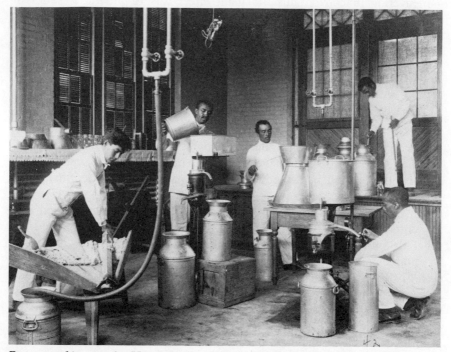

Butter making at the Hampton Institute Dairy (CARPENTER CENTER FOR THE VISUAL ARTS, HARVARD UNIVERSITY)

W. E. B. Du Bois (HARVARD UNIVERSITY LIBRARY)

felt that blacks must, above all, fight for the restoration of their civil rights. In 1905 they met at Niagara Falls, Canada (because no hotel on the American side of the falls would rent them rooms), and launched what they called the Niagara Movement. In 1909, after a race riot in Springfield, Illinois, they met on Lincoln's Birthday to organize, together with white progressives, the National Association for the Advancement of Colored People (NAACP). White men held most of the offices, but Du Bois, its director of publicity and research, was the guiding spirit. In the years after 1909 the NAACP led the drive for equal rights, using as its principal weapon lawsuits in the federal courts. In 1915 it won a first major victory when the Supreme Court invalidated an Oklahoma statute, typical in Southern states, aimed at disfranchising descendants of slaves by means of the previously mentioned grandfather clause. This was a first step toward renewed civil rights for blacks.

three

Theodore Roosevelt: The Emergence of a Modern President

A strong, dynamic President was an essential factor in obtaining effective reform. So reasoned many of the leading exponents of progressivism. They were frustrated at the levels of the city hall, the statehouse, and even the national Capitol in Washington. As a consequence, although they ardently sought to extend democratic institutions, they also wanted a strong progressive in the White House to make full use of presidential powers. Some of them looked specifically to Theodore Roosevelt, who—despite his caution, his tendency to appear far more daring and innovative than he actually was—was in many respects the first of the modern Presidents.

Roosevelt brought to the White House a strength that had not been known there since Jackson and Lincoln. He mobilized public opinion behind him in support of progressive measures at home and operated like a monarch in the realm of world politics. "There adheres in the Presidency," he asserted, "more power than in any other office in any great republic or constitutional monarchy of modern times." He undertook many new things under the assumption that the President might do whatever was not forbidden by the law or the Constitution. "I did not usurp power," he explained afterward, "but I did greatly broaden the use of executive power."

Roosevelt was an accidental occupant of the White House. As Vice President, he took over the presidency after William McKinley's assassination in September 1901. Nor did he enter it as a progressive, even if Mark Hanna, who regarded him as a wild man, lamented, "Now look, that damned cowboy is President of the United States." For when Hanna advised him, "Go slow," Roosevelt replied, "I shall go slow." And he did, through the election of 1904. Like the other men about forty years old who had been McKinley Republicans, Roosevelt needed to be converted to progressivism. As recently as the Pullman strike of 1894, he had written, "I know the Populists and the laboring men well and their faults. . . . I like to see a mob handled by the regulars, or by good State-Guards, not overscrupulous about bloodshed."

Theodore Roosevelt (THEODORE ROOSEVELT COLLECTION, HARVARD UNIVERSITY)

Why, then, did Roosevelt emerge as a progressive? The answer lies in his background and his times. Born into one of the Knickerbocker families of New York City, he had been brought up among those of comfortable income and assured social position who looked with scorn at the robber barons and with fear and loathing at the political bosses and their underlings. His generation at Harvard was distinguished by its indifference to all worlds but its own. Roosevelt broke with it, not in its patrician conservatism, but in its aloofness. His background, unusual for an American, rather resembled that of the English Tory reformers of the era. Like them, he plunged into politics when few American gentlemen would do so; like them, he wished to be one of the governing class.

Roosevelt served a lengthy apprenticeship. He was successively a New York State assemblyman, candidate for mayor of New York City, Civil Service Commissioner, New York City police commissioner, Assistant Secretary of the Navy, and governor of New York. He learned all of the rules of professional politics and, like the most gifted practitioners, how to break them with profit upon occasion.

Roosevelt's varied and exciting experiences endeared him to his followers. As a rancher, he had helped capture outlaws in the Wild West and turn them over to justice; as head of the New York City police, he had labored almost superhumanly to try to stamp out crime and vice; as commander of the Rough Riders, he had charged up San Juan Hill. It is not surprising that for years after his death he continued to be the Boy Scouts' ideal, for he had lived out the daydreams of many of them. More important, his adventures illustrate his love for direct action and his bellicose morality.

As President, Roosevelt continued to function as though he were a deputy sheriff or a police commissioner or a cavalry colonel dedicated to upholding law and order. He did not lose his conservative fear that festering injustice would lead to a bloody upheaval in the United States. Through righting wrongs—the proper kind of police action—he would prevent this cataclysm. Moderate reforms to restrain social malefactors could ease the explosive pressure of malcontented masses. It was for conservative ends that he began to adopt progressive means. He had made a beginning as governor of New York when, facing the problems modernization was bringing, he began to fabricate the policies for which he came to stand as President. As governor, he signed a bill limiting workers on state contracts to an eight-hour day. It was excellent politics to favor such measures, as he could not have helped seeing. More important in his eyes, it was essential justice. "We Republicans hold the just balance," he explained to Boss Thomas C. Platt, "and set our faces as resolutely against the improper corporate influence on the one hand as against demagogy and mob rule on the other."

Manifestly the kind of progressivism that Roosevelt came to epitomize as President was compatible with conservatism. It was exactly the kind that appealed to the prosperous young men in cities and towns throughout the country. Thus White, thinking he was undergoing a complete transformation in his beliefs, became Roosevelt's man. The President, working toward the campaign of 1904, accepted the pledge of fealty. "I want it understood," he wrote White, "that the prime movers in forcing my nomination are men like you . . . , like the farmers, small businessmen and upper-class mechanics who are my natural allies."

For Roosevelt, as for White and the multitude of progressives who had reacted strongly against Populism, the conversion to a program of reform was logical. They were ready to try new means to obtain ends in which they had always believed.

As a rather uncertain fledgling President, only forty-two years old when he took office, Roosevelt had little inclination to put a vigorous progressive program into operation. He later admitted: "I cannot say that I entered the presidency with any deliberately planned and far reaching scheme of social betterment." His greatest ambition obviously was to be elected President in his own right.

Even had Roosevelt possessed a detailed plan of legislation, he could have done little to forward it in the fall of 1901. Congress, like most of the governmental machinery in the United States from the municipalities up, was under the control of old-style politicians.´ "Uncle Joe" Joseph Cannon, as Speaker of the House, operated under the autocratic powers "Czar" Thomas B. Reed had seized in 1890. Though genial, Cannon so firmly controlled appointments to committees and debates on legislation that the few progressives beginning to appear in the House were obliged either to cooperate or to sit as impotent witnesses to Cannon's dictatorship. The Senate was under the domination of an intelligent and competent oligarchy of conservatives. The most commanding of them was tall, austere Nelson Wilmarth Aldrich, a wealthy banker of Rhode Island.

Roosevelt realized how futile it would be to thrust his spear single-handedly against the conservatives in Congress. For the time being, therefore, he was cautious and conciliatory toward their leaders. As he planned his first annual message to Congress, his strategy obviously was to try to attract a wide following without alienating these powerful men. "Before I write my message," he wrote Aldrich in 1901, "I should like to have a chance to go over certain subjects with you." Roosevelt wrote to Senator Chauncey Depew of the New York Central Railroad: "*How* I wish I *wasn't* a reformer, oh, Senator! But I suppose I must live up to my part, like the Negro minstrel who blacked himself all over!"

Roosevelt dispensed patronage throughout the Midwest in a manner calculated to break Hanna's control over the party, although the policies of the two men were in reality basically similar. It made little difference whether these appointments took Roosevelt to the left or right. Henry Clay Payne of the Old Guard was appointed Postmaster General. Payne, through his wide distribution of spoils, helped rally right-wing Republicans and Democrats behind Roosevelt. Finally, Roosevelt cemented alliances with businessmen in the North and reshuffled the unstable Republican organizations in the South. In the South he reversed Hanna's "lily-white" policy to appoint some qualified blacks to office. Indeed, it was to discuss appointments that Roosevelt took the sensational step of inviting Booker T. Washington to the White House in the fall of 1901.

While playing the game of political patronage, Roosevelt markedly improved the quality of officeholders. Gradually, he was able to pull into public service a group of distinguished men, both old and young, of a kind that previously had shunned government work. Henry L. Stimson, who had been earning enormous fees as a corporation lawyer, became United States attorney for the New York City area and brought into his office a group of brilliant and idealistic young lawyers, including Felix Frankfurter.

Partly because Roosevelt had attracted into the government progressives of stature, bound to him by strong ties of personal loyalty, and even more because he had won over or neutralized the Republican machine, he was in firm control of the party by 1904. He had not made it progressive, but he had made it answerable to him. Hanna died early in the year; had he lived and felt the inclination, he could have mustered little strength against Roosevelt at the convention.

JUSTICE FOR TRUSTS

While Roosevelt was quietly taking over the Republican machinery, he was spectacularly building an excited national following. He launched a series of attacks upon the corporate plutocracy—attacks that were vigorous but at the same time moderate.

In his first annual message to Congress, December 3, 1901, he set forth his basic policy toward trusts:

> There is a widespread conviction in the minds of the American people that . . . trusts are in certain of their features and tendencies hurtful to the general welfare. This . . . is based upon sincere conviction that combination and concentration should be, not prohibited, but supervised and within reasonable limits controlled; and in my judgment this conviction is right.

Roosevelt's position on trusts was ready-made for burlesque by Finley Peter Dunne's character, Mr. Dooley: "Th' trusts, says he, are heejoous monsthers built up be th' enlightened intherprise iv th' men that have done so much to advance progress in our beloved country, he says. On wan hand I wud stamp thim undher fut; on th' other hand not so fast."

Specifically, Roosevelt asked for legislation to give the government the right to inspect and examine the workings of great corporations and subsequently, to supervise them in a mild fashion. What he desired first was the power to investigate them and publicize their activities; on the basis of these data Congress could later frame legislation to regulate or tax the trusts. Consequently, he requested the establishment of a Department of Commerce and Labor, containing a Bureau of Corporations to carry on investigations. Congress set up such a department in 1903.

The establishment of a great railroad monopoly in the Northwest, after a bitter and spectacular stock-market battle in 1901, gave Roosevelt an opportunity to begin prosecution under the Sherman Antitrust Act. And so he did, even though his avowed purpose had been to regulate, not destroy, and to stamp underfoot only "malefactors of great wealth," while sparing large corporations that were benign. The new Northern Securities Company had emerged out of the struggle for control of the Northern Pacific between E. H. Harriman of the Union Pacific on the one side and James J. Hill of the Great Northern and J. P. Morgan on the other. In the eyes of progressives these men were malefactors.

Morgan, feeling his position challenged, hastened to the White House, accompanied by Senators Hanna and Depew. According to Roosevelt, Morgan declared: "If we have done anything wrong, send your man to my man and they can fix it up." Morgan, Roosevelt later remarked, "could not help regarding me as a big rival operator, who either intended to ruin all his interests or else could be induced to come to an agreement to ruin none." Roosevelt was not set upon ruining Morgan, but to the joy of progressives he was using his power as President to discipline industry.

When, in 1904, Roosevelt won the case and the Supreme Court dissolved the Northern Securities combine, it in no material way injured Harriman, Hill, or Morgan. But it convinced progressives that Roosevelt, however cautious his avowed policies might be, was a heroic "trust buster."

Trust busting was popular and proceeded rapidly. Roosevelt's attorneys obtained twenty-five indictments altogether and instituted suits against the beef, oil, and tobacco combinations. In these the government was ultimately successful, but the Supreme Court instituted a rule of reason, declaring in effect that the Sherman Act prohibited only unreasonable restraints upon trade. Even though President Taft initiated ninety more suits and obtained forty-three additional indictments, the results of trust busting were disappointing.

Government and Labor

Presidential intervention in labor disputes was nothing new—there had been, for example, the Pullman strike—but the government had usually acted as a strikebreaker for the employers. Now Roosevelt was ready to make the government an impartial arbiter instead. Here again, as in dealing with capitalists, he wished the government to be paramount over the conflicting economic forces and neutral in dealing with them. Organized labor, as long as it was well behaved, did not frighten the progressives nearly as much as did organized capital. The unions were comparatively weak; despite the great upsurge of the American Federation of Labor (AFL) in the 1890s, by 1900 only about 4 percent of the working force, even excluding agricultural laborers, was organized.

Injustice toward workers was most extreme in anthracite coal mining. Eight coal railroads under Morgan's domination held a virtual monopoly over the industry. Wages were substandard, hours long, and the accident rate shockingly high. The workers, under John Mitchell, struck in May 1902, for an eight-hour day, a 20-percent wage increase, and recognition of the union. Mitchell so effectively presented the miners' claims, and George F. Baer, spokesman for the operators, was so truculent that public sympathy was aligned with the strikers. Baer foolishly asserted the divine right of the operators to deal with miners as they saw best. He remained adamant when Roosevelt called operators and miners to the White House early in October to ask them to accept arbitration. In contrast, Mitchell was quite willing to accept. Roosevelt eventually persuaded Morgan to force arbitration upon the operators. Even so, the miners after their long strike failed to gain union recognition and obtained only a 10-percent wage increase.

The coal strike and its settlement were evidence of "a honeymoon period of capital and labor," stretching from McKinley's inauguration through Roosevelt's first term. Union membership jumped from less than a half-million to over 2 million. Monopolistic companies could well afford to deal liberally with unions, since the companies could thus avoid work stoppages in prosperous periods and pass on increased labor costs to the

Powder men in the Perrin coal mine, about 1902 (THEODORE ROOSEVELT COL-
LECTION, HARVARD COLLEGE LIBRARY)

consumers. It was altogether fitting that Hanna, the high priest of modern
big business, should assume the presidency of the National Civic Federation, which was founded in 1901 to bring about friendly relations between
capital and labor, and that Samuel Gompers should become vice president.

Not all laborers were ready to accept the assumption of leaders like
Gompers and Mitchell that differences with capitalists could easily be adjusted around a conference table. The Socialist minority within the AFL
succeeded in capturing unions of machinists and miners. Socialists won
municipal elections in Milwaukee, Schenectady, and Berkeley. Militant
Western miners in 1905 founded the Industrial Workers of the World
(IWW), which tried to organize the great masses of unskilled workers,
mostly immigrants, whom the AFL ignored. The IWW, a syndicalist organization, aimed ultimately to form one big union including all workers,
hold one big strike, and thus paralyze and then take over the government.
Its members, popularly known as Wobblies, were accused of responsibility
for acts of violence. Employers and state and local authorities certainly
did not hesitate to use violence against the Wobblies. Two episodes,

neither of which was the work of the IWW, especially outraged orderly progressives. These were the murder of a former governor of Idaho and the dynamiting of the plant of the Los Angeles *Times*, which was militantly antiunion.

Such episodes prompted many progressives to listen to the antiunion slogans of the National Association of Manufacturers (NAM) and kindred organizations. The NAM, which proclaimed itself against union recognition in 1903, was made up predominantly of men who ran small plants and were dependent upon low labor costs to survive in highly competitive markets. It called the open shop the American Plan and the independent workman (strikebreaker) the American hero. President Charles W. Eliot of Harvard gave formidable support by asserting that nothing was "more essential to the preservation of individual liberty" than protection of the independent workman.

The manufacturers had the backing of federal judges. The most spectacular court blow against collective bargaining grew out of the Danbury Hatters' strike of 1902. The courts held that the union's efforts to obtain a nationwide boycott of Loewe hats was a violation of the Sherman Act and assessed triple damages of $240,000 against the union. In another boycott case, involving the Buck's Stove and Range Company of St. Louis, a federal court issued a sweeping injunction that forbade the AFL to carry on the boycott, to include the company in a "We Don't Patronize" list in its newspaper, or even to mention the dispute orally or in writing. When Gompers and other AFL officials defied the injunction by mentioning the dispute, they were sentenced to prison for contempt of court. The sentences were never served, but the principle of the injunction stood. Union officials began a concerted and vigorous campaign to exempt labor organizations from the Sherman Act and to outlaw antilabor injunctions.

Gompers and his followers demanded an end to governmental discrimination against them; they were not asking for welfare laws. To some extent, Roosevelt sympathized with them. He denounced the Buck's Stove decision and inveighed against court abuse of injunctions. But he was more interested in paternalistic legislation for labor, similar to that being proposed in many state legislatures. He asked Congress for laws to regulate the hours and working conditions of women and children, establish employers' liability for accident compensation, and improve railroad safety measures. For the moment he made no headway.

Indeed, if Roosevelt had obtained legislation, the courts would have invalidated most of it, for they were striking down most state laws as rapidly as they were enacted. The Supreme Court held, in the *Lochner* case in 1905, that a New York law limiting hours of bakers, who pursued an unhealthy occupation, to ten a day or sixty a week was unconstitutional under the Fourteenth Amendment because it violated the right of the bakers to make contracts as they saw fit. Justice Oliver Wendell Holmes, who had been appointed to the Court by Roosevelt because of his enlightened views on labor, tartly dissented: "Some of these laws embody convictions or prejudices which judges are likely to share. Some may not.

But a constitution is not intended to embody a particular economic theory, whether of paternalism and the organic relation of the citizen to the state or of laissez faire." Progressives soon won a respite from the Supreme Court's distaste for government regulation, but this came only after Roosevelt had been reelected and progressivism had won an even greater hold over the American public.

THE 1904 MANDATE FOR REFORM

Roosevelt's rather strange political anxiety had led him to plan exceedingly cautiously for the election of 1904—in some respects too cautiously. At the convention, he was careful not to antagonize the right wing of the party. Democrats veered even more sharply to the right. They abandoned Bryan to nominate Cleveland's former law partner, Alton B. Parker. When Roosevelt, fearing that Wall Street was putting $5 million behind Parker, allowed his campaign manager to tap the trusts, the money came pouring in. Businessmen might call Roosevelt the "mad messiah," but they were not really afraid of him. Despite the Northern Securities decision, Harriman personally contributed $50,000 and Morgan, $150,000; far more came from their associates. The steel, beef, oil, and insurance trusts, and the railroads all aided. Roosevelt was not altogether aware of the source of all the donations, nor did he feel he was putting himself under obligation, but they were a revealing commentary upon his record.

Roosevelt's apprehensions had been groundless. After a dull campaign he won by a popular majority of 2.5 million votes. While businessmen were convinced that he was safe, progressives were confident he would lead in reform. In state elections throughout the nation progressives were generally victorious. As a sidelight, the Socialists under Eugene V. Debs (often regarded as a left-wing offshoot of the progressives), received 400,000 votes, four times as many as in 1900. Their growth gave Roosevelt a convincing argument that sane and slow reform was essential to forestall a violent upheaval.

Roosevelt accepted his 1904 victory as a mandate for progressive reform. He was now freed from his earlier preoccupation with winning reelection, having announced that he would not seek another term. He continued to operate from the political center, offending big businessmen who had contributed to his campaign and, at the same time, offending Midwestern progressives who took up what he termed "the La Follette type of fool radicalism."

While leaving the tariff alone, Roosevelt now exercised his presidential leadership to obtain more effective railroad-rate regulation. The courts had practically nullified the Interstate Commerce Act of 1887. By a series of intricate maneuvers Roosevelt managed to force a new regulatory law through Congress. At one point he seemed to join Senator La Follette in demands for really drastic regulation of railroads. La Follette wished to give the Interstate Commerce Commission (ICC) power to evaluate railroad property as a base for determining rates. He felt betrayed when Roosevelt abandoned him. Although the Hepburn Act of June 1906 was in La Follette's eyes only half a loaf, it was at least the beginning of effective railroad regulation. It enpowered the ICC to put into effect reasonable rates, subject to later court review; extended its jurisdiction to cover express, sleeping-car, and pipeline companies; separated railroad management from other enterprises such as mining; prescribed uniform bookkeeping; and forbade passes and rebates.

It was a large half-loaf, and La Follette and his supporters in Congress soon were able to obtain the remaining part. In 1910 insurgent Republicans and Democrats passed the Mann-Elkins Act, abolishing the long-and-short-haul evil, further extending the jurisdiction of the ICC, and strengthening other features of the Hepburn Act. The ICC could now suspend proposed new rates up to ten months and could demand proof from the railroads that they would be reasonable. Finally, in 1913, La Follette's long agitation resulted in passage of a law authorizing the ICC to evaluate railroads and to set rates that would give a fair return of profit.

CONSERVATION OF RESOURCES AND HEALTH

One of the many reasons for the clamor for lower freight rates had been to cut the rising cost of lumber. The best forests of the Great Lakes area were cut over, and the increasing amounts of lumber coming from the Pacific Northwest had to bear the heavy cost of transportation eastward. Furthermore, trees were being felled faster than they were being grown. It was one of many signs that progressives must abandon the profligate ways of pioneering America.

Roosevelt, ardent sportsman and naturalist that he was, along with his chief forester, Gifford Pinchot, and most Eastern progressives, felt that the United States must develop great national forests like those of the European countries. Clothing his actions in the terminology of the progressive struggle against the vested interests, he rapidly extended the government reserves. He had to operate as best he could, at times with doubtful legality, under existing laws. The very Westerners in Congress who zealously supported his other policies not only blocked new legislation but fought to repeal the old. Furthermore, behind them were not just the big Western business interests, which at times were not hostile, but often the small businessmen of the towns and the small lumbermen, ranchers, and grazers. In 1907 Western congressmen succeeded in attaching a rider (unrelated amendment) to an appropriation bill, prohibiting the President from withdrawing further lands. Roosevelt could not veto the appropriations bill without calamitous effects. He acted swiftly, first to withdraw practically all remaining forests in the public domain, and then to sign the bill. All together he added about 125 million acres to the national forests and reserved 4.7 million acres of phosphate beds and 68 million acres of coal lands—all the known coal deposits in the public domain.

These coal lands again became a topic of public debate in the 1970s, when large-scale strip mining of them began.

Simultaneously, Roosevelt prepared the way for a new government policy on electric power by reserving 2,565 water-power sites. These were the years when expanding private utility companies were interested in obtaining them. He also vetoed a bill to permit private exploitation of the power at Muscle Shoals on the Tennessee River, which a generation later became the heart of the TVA. Roosevelt's actions left the way open for

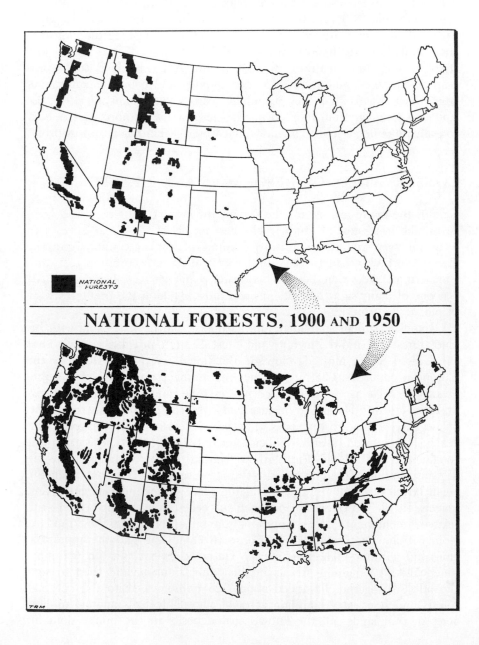

NATIONAL
FORESTS

NATIONAL FORESTS, 1900 AND 1950

government development of huge power projects, a program as popular in the West as the withdrawal of other land was unpopular.

It was not the President, but a Democratic senator from Nevada, Francis G. Newlands, who proposed an extensive federal reclamation program for the West. Roosevelt endorsed it, and to a considerable extent he was able to win political credit for the Newlands Reclamation Act of 1902. It provided that money from the sale of Western lands should go into a revolving fund to undertake irrigation projects too large for private capital or state resources. Eventually, the government built huge dams for the development of power and storage of water and opened up extensive systems of canals to carry the water to arid lands. Already by 1915 the government had invested $80 million in twenty-five projects, the largest of which was the Roosevelt Dam on the Salt River of Arizona. The principle of government aid in irrigation and power development in the West had become firmly established.

In the same fashion that the progressives were trying to regulate natural resources scientifically, they undertook to legislate the nation into better health. Again, many of the early laws were inadequate and were of significance mainly for the precedents they set.

Within the Department of Agriculture Dr. Harvey Wiley had long agitated for the protection of consumers from dangerous foods and adul-

Roosevelt Dam, Arizona (THEODORE ROOSEVELT COLLECTION, HARVARD COLLEGE LIBRARY)

terants. The muckrakers also had made the public shockingly aware of the disgusting and poisonous things they were sometimes eating. None created a more shocked reaction than Sinclair, who wrote a powerful novel of protest against exploitation of immigrant labor in the stockyards and incidentally included nauseating descriptions of the preparation of meats. When *The Jungle* appeared in 1906, it hit Americans' stomachs as much as their consciences, even in the White House.

Roosevelt was horrified, and when a commission verified the descriptions in Sinclair's book, he sought reform. The result was two pieces of legislation passed in June 1906. One was the Meat Inspection Act, which, while fairly ineffective at first, over a period of time did much to bring about eradication of some animal diseases, especially tuberculosis. The other was the Pure Food and Drug Act, which bore the impressive descriptive title, "An Act for preventing the manufacture, sale, or transportation of adulterated or misbranded or poisonous or deleterious foods, drugs, medicines, and liquors, and for regulating traffic therein, and for other purposes." Although the law carried only weak penalties, it eliminated many harmful foods and preparations from drugstores and groceries.

THE PANIC OF 1907: A WARNING

Although Roosevelt's followers believed that he was leading them into the millennium, the panic of 1907 bluntly illustrated the serious flaws still plaguing the American economic structure—and the President's unwillingness to go too far in trying to remedy them. Speculation and mismanagement during the boom years following the Spanish-American War led to a sharp break in prosperity in 1907. It was a rich men's panic at the outset, involving an international tightening of the money market and the failure of thirteen New York banks and of several railroads. The result was wage cuts and layoffs for large numbers of poor men.

Businessmen were quick to lay the blame upon the "mad messiah" in the White House, the muckrakers, trust busters, and progressive legislators. They were incorrect; progressive suits, investigations, and laws do not seem to have been responsible. Antitrust suits had not cut corporate earnings, and regulatory laws such as the Hepburn Act had so reassured investors in both America and Europe that large funds had poured into Wall Street to enable further promotions. Roosevelt, nevertheless, was sensitive to the criticisms and quick to conciliate Wall Street. Judge Elbert H. Gary and Henry Clay Frick called upon him one morning to tell him that unless United States Steel took over shares of the Tennessee Coal and Iron Company from a New York banking house, it would fail and thus threaten a widespread industrial smash-up. They wanted assurance that the government would not consider the purchase a violation of the Sherman Act. Roosevelt tacitly agreed. United States Steel was thus able to buy out a vigorous competitor at a bargain price, further stifle competition, and hold back the development of the iron and steel industry in the South. It shackled Southern steel to the Birmingham differential price scale. This meant that the steel mills in Alabama were forced to charge the same price as Pittsburgh mills, plus a $3-a-ton differential, plus freight from Birmingham.

The real causes of the panic were an inefficient and inelastic credit system, the high degree of "water" in the capital structure of railroads and the new trusts, and the high profits contrasted with the low wages—and thus low buying power—of the workers. By 1909 the economy had swung upward but continued to wobble between upswings and relapses until war prosperity rescued it in 1915.

The panic of 1907 and the economic instabilities that persisted afterward were alarming to progressives. As they began to investigate the serious flaws in the economic structure, they began to propose more elaborate measures for stabilizing the economy. Gradually, many of them were shifting away from their original view that the imposition of a few simple prohibitions would suffice to restore the free flowing of a laissez-faire economy. Some began to demand more elaborate machinery even though it would mean an increasing role for the government. These demands would be difficult to obtain, for their proposals not only could not command a majority in Congress but also went considerably beyond the modest limits of Roosevelt and appealed even less to his successor.

four

A Rift in Republican Ranks

The surge toward national progressive legislation continued to gain impetus during the presidency of William Howard Taft. Progressive strength did not grow smoothly. Rather, as the electorate pressed for progressive measures, strategically placed opponents in Congress struggled to retain the old order. Nor was Taft as effective a presidential leader as either his predecessor or successor in his efforts to retain control over both the liberal and conservative wings of his party. The result was an explosion in Republican ranks that embittered Taft and angered Roosevelt. The rift between Roosevelt and Taft was momentous, for it made possible the election of the Democratic progressive Wilson in 1912.

TAFT: AN ADMINISTRATOR OF JUDICIAL TEMPERAMENT

According to recent biographers, Taft was a more able President than he has usually received credit for being. He brought to the White House unusual experience as an administrator and judge and a deep respect for the law. The tendency of some progressives, even Roosevelt, to obtain their ends without due regard for the law bothered him. Although he regarded Roosevelt's objectives as having been justifiable, he commented in 1910 that Roosevelt "ought more often to have admitted the legal way of reaching the same ends." This colorless way of speaking was another marked contrast between Taft and Roosevelt. Taft lacked Roosevelt's pungent, lively fashion of attracting public attention; he had difficulty in building public support for his programs and in persuading Congress to enact them.

Roosevelt chose Taft to be his successor as the Republican candidate for President in 1908 in the hope that Taft would be the vehicle for enacting his policies. Roosevelt was so convinced that these policies were the only right solution to the nation's problems—and he so loved being President—that he might very well have defied the no-third-term tradition had he thought he could win against the considerable opposition building among more conservative Republican leaders. As it was, caution led him to support his loyal lieutenant, Taft.

Taft, the son of a prominent Republican in Cincinnati, had, despite his own distaste for politics, risen rapidly in office: judge on the Ohio Superior Court, Solicitor General of the United States, judge on a federal circuit court, president of the Philippines Commission, governor general of the Philippines, and Secretary of War. At a time when the nation was eager for progressive domestic reform, Taft was known less for his background as a former federal judge than for his notable achievements as one of the first viceroys of the new American empire. Between 1900 and 1908 he traveled over 100,000 miles on assignment to Manila, Rome, Panama, Cuba, and within the United States. He was a glamorous figure in an age that admired big men who labored strenuously in distant places. His achievements were almost all in the realm of colonial or foreign policy; he had little to do with Roosevelt's domestic policies, although privately he subscribed to almost every one of them. If he was to the right of Roosevelt, it was only by a hairline.

Thus in 1908 Roosevelt had no difficulty in securing the nomination of Taft. The smooth-running Republican machinery followed Roosevelt's bidding and gathered the votes of the delegates: organization men, officeholders, and Southern Republicans.

Business moguls preferred the gingerly progressive Republican candidate to the more forthright Bryan, running forlornly for a third time. John D. Rockefeller wired Taft congratulations on the nomination; Morgan remarked, "Good! good!" Carnegie sent a campaign contribution of $20,000. This did not mean that Taft had capitulated to Wall Street; indeed, he

President William Howard Taft playing golf (HARVARD COLLEGE LIBRARY)

was more careful about accepting corporate campaign contributions than Roosevelt had been in 1904.

Taft campaigned as the champion of smaller business interests. In his acceptance address he promised that he would perfect the machinery for restraining lawbreakers and at the same time interfere with legitimate business as little as possible. Most important, he appealed to small-business and middle-class concern over the rising cost of living by firmly promising a reduction in the tariff.

The election result was a foregone conclusion, a sweep for Taft. The electoral vote was 321 to 162, but there were portents of national unrest in the victory. Taft's lead over Bryan was only half the size of Roosevelt's plurality in 1904; several Western states shifted to Bryan, and several others in the Midwest elected Democratic governors even though they gave their electoral votes to Taft. Republican progressives, pleased at the outcome, proclaimed: "Roosevelt has cut enough hay; Taft is the man to put it into the barn." Republican conservatives rejoiced that they were rid of the "mad messiah."

Certainly Taft's intention was to load Roosevelt's hay into the barn, but the hay soon was drenched by violent political storms. Partly the fault was Taft's lethargy; it had never been his nature to move rapidly, whether because of his corpulence or his desire to abide by the details of the law. An unfriendly critic once wrote during his administration that Taft was "a large, good-natured body, entirely surrounded by people who know exactly what they want." The implication that Taft did not know what he wanted is not correct. But it is true that either he lacked the political skill to obtain it or he looked upon use of his great executive power to this end as being unprincipled. Later, when Roosevelt reminisced, "I did not usurp power, but I did greatly broaden the use of the executive power," Taft warned against so unsafe a practice.

At times Taft's methods seemed those of the judge rather than the politician. Thus he expected that the greatest problem of his administration would be coping with corporations, and he felt that lawyers could best do this. So he filled six of his nine cabinet positions with lawyers. He apparently forgot that he had pledged himself to retain any of Roosevelt's cabinet who might wish to stay; he replaced the conservationist Secretary of the Interior, James R. Garfield, who in his zeal had gone beyond the law, with a Seattle lawyer, Richard A. Ballinger, who was ready to apply the strict letter of the law, even though it might deal a blow to conservation. Later, the Ballinger-Pinchot controversy would cause him trouble.

Taft himself was well aware of the great contrast between himself and his predecessor. He wrote a revealing farewell letter to Roosevelt, who was embarking for an African big game tour:

> When I am addressed as "Mr. President," I turn to see whether you are not at my elbow. . . .
> I have not the facility for educating the public as you had through talks with correspondents, and so I fear that a large part of the public

will feel as if I had fallen away from your ideals; but you know me better and will understand that I am still working away on the same old plan.

Had Taft been the most skilled of presidential leaders, he would have had trouble putting the "same old plan" into execution. Part of the fault was Roosevelt's, because in his last months in office he had outlined to progressives exciting proposals that the conservatives in Congress had ignored. His dazzled following blamed the nonenactment of these proposals upon the Old Guard congressional leadership, especially that of Aldrich in the Senate and Speaker Cannon and the rules committee in the House. One progressive congressman asserted in 1908, "President Roosevelt has been trying to cultivate oranges for many years in the frigid climate of the Committee of Rules, but what has he gotten but the proverbial lemons?"

At campaign time "Uncle Joe" Cannon was a homespun, tobacco-spitting man of the people; in the House he was the reactionary friend of corporate interests. Progressives resented his power, and a growing number of them in the House were ready to revolt against him. Taft personally sympathized with them, but they were not yet powerful enough to succeed in their revolt, and on the advice of Roosevelt he did not encourage them. Rather, like both his predecessor and his successor, he sought to obtain his program through negotiation with the powerful leaders in Congress rather than through overthrowing them. Unfortunately, even from the outset Taft seemed incapable of negotiating with the Old Guard without giving the impression that he had joined them.

"New Wine in Old Bottles" by J. N. Darling, for the Des Moines Register

INSURGENCY, THE TARIFF, AND CONSERVATION

The first fiasco, in the eyes of progressives, occurred when Taft called Congress into special session to enact a lower tariff. "I believe the people are with me," he had written in January 1909, "and before I get through I think I will have downed Cannon and Aldrich too." But having proclaimed a tariff crusade, he remained behind while Midwesterners carried their lances into battle. They were not free traders like some Southern Democrats, but they did want to weaken trusts by exposing them to foreign competition. The way to do this, they thought, was to lower tariff rates substantially. They thought the President was behind them, but he failed to send Congress a fighting message or to intervene with his patronage powers when congressmen began to succumb to the blandishments of lobbyists and logrollers.

The Payne-Aldrich tariff passed Congress over the votes of Midwest Republicans and was signed by Taft on August 5, 1909. He said it was not a perfect bill but represented "a sincere effort on the part of the Republican party to make a downward revision." Also it provided for the Tariff Commission to make scientific studies of rates—an appealing idea to some progressives, who felt that the tariff, like most problems, should be determined scientifically and taken out of politics.

Nevertheless, the Payne-Aldrich tariff seemed to favor Senator Aldrich's New England at the expense of the rest of the country. On a tour around the country in the fall of 1909, Taft tried to defend the new tariff in a hastily prepared speech delivered in the heart of the area of resentment, Winona, Minnesota. One line from that speech made damaging headlines against the President. He said: "On the whole . . . the Payne bill is the best bill that the Republican party ever passed." The remainder of the trip

"Revising the Tariff Downward (?)" by J. N. Darling, for the Des Moines Register

through the Midwest, wrote a reporter, was "a polar dash through the world of ice."

In 1911 Taft further alienated Midwesterners when he submitted to the Senate a reciprocal trade agreement with Canada, an agreement that would have lowered tariffs on both sides and in effect would have brought the two countries into an economic union. Many Eastern manufacturers, seeing larger Canadian markets for their goods, were enthusiastic, but the Midwesterners, fearing a flood of competing Canadian farm products and raw materials, were bitterly hostile. La Follette complained: "It singles out the farmer and forces free trade upon him, but it confers even greater benefits upon a few of the great combinations sheltered behind the high rates found in the Payne-Aldrich tariff." He and his cohorts formed a strange alliance with die-hard members of the Old Guard but were defeated by Eastern Republicans and Southern free-trade Democrats. The Senate approved the reciprocity arrangement, 55 to 27. But the Canadian parliament refused to act, for many Canadians feared that tariff reductions might somehow lead to Canada's being annexed by the United States.

The progressive Republicans of the Midwest had cut loose from Taft. They blamed him, unjustly, for their failure to oust Speaker Cannon in 1909. By 1910, without the presidential blessing, they were strong enough to resume the effort. Under the leadership of George W. Norris they breached Cannon's formidable parliamentary defenses and opened a fierce debate that raged for nearly thirty hours. It ended with Cannon's removal from the rules committee, which henceforth was to be elected by the House. He remained as House Speaker, but he was no longer the obstacle he had been to progressive legislation.

Meanwhile, through the sensational Ballinger-Pinchot controversy Taft lost the sympathy of most of Roosevelt's following in the urban East and the Far West. Taft's new Secretary of the Interior, Ballinger, wished to distribute to private interests the natural resources in the public domain. His viewpoint was dominant among businessmen of the West, who wished themselves to prosper and to see their region grow. But Taft had left in charge of the forestry service in the Department of Agriculture Roosevelt's ardent admirer, Gifford Pinchot of Pennsylvania, who believed in managing and developing forest resources rather than leaving them untouched; Pinchot looked upon Ballinger as a would-be despoiler of the nation's resources. Ballinger was dedicated to developing the West through private enterprise, free from government interference. Pinchot, although friendly with many of the economic interest groups of the West, wanted overall federal regulation. A violent clash between these two men was almost inevitable.

The occasion was the spectacular charge that Ballinger was conniving to turn over valuable coal lands in Alaska to a Morgan-Guggenheim syndicate. Taft, accepting Ballinger's rebuttal, publicly exonerated him. Although Taft was sympathetic toward conservation, he, like Ballinger, thought that the Roosevelt administration had withdrawn much of the lands in Alaska and elsewhere illegally. To a protesting progressive congressman Taft explained, "It is a very dangerous method of upholding reform to violate the law in so doing, even on the ground of high moral principle, or saving the public."

Roosevelt progressives throughout the country championed Pinchot as the defender of the national domain against the corrupt onslaught of big business. Pinchot, by going over the President's head directly to Congress, provoked Taft to discharge him for insubordination. A congressional committee investigated and, since the Old Guard dominated it, reported in favor of Ballinger. To the end Taft stood by his Secretary of the Interior, whom he correctly considered to be an honorable man. But in refusing to dismiss Ballinger as an anticonservationist, Taft opened a rift between himself and the Roosevelt following that was as wide and deep as the one separating him from the La Follette supporters.

T.R. AGAINST TAFT

As early as the tariff fiasco in 1909, progressives had begun to look to the African jungle for their next presidential candidate. In the middle of June 1910, loaded with trophies from Africa and fresh impressions of reform from Europe, Roosevelt returned. Observers noted that his first hello was to Pinchot and that he turned down Taft's invitation to the White House. Indeed, he had already met Pinchot in Europe, bearing messages from progressives, and had come to the conclusion that Taft had "completely twisted around the policies I advocated and acted upon."

Furious with Taft for helping bring about the split in the party, Roosevelt determined to do all he could to reunify it. He told reporters he

"Back in the Old Place" by Nelson Harding, for the Brooklyn Eagle

was seeing all Republicans—"regulars and insurgents, party men and independents." But at Osawatomie, Kansas, on September 1, he delivered a speech that returned him to command of the progressives. At Osawatomie he proclaimed the doctrines of the New Nationalism, emphasizing that social justice could be attained in the nation only through strengthening the power of the federal government so that the executive could be the "steward of public welfare." Men thinking primarily of property rights and personal profits "must now give way to the advocate of human welfare, who rightly maintains that every man holds his property subject to the general right of the community to regulate its use to whatever degree the public welfare may require it." Going beyond these generalizations, frightening enough to the Old Guard, Roosevelt listed some specific proposals: graduated income and inheritance taxes, workmen's accident compensation, regulation of the labor of women and children, tariff revision, and firm regulation of corporations through a more powerful Bureau of Corporations and ICC. From the Mississippi westward progressives were ready to acclaim him as the next presidential candidate, but among his right-wing enemies, Lodge warned him, he was regarded as "little short of a revolutionist."

Progressive Republicans of the Midwest hoped they could wrest the presidential nomination from Taft in 1912. In January 1911 a group of them formed the National Progressive Republican League to work for the nomination of La Follette. But a great majority of the progressive Republicans continued to hope that Roosevelt could be persuaded to run.

With Roosevelt receptive, many of La Follette's supporters switched to him with indecent haste after La Follette on February 2, 1912, exhausted and worried, delivered a rambling, repetitious talk. Roosevelt thus acquired new recruits, but he also won the undying hatred of La Follette and his loyal Midwestern progressive following. Nevertheless, in the primaries Roosevelt demonstrated that he was overwhelmingly the presidential choice of Republican voters.

The nomination at the Republican convention would depend upon the seating of the delegates; more than a third of the seats were contested. The Republican National Committee, made up almost entirely of loyal Taft supporters, allowed Roosevelt only 19 out of 254 contested seats, and thus in advance counted him out of the nomination.

Roosevelt had come in person to the convention to direct his forces, and the night before it opened he told a hysterically cheering throng of 5,000 that he would not be bound by the convention if it failed to seat his contested delegates. He concluded thunderously: "We stand at Armageddon, and we battle for the Lord." As good as his word, he bolted, leaving the conservatives in complete command at the Republican convention. With Roosevelt's one-time friend Elihu Root presiding, Warren G. Harding, one of the most regular of the regulars, mellifluously nominated Taft, who was chosen on the first ballot.

During the Republican convention, Roosevelt had agreed to the formation of a new, Progressive party when Frank Munsey, the newspaper magnate, and George W. Perkins, of United States Steel and International

Harvester, promised him financing. Announcing his willingness to run, Roosevelt said he was as fit as a bull moose, giving the party a symbol as well as a name. When the Progressives met at Chicago in August to nominate Roosevelt formally, the conclave was far more symbolic of progressivism than of ordinary American politics. Missing were La Follette and his following, five of seven governors who had signed a call for Roosevelt in January, and notable Republican insurgents such as Norris of Nebraska and William E. Borah of Idaho.

The convention was more like a camp meeting than the gatherings to which Roosevelt was accustomed. The delegates sang "Onward Christian Soldiers" and closed the convention with the "Doxology." A newspaperman thought Roosevelt looked bewildered as he acknowledged their almost fanatical hymn-singing welcome, for "they were crusaders; he was not." If so, the disparity was not openly apparent, for in his "Confession of Faith," Roosevelt castigated both of the two old parties as representing "government of the needy many by professional politicians in the interests of the rich few." He offered his followers the full array of advanced progressive reform—all the changes in the machinery of government, all the economic and social legislation. Once more he singled out the courts for attack. At the end of the campaign he asserted in words foreshadowing a great struggle a quarter-century later, "We stand for the Constitution, but we will not consent to make of the Constitution a fetish for the protection of fossilized wrong."

What was distinctive and different about Roosevelt's program was his willingness to accept big business, if it was regulated through a national industrial commission. A federal securities commission should police stocks and bonds. In the program of New Nationalism there was much to appeal to the progressives of the cities, whether reformers or businessmen, but little of interest to farmers and much paternalism but no guarantee of collective bargaining for organized labor. In an effort to win disgruntled Southern businessmen away from the Democratic party, Roosevelt endorsed a lily-white (excluding blacks) Progressive party for the South.

Altogether, Roosevelt's New Nationalism represented the ultimate in urban progressivism. When the votes were counted, Roosevelt had run 10 percent better in the eighteen largest cities than in the country as a whole. His program owed much to the thinking of Herbert Croly, who in the *Promise of American Life* blue-printed a powerful federal government that would regulate in the interest of the whole nation the forces of big business and small, agriculture, and labor. It owed much also to the enlightened capitalists like Frank Munsey and George W. Perkins, who saw the solution of the monopoly program in regulation rather than destruction. Its basic significance was in firing the imaginations of young men who a score of years later tried to put the program into effect in the early New Deal.

For the moment the Progressive insurrection spelled political disaster for Roosevelt personally and for his zealous followers. Why had he, who had always been "regular," split from his party? Perhaps it was his strenuous philosophy of sportsmanship that led him to charge to defeat in 1912 rather than retreat to ultimate victory in 1916 or 1920. "I wish to Heaven I was not in this fight," he wrote privately, "and I am in it only on the principle, in the long run a sound one, that I would rather take a thrashing than be quiet under such a kicking." It was misplaced gallantry, for like an unwitting Pied Piper he had led the idealistic young Progressives out of the Republican party, and the Old Guard were not disposed to let them back except on terms of unconditional surrender. W. P. Hepburn exulted at the time of the exodus that it would eliminate "the guerillas and insurgents" and restore the Republican party to its old conservatism. Thus Roosevelt's candidacy relegated progressives to a weak minority in the Republican party.

THE APPEAL OF THE NEW FREEDOM

Between the Progressive bolt of the Republican convention and their nomination of Roosevelt, the Democratic party met at Baltimore, exultant with the heady knowledge that, although they were a political minority, they almost certainly were nominating the next President. Bryan, who long had dominated the party, stood aside while four contenders battled for the nomination. They were Governor Wilson of New Jersey, Speaker Champ Clark of Missouri, the right-wing Governor Judson Harmon of Ohio, and Representative Oscar W. Underwood, the champion of Southern conservatism and a low tariff. Wilson's spectacular reform achievements in New Jersey had early made him the favorite of Democratic progressives in Eastern cities, and he took a quick lead for the nomination as he crisscrossed the nation to make hundreds of inspiring speeches denouncing special privilege and heralding the new progressive order. Yet, in 1912, he emerged from the primaries and state conventions with only 248 delegates to Clark's 436. Underwood swept most of the South.

It was little short of a miracle that Clark, who had the rural Democrats and most of the bosses behind him and who obtained more than a majority of the votes on ballot after ballot (it took two-thirds to win the nomination), nevertheless failed. The main reason for the miracle was that the Wilson and Underwood forces stood firm, blocking Clark's nomination, while Wilson's managers negotiated deals with the machines and with Underwood's following. To some slight extent Clark's defeat may have been due to Bryan, who threw his support to Wilson at a critical moment in the convention struggle.

Wilson won the nomination without badly splitting the party. Backed by a progressive platform, he appeared before the electorate in armor at least as shiny as Roosevelt's. He was able to win over Bryan's rural and small-town following with the same religious appeal, the same denunciation of the Wall Street money trust, that the "Great Commoner" had always used. Some well-educated people who had always scorned Bryan as a fool came to worship Wilson as a saint.

Thus Wilson was able to hold Democratic progressives, while Roosevelt was able only to pull progressives out of the Republican party. As for Taft, after several sad speeches, so conservative that they might have been written by Aldrich, he lapsed into silence. The Socialists, at the peak of their strength under Debs, criticized all three major candidates as defenders of capitalism. The main effect of the Socialists was to serve as a bugaboo for progressive leaders, who could warn that the only alternative to their own safe, moderate programs would be the drastic remedies of socialism. Even in 1912, their heyday, the Socialists attracted only 901,000 votes, 6 percent of the total votes cast.

Because of the three-cornered contest Wilson carried the electoral college overwhelmingly, with 435 votes to 88 for Roosevelt and only 8 for Taft. Wilson had received less than 42 percent of the popular vote, fewer votes than Bryan in any of his three campaigns. Yet, in view of the combined Democratic and Bull Moose totals, the newly elected President had an overwhelming progressive mandate.

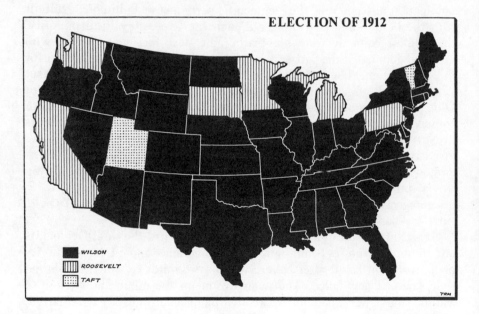

ELECTION OF 1912

WILSON
ROOSEVELT
TAFT

five

The New Freedom Triumphs

As President, Wilson demonstrated remarkable skills by not only securing the passage of most of his own program, the New Freedom, but also much of Roosevelt's New Nationalism.

Wilson, the lean, lantern-jawed son of a Southern Presbyterian preacher, looked as well as acted the part of a progressive crusader. Born in the Valley of Virginia, brought up in Confederate Georgia and the South Carolina of Reconstruction, Wilson had matured in an atmosphere of romantic nostalgia for the lost cause and Calvinistic ardor for what was right and moral. In his emotions he was devoted to his kinfolk and fervently religious. His aspiration had always been to become a political leader, but when as a beginning lawyer in Atlanta he had found the road dull, he had taken a doctor's degree at Johns Hopkins. He had become a professor of political economy and later president of Princeton University. At Princeton, his lectures, evoking images of the selfless Founding Fathers, inspired his students with a respect for an idyllic American past. His graceful writings were also more inspirational than analytical. Wilson drew his own intellectual strength from the Bible and from the political essays of the English conservatives, especially Edmund Burke and Walter Bagehot. The British parliamentary system was his ideal, and as President he was to pattern himself more on Gladstone than on Jefferson.

Both as president of Princeton and as governor of New Jersey, Wilson demonstrated the courageous strength and alarming weaknesses that would characterize his presidency. Both times he fought through major reform programs and then, because of personality difficulties, lost control. He had the vision to inspire multitudes but was dogmatic and distant with individuals. On occasion he demonstrated rare skill as a practitioner of the arts of political persuasion and compromise. On other occasions, often when he was exhausted or ill, his sense of virtue, backed by stubbornness, could lead him away from political accommodation into bitter deadlock. Out of the same characteristics came the glory of Wilson and his ultimate tragedy.

President Woodrow Wilson (NATIONAL ARCHIVES)

In 1912, and for some time thereafter, only the glory was apparent. The distance between the positions of the Democratic party and the new Progressive party was not as great as campaign oratory made it seem, just as personality more than principles separated Wilson from Roosevelt. Nevertheless, the differences in platform were significant in the campaign and in Wilson's future program as President.

Wilson's New Freedom program emerged as the campaign unfolded. His conversion to progressivism had come only two or three years before, and he had continued to cling to the states'-rights position that the task of the federal government was the purely negative one of destroying privilege. Thus Wilson hoped to restore the good old days, which in reality had never existed, by re-creating full opportunity for the small enterpriser. Roosevelt's New Nationalism, Wilson charged, would mean the federal licensing of the juggernauts of big business to crush the American people. In contrast, Wilson proclaimed his New Freedom as the fight for emancipation of the small businessman, the "man on the make." He proclaimed: "If America is not to have free enterprise, then she can have freedom of no sort whatever."

ENACTING WILSON'S PROGRAM

Few Presidents have taken more seriously their electoral mandate or worked more effectively to transform it into law than did Wilson. He brought back into the White House a firm belief in positive presidential leadership. As he assembled a cabinet and advisers, his only shortcoming was his tendency to gauge his subordinates by their complete, unquestioning willingness to accept his point of view. Senator John Sharp Williams once declared, "He was the best judge of measures and the poorest of men I ever knew."

The closest of Wilson's advisers was the shrewd and ubiquitous Colonel Edward M. House, who, through intelligent service and the refusal to accept a cabinet position, virtually shared presidential powers as Wilson's alter ego until 1919. He served as agent for Wilson in negotiations first with the men of economic power in America and later with those of political power in Europe. His discretion and anonymity were so consummate that one contemporary remarked, "He can walk on dead leaves and make no more noise than a tiger." It was House who gathered data for Wilson on the cabinet choices.

The cabinet, as was politically necessary, represented the wide range of factions within the Democratic party. Bryan had to be offered the appointment as Secretary of State in recognition of his long leadership of the party. William Gibbs McAdoo, an energetic, ambitious New York entrepreneur from Georgia, became Secretary of the Treasury; Albert S. Burleson, an adroit Texan, as Postmaster General became the political expert in the cabinet. Representative William B. Wilson, earlier secretary-treasurer of the United Mine Workers, became the first Secretary of Labor, establishing a twenty-year precedent that the office should be filled by a labor leader. It was the most Southern cabinet since the Civil War; half of its members were Southerners, at least by birth.

Over his cabinet and Congress Wilson exerted strong leadership as though he saw in himself the personification of the will of the people. He remarked that first summer, "No one but the President seems to be expected . . . to look out for the general interest of the country." In this spirit he cajoled and drove the Democratic majority in Congress into writing the New Freedom into law. A good many of the Democrats were energetic, responsible progressives who were new to the Congress and took no urging, but above them in many important committee chairmanships were the Conservative Democrats. They were ready to cooperate with Wilson, although less enthusiastically, because they realized that the only opportunity for the Democrats, a minority party, to stay in power was to enact a positive program. Thus Wilson possessed what Roosevelt had lacked, a congressional majority behind him. What he added to Roosevelt's presidential leadership was firm control over the party majority in Congress. Wilson did not wield his patronage powers as young progressive Democrats would have liked, to remodel the party by destroying conservative Democratic control in the many states where it persisted. In order not to jeopardize his legislative program, he accepted the advice of Burleson and rewarded the faithful old-line Democrats in Congress even though he thus helped stifle progressivism in several Southern states. In effect, he occasionally sacrificed progressive men in order to obtain immediate progressive measures. Wilson may not have been too displeased, since the fervent young progressives were less manageable than the older and more conservative Democrats. "My head is with the progressives in the Democratic party," he once told his secretary, Joseph Tumulty, "but my heart, because of the way they stood by me, is with the so-called Old Guard. They stand without hitching."

Wilson promptly undertook what Roosevelt had avoided and Taft had failed to achieve—a substantial lowering of the tariff. On the day he took office he called a special session of Congress. When it met, he did what no other President since Jefferson had done: he appeared before Congress in person. His short graphic message was aimed less at congressmen than at their constituents. It brought to a blaze the sentiment for real tariff reform. With the President's active support, Underwood introduced a bill in the House providing for tariff cuts substantial enough to bring European manufacturers into competition with Americans.

Proud of their handiwork, the Democrats proclaimed that the Underwood-Simmons tariff would cut the cost of living. The law brought the rates down from the Payne-Aldrich level of about 37 percent to 29 percent and added many imports to the free list. The economic upheavals of war came too soon for any proof that it aided consumers or did not injure business. Conclusively, the measure did demonstrate that the Democrats could unite to enact against great hazards a significant piece of reform legislation.

To make up for the loss of revenue under the new tariff, Representative Cordell Hull drafted a section for the bill, providing for a graduated income tax under the Sixteenth Amendment. Hull cautiously set the rates exceedingly low. Then, to his delight, progressive Republican and Democratic senators forced substantially higher rates upon the conservatives and the administration. This first modern income tax imposed a 1-percent tax upon individuals and corporations earning over $4,000, and an additional 1-percent tax on income over $20,000, ranging up to a maximum of 6 percent on income over $500,000. The income tax was the beginning of a great change in the American tax structure. Although more slowly than England and some other nations, the United States was beginning to place a proportionately greater share of the cost of government upon the rich. In so doing, it was beginning to chip away at the enormous disparity in incomes in the United States.

Rather than lose momentum, President Wilson held Congress in session through the sweltering summer to begin work on banking reform. In 1911 he had declared, "The great monopoly in this country is the money monopoly. So long as that exists, our old variety and freedom and individual energy of development are out of the question." A House investigating committee headed by a Democrat, Arsene Pujo, early in 1913 published frightening statistics to back Wilson's accusation. The figures, to which

Louis D. Brandeis gave wide circulation in a series of articles entitled "Other People's Money," indicated that small banks were depositing their surpluses with larger ones, which in turn deposited with a few great investment bankers concentrated on Wall Street. These bankers with their enormous capital, representing the aggregate savings of millions of people, were able to demand control over corporations in return for granting them financing, "the lifeblood of business." The Morgan-Rockefeller empire held "in all, 341 directorships in 112 corporations having aggregate resources or capitalization of $22,245,000,000." In 1913 the entire national wealth was estimated at less than ten times this figure. The tightness of the control through the directorships was illustrated by the remark of a railroad president in 1905: "Wherever Morgan sits on a board is the head of the table even if he has but one share."

To President Wilson the evidence indicated a need to break the money trust. At the same time, paradoxically, one of the serious ills of the American banking system was its decentralization and independence, except through the loose tie of urban clearing houses. As a result also of the defective functioning of the national banking system, in time of financial crisis and deflation it was difficult for banks to draw upon their reserves or to expand their currency. After the panic of 1907 Congress passed the Aldrich-Vreeland Act as a makeshift to permit greater expansion of the currency in time of economic distress. Aldrich recommended, through the National Monetary Commission in 1912, a broader base for currency and the establishment of a great central bankers' bank under bankers' control. Wilson and the even more vehemently anti–Wall Street Bryan wing of the Democrats feared Aldrich's proposal would strengthen the money trust. But Democrats and Republicans alike agreed that banking reform was needed; both parties had promised it in their platforms.

The conservative Democrat Representative Carter Glass proposed a system with perhaps twenty privately controlled but decentralized bankers' banks (reserve banks). Bryan and his followers favored decentralization, but they did want firm government control. It was no easy task for Wilson to satisfy the agrarians without frightening the bankers, especially since he wished to cap the system with a supervisory board. A struggle developed over whether it should be under banker or government control. Under the influence of Brandeis, Wilson accepted the minimum progressive specifications, that the federal government exercise exclusive control over the Federal Reserve Board and stand behind the Federal Reserve notes. With Bryan mediating and Wilson brandishing every presidential power in his armory, the measure finally went through both houses and was signed by the President on December 23, 1913. It was the most important piece of domestic legislation in his administration.

The Federal Reserve Act created twelve regional banks. Each was to serve and be owned by the banks of its district. The Federal Reserve Bank would rediscount their notes, issue a new type of paper currency, Federal Reserve notes, and fulfill other banking functions for member banks and the government. The act required national banks to become members and encourage other banks to do so. Although the American Bankers' Association had criticized the legislation, nearly half the nation's banking resources were represented in the system within its first year of operation and four-fifths by the late twenties. Nor did bankers have any cause to fear the Federal Reserve Board, to which Wilson appointed conservative, sympathetic men. When the list was announced, a progressive Republican senator exclaimed that it looked as though the president of the National City Bank had selected it.

The Federal Reserve System was a notable advance in banking regulation, providing as it did for a more elastic currency, essential at harvest time in agricultural areas, and in periods of crisis thoughout the nation. It did not destroy the so-called money trust, but it did mark a significant start toward a decentralization of capital in the United States. It did not serve as a safeguard against panic and depression, although it could to some extent counteract deflationary flurries. Its cautious board failed at times to regulate the discount rate and use its other powers properly; many of the important regulations that the Pujo Committee had prescribed had not been enacted. Thousands of banks outside of the system were to fail, and the Federal Reserve was to demonstrate its impotence to cope with the great crash of 1929 before new reform legislation was enacted to strengthen it.

There remained the overall problem of the trusts. Wilson had promised to accept legislation abolishing interlocking directorates, but on January 2, 1914, only a few days after he had signed the Federal Reserve Act, the House of Morgan proclaimed that it was voluntarily relinquishing thirty directorships. Wilson decided to go ahead with the legislation anyway, but neither he nor various factions of Democrats in Congress could agree upon where to go. A strong agrarian minority wanted drastic legislation: strict stock-exchange regulation, destruction of the interlocking ties of the money trust, limitation of production by each trust to a third of the product of the particular industry; and a graduated corporation tax so stiff that it would destroy giant combinations. Organized labor, on the other hand, was insistent that it be completely exempted from antitrust legislation. Wilson was strongly opposed to such drastic solutions. Since he felt most businessmen were public spirited, he sought no more than clear rules for their guidance.

Consequently, as several antitrust bills began their course through Congress in 1914, Wilson shifted to follow the lead of Brandeis away from the rather negative court approach earlier envisaged in the New Freedom and toward the regulatory solution of the New Nationalism. He gave his strong support to a bill outlawing unfair trade practices and establishing the Federal Trade Commission to prohibit unfair methods of competition such as price discrimination or exclusive dealing contracts. The commission would police business through cease-and-desist orders, engaging in prevention as well as punishment. Thus Wilson intended to stop monopolistic practices at an early stage and protect legitimate business, small as well as large.

Simultaneously, Wilson lost interest in the Clayton Antitrust bill.

Conservatives in Congress put qualifying clauses around the sections outlawing interlocking directorates or stockholdings and exclusive selling contracts, so that the clauses, as a progressive Republican senator complained, did not have enough teeth to masticate milk toast. Labor, as the American Anti-Boycott Association reported with satisfaction, gained nothing of practical importance from the bill. It contained no more than a platitude that labor was not a commodity and a declaration that unions were not conspiracies in restraint of trade. Although the clause did not cover activities of unions such as the secondary boycott, President Gompers of the AFL chose to hail the Clayton Act as "Labor's Magna Charta" and insist that organized labor was now exempted from antitrust prosecution. This assumption served merely to make bitterness and resentment greater when courts continued in the twenties to follow their earlier inclinations. The Sherman and Clayton Acts might be impotent against trusts, but they were a stout club for disciplining boycotters and strikers.

Samuel Gompers (NATIONAL ARCHIVES)

In practice Wilson's antitrust program was much like those of his predecessors. In the Federal Trade Commission he had accepted the principle of regulation as opposed to dissolution, but the men he appointed to it were so inept or so sympathetic toward business that Brandeis dismissed them as a "stupid administration." Wilson's Attorney General, James C. McReynolds, as an assistant attorney general in the Roosevelt administration and special counsel in the tobacco suits, had come to favor consent decrees over trust busting. He continued the policy of the Taft administration and announced that large corporations doubtful about their legality could straighten out their affairs with the friendly cooperation of the Department of Justice. By December 1913 he had thus obtained a spectacular settlement with the American Telephone and Telegraph Company, which dropped control of the Western Union Telegraph Company. Prosecutions continued, but their main effect was either political (to placate anti–Wall Street sentiment) or persuasive (to bring about consent decrees). The appropriation and staff were too small for effective regulation or prosecution. With more men and money the Department of Justice would still have lost in the courts, for the Clayton Act had done nothing to counteract the Supreme Court's limiting rule of reason.

The debate over antitrust legislation during the first half of 1914 coincided with a deepening depression. It came because the United States, still a debtor nation easily affected by European money markets, suffered from credit restrictions growing out of European pessimism over the Balkan wars and the likelihood of a bigger war. Within this country businessmen blamed the depression upon the Underwood tariff and the other legislation of the New Freedom. Wilson tried to placate business titans through friendly conferences and mild administration of his new reform legislation. He assured the leaders that he opposed only business that expanded "by methods which unrighteously crushed those who were smaller." From its inception the New Freedom had been a comparatively limited, state-rights, negative program, aimed at eliminating the economic evils of America so that free enterprise could flourish. Progressives in Congress had forced Wilson further than he had intended to go in the basic legislation of his first eighteen months in office. By the fall of 1914, when business at home was unsettled and war had broken out abroad, he was ready to proclaim the completion of the New Freedom. The future would be one of business cooperation under the new regulatory legislation.

RETREAT AND ADVANCE

Through 1914 and 1915, to the disappointment of many advanced progressives, Wilson again and again applied the brakes to reforms. With a states'-right answer he turned aside the plea for woman suffrage. He condoned the actions of his Southern cabinet members when they introduced Jim Crow into the administration to an unprecedented degree. Only the angry protests of Northern liberals brought some reversal. He opposed a bill to establish federally backed land banks to ease credit to farmers, declaring it went beyond the proper scope of the government. He gave no aid to a child-labor bill because he thought it unconstitutional. With marked misgivings, he studied the La Follette seamen's bill of 1915, the work of the eloquent president of the Seamen's Union, Andrew Furuseth, which freed seamen of the fetters of their contracts and improved safety regulations. Wilson "finally determined to sign it because it seemed the only chance to get something like justice done to a class of workmen who have been too much neglected by our laws."

For Wilson the New Freedom might be complete, but not for the progressive Democrats in Congress. At times they expressed their sharp dismay, but they did not have to engage in warfare with him as had the Republican insurgents with Taft. When the election year 1916 opened, two things were apparent. The Progressive party, which had never been much more than a Roosevelt vehicle, was disintegrating. Unless the Democrats, who were normally a minority, presented a new, strong progressive program, they would be swamped at the polls by the reunited Republicans. Wilson accepted the challenge and went beyond the New Freedom, allying himself with the progressives, farmers, and laborers to advocate a series of laws that in some respects enacted the Progressive party program of 1912. From a negative policy of restriction he moved to a positive one of vigorous federal intervention in the economy and society. Strangely, Roosevelt had moved to the right and no longer supported his 1912 proposals.

In January 1916 Wilson appointed Brandeis to the Supreme Court and weathered the conservative uproar to obtain his Senate confirmation. In May he accepted a farm-loan bank system in the Federal Farm Loan Act. At the urging of progressives he applied pressure upon the Democratic leaders in the Senate to obtain a workmen's compensation system for federal employees. He also accepted the first federal child-labor law, the Keating-Owen Act of 1916, which prohibited the shipment in interstate commerce of products manufactured by underage children. It marked not only a significant reversal on the part of Wilson but also a new assumption of federal control over manufacturing through the commerce clause of the Constitution. When the Supreme Court invalidated it in 1918 by a 5-to-4 decision, Congress passed an act levying a heavy tax on the products of child labor. This too President Wilson signed, and this too the Supreme Court ultimately invalidated, with Taft, who in 1921 became Chief Justice, writing the decision.

Despite the setback in prohibiting child labor, the second wave of legislation in the Wilson administration further enlarged the regulatory function of the federal government. After Wilson had failed to mediate a dispute between the railroad brotherhoods and the railroads, he signed an emergency measure, the Adamson Act, to prevent a nationwide railroad strike that would have paralyzed commerce. The measure provided for an eight-hour day at the previous ten hours' pay for all railroad workers. While it attracted national attention, other less well known pieces of legislation brought about even greater changes. Without attracting much attention, they undermined states' rights by granting subsidies on a dollar-matching basis for states to undertake various types of programs. Another effect of these laws, in combination with the new income tax, was to take money out of the wealthier Northeastern areas and redistribute it in the South and West. The first of the laws was the Smith-Lever Act of 1914, which provided money for states to establish extension work in agricultural education. It made formal and national the new system of county agents to advise farmers and facilitated the rise of the powerful American Farm Bureau Federation. The Smith-Hughes Act of 1917 subsidized vocational courses in secondary schools. Most important of all, the Federal Highway Act of 1916 appropriated $75 million to be spent for road building over a period of five years.

Altogether, the first Wilson administration had gone far beyond the limited reform program of the New Freedom in an impressive array of regulatory legislation, built upon the efforts of all the progressives for a decade and more. To a considerable extent, it represented the fruition of most of the main progressive objectives. Wilson was justified in his boast that the Democrats had come close to carrying out the platform of the Progressive party as well as their own. Like many of the products of the progressive spirit, some of the laws were limited and cautious in conception and application. Few of the next generation would accept the exaggerated view of a New York congressman who denounced one of the measures (the Adamson Act) as "the first step away from the old democracy of Thomas Jefferson and the federal policy of Alexander Hamilton to the socialism of Karl Marx."

Stuck on the Lincoln Highway in 1915 (BUREAU OF PUBLIC ROADS, DEPARTMENT OF COMMERCE)

Altogether the progressives had achieved much. They had introduced genuine regulation of railroads, a lower tariff, a better credit system, and the income tax. They had refused to give organized labor the weapon of unlimited collective bargaining but had favored much paternalistic labor legislation. They had failed to curb the growth of large corporations but had established the principle of corporate regulation. Through federal subsidies they were undermining state barriers in order to secure standard reform legislation. Within states progressives passed laws regulating the working conditions of women and even of men, providing workmen's compensation insurance, preventing child labor, and protecting social welfare in a wide variety of ways. On both national and state levels they made advances in the fields of public health and conservation. Also, progressives had put the businessman on the defensive so that he gave at least a semblance of acting in the public interest. The National Association of Manufacturers lobbied against almost every progressive measure; nevertheless, corporations moved toward an era of welfare capitalism. Judge Elbert H. Gary wrote in 1926, "To my personal knowledge many men of big affairs have completely changed their opinions and methods concerning ethical questions in business." Progressivism played a large part in whatever change took place.

In the area of social justice progressives failed to legislate a golden age but wiped out some of the most vile abuses of the nineteenth century. Their improvements in the machinery of government at times creaked or broke down or responded as readily to bosses as to progressives, but they unquestionably made governmental institutions, except for the Supreme Court, much more susceptible to popular will. In the next great wave of reform the leaders did not have to spend years winning control of the machinery of government.

six
Militant Progressivism

The militant morality of the American people during the progressive era extended to the foreign affairs. Police action and government regulation as a means of righting wrongs at home had as a logical counterpart the use of threats of armed intervention to secure justice overseas. A few progressives such as President Theodore Roosevelt were ready to pledge American force to preserve what seemed a just power balance in Europe; many more were ready to risk war to maintain a balance in Asia; and almost all favored the forcefully paternalistic policies in Latin America. A decided majority seems to have favored the maintenance of an American empire; a vigorous minority opposed it. These views split conservative Americans as well as progressives and were reflected in the Senate votes on naval bills and expanionist treaties, in which progressives and the Old Guard were to be found on each side.

The ardent moralistic nationalism that had contributed to America's entrance into the war with Spain in 1898 was still alive. To substantiate it in the new technical age were the new, supposedly scientific, racist doctrines popular in both Western Europe and the United States. These notions explain much of the opposition to the "new immigrants" in the absence of any valid data that they were in any way inferior. (Some data could be given such an interpretation, but it has since proved to be unscientific rubbish.) The popular racist doctrines gave justification for the new colonialism, compounded of equal parts of the old Manifest Destiny and Rudyard Kipling's new "White Man's Burden."

Nationalistic Americans favored building a strong navy for national defense. Nor did they object to its use on ventures in the Western Hemisphere. At the time Marines landed in Veracruz, Mexico, Senator William E. Borah of Idaho, usually regarded as an isolationist, declared, "This is the beginning of the march of the United States to the Panama Canal." Nor did many nationalists object to a strong policy toward the East, particularly China. As in Latin America, they felt the United States as a matter of historic right had an interest.

Progressives, who cheered as the government put down malefactors at home, were often ready to applaud just as loudly when the government extended its police power overseas. Some, like Jane Addams of Hull House, were pacifistic—indeed, among most progressives there was the optimistic feeling that great wars were not only un-Christian but also outmoded—but there seemed none of the urgency about foreign policy that there was in domestic matters. Hence most progressives, preoccupied by reform at home, allowed the Presidents to conduct foreign policy little observed, and little checked. Walter Lippmann, who had graduated from Harvard into the progressive vanguard in 1910, wrote years later, "I cannot remember taking any interest whatsoever in foreign affairs until after the outbreak of the First World War. . . . I remained quite innocent of the revolutionary consequences of the Spanish-American War."

When progressives did pay attention to foreign policy, many of the most idealistic applauded as the United States—through its missionaries, its businessmen, or even its armed forces—brought religion and medicine, economic progress, law and order, and (it was hoped) American democratic institutions to backward areas. Involved in this was the exhilaration of moral adventure, seemingly without risk of major war. It was progressivism by the sword.

Along with these militant moral ideas most Americans of the Progressive era still clung to the reassuring illusion of being somehow safely isolated from any war that might break out in Europe. They would have been incredulous if anyone had suggested that they were drifting toward world conflict. It is easier to see in hindsight that the industrial and technological revolutions in the Western world, along with their economic benefits, had brought heightened competition among the great powers for markets, sources of raw materials—and national prestige. The first years of the twentieth century were marked not only by great social gains among industrial nations but also by a frightening arms race, intensified as these countries split into two rival alliances. The United States scarcely could have remained long disentangled, since it was the greatest industrial nation in the world.

T.R. AND THE BIG STICK

As much as any other progressive, Theodore Roosevelt liked to engage in moralizing about the position of the United States in the world. His most often repeated theme was, as he once put it:

> The just war is a war for the integrity of high ideals. The only safe motto for the individual citizen of a democracy fit to play a great part in the world is service—service by work and help in peace, service through the high gallantry of entire indifference to life, if war comes on land.

This kind of talk rallied the support of many progressives, even those who were revolted by Roosevelt's blatant militarism—his equally incessant extolling of the soldierly virtues as "the most valuable of all qualities." Despite his bombast, he conducted foreign affairs with a sure hand.

Roosevelt's concept of the role of the United States in world politics emphasized sea power. Now that the United States had colonies, it needed to build a navy powerful enough to keep the sea lanes open to them. It also needed to build an Isthmian canal so that naval units could sail quickly from one ocean to another, and not have to make a long and difficult voyage around Cape Horn, as the *Oregon* had done during the Spanish-American War. In addition, it needed to protect the Caribbean approaches to the canal from encroachment. All this predicated a strong naval policy at a time when the key to strength in the world was a powerful fleet. This meant a navy second only to that of Great Britain.

Such were the views of President Roosevelt at the time when Kaiser Wilhelm II was launching Germany upon a gigantic naval race with Great Britain. As Britain began construction of the first dreadnought (large modern battleship) in 1905, both Germany and the United States were building more and larger warships, amid growing alarums of war. Urged on by Roosevelt, the most effective of naval lobbyists, Congress voted appropriations for ten battleships and four armored cruisers between 1902 and 1904. These were more powerful and more widely ranging than the relatively light vessels of the nineties, which had been designed primarily to defend the American coast. By 1906 the American navy was second only to the British, but in the next few years it was surpassed by the German navy.

Roosevelt liked to quote an African proverb: "Speak softly and carry a big stick." This certainly characterized his action in the Far East, as well as in the Caribbean. He hoped to make the Open Door policy effective against Russian expansion in Manchuria. For a moment in 1903 he expressed such indignation over the "treachery" and "mendacity" of Russia that he toyed with the idea of going to "extremes" with her. His practical policy, however, was to encourage Japanese efforts to check the Russian drive. When the Japanese made a surprise attack upon the Russian fleet at Port Arthur, Manchuria, in 1904, he was inclined to cheer, as were most Americans. He warned the French and Germans against aiding Russia, but he did not wish to see the Japanese totally victorious, since this might "possibly mean a struggle between them and us in the future."

Roosevelt pursued this same policy in the peace negotiations. Though the Japanese won a series of spectacular victories, they faced such serious financial difficulties that they asked Roosevelt to mediate. He agreed and called a peace conference at Portsmouth, New Hampshire, in the summer of 1905. But he soon offended the Japanese by opposing their demands for an enormous idemnity. He lost their good will even though he approved their territorial gains at the conference—control over Korea and South Manchuria and annexation of the southern half of Sakhalin Island, which had belonged to Russia.

Japanese-American relations, thus suddenly made worse, were not much improved by a secret Japanese-American agreement that was effected at the time of the Portsmouth conference. President Roosevelt had dispatched Secretary of War Taft from Manila to Tokyo to reach a Far Eastern understanding with the Japanese. In the resulting Taft-Katsura memorandum of July 1905 the Japanese prime minister acknowledged American sovereignty in the Philippines, and the American President recognized the suzerainty of Japan over Korea.

Roosevelt's role in helping to negotiate the 1905 Treaty of Portsmouth won for him the Nobel Peace Prize. His actions did indeed contribute to preservation of the peace by maintaining a power balance between Russia and Japan on the Asian mainland. But in Asian waters Japan had risen to a new ascendancy through her destruction of the Russian fleets. Japan repaired and refloated many of the vessels and rapidly built new ships in the following years. Japan undoubtedly had become powerful enough to seize the Philippines (which Roosevelt came to regard as an Achilles heel) because the American fleet would have had trouble fighting effectively so far from home. Unfortunately, at this same time, the people of Japan and the United States became angry with each other.

In October 1906, within a year after Japan's victory over a great European power, the San Francisco school board ordered the segregation of Oriental schoolchildren. This step was taken in response to the feelings of Californians against the 500 to 1,000 Japanese immigrants coming in each year, feelings which were intensified by lurid "Yellow Peril" articles in the Hearst and other newspapers. Resentment in Japan flared high, and jingoes in each country fanned the flames still higher.

Roosevelt worked skillfully to douse the flames. He persuaded San Francisco to desegregate its schools, and in return in 1907 he negotiated a gentlemen's agreement with Japan to keep out agricultural laborers. Then, lest the Japanese government think he had acted through fear, he launched a spectacular naval demonstration. He sent sixteen battleships of the new navy, "the Great White Fleet," on an unprecedented 45,000-mile voyage around the world. It gave the navy invaluable experience in sailing in formation while demonstrating the danger of dependence on foreign-owned coal-

The "Great White Fleet" sails around the world, 1908 (OFFICIAL U.S. NAVY PHOTO)

ing stations. The Japanese invited this formidable armada to visit Yokohama and gave it a clamorous welcome. Thus Roosevelt came to feel that through brandishing the big stick he had helped the cause of peace.

For the moment, the United States had demonstrated sufficient naval strength to restore an unsteady balance in Asian waters. In 1908, before the fleet had returned home, Japan and the United States negotiated the comprehensive Root-Takahira Agreement. Both countries agreed to support the Open Door in China. The United States tacitly seemed to give Japan a free hand in Manchuria (where rivalry with Russia continued) in return for an explicit guarantee of the status quo in the Pacific. This precarious equilibrium might be destroyed by any future upset in the naval ratios.

At the same time that he was directly engaged in balancing the powers in the Pacific, Roosevelt was participating somewhat less directly in trying to maintain a balance in Europe. American relations with Great Britain were increasingly cordial. In 1903 the British agreed to refer a troublesome dispute over the boundary between Alaska and Canada to a tribunal of three Americans, two Canadians, and one Englishman. To cultivate the friendship of the United States the English member of the tribunal voted against the Canadians and in favor of the American claim. Then the British government made another concession by pulling its naval units out of the Caribbean and leaving it as virtually an American lake.

When Germany and France quarreled over Morocco, Roosevelt was reluctant to involve the United States. "We have other fish to fry," he told Taft in 1905. Nevertheless, he resolved to try "to keep matters on an even keel in Europe." Consequently, he intervened on behalf of the German Kaiser to persuade France and Britain to attend an international conference for establishing the status of Morocco. Germany was protesting because the French had set up a protectorate there. At the conference, which met in Algeciras, Spain, in 1906, the American delegates sided with the British and the French to keep France dominant in Morocco while making some concessions to appease Germany. For the moment, the United States had helped avert, or at least postpone, a war into which it might ultimately be dragged.

THE IRON-FISTED NEIGHBOR

Roosevelt's preoccupation with the American strategy of defense in the Caribbean—especially his almost obsessive fear of German penetration—betrayed him into acting like an iron-fisted neighbor toward small countries to the south. He first used his might impetuously to start work on a canal in Panama.

Before Roosevelt became President, the McKinley administration was negotiating with Britain to remove an old obstacle, the 1850 treaty agreeing that the two countries would jointly construct, operate, and defend any canal to be built in Central America. In 1901 the British, eager to court American friendship, consented in the Hay-Pauncefote treaty to exclusive American construction, operation, and fortification of a canal.

"Here No One Dares Lay a Hand but Myself" by Mayol, for the Buenos Aires Caras y Caretas

The next question was where to locate the canal. There were two possible routes. The shortest one would be across the Isthmus of Panama, but the rights there were owned by a French company, the successor of an earlier company that had tried and failed to dig a canal. For its franchise the French company wanted $109 million, which would make a Panama canal more expensive than a Nicaraguan one. Consequently, both Congress and President Roosevelt favored the Nicaraguan route. But the French company had expert agents—Philippe Bunau-Varilla, its chief engineer, and William Nelson Cromwell, an attorney who had contributed heavily to the Republican campaign fund in 1900—who hastily cut the price of their rights to $40 million. Unless sold to the United States and sold quickly, the rights would be worthless, for they would expire in 1904. This price cut and able lobbying caused Congress and the President to change their minds.

Impatient to begin construction, Roosevelt put pressure upon Colombia, which owned Panama, to conclude a treaty authorizing the United States to dig a canal there. In January 1903 Secretary of State Hay and the Colombian chargé d'affaires Tomas Harrán signed a treaty that was most unfavorable to Colombia. It authorized the United States to construct a canal in return for a payment of only $10 million and an annual rental of $250,000, as compared with the $40 million the French company was to receive. The Colombian senate, as it had every right to do, rejected the treaty.

Roosevelt was too furious to give thought to niceties or to the value of a friendly policy toward Latin America. Fuming that the Colombians were "inefficient bandits," he considered seizing Panama through twisting a technicality in an 1846 treaty with Colombia (then New Granada) guaranteeing the neutrality and free transit of the Isthmus. Roosevelt's intended seizure became unnecessary, because Bunau-Varilla helped organize a Panamanian revolution. There had been many previous revolts, all failures. But at the outset of this one, the United States landed troops from the U.S.S. *Nashville* and, invoking the 1846 treaty obligation to maintain order, prevented Colombian forces from putting down the rebellion. Three days later, the United States recognized the new republic of Panama and, soon after that, negotiated a treaty paying Panama the sum Colombia had rejected, in return for the grant of a zone ten miles wide. The minister from Panama who arranged the treaty was Bunau-Varilla.

Work on the canal proceeded smoothly and efficiently. The elimination of tropical diseases in the area, the digging of the tremendous cuts, and the installation of huge locks at a total cost of $375 million filled Americans with patriotic enthusiasm, though some were ashamed of Roosevelt's ruthlessness. In 1911 he boasted: "I took the Canal Zone and let Congress debate; and while the debate goes on, the Canal does also." It opened in 1914.

Meanwhile Roosevelt was enlarging the Monroe Doctrine. In 1902 he had written to a German friend: "If any South American country misbehaves toward any European country, let the European country spank it." Germany, along with Italy and Great Britain, proceeded to spank Venezuela by blockading her coast. The object was to force the Venezuelan dictator to pay his country's debts to European bankers.

By 1903 Roosevelt had changed his mind. Americans were angered at the news of the German bombardment of a Venezuelan port, and he himself was beginning to fear that the Germans planned to establish a permanent base in Venezuela. He warned the Germans (according to his own later account) that Admiral Dewey had his fleet in the Caribbean and was ready to act in case they tried to acquire any territory. The Germans finally withdrew—as the British and Italians already had done—and agreed to submit the debt question to arbitration.

The Venezuela incident led to a new Caribbean policy usually called the Roosevelt Corollary of the Monroe Doctrine. The Hague Court declared that the powers that had threatened Venezuela had prior claim on payment of their debts; this increased the likelihood of future European intervention in the Western Hemisphere. For Roosevelt, who still believed that small nations must pay their just debts, the only way out seemed a drastic new device. If these little countries could not behave themselves, the United States reluctantly would police them and collect debt payments from them in order to forestall European intervention. Uncle Sam would act as a bill collector for European bankers. Roosevelt declared to Congress in 1904 that the United States might be forced, "however reluctantly, in flagrant cases of . . . wrongdoing or impotence, to the exercise of an international police power."

The occasion for putting the Roosevelt Corollary into operation was the defaulting of Santo Domingo on about $22 million of its debt to European nations. France and Italy threatened to intervene. In effect, the

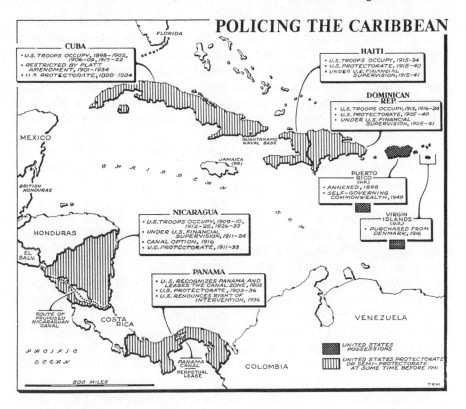

POLICING THE CARIBBEAN

United States established a receivership, taking over Dominican customs, paying 45 percent of the receipts to the Dominican government, and paying the rest to foreign creditors.

As a part of an American strategy of Canal defense, Roosevelt's Caribbean policy was doubtless successful. As a means of securing the support and cooperation of nations to the south, it left much to be desired. Roosevelt's tactics inspired fear rather than friendship.

TAFT AND DOLLAR DIPLOMACY

President Taft was no readier in foreign affairs than at home to exert strong personal leadership as Roosevelt had done. For the most part he left the State Department to his Secretary of State, a former corporation lawyer, Philander C. Knox. Taft and Knox made no real effort to maintain a balance of power in either Europe or Asia. Instead, they concentrated upon promoting American banking and business interests overseas.

In Far Eastern relations, this policy brought to the forefront young Willard Straight, an agent of American bankers, formerly consul general at Mukden, Manchuria. He argued that dollar diplomacy was the financial expression of the Open Door policy, that it would make "a guaranty for the preservation, rather than the destruction of China's integrity." Taft, therefore, was ready to ignore Roosevelt's tacit arrangement with Japan that the

United States would stay out of Manchuria, and to support the right of Americans to invest both there and in China. When British, French, and German bankers formed a consortium to finance railroads in China, Secretary Knox insisted that Americans should also participate. In 1911 they were admitted. Then Knox proposed that an international syndicate purchase the South Manchurian Railroad in order to neutralize it. This led the rivals Russia and Japan to sign a treaty of amity in 1910, thus closing the Manchurian door in Taft's face.

In the Caribbean there were no other great powers to block the amateurish American operations. As a result, a new pattern emerged there of interventions going far beyond Roosevelt's limited ones, to establish firm military, political, and, above all, economic control over several unstable republics to the south. Advocates of this program argued that American investors must be invited in to replace European investors, who otherwise might eventually bring about European intervention. This was a logical step beyond the Roosevelt Corollary.

The new policy began in 1909 when Knox tried to arrange for American bankers to establish a financial receivership in Honduras. He persuaded New York bankers to invest in the National Bank of Haiti. Then he sent marines to Nicaragua to protect revolutionaries, sponsored by an American mining company, who were fighting to overthrow a hostile dictator. Knox negotiated a treaty with the new friendly government giving the United States financial control, but the United States Senate failed to approve it. American bankers, less reluctant, accepted Knox's invitation to move in. By 1912 the new pro-American government was so unpopular that a revolt broke out. Taft sent marines to crush the uprising, and some of them remained as late as 1925. Even more than Roosevelt's policies, those of Taft alienated the neighboring countries to the south.

WILSONIAN INTERVENTION

President Wilson brought to the determination of foreign policy a flair for idealistic pronouncements. He was never unsure of his moral position but was often uncertain how to reach it. He and his Secretaries of State and the Navy, Bryan and Josephus Daniels, were all devoutly religious, war-hating men of good will, who disapproved of the exorbitant money-making sometimes connected with dollar diplomacy. But the temptation to make use of the force at their disposal to uplift their brothers to the south was too great to resist. The need to do so seemed compelling to them, because like their predecessors they felt that they must maintain an American-sponsored stability in the Caribbean as a vital part of national defense.

Wilson expounded his new policies in a speech at Mobile, Alabama, in the fall of 1913. He disavowed imperialist intent. "The United States will never again seek one additional foot of territory by conquest," he declared. Rather, he sought "the development of constitutional liberty in the world."

The Wilson administration not only regularized through treaty the continuing occupation of Nicaragua but also initiated new interventions in Santo Domingo and Haiti—to head off a supposed threat of German intervention. In spite of American customs control, revolution after revolution had swept through and impoverished Santo Domingo. The United States took over all Dominican finances and the police force, but the Dominicans would not agree to a treaty establishing a virtual protectorate. In 1916 Wilson established a military government. During the eight years that this government continued, the United States forcibly maintained order, trained a native constabulary, and promoted education, sanitation, and public works.

On the other end of the island of Hispaniola, the black republic of Haiti was even more revolution-wracked, the violence culminating in 1915, when a mob tore an unpopular president limb from limb. Wilson again sent in the marines, established another military government, and began the task of improving living conditions in Haiti. The marines demonstrated their efficiency in 1918 when they supervised an election to ratify a new American-sponsored constitution. The vote for it was 69,377 to 355. Nevertheless, that year they had to put down a serious revolt, killing some hundreds of Haitians in the process.

There was a persistent fear that the Germans might try to acquire the Danish West Indies. In 1902 the Senate ratified a treaty for their purchase, but the Danish parliament rejected it. Finally in 1917 the United States acquired the poverty-stricken islets, which were then renamed the Virgin Islands, for an exorbitant $25 million. Their value was negative: the United States wanted to make sure they were not in the possession of any potentially hostile power.

MAKING MEXICO BEHAVE

American business interests had invested about $1 billion in Mexico during the regime of a friendly dictator, Porfirio Díaz. They owned over half the oil, two-thirds of the railroads, and three-fourths of the mines and smelters. Popular though Díaz was in the United States, he came to be hated in Mexico because, while he encouraged foreigners to amass huge profits, he suppressed civil liberties and kept the masses in peonage. For the average Mexican there was little of the progress toward democracy or economic security that President Wilson desired. In 1910 the aged Díaz was overthrown by a democratic reform leader, who in turn was murdered and succeeded by the reactionary Victoriano Huerta just before Wilson took office. Wilson turned a deaf ear to American investors who saw in Huerta's presidency an opportunity to return to the "good old days." Rather, he refused to recognize "the government of butchers."

Years of tedious complications followed. Wilson hoped that, by refusing recognition to Huerta's government, he could bring about its collapse and the development of constitutionalism in Mexico. He offered in June

1913 to mediate between Huerta and the opposing Constitutionalists of Venustiano Carranza. Both sides refused.

For several months Wilson pursued a policy of watchful waiting, but when Huerta established a full military dictatorship in October 1913, Wilson began to bring increasing pressure against him. First he persuaded the British (who were obtaining most of their naval oil from Mexico) to stop supporting Huerta. Next he offered to send American troops to the aid of Carranza, but again he was rebuffed, since all Carranza wanted was the right to buy arms in the United States. Wilson granted this in February 1914 by lifting President Taft's arms embargo, but still the Carranzists did not win.

Wilson was in a dilemma: he might have to choose between recognizing Huerta, stronger than ever, or intervening with armed force, which could mean war against all the Mexican factions. Off the coast of Mexico the commanders of American fleet units, engaged in watchful waiting, became increasingly restless. The precipitate action of one of them gave Wilson a way out. In April 1914 one of Huerta's officers arrested several sailors of the U.S.S. *Dolphin* who had gone ashore at Tampico; a superior officer quickly released them and apologized. But the American admiral demanded a twenty-one gun salute to the United States flag in addition. At this Huerta balked. Wilson, deciding to back the admiral, sent all available warships to Mexican waters and asked Congress for authority to take drastic action. Then, anxious to prevent a German ship loaded with munitions from reaching Huerta's forces, Wilson, without waiting for Congress to act, ordered the navy to seize Veracruz. It did so, on April 21 and 22, 1914, but not in the bloodless way that Wilson had anticipated. The Mexicans suffered 126 killed and 195 wounded; the Americans, 19 killed and 71 wounded.

THE UNITED STATES IN MEXICO, 1913–1916

At this difficult point Argentina, Brazil, and Chile offered to mediate. With relief Wilson accepted and sent his delegates to confer with Huerta's at Niagara Falls, Canada, from May to July 1914. As the negotiations went on and on, the Carranzists advanced on Mexico City, finally bringing the result Wilson wished, the abdication of Huerta.

Under Carranza's presidency the Mexican muddle did not clear up but got worse. By September 1914 civil war was again devastating Mexico, as a former general of Carranza's, Francisco ("Pancho") Villa, tried to overthrow him. In October 1915 the United States gave de facto recognition to Carranza's government.

This antagonized Villa, who was still roaming northern Mexico. He tried to bring about a war between the United States and Mexico by shooting sixteen Americans he seized from a train in January 1916. When that failed, in March he raided Columbus, New Mexico, just across the border, killing nineteen more Americans. Wilson retaliated by ordering a punitive expedition under Brigadier General John J. Pershing to hunt down Villa. For this, Wilson had the permission of Carranza, but as Villa drew the American forces 300 miles into Mexico, two skirmishes with Carranza's army almost led to war. Again the peace forces outweighed the jingoes in the United States, and again Wilson accepted compromise. On July 4, 1916, Carranza suggested the appointment of a Joint High Commission to consider the problem. The commission debated into January 1917, when it broke up without establishing a basis for the withdrawal of American troops. By then the United States was so close to war with Germany that Wilson nevertheless withdrew the troops and in March 1917 gave formal recognition to Carranza's government.

Nothing but trouble had come out of Wilson's long and muddled intervention in Mexico. His bad tactics had aroused a hostility among the Mexican people which did not dissipate for years.

In other respects Wilson and his Secretary of State were slightly more

General John J. Pershing in Mexico (NATIONAL ARCHIVES)

successful in improving relations between the United States and Latin America. During 1913 and 1914 they negotiated a treaty with Colombia expressing "sincere regrets" for the Panama incident and paying an indemnity of $25 million. Roosevelt thundered that it was a "blackmail treaty," and his Republican friends in the Senate blocked it until after his death. In 1921 Congress voted to pay the indemnity but omit the apology.

seven
The New Enlightenment

By the opening years of the twentieth century the United States was undergoing an intellectual as well as a material revolution. The evolutionary theories of Darwin had helped introduce a scientific age and gave Americans an explanation of the functioning of human society. Educated people, both conservatives and liberals accepted the concept of Social Darwinism, that society evolved through survival of the fittest. It was an age in which scientific method, whether it was applicable or not, seemed supreme in almost every field of learning.

As for philosophers, in the latter part of the nineteenth century many of them, like Josiah Royce, had helped transplant German idealism to the United States. Idealism in various forms persisted, but by the early 1900s it was attracting far less attention than the distinctly American pragmatism. The dominant philosophy of twentieth-century America, pragmatism, was remarkably fitted to the progressives' need for an essentially scientific system of thought that could encompass their militant morality. Scientific method was uppermost in the thinking of a brilliant mathematical logician, Charles Sanders Peirce, who in 1878 published a paper expounding pragmatism. It did not attract much attention until the turn of the century; pragmatism was a twentieth-century philosophy. In the early 1900s it was William James, a famous psychologist and the brother of the novelist Henry James, who modified and gave wide currency to pragmatism. He sought to reconcile religion and science by developing a pragmatic theory of truth. Morton White has explained in *The Age of Analysis* (1955):

> The test of scientific, metaphysical, and theological truth was made uniform by James. If you want to know whether a theory of any kind is true, try believing it and see whether satisfactory results ensue: that is the brief summary that led some to hail James as a savior and others to caricature him brutally.

James' contemporary John Dewey, who left an indelible impression upon education, emphasized the moral aspects of pragmatism, making it

William James and Josiah Royce (HARVARD UNIVERSITY)

a philosophy of reform, one that would help guide the way to the good society. He felt that what was good, or had value, could be ascertained through carefully conducted experiments. Despite his turgid writing style, Dewey provided progressives with the philosophical system they required. "We were all Deweyites before we read Dewey," declared a progressive political scientist, "and we were all the more effective reformers after we had read him."

CHANGES IN SCHOOLING AND SCHOLARSHIP

In education pragmatism was especially influential. Psychologists emphasized the importance of proper early environment and training. Educators led by Dewey insisted that the schools could best provide the proper environment and training for curing the ills of society. Through their emphasis upon progressive education they touched off a debate that continued vigorously for many decades. Dewey attacked the prevalent classical education for the elite with its emphasis upon memorization and proposed more democratic methods of learning by doing. Schools should develop in the students not merely knowledge but also adjustment to life.

Some of Dewey's more zealous followers fell into excesses, but undeniably his influence did solidly extend education during the era. Kindergartens spread rapidly. The number of public high schools nearly doubled between 1900 and 1914, and the number of students increased two-and-a-half times. There were marked advances in elementary education also, but in 1914 the average child attended only 86 days of a 158-day school year and remained in school little more than six years. Teachers' salaries had increased from about $38 to $66 per month. There were wide variations in the quality of public education between that in Northern suburbs and in segregated schools for black children in the rural South.

Enrollment in higher education more than doubled during the progressive years, reaching over 350,000 by 1910. The quality of education improved markedly as colleges and universities moved from the rigid, classical curriculum to broader course offerings and the elective system. Professional and graduate schools generally improved to such a degree that in some respects they rivaled those of Europe. Professional associations had also come into existence.

The prevailing spirit in higher education as the Darwinian winds swept across the nation was scientific. It brought remarkable improvements in some areas and certain excesses in others. For the social sciences it meant all too often merely a painstaking collecting of data, much as in the cataloging technique of botany and zoology. But it also led to the nationalistic emphasis upon the effect of the frontier in the writings of the historian Frederick Jackson Turner and the skepticism of the economist Thorstein Veblen, who in *A Theory of the Leisure Class* (1899) attacked laissez-faire orthodoxy. Among lawyers there was debate over sociological jurisprudence, which Roscoe Pound described as "a movement . . . for the adjustment of principles and doctrines to the human conditions they are to govern rather than to assume first principles." Law schools rapidly switched to training through the case method; by 1928 three-fourths of the leading law schools employed it.

The experience of universities in training lawyers and social scientists by means of case and laboratory methods fed into politics and the social sciences. Universities provided governments with economists, political scientists, agricultural specialists, and experts on urban problems. Close working relationships developed between legislators and administrators, on the one side, and the university specialists, on the other.

SCIENCE AND MEDICINE MOVE INTO THE LABORATORY

In their scientific laboratories the universities were beginning to support a certain degree of basic or pure research, in addition to the applied research for which Americans had always been notable. Most of the great discoveries were still being made in Europe: the quantum theory in the field of physics, by Max Planck, in 1900; the theory of relativity, by Albert Einstein, in 1905. The strength of Americans was still in applied science and engineering and in the training of an ever-increasing number of technicians for American industry.

Science applied to agriculture finally caught the imagination of farmers. M. L. Wilson, one of the founders of the New Deal agricultural program, recalled, "When I went to Ames [Iowa] to study agriculture in 1902, . . . I was the first boy from that neighborhood to go to an *agricultural* college. Ten or fifteen years later it was becoming an accepted thing for all who could afford it."

By 1900 medical education at a few medical schools, and notably at Johns Hopkins (opened in 1893), had reached a level that compared favorably with that in Edinburgh, Vienna, and elsewhere in Europe. At Johns Hopkins, William H. Welch assembled a brilliant array of doctors who taught in laboratories and clinics by the inductive method. At the same school students did not merely sit in clinics or visit hospitals, practices that had long been commonplace, but served as part of the working staff. Unfortunately, many mediocre and worthless medical schools were in existence throughout the country. When Abraham Flexner made a survey in 1910 for the Carnegie Foundation for the Advancement of Teaching, he discovered that the dissecting room at one school doubled as a chicken yard. The report forced almost half of the medical schools out of existence and helped prod others toward the standards of Johns Hopkins.

The nation had attained excellence in applied medicine, but its record in medical research was considerably below that of Europe. One beneficent outcome of the Caribbean adventures of the United States, beginning with the Spanish-American War in 1898, had been the great discoveries in tropical medicine made by American medical scientists. In 1900 Dr. Walter Reed and his associates proved conclusively that a striped mosquito carried and transmitted yellow fever. Thus in 1901 the army began a widespread extermination program of the insect. As a result, yellow fever cases decreased from 1,400 in Havana alone in 1900 to 37 in all of Cuba in 1901. During the digging of the Panama Canal, Major William C. Gorgas applied the new knowledge so thoroughly that not one case of yellow fever originated there and malaria was virtually eradicated. In Puerto Rico Major Bailey K. Ashford discovered that the cause of the widespread anemia was hookworm, for which he developed an inexpensive cure.

All this knowledge was valuable in the southern United States. In 1909 Rockefeller gave a million dollars for the eradication of hookworm in the South, where almost 60 percent of the schoolchildren had some infestation. With chemicals and vaccines, some of which were important European developments, the nation made encouraging progress in combating venereal diseases, typhus, typhoid, and diphtheria. Sanitariums and a national association successfully combated tuberculosis. Campaigns against mosquitoes and flies, improved sanitation, milk inspection, and, beginning in 1908, the

Major Walter Reed (NATIONAL ARCHIVES)

chlorination of water supplies reflected the new vigor of the state and municipal boards of health. To cap the entire program, the marine hospital service expanded in 1902 and in 1912 became the United States Public Health Service. The national death rate dropped from 17 per 1,000 in 1900 to 13.2 in 1920. In underdeveloped tropical areas also, application of these medical discoveries led to a lowering of the death rate and increases in population.

LETTERS: FROM BACK BAY TO GREENWICH VILLAGE

The progressive generation of intellectuals moved with equal vigor beyond genteel literary traditions. Ohio-born William Dean Howells, the last of the great Boston literary arbiters, in 1881 left the Back Bay for the brownstone fronts of New York, bringing with him a polite realism—a careful, simple rendering of what he saw.

The most talked-about American novelist was another polite realist, the previously mentioned Henry James, who, when he came from Britain for a visit in 1904, had not been in the United States for a score of years. James had never abandoned interest in his own country. In several of his novels he examined the interaction of the representatives of America's newer culture with the sophisticates of the older culture of Europe. James' novels commanded only a limited number of readers in the United States, since to many they seemed to be intolerably involved in style and concerned with little more than the interplay of polite, well-to-do people in drawing rooms. A later generation was more appreciative of them as critiques not only of European ways but also of American society and its prevailing norms.

The age brought naturalism into the arts. Toward the still flourishing genteel and popular writers the new writers expressed unbounded scorn. Henry L. Mencken in his first critical article, which appeared in *Smart Set* in 1908, sneered that "American manufacturers of fiction, having the souls of fudge-besotted high-school girls, behold the human comedy as a mixture of a fashionable wedding and a three-alarm fire with the music of Chopin."

Popular magazines of the period built huge reader circulation on the publication of light, romantic fiction, interspersed for several years with muckraking articles. The popularity of romantic historical novels was so high that Howells, in 1901, lamented, "There is such a spilth of blood that you might expect to see it drip from the printed page." Before 1898 few American novels had sold 100,000 copies; by 1901 this figure was commonplace. Two historical novels of the American Winston Churchill, *Richard Carvell* and *The Crisis*, sold 420,000 and 320,000 copies respectively. By 1904 readers were turning to the adventure stories of Jack London, the sentimentalism of Kate Douglas Wiggin, and the shrewd portrayal of American life, whether middle class or genteel, of Booth Tarkington and Edith Wharton. Popular fiction was sometimes progressive in overtone. London lost a sizable part of his audience when he turned from adventure to socialism, but Churchill kept his when he attacked the railroads in *Mr. Crewe's Career* (1908). The writers who survived for later generations, along with the then popular authors, reflected much of the spirit of the times—Social Darwinism—with an emphasis upon racism and imperialism and preoccupation with success and its reverse image, failure.

Literature raced rapidly down the path of realism or naturalism, far beyond Howells and James, leading deep into the scientific age. Realism, as its detractors pointed out, merely photographed American society in its lower, if not lowest, strata, in sharpest contrast to the romantic literature of the period. Naturalism grew out of the drive of the French novelist Émile Zola and his followers to rip away the curtains of superstition. Some American novelists, inhibited by prevailing moral standards, had in part embraced naturalism, but like Howells they heeded the admonition that "literature must be suited to maiden eyes and ears." Increasingly, younger novelists strained against this restriction, one of their number complaining, "The female reader is the Iron Madonna who strangles in her fond embrace the American novelist."

In 1900 Theodore Dreiser tried to break away from the literary iron maiden to portray, in *Sister Carrie*, a poor girl who, far from suffering punishment for her liaisons with two men, used them to achieve success as an actress. The book was suppressed on the insistence of the publisher's wife and did not reappear for twelve years. In a tumbling, awkward style Dreiser hewed out a series of massive novels that established naturalism in American literature. *The Financier* (1912) and *The Titan* (1914) formed the saga of a ruthless Chicago magnate who destroyed his business competitors and made unscrupulous use of his wealth.

Dreiser's contemporaries, who for the most part did not approach European naturalism as closely as he did, presented American realities in the harsh spirit of revolt. Hamlin Garland ripped the agrarian dream with his sketches of the bleakness of farm life. Frank Norris, as a well-to-do young man, went to Paris to learn to paint; but he returned to America to write. Influenced by Zola and Kipling, his novels blended a powerful naturalism with overtones of romanticism. Striving for a "big, epic, dramatic thing," Norris embarked upon a trilogy but died at the age of thirty-two before he could complete the third volume. The first volume, *The Octopus* (1901), told of the struggle between the wheat ranchers and the railroad interests in California. The action of the second volume, *The Pit* (1903), shifted to the grain markets of Chicago. Ellen Glasgow succeeded in carrying to completion a large-scaled fictional project, a series of twelve novels that systematically examined the changing ways of the American South. The daughter of a socially prominent Richmond family, she consciously broke with Southern womanly tradition by publishing in 1897 *The Descendant*, the hero of which was of illegitimate birth and poor-white background.

Though few of the leading poets sang the themes of progressivism, the new stirrings wrought changes in poetry. Edwin Arlington Robinson, living in secluded poverty and writing a dignified and beautiful blank verse, received from President Roosevelt, an admirer of his verse, an appointment to the New York custom house. Robert Frost, ignoring in his poetry both progressive reform and poetic fashions, wrote of New England folk and countryside, and was in turn ignored by American publishers. His renown began only at the end of the era. The visionary poetry of Vachel Lindsay, when analyzed layer by layer, seemed to reveal no more than the evanes-

Frank Norris (HARVARD UNIVERSITY LIBRARY)

cent bubbles of a child's dreams; but in about twenty of his poems he caught something more: the rhythms and cadences of the revival tent, the street parade, and the carnival. Carl Sandburg in his free verse caught even more of the cadence and movement of the common people. Besides writing poetry, he was a collector of folk songs and the author of a six-volume biography of Abraham Lincoln (1926–1939), whom he helped elevate still higher than ever before in the hierarchy of folk heroes.

The first magazine to publish Sandburg and many other American poets of the era was *Poetry: A Magazine of Verse*, which Harriet Monroe founded in Chicago in 1912 for the publication of poetry of both a traditional and an experimental nature. The first number published two poems by an expatriate in London, Ezra Pound, who thereafter continued to proclaim in *Poetry* the dogmas of a small London group calling themselves the Imagists, who sought to create a new type of sharp, severe free verse. Amy Lowell went from Boston to London and eventually took command of the movement, and Pound moved on to other experiments in poetry.

The work of expatriate American artists in London and Paris was less exciting in American terms than the "Little Renaissance" that had begun among poets, novelists, playwrights, and artists in Chicago and spread to New York and other American cities. In the closing years of the Progressive era many brilliant young writers and artists were serving their apprenticeships in Greenwich Village. John Butler Yeats wrote in 1912, "The fiddles are tuning as it were all over America."

MUSIC, PAINTING, ARCHITECTURE, AND THE CINEMA

Although American composers during the Progressive era failed to make a niche for themselves comparable to that of the writers and artists, musical performance moved into golden years. If a concertgoer of today could go back and attend the performances at the new Symphony Hall in Boston in October 1900, he would find that little has changed in the decades following that opening. Modeled after a Greek theater by Charles F. McKim of the New York firm McKim, Mead, and White, this concert hall was the first in the world to be constructed in conformity with acoustical research. The observer from a later day would find everything familiar except the costumes of the women at the first regular concert. The Boston Symphony Orchestra, opening its twentieth season, played Weber's Overture to *Euryanthe*, Handel's Organ Concerto No. 4 in D Minor, the ballet music from Schubert's *Rosamunde*, and Beethoven's Fifth Symphony.

Throughout the nation distinguished symphony orchestras came into existence, and galaxies of performing stars made memorable the concert and opera seasons. In the years since the Civil War symphony orchestras had become permanent organizations, able to give an increased number of concerts and expand their repertoires. The works of Beethoven continued to dominate orchestra programs throughout the first half of the twentieth century but did drop from about a quarter of the repertoire to about an eighth, making room for the romantic Wagner and Tchaikovsky, who soared to a high peak of popularity in 1906–1910. Brahms, Mozart, and Bach were trailed by a galaxy of the modern composers, with an occasional American composer at the bottom. Even then, the Boston Symphony led all other orchestras in performing American music, allotting it about 6 percent of its repertoire. Americans hoped that at last they had acquired a great composer in Edward MacDowell, whose music was performed more often than that of any other American composer, but it failed to impress critics as being comparable to the best European work.

Victor Herbert, born in Dublin in 1859 and trained in Germany, established himself in America as an orchestra conductor and as the composer of a long series of excellent light operas: *Babes in Toyland* (1903), *Naughty Marietta* (1910), and many others. Musical comedy, even further removed from opera, was developing rapidly, with hits like George M. Cohan's *Forty-five Minutes from Broadway* (1906), and in this field American music proved to be eminently successful.

During these years jazz was in its infancy and was confined to New Orleans. It did not burst upon the nation until about 1917. Ragtime, one of the elements of jazz, had become the national musical passion by the turn of the century, but it was at the point of being forgotten when in 1911 Irving Berlin briefly revived it with *Alexander's Ragtime Band*.

The trends in art nearly paralleled those in literature. One critic wrote in 1902 that the underlying theme of art that was not official, commercial, or fashionable "is sadness, heart-searching, misgiving, melancholy—now spiritual, now sensuous—revolt against surrounding circumstance." It was a revolt against the prevailing academic style, typified at its best in the fashionable, lively portraitures by John Singer Sargent.

Parallel to Sargent in the early 1900s were several well-established painters: the romantic realist Thomas Eakins, who was painting dark and sober portraits that seldom pleased the sitters, and the popular Winslow Homer, who was delighting both the critics and the middle-class public with his pictures of the sea and the sky. Another painter, a romantic visionary who worked almost unnoticed, was Albert Pinkham Ryder.

It was out of romantic realism and French Impressionism that the most effective painters of the Progressive era developed. By the early 1900s the work of several of the French Impressionists had become accepted in the United States: masters of light, form, and color like Renoir, Monet, and Pissaro. Impressionism had touched Sargent; it dominated Mary Cassatt and Childe Hassam. Hassam had painted New York's Union Square as Monet had painted Les Grands Boulevards of Paris. Robert Henri developed a more distinctly American Impressionism, painting urban scenes and portraits in the manner of Pissaro and Franz Hals respectively, while employing Sargent's broad, descriptive brush strokes. Henri gave instruction and leadership to a new school of American painters whose work has often been compared to that of the contemporary progressive novelists. These dark Impressionists, as an art critic, John I. H. Baur, has called them, were more popularly called the Ashcan School because of their insistence upon portraying the grimmer sides of American life. Most of them at one time or another had earned their livings as newspaper and magazine illustrators; one of their number, George Luks, was the illustrator of a comic strip, "Hogan's Alley." Their debt to Hogarth and Daumier was almost as great as to the Impressionist Henri. In 1908 in revolt against the National Academy's refusal to countenance their work, they organized as the Eight and held an exhibition in New York. Some critics denounced them as "the Revolutionary Black Gang," more by reason of their subjects than their techniques. Other critics readily acceded that the group was creating a national art.

Four painters whom critics most often associated with the Ashcan School were John Sloan, George Luks, William Glackens, and Everett Shinn. To soften the dreariness of the slums he painted Sloan used a touch of satire in portraying its men and women, as in "The Hairdresser's Window." Luks dramatically and wittily portrayed individuals, as in "The Spielers." Glackens painted larger canvases in which people as a group seem to form the subject pattern, as in "Roller Skating Rink." In an era when it was boldness to do so, Shinn painted an actress showing her shapely ankle in "The Revue." A pupil of Henri's, George Bellows, caught the vigor and violence of the era in his paintings and drawings of prize fights. In 1910 the Eight and their followers held a second successful exhibit, but they were already at the peak of their reputations as revolutionizers of American art, about to lose their place to even more modern and daring artists.

Americans had become used to the Impressionists and the artists whom they had influenced; they were ill prepared for Cézanne, Van Gogh, Gaugin, Picasso, Matisse, and the nonrepresentational painters. The work of these artists came as a bombshell. It was a gifted photographer, Alfred Stieglitz, who as much as anyone else helped detonate it among painters. The walls of his small gallery at 291 Fifth Avenue, New York City, exhibited one shock after another: in 1908 Rodin and Matisse, followed in the next three years by Toulouse-Lautrec, Cézanne, and Picasso.

Only a small number of artists and art lovers were aware of what was going on at Stieglitz's 291 gallery until, in 1913, modernism burst upon the American public through a huge exhibition assembled at the Sixty-ninth Regiment Armory in New York City. Most of the 1,600 exhibited works were conservative, but a group of French moderns left the critics wide eyed. "American art," wrote one of the promoters of the exhibit, "needs the shock that the work of some of these men will give." Certainly, the classicists reacted strongly, but the public was less outraged than the critics and became accustomed to seeing modern art. The Metropolitan Museum purchased one of the exhibited Cézannes, the first public museum in the United States to acquire a Cézanne painting. The total effect of the armory show and Stieglitz's exhibits was to lead many young artists far beyond the Ashcan revolt to explore the fields of expressionism and abstraction.

The Armory Show, New York City, 1913 (MUSEUM OF MODERN ART)

Classic forms continued to dominate architecture. "The White City" of the Chicago Columbian Exposition of the 1890s had exalted the reputation of Charles F. McKim and had established the Greek or Roman temple as the model for public buildings. Louis Sullivan won few followers when he proposed types of architecture he regarded as better suited to America, in which "form follows function." While Sullivan continued into the early 1900s designing commercial structures, his gifted assistant, Frank Lloyd Wright, had left him in 1893 to follow his own bent in domestic architecture.

In 1900 Wright built the first of the prairie houses. In designing public buildings and factories, as well as homes, Wright tried to make his architecture fit the surroundings, both in appearance and in historic spirit, yet he used modern materials and the newest engineering techniques. Nevertheless, until the late twenties Wright's designs influenced European architecture more than that of the United States. The most that can be said for Americans is that they did revert to the graceful colonial styles for their homes.

Like architecture, the American theater during the progressive era leaned more to commercial than aesthetic interests. It was an expanding business, dominated by a nationwide syndicate that prospered on romantic plays, popular vaudeville, and matinée idols. Experimental realism had made a beginning, but only in the realm of little-theater groups such as the Provincetown Players and the 47 Workshop of Professor George P. Baker of Harvard, later of Yale. These could hardly appeal to wide audiences, who were soon to be won over to the motion picture.

Frank Lloyd Wright's Taliesin East, 1911

At first, to theatergoers and the theatrical world in general, the idea of the motion picture offering serious competition to the stage appeared ludicrous. The first film to tell a continuous story was a melodrama, *The Great Train Robbery*, produced in 1903. This stage of motion picture development was short. By 1915 the lengthy, impressive feature film had

On the Edison Studio set, 1914 (MUSEUM OF MODERN ART/FILM STILLS ARCHIVE)

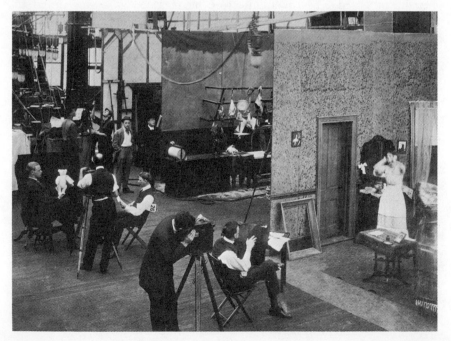

arrived with *The Birth of a Nation.* It was as significant in marking the coming of age of a new art form as it was deplorable in its glorification of the Ku Klux Klan. A motion picture monopoly movement had begun in 1909 and had been smashed by the government in 1914, but motion pictures had become a multimillion-dollar industry and were moving into large and ornate theaters.

Thus in many ways the first years of the twentieth century swept Americans far beyond the old nineteenth-century patterns of life. World War I was to sweep them even further.

eight
Making the World Safe for Democracy

In August 1914 the great war that broke in Europe seemed incredible to Americans; the possibility that they might become involved seemed inconceivable. Yet in less than three years they reluctantly embarked upon the great crusade, in the words of President Wilson, "to make the world safe for democracy."

WAR IN EUROPE

Bryan, before he took office as Secretary of State, suggested to Wilson a scheme for "cooling-off" treaties with all the nations of the world. These would provide that disputes should go to permanent commissions for a one-year investigation before any party could strengthen its armaments or go to war. This proposal was in keeping with the progressive theory that war was unthinkable and that all disputes could be settled through reasonable discussion. Bryan negotiated thirty such treaties with large and small nations—but none with Germany.

The problem of the European balance of power gave Wilson at least slight concern in May 1914 when he authorized Colonel House to sail abroad to try to bring an end to the arms race. Within a few months Europe became Wilson's greatest cause for anxiety, as fate directed his administration toward an overwhelming concern with foreign affairs.

Americans paid little attention to the minor alarms that followed the assassination of the Austrian Archduke in Sarajevo, Bosnia, at the end of June. Balkan crises were familiar and boring news; events in Mexico, where Carranza was driving out Huerta, seemed more sensational. Even when Austria-Hungary declared war on Serbia on July 28, Americans were not shocked, but the week that followed left them stunned. The declaration of war against Serbia triggered a chain reaction of threats and counter-threats, commitments and countercommitments among the alliances. It detonated an explosion that no one seemed really to want but no one seemed able to avoid. By August 5 Britain, France, and Russia were at war with Germany and Austria-Hungary. The explosion had blown to bits the comfortable, optimistic Europe that had seemed so safe and stable.

Bewildered Americans congratulated themselves that at least the explosion could not extend to their shores; the New World was still secure. A sizable number, who were of German ancestry or had been educated in German universities, automatically saw the war as a valiant German struggle against the cruel despotism of Czarist Russia. And most Irish Americans sympathized with Germany as the foe of their ancient oppressor, England. But the vast majority of the people, with greater educational, economic, or sentimental ties to Britain and France, were shocked by the German invasion of Belgium in defiance of a treaty. They were pro-Allied without being at all sure what the war was about. Almost none of them in August 1914 envisaged American entrance into the war. There was no clear call for an American democratic crusade.

With the outbreak of war in Europe Wilson feared that Japan would take advantage of the preoccupation of the Western powers to expand in the Orient. He reverted to a balance-of-power policy to try to stem the Japanese tide as much as possible. Japan declared war upon Germany and seized the German holdings on the Shantung peninsula of China; this the United States could not criticize. Next Japan tried to impose upon the Chinese a treaty embodying twenty-one demands that would have made China virtually a protectorate. At this point (in 1915) the American government, with the aid of the British, exerted such strong pressure that Japan abandoned the treaty.

But the United States appeased Japan in the Lansing-Ishii Agreement of November 2, 1917. This recognized that Japan had "special interests in China, particularly in the part to which her possessions are contiguous." The Japanese were pleased, because in translating the ambiguous document into Chinese they could give the impression that the United States approved their policy. Secretary of State Lansing was satisfied because he felt that he had protected China for at least the duration of the European war. For both nations, if they held to their policies, there was trouble ahead.

Blockade and Submarine Warfare

In 1914 President Wilson had proclaimed neutrality and, going beyond that, had called upon the American people to remain impartial in thought as well as in action. Yet from the beginning he himself took one attitude toward the Allies and quite a different attitude toward Germany.

The immediate problem for Wilson was domestic: to bolster the economy, which was staggering under the impact of war. As European nations sought to liquidate their investments in the United States, Wilson closed the stock exchange to prevent panic and discouraged loans to belligerents in order to preserve the gold reserve. (Secretary Bryan asserted that such loans by banks would be unneutral.) Then war orders began to turn the panic into a boom.

Americans soon learned that the nation in control of the seas would countenance no neutral trade with the enemy. President Wilson acquiesced, though not without protests, as the British developed and tightened their system of control. The United States could have retaliated with an embargo, but this would have created serious economic distress among American farmers, and it would have hurt industry. Besides, the basically pro-Allied sympathies of the administration and a great majority of the people made so drastic a step unthinkable. Hence the United States accepted the British blockade of the Central Powers but was not so ready to accept a German counterblockade.

Blockade warfare became essential to the strategy of both the British and the Germans. The development of rapid-firing cannons and of machine guns made frontal assault prohibitively expensive, so that the war in Europe settled down into an exhausting trench warfare between the combatants. The counterpart on the high seas was the blockade. From the outset Great Britain made use of her superior navy to wage economic warfare against Germany. Gradually, she extended the contraband list. She even seized American vessels carrying foodstuffs to neutral countries, on the grounds that such shipments might release supplies that could go to Germany. Americans complained that the British were using the controls to benefit British firms at the expense of American business.

On the whole, the British blockade proved to be no economic handicap for the United States, since by early 1915 heavy war orders were arriving that more than filled the trade gap it had created. While trade with the Central Powers almost came to an end, that with the Allies between 1914 and 1916 jumped from $824 million to $3,214 million—a staggering figure for that time. In March 1915 the government relaxed its regulations to allow the Allies to float huge loans in the United States for financing their purchases. In effect, the United States, embarking upon the greatest boom in its history, was becoming the great arsenal for the Allies.

This the Germans could not permit. During the first weeks of the war, they imposed no blockades but concentrated upon trying to win a decision in France. The German armies drove deep but were halted short of Paris in the Battle of the Marne in September 1914. While on the Russian front great armies continued to move back and forth for several years, in the west the war turned into the grinding attrition of trench combat along lines extending from the North Sea to Switzerland. As a stalemate developed along the Western Front, Germany turned toward the submarine as a possible means of breaking the British blockade. Submarines had the advantage of surprise but were so vulnerable to attack by an armed ship that they could scarcely follow the accepted rules of international law. These rules called for visit and search of enemy merchantmen and allowed sinking only if provision were made for the safety of passengers and crew. The sinking of merchant vessels without warning seemed to Americans to add a new and frightful dimension to warfare.

Beginning on February 4, 1915, Germany announced that she would sink enemy vessels in a broad zone around the British Isles. This policy, the Germans explained, was in retaliation for the British food blockade, which they claimed would starve women and children in Germany. President Wilson declared on Febuary 10 that he would hold Germany to "strict accountability" for unlawful acts.

A serious crisis came when, on May 7, 1915, a submarine fired a torpedo without warning into the Cunard liner *Lusitania*. The ship went down in eighteen minutes, drowning 1,198 people, among them 128 Americans. "An act of piracy," Theodore Roosevelt called it.

A few days earlier, April 22, the Germans had launched against the Allied lines at Ypres a new weapon of frightfulness, poison gas. On May 13 American newspapers carried lengthy excerpts from an official British report on almost unprintable alleged German atrocities in Belgium. Although it bore the respected name of the former ambassador to the United States, Lord Bryce, this report contained fabrications. Yet few Americans questioned its authenticity, for by this time most people were ready to believe almost anything against Germany. Even in their revulsion, however, they were not ready to fight.

Wilson came close to the point of coercion over the *Lusitania* incident in the ensuing exchange of notes with Germany. In his first note he virtually demanded that Germany end her submarine blockade. When the Germans sent an argumentative reply, he drafted an even stronger second note—so strong that the peace-minded Secretary Bryan resigned rather than sign it. Wilson appointed the counselor of the State Department, Robert Lansing, an expert in international law, to be the new secretary. Lansing was ready to take an adamant position. Wilson had said: "There is such a thing as a man being too proud to fight." Yet he was ready to risk war rather than surrender to Germany what he considered to be American maritime rights.

New trouble developed in the early months of 1916 when the Allies began arming merchantmen and ordering them to attack submarines. On February 10, 1916, Germany gave notice that she would sink them without warning. Wilson reiterated his doctrine of strict accountability, and on March 24, when the channel steamer *Sussex* was torpedoed, he threatened to break off diplomatic relations if Germany did not abandon her unrestricted submarine campaign. He made the threat at a time when Germany still lacked sufficient submarines to maintain a tight blockade and did not wish to bring the United States into the war. Consequently, on May 4 the German foreign office pledged that submarine commanders would observe rules of visit and search. The President had won a diplomatic victory, and relations with Germany became less tense during the eight months that followed.

Preparedness—or Pacifism?

With the outbreak of war, generals and admirals, who in peacetime attracted little attention, began to gather followings as they raised a hue and cry for increased defenses. President Wilson through his pacifist Secretary of the Navy, Daniels, was able to muzzle the navy rather effectively. Its demands for a huge fleet-building program and its warnings of the catastrophe that faced America if the British Grand Fleet collapsed appeared for the most part indirectly through friendly politicians and publicists. Roosevelt's close friend Major General Leonard Wood, who had just finished a term as Chief of Staff, was not so easily silenced. The Secretary of War, Lindley M. Garrison, was a zealous advocate of preparedness, and several influential civilians like Roosevelt constantly made the headlines with their warnings.

The army was much less ready than the navy to fight a major war. The establishment of the General Staff and other administrative reforms had come into effect in the Roosevelt administration, but the older officers were still antagonistic toward such changes. The Quartermaster Corps in 1913 was thinking about using trucks but as yet was not seriously testing them. The air force, consisting of seventeen planes, was part of the Signal Corps; its 1913 appropriation was $125,000. The army numbered less than 80,000 men, a large part of whom were required to maintain the posts within the United States. The National Guard was somewhat larger but was scarcely professional.

Wilson opposed new armaments, and so did public opinion, until the crisis over submarine sinkings frightened the nation into preparedness. In November 1915 the President proposed a long-range program that by 1925 would give the United States a navy second to none and would reorganize the army and provide a reserve force of 40,000 men. This proposal touched off a hot debate in Congress and throughout the country. Large numbers of those who had been agrarian progressives of the West and South rallied behind the House majority leader, Claude Kitchin of North Carolina, to block the army program. Throughout the country the pleas of Bryan and peace organizations strongly appealed to farmers and workingmen. Wilson took the issue to the country in a series of speeches in January and early February 1916, but the House would not budge.

Wilson had to compromise. He accepted the resignation of Secretary of War Garrison and appointed in his place Newton D. Baker, an able Ohio progressive who had opposed preparedness only a few weeks earlier. Ultimately, Congress passed legislation providing for substantial increases in the army, the navy, and merchant shipping. The Merchant Marine Act of 1916 established the United States Shipping Board, which was empowered to own and operate vessels and regulate shipping.

Conservatives wished to finance the defense expenditures through bonds, but the administration proposed new, heavier taxes. Progressives denounced the tax proposals as falling too heavily upon the masses. In Congress the progressives fought through a tax measure frankly aimed at making the wealthy, whom they blamed for preparedness demands, pay the bill. The Revenue Act of 1916 levied income and inheritance taxes heavily upon the rich for the first time in American history.

In 1916 Democrats and Republicans fought the presidential campaign over the issue of foreign policy before a seriously divided people. At the Democratic convention the keynoter began citing Wilson's interchanges with Germany, and the crowd whooped with enthusiasm. "What did we do? What did we do?" the delegates chanted, and the keynoter responded: "We didn't go to war, we didn't go to war." Out of the convention came the slogan (which Wilson himself never used) "He kept us out of war." The Democrats went into the campaign far stronger than had been expected of a minority party battling against the reunited Republicans. Many of the former Bull Moosers, Republican farmers in the Midwest, and workers who had once voted for a full dinner pail now favored the Democrats. In part they did so because of Wilson's progressive domestic policy but still more because of their hope that the President could continue to keep the country out of the war.

As for the Republicans, they persuaded Charles Evans Hughes, who had an impeccable progressive record, to resign from the Supreme Court and accept the nomination. Primarily because of the whooping of Roosevelt and others on the sidelines, the Republicans gradually began to look like the war party. Hughes, under pressure from militant Republicans, wired Roosevelt congratulations on warlike speeches. This and Hughes' own remarks led voters to believe that he was more likely than Wilson to adopt a militant policy.

Wilson warned that a Republican victory would mean intervention in Mexico and war in Europe. The lure of progressivism and peace were still so irresistible in 1916 that the Democratic party, though normally a

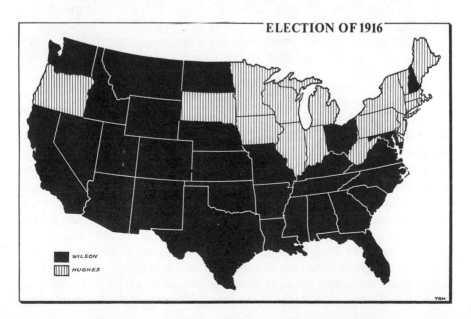

ELECTION OF 1916

WILSON
HUGHES

minority, squeezed through to victory. On election night returns from the East were almost solidly for Hughes; he appeared elected. Then, as returns from the West came in, the picture began to change, though it was not until Friday that Wilson's election was certain. The Democrats also retained a precarious control over both houses of Congress.

"A Fearful Thing"

So far as elections can be regarded as national plebiscites, Wilson had received a narrow mandate to continue along the path of progressivism and peace. Undoubtedly, he intended to follow such a course. Since the outbreak of the war he had repeatedly sought means to bring the warring nations into a peace conference. But both sides had invested too heavily in the conflict, and were still too hopeful of gaining from their investment, to talk of a negotiated peace.

Immediately after the election, in November 1916, Wilson renewed negotiations looking toward a settlement. The Germans, successful on the Russian front, for a while appeared to be willing. But the top German generals did not want any conference at all. Nevertheless, on January 22, 1917, Wilson spread his plan before the Senate, calling for a lasting peace that the American people would help maintain through a league of nations. It would be a peace with freedom of the seas, disarmament, national self-determination for subject peoples, and equality among nations. "Peace among equals"—a lasting peace—could come only through "peace without victory."

On January 9 the military leaders of Germany had decided upon one final cast of the iron dice. They had resolved to return to unrestricted submarine warfare even though it would bring the United States into the war. They hoped that they could crush France on land and starve Britain from the sea before America could make her weight felt. On January 31 the German ambassador announced that, beginning the following day, submarines would sink all ships, enemy or neutral, in a broad zone around the British Isles.

President Wilson now faced a dilemma of his own making. He had in effect during the previous eighteen months drawn a narrow line—the right of American citizens and vessels to travel on the high seas in time of war—and threatened Germany with war if she transgressed it. How could Wilson take the United States into a war against Germany for such a limited end and still bring about the kind of peace he wanted, a just peace among equals, a peace without the victor dictating to the vanquished?

Gradually, events carried Wilson toward war. On February 25 the British turned over to him an intercepted note from the German foreign secretary, Arthur Zimmerman, proposing that in the event of war Mexico should attack the United States and receive in return her lost provinces north of the border. Americans were infuriated. At about the same time, the Russian revolution eliminated one of the moral problems in Wilson's mind by replacing a despotism among the Allies with a constitutional monarchy. (This government lasted only until November 1917, when Lenin and the communists came into power.)

On March 18, 1917, news came that submarines had torpedoed three American ships. On March 20 the cabinet unanimously advised the President to ask Congress for a declaration of war. On the evening of April 2, 1917, President Wilson delivered his war message to Congress. After enumerating the German trangressions of American neutral rights, he declared:

> It is a fearful thing to lead this great peaceful people into war, into the most terrible . . . of all wars. . . . But the right is more precious than peace, and we shall fight for the things which we have always carried nearest our hearts—for democracy, . . . for the rights and liberties of small nations, for a universal dominion of right by such a concert of free peoples as shall bring peace and safety to all nations and make the world itself at last free.

Four days later, Congress passed the war declaration and the President signed it.

WAR WITHOUT STINT

President Wilson had called for war "without stint or limit." In this spirit the American government proceeded to mobilize economic resources on a grand scale, to launch massive campaigns against German submarines in the Atlantic and against German armies in France, and to indoctrinate the American people for enduring the burdens and the sacrifices of the total war.

Controlling the Economy

Clumsily at first, but steadily and impressively, the unprepared nation built a gigantic war machine. Nearly 5,000 government agencies were set up

The sinking of the Illinois, *March 18, 1917* (OFFICIAL U.S. NAVY PHOTO)

to see that men, money, and materials were directed toward the war effort. These agencies brought an unprecedented degree of regulation and control to American economic life.

Troops had to be raised, the army enormously enlarged. Roosevelt, elderly and ill, still seemed to think in terms of the Spanish-American War; backed by a clique of Republican senators, he fought for permission to take a volunteer division to the Western Front. Speaker Champ Clark was so incensed at the prospect of a draft that he asserted from the floor of the House during debate: "In the estimation of Missourians there is precious little difference between a conscript and a convict." For weeks the debate went on, but in the end Roosevelt was turned down, and the Selective Service Act was passed.

During the debate, it had become clear what a large figure in both money and men the President must write into the blank check that Congress (and the American people) had signed. In April British and French missions arrived and made clear for the first time their desperate need for money, men, and ships if they were to stave off imminent defeat. Congress soon authorized the Treasury Department to borrow $7 billion, of which $3 billion were to go as loans to the Allies.

To finance the war Secretary of the Treasury William G. McAdoo raised about one-third of a $32 billion total through taxation. He felt that additional taxes would put too heavy a burden on low-income groups. The War Revenue Act of 1917 imposed a great variety of excise taxes and income taxes steeper than any before—so steep as to take two-thirds of a $2 million income. Altogether, the taxes on individual and corporate incomes, excess profits, and inheritances provided 74 percent of the war tax revenues. There was one conspicuous loophole: many corporations distributed to their stockholders stock exempt from taxes rather than giving them dividends.

In his borrowing policy McAdoo tried, again, to keep the burden of the war from falling too heavily upon the poorer people. He sought to sell as many Liberty Bonds as possible to them so that they, not richer people, would reap the ultimate profit. Despite McAdoo's efforts, those with moderate incomes (under $2,000 a year) probably purchased no more than 30 percent of the $23 billion worth of bonds sold.

During the preparedness period, in August 1916, Congress had approved the establishment of a Council of National Defense, consisting of six cabinet members, and an Advisory Commission made up of representatives of industry, transportation, business, and labor. In July 1917 the council set up a centralized War Industries Board to coordinate government purchases. Wilson reorganized this board, conferred upon it sweeping powers over industry, and appointed as chairman a Wall Street broker, Bernard Baruch.

Food was almost as vital as munitions for the Allies. At the suggestion of the Council for National Defense, a Food Administration was set up by the President. After vigorous debate it was later authorized by Congress in the Lever Act of August 10, 1917. Its administrator was one of the

Fourth Liberty Loan Parade, New Orleans (NATIONAL ARCHIVES)

most spectacular civilian heroes of the war, an American mining engineer, Herbert Hoover, who had supervised the relief feeding of Belgium. His task was to increase food production, cut waste, substitute plentiful for scarce foods, and protect consumers from speculators. Hoover, in keeping with his experience in Belgium, wished to be an administrator, not a dictator, and to run his program on a voluntary basis as far as possible. To a remarkable degree he was able to enlist the patriotic support of the public in conserving food and observing meatless and wheatless days. His slogan, seen on widely distributed posters, was "Food will win the war."

The shortage of wheat was especially critical because 1916 had been a bad crop year. Hoover encouraged wheat production by guaranteeing the purchase of the entire 1917 crop at $2.20 per bushel, a figure high enough to assure farmers a substantial profit. Wheat acreage jumped from 45 million in 1917 to 75 million in 1919, and the land produced bumper crops.

Hoover opposed retail price fixing, which he thought would lead to black markets, but he did protect consumers from speculation. Food prices went up gradually.

The Lever Act, which established the Food Administration, also authorized a Fuel Administration, which fixed the price of coal high enough to bring submarginal coal mines into operation and increase bituminous coal production by about 50 percent. In spite of this increase, the fuel shortage became so acute that the Fuel Administration had to order a series of coal holidays for Eastern industries in the early months of 1918.

In order to guarantee war production in German-owned factories in this country, especially those producing chemicals, these and all other German assets came under the custody of an alien property custodian, A. Mitchell Palmer. The Trading-with-the-Enemy Act of October 1917 provided for their seizure and administration. Palmer obtained additional authority to sell German property, which he utilized especially to license dye and chemical patents to American industry. This was punitive toward the Germans, immensely profitable for some American businessmen, and helpful for the development of a strong chemical industry in the United States.

The Aircraft Production Board failed to produce a promised 22,000 airplanes by July 1918—a ridiculous figure, since neither side on the Western Front ever had as many as 2,500 planes at one time. The failure to fulfill this overoptimistic promise led to harsh criticism. By the time the armistice was signed, the United States had delivered to France 1,185 De Haviland bombers and 5,460 Liberty motors.

In April 1918 President Wilson established the National War Labor Board, to serve as a kind of supreme court for labor disputes. Labor and industry each provided five representatives for the board; the two chairmen represented the public. The War Labor Board would not countenance strikes or lockouts but recognized the right of unions to organize and bargain collectively. It favored the eight-hour day, the establishment in any given area of the wages prevailing in it, the maintenance of a basic living standard for workers, and equal pay for women who did equal work. Like

Manufacturing Curtiss OX-5 airplane engines (NATIONAL ARCHIVES)

some other war agencies, it had to function through persuasion or use of the President's war powers.

President Gompers of the AFL did much during the war to enhance the prestige of organized labor. He sat with industrialists on the Council of National Defense and pledged to see that there would be no strikes, in return for recognition of unionism and wage increases. He also cooperated in the government onslaught against labor radicals, which meant the Industrial Workers of the World (IWW), who were engaging in sabotage in the West. The IWW almost disappeared, while membership in other unions jumped from 2,716,900 in 1914 to 3,104,600 in 1917 and 4,169,100 in 1919. Still, this was no more than one-eighth of all wage earners.

DELIVERING THE GOODS

Increased production and stringent economy within the United States would be of no avail unless supplies could be delivered to Europe. Into the winter of 1917–1918 transportation difficulties plagued the nation. Railroads could not get raw materials to Eastern factories or munitions to ports, even through cooperation with a voluntary Railroad War Board. On December 28, 1917, Wilson put the railroads under a Railroad Administration headed by Secretary of the Treasury McAdoo. He utilized expert railroad men to run the lines as one unified system. Railroads could draw upon a half-billion-dollar revolving fund for improvements and received rent equivalent to their average earnings in 1914–1917. The transportation

Women working on fuses for artillery shells (NATIONAL ARCHIVES)

Launching the first freighter at Hog Island, August 1918 (NATIONAL ARCHIVES)

snarl was so effectively untangled that a freight-car shortage of 150,000 in 1917 was transformed into a surplus of 300,000 by the end of 1918.

Shipping was a still greater and more persistent problem. By the summer of 1917 submarines had sunk nearly a quarter of the British merchant fleet; that of the United States was relatively small and mainly committed to coastal trade. The Emergency Fleet Corporation under the Shipping Board eventually began to make remarkable progress in building new shipyards to turn out 1,700 ships of steel and 1,000 of wood.

The enormous outpouring of goods indicated the potential for higher living standards in postwar America. The government economic controls set a precedent for controls in time of future emergency or war. But during World War I, Americans enthusiastically hailed the feats of production because they contributed to the crushing of the German forces.

nine

Victory and Isolation

While the American people were transforming their nation's vast resources into the sinews of war, the armed forces were striving to tip the scales of battle against Germany on the high seas and along the battle line in France. A third great mobilization, that of the minds of the people of the United States, brought an almost hysterical support for the war. President Wilson and the administrators in Washington intended to teach them the significance of the war and the necessity to build a just and lasting peace. Many Americans of both major parties viewed the war and the peace that was to follow with truly Wilsonian dedication, but among many others the indoctrination seemed to lead to conformity rather than understanding and to engender more hatred than idealism. This threatened tragedy, for while the course of the war on the battlefield was determining its military conclusion, its path in men's minds was helping shape its ultimate outcome. What victory would mean to either the world or the United States was far from clear as the battles unfolded; yet in the conduct of the war were to be found some of the clues to the peace.

COUNTERING THE SUBMARINE MENACE

For many months after April 1917 it seemed quite possible that the Allies would lose the war. The Germans had acted to provoke American entrance, taking the calculated risk that they could destroy the French armies and starve the British people before the United States could intervene decisively. They came close to making good on this risk.

None of the huge mobilization of men and matériel in the United States would benefit the Allies until it had reached the Western Front. For every American soldier in France there would have to be about four tons of shipping in continuous operation; there must be a "bridge of ships" across the Atlantic. Yet German submarines were sinking ships faster than they could be built. In the second quarter of 1917 one out of every four ships that left Great Britain on a transatlantic crossing never returned. If this continued, by October 1917 there would not be sufficient tonnage to carry on the war. The British had no solution. Fortunately, the American navy was able to bring both fresh resources and an effective defense scheme. It sent all the destroyers to Queenstown, Ireland, to aid in the antisubmarine patrols; by July 1917 there were already thirty-five stationed there. At home the navy suspended building battleships to begin construction of 250 destroyers and 400 submarine chasers.

War vessels escorted fleets of transports and supply ships across the Atlantic to protect them from submarine attacks. At first, the British admiralty had opposed the use of such convoys and kept most of its destroyers as a curtain to protect the Grand Fleet and the channel ferries. Eventually, however, United States Admiral William S. Sims broke down the resistance of the admiralty, so that a convoying system was well established by August 1917.

Sinkings, which had totaled nearly 900,000 tons in April 1917, dropped to 350,000 tons by December 1917 and to only 112,000 tons by October 1918. This was primarily a British achievement, but the United States contributed to it substantially. The British provided 70 percent of the escorting ships, the French 3 percent, and the Americans 27 percent.

The American navy grew enormously in size and efficiency. By the time the armistice was signed, it had 200,000 men and 834 vessels convoying across the Atlantic or serving in European waters. It had grown in overall size to 533,000 men and 2,000 ships. It performed great feats in moving men and supplies across the Atlantic.

A convoy in the danger zone, and (inset) a camouflaged warship (OFFICIAL U.S. NAVY PHOTOS)

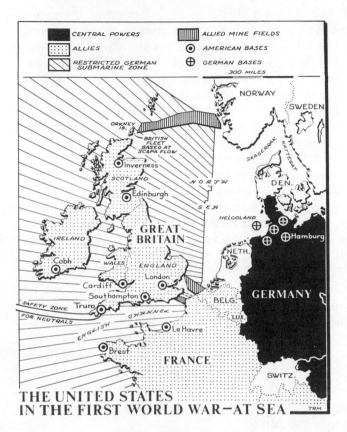

THE UNITED STATES
IN THE FIRST WORLD WAR—AT SEA

Submarine Sinkings and Shipbuilding, 1917–1918

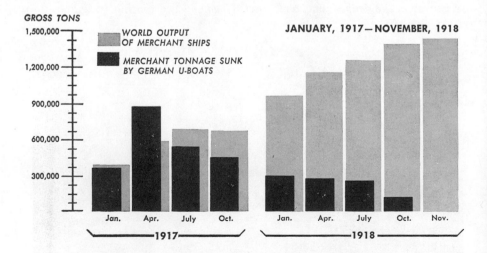

The AEF in France

American strategic plans were drawn up after the country entered the war, and essentially these plans were developed in France at the headquarters of the commanding general of the American Expeditionary Force (AEF), John J. Pershing, a highly intelligent officer and a driving personality.

Pershing's goal was to build an American force in France numbering 1 million men by June 1, 1918. Many obstacles stood between him and his objective, as he came to realize after he arrived in Paris on June 14, 1917. The dispirited Allies stood on the defensive against the desperately aggressive enemy; they needed fresh American troops but wished to use them piecemeal as reinforcements along their own weary lines. They did not like Pershing's insistence that the Americans should operate as a separate army; they had no reason to trust the untried American soldiers or officers. In truth, there had been nothing in American military activities during the Spanish-American War and the Mexican intervention to warrant confidence. But General Pershing stood firm, with President Wilson behind him.

In the winter of 1917–1918 the Germans knocked the Russians out of the war. Lenin and his followers in Russia overthrew the constitutional government of Kerensky and opened peace negotiations. Meanwhile, the Germans along with the Austrians delivered a near-fatal blow to the Italians at Caporetto. The stunned Allies organized a Supreme War Council and looked desperately to the United States for manpower. Pershing gradually had been building port facilities, running railroads across France, and constructing training camps and supply dumps. As a trickle of troops began to arrive, he tried to give them three months' training before putting them into combat. While the number was small, he was willing to brigade his units temporarily among the Allies to give them experience and to

The U.S. Army in World War I

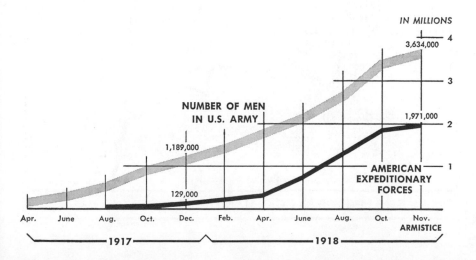

meet emergencies. Thus the First Division went into action with the French in Lorraine in October 1917 and took over a quiet sector of its own near Toul in January 1918.

In the early months of 1918 Germany moved troops from the east and slammed them against the Allies in a series of great offensives designed to end the war before a significant number of Americans could arrive. The Germans had not succeeded by July 1, when Pershing had his million soldiers in France.

On May 30 the Germans had crossed the Marne River at Château-Thierry and threatened Paris fifty miles away. American and French troops, under the French command, fought to blunt the German drive. After a week of bitter counterattacking the Americans recaptured Belleau Wood and thus helped stabilize the line. A little further south at Reims, in the great bulge toward Paris, the Germans tried on July 15, the morning after Bastille Day, to crash through the French lines. Some 85,000 American troops helped repel the German thrust. By July 18 the German offensive was over; and the Allies began a counteroffensive, with American divisions participating, to liquidate the Marne salient (outward projection in the battle line). By August 6 it was gone.

In the months that followed, as American troops disembarked at a rate averaging 263,000 per month, the reinvigorated Allies pressed the ex-

THE FIVE GREAT GERMAN OFFENSIVES OF 1918

Fourteen-inch railway gun firing at railroad and troop center (NATIONAL AR-CHIVES)

hausted Germans from Lorraine to the North Sea. On August 12 Pershing for the first time launched an offensive under his own command. He directed the First Army, consisting of 550,000 American troops, against the St. Mihiel salient protruding south of Verdun. Within thirty-six hours the drive had succeeded.

On September 26, 1918, the Americans began to advance along a 24-mile front in the Argonne Forest, as part of a grand, 200-mile-wide offensive, which was to continue for a total of forty-seven days. The American troops fought through what Pershing described as a "vast network of uncut barbwire, the deep ravines, dense woods, myriads of shell craters, and a heavy fog." The Allied high command had not imagined the Americans could make much progress against these obstacles, but after October 4 the regrouped army advanced. By the end of the month it had overrun almost all of the enemy's fixed positions, was beyond the Argonne Forest, and was driving toward vital German communications. On November 7 the Americans established bridgeheads across the Meuse River, planted their guns looking down on the famous fortress of Sedan, and cut the railroad that carried German supplies to the front. It had been the greatest battle in which American troops had ever fought. The 1.2 million soldiers had used a greater weight of ammunition than had all of the Union forces through the four years of the Civil War.

Captain Edward V. Rickenbacker (center) and other pilots of the 94th Pursuit Squadron (NATIONAL ARCHIVES)

During the Argonne fighting, other American divisions were deployed elsewhere along the front. All together, Americans participated in thirteen major operations, of which only two were under Pershing's command. By early November the weight of American troops was becoming irresistible; 2 million of them were serving in France.

All along the line millions of Allied troops had pushed back the Germans, whose reserves were gone, regiments weakened, and communications threatened. They faced an invasion of their own country. They began to seek an armistice, a temporary cease-fire. Pershing, convinced that the Allies should demand a surrender instead, would have liked to push on to Berlin, to make the Germans really feel the war. The day after the Americans reached Sedan, German envoys crossed the lines to meet the Allied Commander in Chief, the French General Ferdinand Foch, and receive armistice terms from him—terms so stiff that a resumption of hostilities would be impossible. The Germans accepted, and on November 11, 1918, the armistice went into effect.

Rejoicing Americans credited their armies with winning the decisive battles—"We won the war." Beyond question they had supplied the margin of victory. Yet the really crushing burden of the war had not fallen upon the American troops or the American people. The United States lost 112,000 men from enemy action or disease; 237,000 more were wounded. By comparison 1,385,000 French and 900,000 British died. Only 7 percent of the soldiers from the United States were casualties, compared with 73 percent of those from France and 36 percent of those from the British Empire.

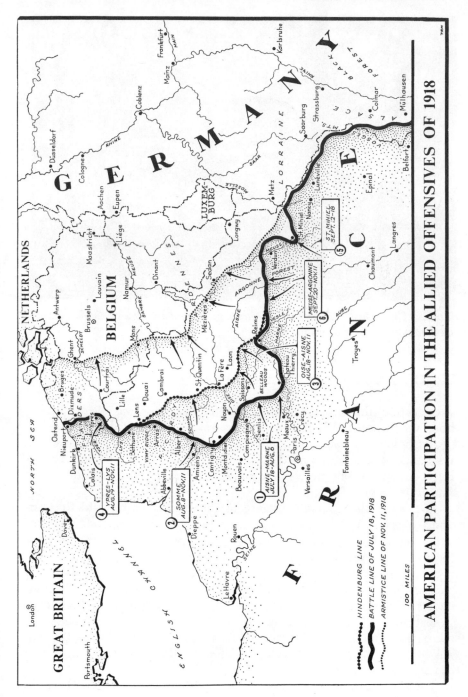

AMERICAN PARTICIPATION IN THE ALLIED OFFENSIVES OF 1918

Stanford University Section of the American Ambulance Field Service leaving for the front (NATIONAL ARCHIVES)

PEACE IDEALS AND WAR HATREDS

Even before the armistice the thoughts of Americans were turning from war to peace. The conduct of the war had depended upon production at home and operations of the armed forces abroad. The pursuit of a satisfactory peace depended—in a democratic nation like the United States—upon a much more subtle and difficult factor, the attitude of the American people.

Ever since the hesitant entrance of the United States into the war, official agencies and private groups, from President Wilson and the Committee on Public Information to the yellow press, had sought to mold the minds of Americans. In conflicting ways they tried to explain the significance of the war, encourage Americans in its vigorous pursuit, and prepare them for the peace to follow. As is all too easy in such circumstances, Americans learned readily to hate the Germans and German sympathizers but prepared themselves less well to assume a commanding role in maintaining a just peace in the postwar world. This in the end was to be the tragedy of President Wilson, of the American people, and consequently of all mankind.

Even before America entered the war, President Wilson had begun a series of idealistic addresses outlining the nature of the postwar world he wished to see emerge. He talked then of "peace without victory" and the right of the several submerged nationalities in Europe to organize governments of their own choosing. He asserted too that the American people would be willing to join a postwar association of nations. Many Americans of good will, like the members of the League to Enforce Peace, thrilled to Wilson's words. But his speeches remained merely words, since Wilson had not bound the Allies to his conditions as a basis for American intervention. And he seemed to reinforce the distinction between the United States and the Allies through the fiction that America was fighting Germany separately as an "associated power."

After American entrance Wilson had discovered that the Allies had made secret treaties among themselves. These treaties divided among the Allies the enemy's colonies as spoils of the war. The new Bolshevik government of Russia publicized some of the treaties; their terms seemed to run counter to the idealism for which Wilson was exhorting Americans to fight. Wilson was sure that in time he could counteract the treaties and force the British and French to accept a just peace. On January 8, 1918, he expounded his own war aims, under fourteen headings, in a speech before a joint session of Congress.

His Fourteen Points, coming at a time when all the belligerent peoples were overwhelmingly weary of the war, met with an enthusiastic response among liberals and working people in the United States, in the Allied nations, and throughout the world. Many Germans as well welcomed them and a later clarification of them, "the five particulars," as the promise of a democratic Germany that could assume a position of equality in the community of nations. They were the most stirring and effective piece of propaganda the war produced.

It was not clear that Wilson had the American people behind him, even though his Committee on Public Information had been engaged in a large-scale effort to sell the war. George Creel, a progressive newspaperman who had worked in the 1916 presidential campaign, headed the committee. He persuaded newspapers to engage in voluntary self-censorship, an idea not entirely palatable to them. The committee disseminated countless tons of propaganda and enlisted the services of 150,000 writers, lecturers, actors, and artists. Throughout the country 75,000 such volunteers arose to speak on almost every conceivable occasion. Throughout the United States and the world 75 million pieces of printed matter carried the American view of the war. Much of what the Creel Committee disseminated was idealistic, in keeping with Wilson's speeches and the Fourteen Points, depicting the war as a great crusade for humanity. Much also, unfortunately, appealed more to fear and hate than to a spirit of altruistic sacrifice.

Throughout the country spread a hysterical hatred of all that seemed unpatriotic. Congress reflected and encouraged the hysteria by passing stern laws for the suppression of dissent. The Espionage Act of June 15, 1917, provided penalties running up to a $10,000 fine and twenty years' imprisonment, not only for those engaged in espionage, sabotage, and obstruction of the war effort but even for those who should "willfully cause or attempt to cause insubordination, mutiny, or refusal of duty" or "willfully obstruct the recruiting or enlistment service." The law also empowered the Postmaster General to ban from the mails any matter that in his opinion was seditious. The Trading-with-the-Enemy Act of October 1917, established censorship over international communications and the foreign-language press (in addition to authorizing various types of economic warfare against the Germans).

These measures were vigorously, and at times capriciously, enforced, but the administration sought still greater punitive powers to discipline the disloyal. Congress responded with the Sabotage Act of April 20, 1918, aimed primarily at the IWW, and the Sedition Act of May 16, 1918. The Sedition Act, modeled after a Montana statute for suppressing the IWW, was harsh beyond any previous legislation in American history. The enforcement of these laws was almost as stern as any lynch mob could desire. Over 1,500 were arrested for seditious utterances, though only 10 were taken into custody for sabotage. The force of the laws continued unabated after the armistice. In the fall of 1918, after a four-day trial, the Socialist leader Debs, who had been pacifist, not pro-German, was sentenced to ten years in a federal penitentiary under the Espionage Act; in March 1919 the Supreme Court upheld his conviction.

Whatever pacifist or pro-German offenders escaped the federal net were likely to be caught in the meshes of state sedition laws or to suffer the wrath of vigilantes. The furor was rather ludicrous in some ways, as sauerkraut became "liberty cabbage" and hamburger, "liberty sausage." It was a bit less funny to ban all German music, the teaching of the German language, or the keeping of German books in public libraries, as was done in many places. And it was frightening when a vigilance committee in Minnesota, having forbidden a pastor to speak German, caught him praying at the bedside of a dying woman who spoke only German, tarred and feathered him and rode him out of town on a rail. Sadly at the time of the armistice there was more of this bellicose feeling than of the spirit of the Fourteen Points.

REPUDIATION AT THE POLLS

Wilson planned to attend the peace conference in person, and there he hoped to represent the masses of the world. Before the conference began, however, he had cause to wonder whether he would have even the people of the United States behind him. Though the war had raised the income of millions of previously low-paid Americans, the Wilson administration failed to get the approval of a majority of the voters in the congressional elections of 1918. Throughout the war Wilson had faced dissension within his own party as some of his congressional leaders of agrarian progressive background fought drastic war measures, helped impose heavy taxation on the more well-to-do, and hurried through wartime prohibition and a prohibition amendment to the Constitution. City Democrats were particularly unhappy over losing their beer. Southern Democrats prevented the limiting of the price of cotton, while the price of wheat was controlled. The Midwestern grain belt, as a result, reacted angrily against all Democrats.

Dr. Ernst Kunwald, former conductor of the Cincinnati Symphony Orchestra, being arrested as an enemy alien (NATIONAL ARCHIVES)

Even before the 1918 elections it seemed likely that conditions at home would influence voters more than policies abroad. Nevertheless, with the war obviously almost over, the President put the election on the basis of high international policy. On October 24 he declared: "The return of a Republican majority to either house of the Congress would . . . be interpreted on the other side of the water as a repudiation of my leadership." This outraged those Republicans who had supported him in his foreign policy, since he had earlier declared "politics is adjourned" for the duration of the war. The fact that the Republicans captured both houses of Congress in 1918 would itself have a serious effect on foreign policy; the effect was exaggerated by Wilson's ill-considered appeal.

THE ARMISTICE

Repudiation at the polls created a sad atmosphere for Wilson's assumption of peace negotiations. The President, like the nation, was tense and tired, but he was ready to drive ahead. He strove to pull his own country and the reluctant Allies with him in his determination to make the Fourteen Points and especially the fourteenth—the League of Nations—a reality.

The pulling and hauling with the Allies went on through most of October 1918, during the negotiations that led to the armistice. The Germans sought through Wilson an armistice based on the Fourteen Points. The Allies denied even knowing what these points were, for the Allies were by no means ready to give up their claims for reparations and annexations. Only after Wilson had twice threatened to negotiate a separate peace were they willing to present a united façade. The Allies seemed to agree to the Fourteen Points in entirety, except for explicit reservations on reparations and freedom of the seas, and this apparent agreement led the Germans to expect generous treatment. Further misunderstanding developed because, while the Allies laid down military and naval terms that would make it impossible for the Germans to resume warfare, they used the term "armistice," which meant a negotiated pause in hostilities, rather than the word "surrender." What followed at Versailles was a conclave of victors dictating to a vanquished country, not a negotiated peace or the peace without victory that Wilson had once recommended.

The armistice that went into effect on November 11, 1918, provided that the Allies would negotiate peace on the basis of the Fourteen Points. The Germans agreed to withdraw their forces from France and Belgium and to surrender huge quantities of matériel. They accepted what was virtually the unconditional surrender of their fleet. While the peace was being drafted, the Allied blockade continued.

To the Allies as they assembled in Paris there seemed no need to consult Germany on the nature of the peace. Indeed, the only obstacle to the kind of postwar world they had planned in their secret treaties was President Wilson. He made the unprecedented decision to leave the United States and attend the peace conference in person. Colonel House and other advisers urged him not to go.

Wilson seriously miscalculated in refusing to take with him as one of the peace commissioners a leading Republican like Elihu Root or William Howard Taft. He would have done well, too, to include one of the powerful Republican senators, since it would take many Republican votes to muster the requisite two-thirds majority for ratification of the treaty by the Senate. Nevertheless, Wilson took only a nonpolitical Republican diplomat, Henry White, and relied neither upon him nor upon the other commissioners.

Arriving in Europe in December 1918, before the other European leaders were ready to confer, Wilson toured France, Italy, and England. Wherever he went, hysterically cheering crowds greeted him; everywhere boulevards and plazas were renamed for him. The cheering millions reinforced his feeling that he was the spokesman for humanity. He was not aware that in each nation these masses looked to him to obtain for them much that ran contrary to the Fourteen Points. A little later, when he fought against some of their national claims, their adulation evaporated into disillusion.

Wilson at Versailles

The sessions of Paris began January 12, 1919, in an atmosphere of idealism tinctured with national aggrandizement, amidst glittering scenes reminiscent of the Congress of Vienna. To the east, however, there was an urgency born of imminent starvation and the threatening spread of communism. Hoover, trying to get food into central Europe to fend off both threats, declared: "The wolf is at the door of the world." One of the greatest difficulties was that Russia, where Red Bolsheviks were still fighting White counterrevolutionaries, was entirely unrepresented.

At the outset Wilson had to struggle to prevent a division of spoils under the secret treaties. He tried to block the Japanese from obtaining permanently the German treaty rights in the Shantung peninsula of China and the former German islands north of the Equator in the Pacific, which could be Japanese strongholds. He had to give way, however, to the insistence of the British that they honor the treaty promises with which they had lured the Japanese into the war. Wilson with more success persuaded the Allies to hold former German colonies and Turkish territories on a basis of trusteeship responsible to the League of Nations. This was the new and unprecedented mandate system.

Simultaneously, Wilson worked on the drafting of the League Covenant. He insisted that it form the first part of the treaty and be inseparable

Red Cross official supervising the unloading of American flour in eastern Poland
(NATIONAL ARCHIVES)

from it, and he labored long and hard to draft it in meticulous detail. In the League Covenant he saw the one possible way of overriding the vengeful selfishness that seemed dominant among the victorious nations. Whatever imperfections and inequities there were in the treaty he thought could be rectified through the League: through it and it alone the world could avoid future wars. In the League he envisaged a potentially powerful (but not armed) international organization through which the nations of the world could share responsibility in maintaining the security of all against any aggressor.

At the end of February 1919, as Congress prepared to adjourn, Wilson came home to sign bills. He brought with him the League Covenant, determined that he would force the Senate to accept it without compromise. The acclaim with which Bostonians greeted him, the friendliness of editorials in most newspapers, and the energy with which large and influential organizations advocated the League—all encouraged him to think public sentiment was overwhelmingly behind him. When Colonel House warned him he must be prepared to compromise with the Senate, he retorted: "I have found that you get nothing in this world that is worth-while without fighting for it."

A stiff fight was taking form. In the Senate, on March 4, 1919, Henry Cabot Lodge produced a round robin signed by thirty-nine senators, a

The "Big Four" in Paris: (left to right) David Lloyd George of Great Britain, Vittorio E. Orlando of Italy, Georges Clemenceau of France, and President Wilson (NATIONAL ARCHIVES)

number sufficient to block the treaty, announcing that they would not accept the covenant in its existing form. Wilson, about to reembark for Paris, retorted angrily. But back at the conference he did obtain some of the amendments upon which the Senate would obviously insist. These provided that a nation need not accept a mandate against its will, that a member could withdraw with two years' notice, that the League would not regulate immigration and other internal matters, and that it would not infringe upon the Monroe Doctrine. The Republican senators, however, were not appeased. Many of them saw in the struggle over the covenant a means of embarrassing Wilson, stripping him of some of his glory, and developing a winning issue for the campaign of 1920.

While Wilson was obtaining revisions to the covenant, the conference was also grappling with the critical problem of Germany and the remaking of the European map. Together with the British prime minister, Lloyd George, Wilson resisted the French proposal to break up western Germany into buffer states. He did sanction the return of Alsace-Lorraine to France and the establishment of a strong Poland and Czechoslovakia on Germany's borders, all in keeping with the national self-determination clauses of the Fourteen Points. He also supported German demilitarization, long-term Allied occupation of the west bank of the Rhine, and an Anglo-French-American mutual defense pact (which was never ratified). If maintained, these security provisions should have prevented the resurgence of Germany as a military menace to the West.

Elsewhere the remapping of Europe proceeded rather fitfully. Italy obtained the Brenner Pass area, in which 200,000 Austrians lived, then was outraged at not also receiving Fiume, which Wilson felt must be a port for the new nation of Yugoslavia. In this region and others the economic needs of nations conflicted with the principle of national self-determination of peoples. Back in the United States, ethnic groups were ready to clamor for more for their native countries. The Irish in the United States insisted that Wilson should fight for national self-determination for Ireland, which was wracked by civil war. Wilson took up the matter privately with Lloyd George but did not make a public stand.

Wilson's most important departure from the Fourteen Points was his acceptance of British and French demands for heavy reparations from the Germans. Even before the armistice he had partly accepted the demands that Germany pay for civilian damages. At the conference he permitted these demands to cover even pensions for veterans; the astronomical sum was to be set later by a reparations commission. Meanwhile, though Wilson himself for years had taken an economic-determinism view of the origins of the war, the other powers insisted that Germany must accept sole responsibility for starting it. The war-guilt clause and the reparations bill embittered the German people. Even in the United States the harsh peace meted out against Germany disillusioned many liberals and alienated them from Wilson. They regarded the treaty as a "hell's brew" that would ultimately lead to another war.

The League Rejected

Wilson returned to the United States confident that the Senate, despite the difficulties Lodge was stirring up, would ratify the treaty. On July 10, 1919, when he presented it to the Senate, he asked rhetorically: "Dare we reject it and break the heart of the world?"

Through a combination of coercion and compromise he might have brought about ratification. But he was suffering from hardening of the arteries and, while in Paris, had been so ill that he may have been close to a stroke. His physical condition robbed him of political suppleness; instead of using patience and tact, he was more likely to shower his opponents with self-righteous anger.

Wilson's opponents in the Senate were moved by both principle and partisanship. The fourteen "irreconcilables" were men of conscience, of Midwestern or Far Western progressive tradition, such as Republicans William E. Borah of Idaho, Hiram Johnson of California, and La Follette of Wisconsin and Democrat James Reed of Missouri. They acted from a deep conviction that their nation could best be served by staying out of the League. Other opponents with less conviction were more concerned with constructing a winning issue for the Republicans in the 1920 election than they were with assuring the future of the world. Senator Lodge, applying all his brilliant intellect to his loathing for Wilson, was ready, as chairman of the Senate Foreign Relations Committee, to use every possible tactic to obstruct, delay, and defeat the treaty. Public sentiment seemed to favor ratification, and Lodge needed time to marshal forces against it. Consequently, after it reached the committee he spent the first two weeks reading aloud every word on its nearly 300 pages. Next, he held six weeks of public hearings, listening to the complaints of every disgruntled minority.

From the White House, Wilson did some conferring with Republican senators. He explained to them that he considered the collective-security provision of Article X (according to which League members guaranteed one another's territorial integrity) to be more of a moral obligation upon the United States than a legal one—but to Wilson moral obligations were the more important. The senators were not impressed; it began to appear that Wilson would have to accept some of Lodge's reservations if he wished to obtain ratification. When one senator told him this, he retorted: "Never! Never! . . . I'll appeal to the country!"

So Wilson, at the end of his physical resources, against the stern warnings of his physician, undertook a cross-country speaking tour, writing his speeches as he went along, delivering them night after night. In twenty-two days he traveled over 8,000 miles, giving thirty-six addresses averaging an hour in length. At first the halls were not entirely filled, nor were his speeches always well polished. As the tour proceeded, he gained larger and more enthusiastic audiences and grew more eloquent in his moral fervor. Had it been possible to sway the United States Senate through public opinion, the tour might have been a success. But Wilson became more and more frail. Finally, after speaking at Pueblo, Colorado, September 25, he suffered such acute headaches that he had to cancel the tour and return to Washington.

Then he suffered an acute stroke that partially paralyzed his left side. For two weeks he was close to death, and for six more weeks so seriously ill that he could attend only to what little business his devoted wife and doctor thought would not unduly upset or fatigue him. When some officials tried to see the President on vital matters, Mrs. Wilson turned them away, saying: "I am not interested in the President of the United States. I am interested in my husband and his health."

At this critical juncture the Senate Foreign Relations Committee finally reported the treaty, recommending forty-five amendments and three reservations. Lodge managed to marshal the Republican senators so well that in November he obtained adoption of fourteen reservations. By this time Wilson had recovered sufficiently to give stern directions to the Democratic minority: they must vote only for the treaty without any reservations whatsoever. Although none of the Lodge reservations would have devitalized the League, Wilson preferred no ratification of the treaty to ratification with reservations. While he was by no means his old self, he was able to exert power enough to maintain discipline over the loyal Democrats. When the vote came on November 19, 1919, forty-two Democrats joined with the thirteen Republican irreconcilables to vote down the treaty with reservations. Next the Senate voted on ratification of the treaty without reservations. There were thirty-eight senators, all but one of them a Democrat, who voted for it; fifty-five voted against it.

On the day of the final vote, March 19, 1920, when the Senate considered the treaty with fifteen reservations, it came within seven votes of receiving the requisite two-thirds majority. By this time President Wilson was looking to the election of 1920 as a "solemn referendum" on the League issue.

ten

The New Era

In times of stress Americans dream of an earlier, happier time. Thus as they emerged, disillusioned, from World War I, they looked backward to the mirage of the prewar past. They were weary of wartime regimentation and of talk about world responsibilities, which isolationists warned would mean involvement in future wars. They rejoiced in the speed with which wartime regulations were scrapped and at the polls in 1920 overwhelmingly voted away the Wilsonian order of things. But nothing could restore what had once been, for both progressivism and the war had brought lasting changes.

THE LEGACY OF PROGRESSIVISM AND THE WAR

American political life in the 1920s was not a break from previous development; it was more, too, than a reactionary interlude between the New Freedom and the New Deal. Much of what Wilson had stood for remained, for the pattern of the twenties grew out of American experience in the war and the Progressive era. A good bit of the progressivism that persisted in the decade represented the dark side, the narrowness and hatreds that could sometimes be involved in the movement. Many a man who had voted for Bryan or Roosevelt was now determined to fight for his cherished small-town way of life, and if the ballot failed, he would resort to the bedsheet of the Ku Klux Klan. Much of the positive side of progressivism survived as well, in the persisting demand throughout much of the South and West for government regulation or dissolution of monopolies, development of water power, and similar reforms. Men like La Follette and Norris still proclaimed these objectives in the Senate, where they formed an impotent but vocal minority. Progressivism persisted in the urban East also, in drives for more efficient government and better service to communities. Men like Governor Alfred E. Smith of New York

128

Troops returning on the Leviathan, *December 1918* (NATIONAL ARCHIVES)

led these campaigns on the state level; Secretary of Commerce Hoover was one of their champions in the national government. Progressivism had disappeared from the White House and could no longer command a majority in Congress, but it remained a significant force through the 1920s.

As for the war, it had raised the living standard of factory workers and built a powerful labor movement; it had created great shifts in population and accompanying tensions. It had given a temporary bonanza to the farmer, stepped up the mechanization of agriculture, and brought the plow to tens of thousands of acres of semiarid prairie grasslands. Much of this transformation had been painful and led to further difficult adjustments in the twenties. The war also had changed styles and fashions and molded consumer demands into new channels. In little ways (such as the introduction of wrist watches for men, shorter skirts for women, and cigarettes for both) and in major ways that involved basic shifts in the economy it was changing the patterns of life for most Americans.

The wartime production miracles and the clever new writings of American public relations experts and advertising men renewed the nation's faith in business. Even before the war the Supreme Court's rule of reason had so impressed the masses that they were beginning to make distinctions, illusory though they might be, between virtuous large-scale businesses of which they should be proud and the wicked trusts they should police. The worship of science and technology continued unabated, but now Americans felt that the new knowledge could best be applied by business. The heroes of the 1920s were the business leaders in the great industries. The bright young men no longer flocked to Washington, nor did they hurry to establish their own small businesses. Rather, they aimed for the board room or the industrial laboratory of a large corporation.

Business moguls, for their part, had abandoned their open contempt for the public and talked the new language of service. They promised to create even higher living standards in the years ahead. The price they asked was simple—merely that the government aid and protect them and not interfere with them. This the government was ready to do. "This is a business country," Calvin Coolidge proclaimed, "and it wants a business government." Thus the nation once again embarked into a business age. This phase was called simply the New Era.

The pattern of the New Era unfolded slowly and hesitantly in the years after the war. There were some—not radicals but old progressives—who would have made it quite the reverse of an age of big business, who would have liked to see the continuation of wartime government regulation or ownership. At the close of the war the government owned most of the nation's commercial radio facilities (used as yet only for sending messages), commanded a vast merchant fleet, and controlled the railroads.

The call for nationalization, which frightened many Americans, went beyond the old progressive bounds. Congress was not willing to go so far but did pass the Esch-Cummins Transportation Act of 1920, establishing as tight federal control over railroad rates and securities as any progressive had ever visualized. Railroads suffered from the new rigorous competition of motor vehicles and other carriers and were seldom able to earn the 6-percent return the ICC allowed.

Western progressives obtained two measures to stave off corporate onslaughts. One, the General Leasing Act, was intended to protect the naval oil reserves from oil companies that for some years had been trying to obtain them. It also authorized the leasing of other mineral and oil lands on terms favorable to the government. The other measure, the Water Power Act of 1920, was a first tentative step toward federal regulation of power. It established a Federal Power Commission (consisting of the Secretaries of War, the Interior, and Agriculture) to license the construction and operation of hydroelectric plants on public lands and to regulate rates on power from these plants when it passed across state boundaries.

Soon after the war Congress helped bring to fruition two other progressive dreams. In June 1919 it approved the women's suffrage (Nineteenth) amendment, which was ratified in August 1920. In October 1919, over the veto of President Wilson, Congress passed the drastic Volstead Act implementing the prohibition (Eighteenth) amendment, submitted by Congress in December 1917 and ratified by January 1919. Several states had passed laws outlawing hard liquor but permitting the sale of weak beer, which might have been an adequate sop to the millions of urban opponents of prohibition. The Volstead Act prohibited all liquors containing more than 0.5 percent of alcohol. To jubilant members of the Anti-Saloon League and the Women's Christian Temperance Union—the two groups most responsible for bringing about prohibition—this meant the enforcement of morality. To opponents it meant an unjustifiable infringement on personal liberty.

In total, these pieces of legislation seemed to be the last surge of pro-

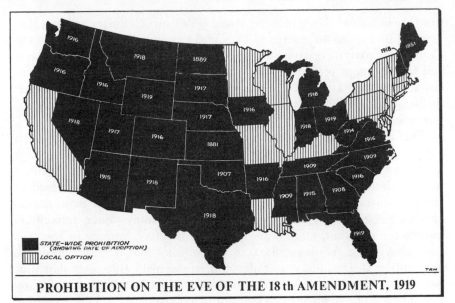

STATE-WIDE PROHIBITION
(SHOWING DATE OF ADOPTION)

LOCAL OPTION

PROHIBITION ON THE EVE OF THE 18th AMENDMENT, 1919

gressivism as the new order emerged. The rapid scrapping of wartime controls pointed the main direction that the twenties were to take.

THE RED SCARE

The sudden dropping of controls allowed prices to soar, to the dismay of consumers and organized labor. On the price index (in which 1913 prices had an index of 100) manufactured goods rose from 198.4 in 1918 to 239.5 in 1920; food prices kept pace. Suddenly, in 1921, prices dropped, and a brief recession followed, giving way to full recovery by 1923. Meanwhile, fears of radicalism, heightened by the spread of communism in Russia and elsewhere in Europe, provoked a hysterical spirit of reaction in America.

Union workers tried to preserve their wartime economic gains by striking for higher wages as living costs went upward. In 1919 a great wave of strikes spread across the country, involving about 4 million workers. In many of these strikes—such as those conducted by longshoremen, printers, and laborers in the clothing, textile, telephone, and other industries—the strikers succeeded in raising their living standards. In the process they alienated much of the public, which was quick to accept the industrialists' explanations that higher wages were responsible for higher prices and that the strike leaders were radicals.

The outbreak of a steel strike in September 1919 brought antilabor feelings to a boil. The grievances of the workers were serious. They were working an average of nearly sixty-nine hours per week for bare subsistence wages. Despite the workers' valid claims, United States Steel was able to swing public sentiment away from the strikers by claiming that the leaders were communists. The chief organizer, William Z. Foster, once a follower of Bryan, was to emerge in 1924 as the presidential candidate of the Communist party. The company brought in black strikebreakers, and state and federal troops prevented picketing. In rioting at Gary, Indiana, eighteen strikers were killed. Within a few weeks tens of thousands of strikebreakers under armed protection were operating the plants at three-quarters capacity, and by January the workers were starved out.

Public opinion turned even more firmly against organized labor when a police strike broke out in Boston. The policemen were working long hours on prewar salaries under unpleasant conditions. After their organization, the Boston Social Club, obtained an AFL charter and threatened to strike, a Mayor's Citizens Committee prepared to meet their demands except for recognition of their union. The police commissioner, responsible only to the governor, refused and dismissed nineteen leaders. In response the police struck. As mischief-makers and rowdies took over, horrified citizens put on their military uniforms and, armed with rifles and shotguns, began patrolling the streets. The mayor mobilized state troops and restored order. The following day Governor Coolidge, who had done nothing to prevent the strike or preserve the peace, suddenly acted. He ordered in troops and backed the decision of the police commissioner never to reemploy any of the strikers. When President Gompers of the AFL appealed to Coolidge, the governor wired back: "There is no right to strike against the public safety, anywhere, anytime." This one telegram made Coolidge a formidable contender for the Republican presidential nomination in 1920.

In Washington Attorney General A. Mitchell Palmer was becoming prominent through his war on both labor and radicals. When the new president of the United Mine Workers, John L. Lewis, took the bituminous coal workers out on strike in November 1919, Palmer smashed the strike with federal court injunctions.

Palmer attracted even more attention with his crusade against Reds. Throughout the country the violent suppression of alleged pro-German activities during the war had been continued in the persecution of the IWW, the Socialists, and all other left-wingers. Both Congress and the New York state legislature denied seats to Socialists. By 1920 one-third of the states had enacted criminal syndicalist laws to punish radicals. The New York law prohibited "advocating, teaching, or aiding and abetting the commission of crime and sabotage, or unlawful acts of force and violence or unlawful methods of terrorism as a means of accomplishing a change in industrial ownership or control, or affecting any political change."

Bombings and attempted bombings captured the headlines. A bomb damaged the front of Palmer's home in June 1919; bombs addressed to a number of government leaders were discovered in the mails; a year later an explosion on Wall Street killed thirty-eight people. Four members of the newly founded American Legion were killed in an attack on IWW headquarters in Centralia, Washington, on Armistice Day 1919. These incidents furnished the material out of which the newspapers, with some aid from Palmer, built a great national panic. Within the country there were very few radicals to undertake a revolution: IWW membership was down to 35,000 and continued to decline; the Socialist party numbered 39,000 and was not revolutionary anyway; the Communist-Labor party (left-wing Socialists) had 10,000 to 30,000 members; and the Communist party, organized September 1, 1919, had 30,000 to 60,000.

Palmer's goal was to ferret out and eliminate the communists. He proposed a sedition bill so drastic that Congress would not enact it; then he proceeded anyway without it. The Labor Department had already arrested and deported to Finland 249 Russian communists. Nevertheless, Palmer, without advance notice to the Labor Department, conducted a great red roundup on January 1, 1920, jailing some 6,000 suspects. Communists who were United States citizens he turned over to the states for prosecution. The aliens came under the jurisdiction of the Labor Department, which gave them fair treatment. Only 556 proved communists were deported.

In Massachusetts a payroll robbery and murder in April 1920 led to the trial and conviction of two anarchists, Nicola Sacco and Bartolomeo Vanzetti. Many believers in civil liberties felt that the two men were being prosecuted more on the basis of their radicalism than on the criminal evidence. Ultimately, throughout the country and in Western Europe as well, outraged liberals and radicals demanded the release of the two men, but in August 1927 they were executed. The Sacco and Vanzetti case was a *cause célèbre* of the 1920s.

The KKK and the Blacks

If there had been a blaze of revolution, which was improbable, it was indeed under control, but the backfire of intolerance swept out of control and began to sear the country. Not only radicals, but labor organizers, aliens, Catholics, Jews, and blacks became its victims.

Intolerance was organized in the Ku Klux Klan, which in 1915 had been revived in Atlanta, Georgia, and soon spread throughout the country, claiming 5 million members at its height in the 1920s. White-robed and hooded Klansmen used fiery crosses, threats, torture, and murder to intimidate minority groups and other people they considered un-American or immoral. The Klan became a political power in many states, most notably in Indiana, where a Klansman made himself governor and virtually dictator for a time.

No group suffered more severely than the blacks. For hundreds of thousands of them the war had offered an opportunity to break out of the narrow caste structure of the South. Some 400,000 served in the army, half of them in Europe, where the local people usually drew no color line. Several hundred thousand more moved into the industrial North, where there was less discrimination against them than in the South. Even in the North, however, they suffered from wretched housing, low pay, and the animosity of unskilled white workers who feared their competition.

In both North and South, blacks faced explosive resentment against

A Ku Klux Klan meeting—not in the Twenties but in 1948 (NATIONAL ARCHIVES)

them. In order to intimidate them back into their former subservience, Southerners resorted to the terrorism of the Klan and to lynchings, which increased from thirty-four in 1917 to more than seventy in 1919. Terrible racc riots broke out, beginning in July 1919, in twenty-six towns and cities, mostly in the North. Hundreds of persons were killed or wounded, and millions of dollars' worth of property was destroyed. The worst of the outbursts began on a Chicago bathing beach and continued through thirteen days of pillaging and burning in the black district; 23 blacks and 15 whites were killed, 500 were injured, and 1,000 families, mostly black, were left homeless.

These terrors led numbers of blacks to follow a persuasive Jamaican who promised a way out of their persecution through black separatism and nationalism. In return for their contributions he promised to take them home to an African empire. Marcus Garvey mismanaged their funds and in 1923 was convicted of swindling, but black nationalism persisted.

PRESIDENT HARDING'S NORMALCY

The 1920 election took place amid these tensions and struggles, making a solemn referendum on a league of nations impossible. Only an ill man sequestered from the flow of events, as President Wilson was, could have expected such a thing. A Democratic victory was so improbable that Republican leaders felt no compulsion to put forth any of their strong candidates.

The two leading contenders were Leonard Wood and Frank O. Lowden. General Wood, an ardent conservative nationalist, commanded most of Roosevelt's former following and collected a campaign chest of startling proportions ($1,773,000) with which he battled Lowden for delegates. Lowden, favorably known as an efficient governor of Illinois, also commanded large campaign funds, totaling $414,000. Progressive Republican charges that both contenders were deeply indebted to big business helped induce party managers to ignore them when the two deadlocked at the convention. Late one night in a smoke-filled hotel room a cabal of senators led by Lodge turned to one of the most regular and pliable of their colleagues, Warren G. Harding of Ohio. The convention nominated Harding on the tenth ballot and chose as his running mate the Massachusetts governor Coolidge. These two were thoroughly conservative candidates running on a thoroughly conservative platform.

The Democrats, assembling at San Francisco, were rather confused because President Wilson, who could have easily designated a candidate, seemed to be waiting with pathetic coyness to be renominated for a third term. This was out of the question. For thirty-eight ballots two of Wilson's cabinet members, his efficient son-in-law McAdoo and his superpatriotic Attorney General Palmer, battled for the nomination. In the end the urban bosses stepped in and secured the nomination of an antiprohibition candidate who might salvage their city tickets for them. This was the former progressive governor of Ohio, James M. Cox. As a gesture toward the Wilsonians, Assistant Secretary of the Navy Franklin D. Roosevelt was nominated for Vice President.

Cox and Roosevelt campaigned arduously to make the election the League referendum that Wilson wished it to be. Harding, following the advice of his managers, made few speeches and took few positions on the issues of the day except to promise a return to what he earlier had called normalcy. He displayed an ambivalence that was politically most successful. On the League he at first gave the impression that he favored adherence, then as city resentment against it flared, gave the impression he was against it. Lest Cox's crusade win away Republican votes, thirty-one distinguished Republicans signed a statement declaring that a vote for Harding was a vote for American entrance into the League with reservations.

The landslide exceeded even the expectations of the Republicans. Harding received 16,152,000 popular votes, 61 percent of the total, and carried every state outside of the Solid South. He even won Tennessee. Cox received only 9,147,000 popular votes. Debs, running on the Socialist ticket while in the Atlanta penitentiary, received 920,000 votes. The sweep brought a Republican majority of 22 in the Senate and 167 in the House.

In voting against Wilsonianism, the electorate brought into power a weak, amiable conservative. Alice Roosevelt Longworth, daughter of a President and wife of the Speaker of the House, reared in the genteel tradition of Republican politics, could not forget the sight of a poker session in the President's study. "Harding was not a bad man," she reminisced. "He was just a slob."

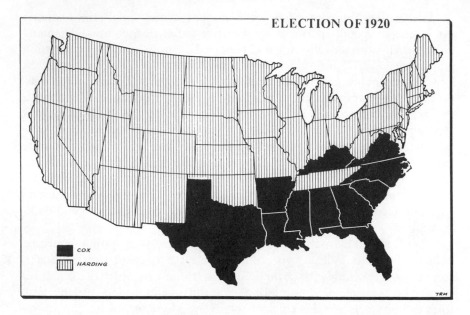

President Harding wished to surround himself with the best-qualified men, and in part he succeeded. When he was persuaded that his friend Albert B. Fall was not of a caliber to be Secretary of State, he placed Fall, a notorious anticonservationist, in charge of the Interior Department. He then appointed the brilliant and distinguished Hughes to be Secretary of State. He placed Hoover, the friend of small enterprise and an expert on efficiency, in charge of the Commerce Department, and made Henry C. Wallace, spokesman for the Midwest farmers, Secretary of Agriculture. Andrew W. Mellon represented big business as Secretary of the Treasury. These able men, pulling in several directions, together with the congressional leaders, developed government policies.

SUBSTITUTES FOR LEAGUE MEMBERSHIP

The task of developing Republican alternatives to Wilsonian foreign policy fell largely on the shoulders of Secretaries of State Hughes (1921–1925) and Frank B. Kellogg (1925–1929). Hughes' policy involved first of all ending the war with Germany by an act of Congress, which was signed July 2, 1921. Hughes then negotiated separate peace treaties with the former Central Powers to secure for the United States the benefits without the responsibilities of the Paris treaties. In time, Hughes permitted American delegations to participate in League conferences on minor matters as long as they did not make commitments. Throughout his years as Secretary of State he was chilly toward every European proposal for collective security. He did, in February 1923, persuade President Harding to recommend that the United States join with reservations the World Court, an almost completely powerless body. But the World Court was an instrument of the League, and while internationally minded Americans ardently favored joining, the irreconcilables in the Senate violently fought it. Each succeeding President through Franklin D. Roosevelt advocated American adherence to the League; each time, through 1935, the Senate blocked it.

Through the Washington Arms Conference, Republicans made it appear that they were taking positive steps to preserve the peace. It was in effect a Republican substitute for entrance into the League. In May 1921 Senator Borah had introduced a resolution calling for a conference to reduce armaments, but the basic impetus for the meeting came from the British, who feared a three-way naval race with the Americans and the Japanese. Japan had emerged from the war stronger than before in China and with troops still stationed in Siberia. It threatened to expand still further, to shut the Open Door in China, and to arm its new island possessions in the Pacific. American public opinion saw an even more serious threat in the Anglo-Japanese alliance. Hence the British, wishing to strengthen their amicable relations with the United States, proposed the conference. Hughes seized the initiative, and President Harding issued invitations.

The arms conference opened on November 12, 1921, the day after burial rites for the Unknown Soldier at Arlington Cemetery. Hughes in his opening speech startled the delegates and won enormous acclaim by dramatically presenting a concrete plan for the reduction in size of the fleets of the United States, Great Britain, and Japan. He proposed a ten-year moratorium on capital-ship construction (battleships, cruisers, and carriers) and the scrapping by the three powers of nearly 1.9 million tons of ships already built or under construction. A British observer declared: "Secretary Hughes sank in thirty-five minutes more ships than all the admirals of the world have sunk in a cycle of centuries."

In the negotiations that followed, Japan agreed to limit her capital ships to a total of approximately 300,000 tons, compared with 500,000 tons each for the United States and Great Britain. In addition the United States pledged itself not to increase its fortifications in Guam and the Philippines. Japan and Great Britain made similar pledges. Thus the Five Power Pact of 1922 provided a ratio of 5:5:3 for the United States, Great Britain, and Japan, and 1.75:1.75 for France and Italy, stopping what otherwise could have become a disastrous armaments race. Two other treaties aimed at guaranteeing the status quo in the Far East. The Nine Power Pact pledged a continuation of the Open Door policy in China. Afterward, Japan restored full sovereign rights to China in the Shantung peninsula and promised to withdraw the Japanese troops from Siberia. The Four Power Pact—among the United States, Great Britain, France, and Japan—represented a mutual recognition of insular rights in the Pacific. Upon its ratification Japan relinquished her alliance with Great Britain.

The Washington treaties lowered the tension between the United States and Japan for nearly a decade. Their one unfortunate result was that the United States relinquished the physical force with which to impose its will in the Far East but retained its moral, economic, and political objectives in that area. The Senate came close to rejecting the Four Power Pact for fear it would commit the United States to some collective security arrangement in the Orient. On the other hand, the popularity of the Naval Limitation Treaty (Five Power Pact) is shown by the fact that only one senator voted against its ratification.

During the Coolidge administration, millions of Americans signed petitions urging the United States to promote a multilateral treaty outlawing war. The French foreign minister, Aristide Briand, proposed a treaty of this kind between France and the United States. Secretary Kellogg responded by suggesting that other countries be invited to join. So, at Paris in 1928, most of the great nations, including the United States, signed a treaty solemnly renouncing war as an instrument of national policy but providing no machinery whatever for enforcement. The treaty evoked much enthusiasm in the United States, for it seemed to offer collective security without any risks.

Hughes tried to extend the good will of the United States toward Latin America. During his first months in office, he was decidedly influenced by Sumner Welles, later one of the chief molders of the Good Neighbor policy. By 1924 Hughes had ended the marine occupation of Santo Domingo and prepared for its end in Nicaragua. He felt that the occupation was still necessary in Haiti.

Hughes moved away from the progressive policy of intervention and tried wherever possible to substitute the nonrecognition of undesirable governments for the landing of the marines. Neither he nor his successor in the Coolidge administration was ready to give up intervention entirely. For a time during the Coolidge administration trouble with Mexico over the rights of American oil companies and renewed marine intervention in Nicaragua seemed to indicate a retreat to the old policies.

Economic Nationalism

In European affairs a persisting and troublesome issue was that of reparations and war debts. The failure of the United States to join the League of Nations had most serious repercussions on this problem, since the League's Reparations Commission, which was not under the chairmanship of an American as had been expected, set astronomically high sums for Germany to pay. Reparations payments depended to a considerable degree upon American private loans to Germany; war-debt payments from the Allies to the United States depended, in turn, almost entirely upon reparations. The American public insisted that the Allies should repay the $10 billion the United States had loaned during the war. Coolidge later epitomized the popular view when he remarked simply: "They hired the money, didn't they?"

The United States pressured the former Allies, through a World War Foreign Debt Commission, to negotiate long-term schedules of debt payments. Between 1923 and 1926 the commission reached agreements with

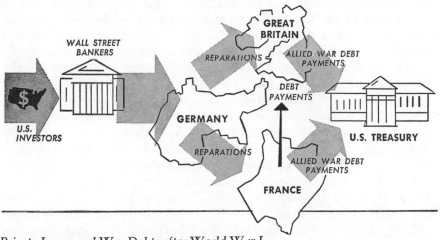

Private Loans and War Debts after World War I

the Allies in regard to their debts (which the United States government insisted bore no relationship to German reparations payments). The administration did not worry about how Germany, France, Italy, and the other debtors could make payments over the high tariff wall that the United States was raising against their exports.

What kept the payments going during the twenties was the huge total of private American loans pouring into German governmental units or corporations—about $2.5 billion between 1923 and 1930. Germany paid about $2 billion in reparations, and the former Allies about $2.6 billion in war-debt payments. Thus the Germans were paying the Allies, and the Allies were paying the United States, with dollars that Americans were lending to the Germans.

As soon as the Republicans had come into power in 1921, they enacted an emergency tariff measure to raise the low Underwood rates. In 1922 they passed the Fordney-McCumber Act providing protection especially for agriculture, the chemical industry, and manufacturers threatened by Japanese and German competition. The tariff gave agriculture little real protection, but it provided industrialists with several benefits. It accepted the principle that, when foreign firms had costs of production lower than their American competitors, the tariff should be high enough to offset the differential. It prohibited most competing imports and led to higher prices at home. Other nations followed the American lead in economic nationalism; by 1928 about sixty countries had raised their tariffs.

Immigration Restriction

Along with high walls against competing goods, Congress finally succeeded in erecting barriers against incoming foreigners. The movement to curtail immigration came to a spectacularly successful climax with the beginning of the Harding administration. Racist objections to the "new immigrants" and the unionists' fear that the newcomers were perpetuating a pool of cheap labor in the United States were reinforced by the new allegation that some of them were radicals. This led employers who had previously favored immigration to switch to the restrictive side.

In 1921 Congress passed an emergency immigration act, setting up a quota system: immigrants from any country could not exceed 3 percent of the number of persons of their nationality who had been in the United States in 1910. This cut the number of immigrants from 800,000 in the year ending June 30, 1921, to about 300,000 in the following twelve months. Racists still were not satisfied, so that Congress in 1924 enacted the National Origins Act. This measure not only banned the people of East Asia entirely but set a quota of 2 percent for Europeans based on the 1890 census. It cut the yearly total to 164,000, heavily weighted in favor of those from northwestern Europe. On July 1, 1929, an overall limit of about 150,000 immigrants a year went into effect, but during the entire depression decade of the thirties the total net immigration was less than 70,000. The great flood of so many decades had been reduced to a few drops.

Excluding all aliens ineligible to become citizens meant excluding the Japanese in particular. It was an unnecessary insult to the Japanese, since the gentlemen's agreement had worked well, and the application of a quota system to Japan would have allowed only a tiny trickle of immigrants. Indignation in Japan against the act of 1924 was so extreme that Hughes lamented privately: "It has undone the work of the Washington Conference and implanted the seeds of an antagonism which are sure to bear fruit in the future."

Effects of the Quota Acts on Sources of Immigration

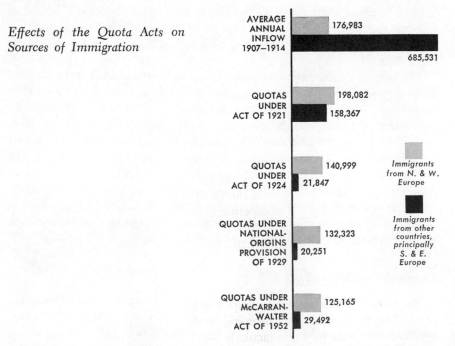

AVERAGE ANNUAL INFLOW 1907–1914	176,983	
	685,531	
QUOTAS UNDER ACT OF 1921	198,082	
	158,367	
QUOTAS UNDER ACT OF 1924	140,999	Immigrants from N. & W. Europe
	21,847	
QUOTAS UNDER NATIONAL-ORIGINS PROVISION OF 1929	132,323	Immigrants from other countries, principally S. & E. Europe
	20,251	
QUOTAS UNDER McCARRAN-WALTER ACT OF 1952	125,165	
	29,492	

THE HARDING DEBACLE

Altogether, the Harding administration seemed to stand for a business-men's nationalism. In domestic as well as foreign policies the President seemed to be carrying out his campaign slogan: "Less government in business and more business in government." The Democrats made strong gains in the 1922 elections, reflecting the hard times that followed the war, but the return of prosperity soon afterward heightened Harding's popularity. He occasionally was even vigorous in his humanity. He took a step Wilson had curtly declined; on Christmas Day, 1921, he pardoned the Socialist Debs. At the urging of Hoover he pressured the steel companies into granting an eight-hour day to their workers. The press of the country, overwhelmingly Republican, created the illusion that Harding was an exceptionally fine President.

Behind the façade rot had set in. With singularly bad judgment Harding had placed a number of his poker-playing and drinking companions into positions of trust, where they betrayed him and the American people. Probably Harding never knew in detail how shockingly they were looting the government, but he knew enough to be heartsick. One of the "Ohio Gang," Attorney General Harry Daugherty's friend Jesse Smith, had been engaging in large-scale "fixing" in the Department of Justice. After Harding ordered him out of Washington, Smith committed suicide. The director of the Veterans' Bureau, Charles R. Forbes, engaged in such colossal thievery that the total loss ran to nearly $250 million. When Harding received intimations of the corruption, he allowed Forbes to flee the country and resign. Ultimately, Forbes served a two-year penitentiary sentence for defrauding the government.

The most spectacular fraud involved the rich naval oil reserves at Teapot Dome, Wyoming, and Elk Hills, California. Secretary of the Interior Fall persuaded Harding to transfer the oil reserves to his department, then secretly leased them to Harry F. Sinclair and Edward L. Doheny. Fall, who had been in financial straits, suddenly became affluent. An investigation headed by Senator Thomas J. Walsh of Montana during the fall and winter of 1923 and 1924 uncovered the reason. Sinclair had loaned Fall $308,000 in cash and government bonds and a herd of cattle for his ranch; Doheny had loaned him $100,000 more. In 1929 Fall was convicted of bribery, fined $100,000, and sentenced to a year in a federal penitentiary.

In the summer of 1923 Harding journeyed to Alaska. Tired and depressed, he responded wanly to the cheering throngs, who had no inkling of the mess in Washington. He never had to face the exposure of the corruption because upon his return to Seattle he became ill. It was reported that he had been poisoned by seafood, but actually he had suffered a serious heart attack. He seemed to improve, so he continued to San Francisco. There he had a second attack and suddenly died. In the months that followed, as exposure after exposure crowded the headlines, his reputation collapsed.

By his sudden death Harding had escaped certain ignominy and had spared his party from it as well. His successor, Coolidge, was all that he was not, a man of impeccable integrity and efficient conservatism. In many respects Harding had symbolized the years immediately after the war. Just as his fine presidential appearance had covered appalling weakness, so had the notion of normalcy covered much that was cruel, greedy, or short-sighted.

President Harding speaking on his Western trip (NATIONAL ARCHIVES)

eleven
A Precarious Prosperity

The mid-1920s were a golden interlude of prosperity for a large number of American people. The generation that had been young then looked back upon these years with a justifiable nostalgia, for they were rich years, both materially and in cultural advance. It was a short boom, not lasting much more than five years, and it was a precarious one in which millions of people did not share. The flaws in these years require critical examination, but the substantial contributions of the mid-1920s also should be remembered.

COOLIDGE TAKES THE NATION FURTHER RIGHT

It was the singular good fortune of Coolidge to become President of the United States at the only time since the nineties when his largely negative custodial approach to the presidency could bring him popularity rather than disaster. He came to be Chief Executive through a curious mixture of luck, political regularity, and Yankee shrewdness. If it was mainly luck that elevated him to the White House, it was mainly shrewdness that kept him so well established there. Even more than Harding, Coolidge had gone up the ladder of respectable political regularity, missing few of the rungs from minor officialdom in Northampton, Massachusetts, to the Vice Presidency: he had been councilman, solicitor, representative in the legislature, mayor, state senator, lieutenant governor, and governor, at which point he probably would have stopped had it not been for the Boston police strike. Unlike Harding, he had a clear-cut conservative philosophy; he always cooperated wholeheartedly with the big interests because he believed in them, and he fought unwaveringly for what he believed.

To the older circle in Washington, Coolidge's personality was not especially appealing; Alice Roosevelt Longworth remarked that he had been weaned on a dill pickle. To the American public, however, there was an infinite appeal and security in his folksy virtues, so lavishly detailed and praised in the nation's press. Coolidge reinforced this folksy appeal with little homilies drawn from his Vermont boyhood—exhortations (in which he fervently believed) to thrift, hard work, and respect for business. It was the old Puritan ethic in homespun terms, sermons couched in the phrases of the "good old days," urging an acceptance of the new economic oligarchy. For millions of middle-class urban people, only a generation or two away from rural backgrounds, there was a strong attraction in this country philosophy refurbished for the machine age.

Under Coolidge's comforting moral leadership the men of power in the United States could take a calm and even incredulous view of the Harding scandals as they came to light one by one in the winter of 1923–1924. Indeed, the respectable press showered indignation less upon the corrupt officials than upon those pressing the investigations. Two progressive Democratic senators, Thomas J. Walsh and Burton K. Wheeler, appeared to *The New York Times* to be "assassins of character."

Under Coolidge the Republicans seemed so patently incorruptible that the exposures appeared if anything to backfire against the exposing Democrats. Ultimately, Coolidge forced Attorney General Daugherty to resign and helped clean up the scandals. As the election of 1924 approached, the revelations seemed to be doing no appreciable harm to the

President Coolidge in Vermont (HARVARD COLLEGE LIBRARY)

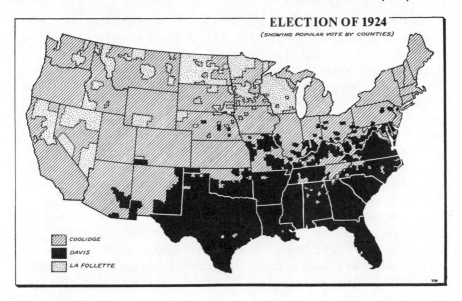

ELECTION OF 1924
(SHOWING POPULAR VOTE BY COUNTIES)

COOLIDGE
DAVIS
LA FOLLETTE

Republican party. The nation appeared ready to heed the party's campaign slogan: "Keep cool with Coolidge."

In 1924 the Democratic party was badly split between its rural and urban wings. Rural Democrats were backing as their candidate McAdoo, the competent heir to Wilsonianism. Strangely, the Teapot Dome scandal, which did no harm to the Republicans, tarnished McAdoo's reputation because he had served as a lawyer for Doheny, the California oil magnate. As for the urban wing of the party, it was advancing the candidacy of the equally competent liberal governor of New York, Alfred E. Smith, who was the son of Irish immigrants and had made his way upward from the Lower East Side of New York. Because of his background and because he was a Catholic and a "wet" (an opponent of prohibition) he was the idol of many new Americans but an anathema to rural Democrats.

Finally, both contenders withdrew, and on the 103rd ballot at the convention in Madison Square Garden the exhausted delegates nominated a compromise candidate, John W. Davis. Originally a West Virginian, Davis as Solicitor General under Wilson had ably defended the legislation of the New Freedom before the Supreme Court. In the years since, he had become a lawyer for J. P. Morgan and some of the great corporations and had amassed a fortune.

While the Democratic convention dragged on, insurgent Republicans and allied representatives of labor held a third convention to organize a Progressive party and nominate La Follette and Burton K. Wheeler. Their platform took an advanced progressive position, attacking monopoly and promising reforms for the farmers and workingmen. The party's support came from farmers, chiefly on the Great Plains, who had earlier formed the Nonpartisan League and the Farmer-Labor party, and from the Railroad Brotherhoods and the AFL.

This third party apparently was a real contrast to the Republican and Democratic tickets, and it served as a made-to-order target for the Republicans. They campaigned to frighten the electorate into choosing Coolidge as the only alternative to the "red radicalism" of La Follette. Before Election Day labor became lukewarm toward La Follette; Republican farmers, as crop prices rose, decided to stay within the party. In its last thrust the old Midwestern insurgency carried only Wisconsin and secured but 16.5 percent of the popular vote throughout the country. Coolidge polled 54 percent, and Davis only 28.8 percent.

In his inaugural, March 4, 1925, President Coolidge, declaring that the nation had achieved "a state of contentment seldom before seen," pledged himself to the maintenance of things as they were. During the prosperous years of the Coolidge era, as revenues came pouring in, the federal government did not greatly enlarge its services. It spent nothing in areas such as public housing and little for farm relief or public works. Arms expenditures were a relative pittance. Consequently, the budget varied little between 1923 and 1929. Meanwhile, the national debt dropped by nearly a quarter.

Favored Business

Big business had a special friend in the government during the 1920s. Mellon, the Pittsburgh aluminum baron who served as Secretary of the Treasury from Harding's inauguration into the Hoover administration, was widely hailed as the greatest Secretary of the Treasury since Alexander Hamilton. His main function seemed to be to preside over tax cuts; cartoonists routinely pictured Mellon slicing a tax melon. So far as he could do so, as a matter of principle, he divided these cuts among the wealthy to give them the incentive to earn more money.

Smaller businessmen also had a strong champion in the government, Secretary of Commerce Hoover. In his own spectacular rise as an international mining engineer, Hoover epitomized the self-made businessman. Denouncing both the radicalism and reaction he had seen in Europe, Hoover set forth his own credo in 1922 in a small book entitled *American Individualism*. It extolled the equality of opportunity that enabled Americans to succeed on their own merits and the "rising vision of service" that led them to develop community responsibility rather than merely to seek "the acquisition and preservation of private property." This had been Hoover's own way of life.

Hoover made the Commerce Department the most active of the departments, as he sought to help small business become as efficient and profitable as big business. Through commercial attachés whom he sent to American embassies he solicited foreign orders for American industry at the same time that he favored the tariff to protect it from overseas competition. Through the National Bureau of Standards he performed innumerable other services for industry, such as standardizing products and eliminating waste.

"*The Traffic Problem in Washington, D.C.*" *by J. N. Darling for the Des Moines* Register

The most significant means of helping small business was the sponsorship of voluntary trade associations similar to the committees of the War Industries Board. By 1921 about 2,000 were in operation. These associations, free from government regulation, could establish codes of ethics, standardize production, establish efficiency, and make substantial savings. They could serve even better than government prohibition of evil practices, Hoover had pointed out, to secure "cooperation in the business community to cure its own abuses." They could also arrive indirectly at higher standard prices, which would bring them good profits. Their real value to highly competitive smaller businesses was to eliminate competition through setting up standardized schedules of quality and prices.

Voluntarism was at the heart of all of Hoover's projects. As the new field of commercial radio broadcasting began to develop, Hoover fostered voluntary self-regulation for it. When the efforts to keep stations off each other's wave lengths completely broke down, he moved toward compulsory government regulation through the Federal Radio Commission, established in 1927. In the same way, the Department of Commerce finally took over regulation of commercial aeronautics through the Air Commerce Act in 1926.

On the whole, business thrived from 1923 to 1929. In part this was due to benign governmental policies. Hoover's laudable efforts to bring about increased standardization and efficiency took the economy further away from free competition and contributed to the increased profits of business and consequently to the concentration of wealth. Secretary Mellon's tax policies helped the rich to become richer, while incomes of poorer people advanced little if at all. The tendency of the courts to frown upon trade-association price schedules helped stimulate mergers.

And mergers helped to sustain the trend toward concentration of business that had begun after the Civil War. During the twenties, 8,000 mining and manufacturing companies disappeared into combinations, and 5,000 public utilities were swallowed, mostly by holding companies. By 1929 chain stores were selling more than a quarter of the nation's food, apparel, and general merchandise. The 200 largest nonfinancial corporations owned nearly half of all corporate wealth, and 22 percent of all national wealth. The 503 persons with the highest incomes received as much money as the total wages of 615,000 automobile workers.

The Decline of Unions

The onslaught against all Americans who did not conform, against any who might disturb the status quo, reacted strongly to the advantage of business leaders, who already basked in the public favor. These leaders were able to reestablish in the minds of many people the feeling that unionism was somehow un-American. In 1920 they began a great open-shop movement to break unions and reduce wages, under the alluring title "The American Plan."

The paternalistic policies of welfare capitalism, together with the antiunion campaign, led to a decline in union membership during the 1920s. Many companies greatly improved working conditions by installing safety devices and improving sanitation. They raised their workers' morale by building attractive cafeterias and promoting athletic teams. Company welfare workers looked into the workers' family problems. By 1926 nearly 3 million workers could look forward to pensions upon retirement. In some companies they could buy stock below market value. Altogether they owned less than 1 percent, but even this did much to change some workers' attitudes. Further, they could voice their grievances through company unions or workers' councils, which were often effective safety valves for the employer. Through devices like these, companies helped fend off unionism from the new mass-production industries like automobile manufacturing.

Within the skilled crafts the AFL continued quietly and conservatively under the presidency of William Green. Its leaders seemed more interested in maintaining labor monopolies, especially in the building trades, than in organizing industrial workers. Membership in the United Mine Workers dwindled after unsuccessful strikes in 1922. Union membership declined from over 5 million in 1920 to around 4.3 million in 1929.

In some industries, like coal mining and textiles in the South, hours were long and wages were pitiful. At Elizabethton, Tennessee, in 1929, mill girls were working fifty-six hours a week for sixteen to eighteen cents an hour. Behind the harried workers was always the threat of legal action if they sought to help themselves through unions. Federal courts were granting injunctions to break boycotts or to enforce antiunion (yellow-dog) contracts. For most workingmen, however, conditions of labor had improved and living standards were up. Real wages increased about 26 percent between 1919 and 1929. They still were far from adequate. The average was less than $1,500 a year at a time when it was estimated that $1,800 was required to maintain a minimum decent living standard.

No Parity for Farmers

While the income of most Americans advanced during the 1920s, that of the farmers drastically declined. In 1920 they lost their price supports at the same time that the bloated wartime European market contracted. At home, as machines released men from heavy manual labor, the consumption of starches dropped sharply.

Within agriculture there were great variations. Truck gardening more than doubled, and dairying and citrus growing increased a third, reflecting the shifts in eating habits. Many such farmers enjoyed satisfactory incomes. At the same time, those on marginal or submarginal lands suffered so acutely that in the five years after 1919, 13 million acres were abandoned. Poor farmers were unable to compete with large landowners who were using new, expensive machinery, which especially helped contribute to the glut of wheat. The number of tractors in use increased from 230,000 in 1920 to 920,000 in 1930, displacing 7,450,000 horses and releasing an additional 35 million acres of land for crops. On the Great Plains speculators bought the lands of bankrupt farmers and grew wheat on it with improved tractors and combines. In the Texas Panhandle alone nearly 3 million new acres were ploughed.

The success of the big operators made the desperation of small farmers even more acute. In the year ending June 30, 1927, the average income of all the 6.3 million farmers was only $548, and out of this farmers had to meet a variety of pressing obligations. Farm income in 1920 was 15 percent of the national total; by 1929 it was only 9 percent. The agricultural population dropped 3 million between 1921 and 1928. Many of those who remained on the farms ceased to own them and became tenants. Distressed farmers, both owners and renters, began to agitate militantly for relief.

Even during the bonanza years of the war, agrarian agitation had stirred the Great Plains. In 1915 wheat growers of North Dakota had organized the Nonpartisan League, pledged to strict regulation of railroads and banks, and state ownership of grain elevators and farm credit agencies. The league won control of the North Dakota government in 1916, then began to organize in adjacent states, and in 1920 joined with other radical groups to form the Farmer-Labor party. The new party had some success in the congressional election of 1922, but by 1924 even La Follette would not accept its support. It was too radical for farmers who were earning $1,000 to $4,000 a year.

These men, the middle 40 percent of the farmers in terms of income, produced 46 percent of the farm products and were solid citizens in their communities. Often acting through the Farm Bureau Federation or the Grange, they sought government price supports. From the outset they

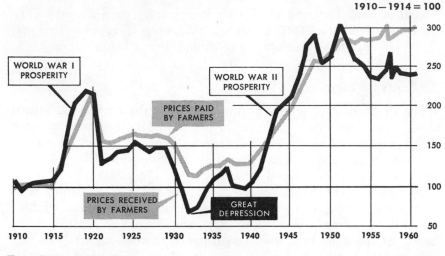

1910-1914 = 100

WORLD WAR I
PROSPERITY

WORLD WAR II
PROSPERITY

PRICES PAID
BY FARMERS

PRICES RECEIVED
BY FARMERS

GREAT
DEPRESSION

Farm Prices, 1910–1961

had powerful strength in the Congress. During the special session of Congress in the spring of 1921, Midwestern congressional leaders from both parties, meeting in the offices of the Farm Bureau Federation, organized a farm bloc.

One price-raising scheme came to dominate the farmers' thinking. Behind the tariff barrier the American protected price for crops should be raised to a "fair exchange value" based on the price of the crop during ten prewar years as compared with the general average of all prices during the same period. This was the parity price. The means of obtaining parity for farmers would be for the government to buy up the surplus at the high American price and sell it abroad at whatever it would bring on the world market. To make up for the loss, an equalization fee or tax would be charged the farmers on their entire crop.

Between 1924 and 1928 Senator Charles L. McNary of Oregon and Representative Gilbert Haugen of Iowa promoted this scheme in Congress. In 1924 the McNary-Haugen bill covered only grain and was defeated in the House, but in 1926 the addition of cotton, tobacco, and rice brought Southern support. In 1927 Congress passed it, but President Coolidge coldly vetoed it as being preferential legislation contrary to the principles of laissez faire. (On the same day he signed an order raising the tariff on pig iron 50 percent.) A year later Congress again passed the McNary-Haugen bill, and Coolidge again vetoed it.

Farmers were well organized, and indeed were on the threshold of victory, but they could not win until they put into the White House a President, either Republican or Democratic, sympathetic to their program. In 1928 the Democratic Smith accepted the farmers' proposals, but few were as yet ready to bolt their party even to obtain price supports. As long as the country as a whole was prosperous, the farmers seemed doomed to be economically depressed.

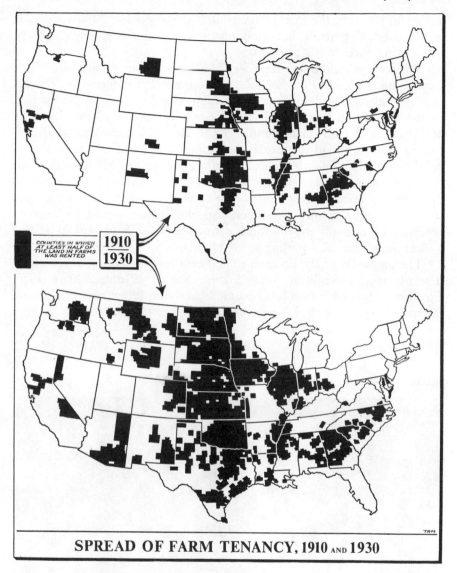

COUNTIES IN WHICH AT LEAST HALF OF THE LAND IN FARMS WAS RENTED

1910
1930

SPREAD OF FARM TENANCY, 1910 AND 1930

NEW WAYS OF LIFE

For those who enjoyed the prosperity and for those who were content to share vicariously in the frolics and foibles of the wealthy through tabloid newspaper accounts, it was a wonderful era. The national wealth of the United States was almost as great as that of all of Europe, and this was the impression newspaper readers and visitors received. It was the era when Florida real-estate salesmen hired the famous orator Bryan to lecture on the climate. Even though only an infinitesimal portion of Americans bought real estate in Florida during the land boom of 1924–1925, the impression was that most people were dabbling in the speculation. So too with the stock market later in the decade. Millions shared in the national frenzies, but most of them did not participate actively while living their sober, quiet lives.

The average middle-class American family owned an automobile. There were 23 million cars in use by 1929, and on Sundays it seemed as though they were all out on the new concrete highways. At home people listened to the radio. The first commercial station, KDKA, broadcast the news of Harding's election in November 1920. By 1924 the National Broadcasting Company had organized a nationwide network of stations, and by 1930 over 12 million American families had radios. Millions also had electric vacuum cleaners and washing machines; many were beginning to buy electric refrigerators. Household appliances were supplanting the housemaid and the hired girl. Food and clothing accounted for only 44 percent of the family expenditures, compared with 58 percent in 1899— a clear indication of the rising living standards.

The prosperity of the twenties spilled over into the educational system. The per-pupil expenditure jumped from $24 in 1910 to $90 in 1930. Free elementary education had become established throughout the nation; illiteracy dropped from 7.7 percent to 4.3 percent. Enrollment in high

Detail from mural "City Life" by Thomas Hart Benton (THE NEW SCHOOL FOR SOCIAL RESEARCH)

schools increased 400 percent, and enrollment in colleges and universities grew almost as fast.

Much money went to bootleggers, the dealers in illicit liquor, a new multimillion-dollar business. The first prohibition commissioner had optimistically announced his determination to see that alcoholic beverages were "not manufactured, nor sold, nor given away, nor hauled in anything on the surface of the earth or under the earth or in the air." But with an insufficient budget and only a few thousand poorly paid agents—and with little or no cooperation from state and local authorities—the commissioner had an almost impossible task in patrolling 18,000 miles of coastline, guarding against the diversion of any of the 57 million gallons of industrial alcohol, overseeing hundreds of millions of medical prescriptions, and checking on 20 million homes to prevent the concoction of home brew, wine, or "bathtub gin."

Gangsters turned to the large-scale smuggling or manufacture and distribution of liquor. In Chicago, "Scarface" Al Capone built an underworld empire that was based on beer and extended out into slot machines, laundries, and labor unions; it grossed about $60 million per year. He guarded it against interlopers with an army of 700 to 1,000 gunmen. Between 1920 and 1927 over 250 men were killed in Chicago gang warfare. Capone miraculously survived both his rivals and the forces of the law until finally in 1931 he was convicted of federal income tax evasion.

New ways of life, alarming to the older generation, swept America. Men wore wrist watches and smoked cigarettes, both of which had seemed rather effeminate before the war. Women seemed to have lost their modesty as they bobbed their hair, applied lipstick, donned short skirts and silk stockings, and unblushingly began using words previously reserved

Prohibition officers at Detroit on the seized tug "Geronimo," June 1928
(NATIONAL ARCHIVES)

for males. Younger people talked frankly and openly about sex. It was talk that frightened their elders, and it was made doubly frightening by the disappearance of chaperons and the availability of automobiles. Compounding the evil in the eyes of elders were the many new road houses and speakeasies, where young people flouted prohibition by drinking beer or cocktails. There too they listened to jazz and danced the new steps like the Charleston, which some preachers denounced to their flocks as lascivious. It seemed to many critics that Gertrude Stein had correctly labeled this the "lost generation"; these people could not believe that in time the "flaming youth" would mature into censorious middle age.

Motion pictures flamboyantly heralded the new moral code and together with tabloid papers helped fabricate false stereotypes of the period. An estimated 50 million people a week went to theaters to see the "it" girl, Clara Bow, the glamorous Rudolph Valentino, the comedian Charlie Chaplin, gangster pictures, Westerns, and great spectacles like the first film version of *The Ten Commandments*. These helped standardize American habits and not always in the most edifying way. Further, since nine-tenths of the world's motion pictures were made in the United States, they brought curiously distorted notions of American culture to other countries. In 1927 a revolution struck the motion-picture industry when the first important all-talking picture, *The Jazz Singer*, starring Al Jolson, was a phenomenal success. Motion pictures also began to carry American speech around the world.

In journalism the twenties brought an even greater sensationalism than the nineties in some mass-circulation city papers. From Britain came the idea of the half-sized tabloid, which led to the founding of the *News, Mirror,* and *Graphic* in New York City, and similar papers throughout the country. Tabloid journalism came to mean what yellow journalism had meant earlier, with the addition of a strong emphasis upon serial comic strips and sensational photographs. Millions of readers followed the gang wars in Chicago and murder trials in New York and elsewhere. Even *The New York Times* had to capitulate its dignity to reader demands and lavish front-page space upon one spectacular murder trial, the Hall-Mills case, concerning the murder of a minister and a choir singer.

Among magazines the *Saturday Evening Post*, with its conservative editorials and well-written stories, mirrored the era as faithfully as did President Coolidge. Close behind it in capturing the popular spirit was a reprint magazine founded in 1921, *Reader's Digest*, which filled its readers with inspiration and optimism, and guided them effortlessly through what they might consider difficult, serious subjects. It was the beginning of predigested reading. Much the same formula went into *Time*, the first of the news magazines, founded in 1925. In its liveliness, *Time* was one of the magazines tailored for the college graduates of the twenties. Another was the gay, sophisticated *New Yorker*, founded in 1925, which, with its clever cartoons and polished articles and stories, soon eclipsed the older *Life* and *Judge*. But the magazines that best typified the iconoclastic spirit of the intelligentsia and its rejection of middle-class values were *Smart Set* and the *American Mercury*. Their editors, Henry L. Mencken and George Jean Nathan, ridiculed the shibboleths of the decade but more than that introduced to their readers many of the most vigorous writers of the era.

Writers, Artists, Musicians

Seldom before in American history has such a remarkable galaxy of new writers appeared at one time. There was as much negativism from the expatriates in Paris as there had been before the war from Greenwich Village; many took perverse delight in damning the United States as a dollar-grubbing philistine civilization. Despite this spirit, it was not a generation lost to letters, nor were the voices of protest ignored.

Sherwood Anderson, giving up his paint factory, wrote tart Freudian sketches of small-town America in *Winesburg, Ohio* (1919). Sinclair Lewis more spectacularly exploited the same vein in his satiric *Main Street* (1920) and *Babbitt* (1922). His onslaught against business philistinism, in a long series of novels, at times verged close to caricature, but in time brought Lewis a Nobel Prize. With far more pessimism, utilizing experimental episodic techniques, John Dos Passos dissected the life of the metropolis in *Manhattan Transfer* (1925). Theodore Dreiser came into his own in 1925 with *An American Tragedy*, which analyzed with compassion both the psychological and environmental factors that led a young man to consider drowning his mistress.

The novelist who best embodied the jazz age in both his personal life and his writing was F. Scott Fitzgerald, catapulted to success with *This Side of Paradise* (1920). Young novelists who helped set patterns for later decades were Ernest Hemingway and William Faulkner. Hemingway stated the reaction against war most vigorously in his novel of disillusion, *A Farewell to Arms* (1929), which also helped set a new literary style. Faulkner, analyzing the South with morbid intensity in novels like *The Sound and the Fury* (1929) and *Sanctuary* (1931), developed an abstruse stream-of-consciousness technique that profoundly influenced other writers.

In drama these were the golden years of Eugene O'Neill, who drew from Ibsen, Strindberg, and Freud to develop American plays that were both critical and popular successes. *The Emperor Jones* (1920), *Anna Christie* (1922), *Strange Interlude* (1928), and other plays won O'Neill three Pulitzer Prizes in the decade and helped maintain him in the forefront of American dramatists a decade later. A number of other young playwrights wrote for the experimental stage, which flourished at scores of colleges and cities, even while motion pictures were superseding the old legitimate theater circuits.

In poetry two of the most significant writers were expatriates from the United States. These were T. S. Eliot in London, whose *The Waste Land* appeared in 1922, and Ezra Pound, who settled in Italy, where he

Eugene O'Neill (NATIONAL AR-
CHIVES)

wrote *Cantos* and embraced fascism. At home Edna St. Vincent Millay
typified the twenties with her hedonistic love poetry, while Robinson
Jeffers turned to dark naturalistic themes. Older poets like Edwin Arlington Robinson and Robert Frost continued to write in established veins,
and numerous young poets experimented with innovations in techniques
and topics.

American authors continued to produce along lines that in many
cases had been pioneered before the war. As early as 1915 Max Weber
had experimented with totally abstract art, but abandoned it by 1920,
not to return again until the early forties. About 1920 Georgia O'Keeffe
and Charles Sheeler turned from abstraction or semiabstraction, to a
sharp, precise realism in which abstract design was dominant. Miss
O'Keeffe's paintings of bleached cattle skulls or the interior of lilies, rendered in bright colors and meticulous detail, often portrayed abstract
patterns, or, sometimes, a wealth of feminine symbolism. Sheeler, working with lens as well as brush, explored the artistic potentialities of industrial forms.

Architects filled the great cities with skyscrapers and were active in
city planning. Some of the surplus wealth of the twenties poured into
European painting; Mellon matched his ingenuity in keepng taxes down
with his lavish purchases of old masters, some of them from the dollar-
hungry Soviet Union. By 1930 American art galleries owned $2 billion
worth of paintings. Along with this went a rapidly widening popular
appreciation of fine art.

In music the twenties were notable for the rise of jazz, "the most
important musical expression that America has achieved." It had originated among black musicians in the South, particularly in New Orleans,
who drew upon their African heritage in composing and playing tunes
with improvised harmonies and a syncopated beat. Among the outstand-

"River Rouge Plant" by Charles Sheeler (WHITNEY MUSEUM OF AMERICAN ART)

ing black creators of jazz were the guitar-playing singer Huddie Ledbetter ("Leadbelly") and the band conductor William C. Handy, the "father of the blues," whose compositions include *St. Louis Blues* (1914). The new music first became widely known when jazzmen moved with the general black migration northward during and after World War I. The great trumpet player Louis ("Satchmo") Armstrong, for example, went from New Orleans to Chicago in 1922 to join a band that helped spread jazz through phonograph recordings. Meanwhile, white musicians had begun to take up the new form, modify it, and make it increasingly popular and even respectable by treating it as serious music. Prominent among them were the composer George Gershwin, who incorporated jazz elements in his *Rhapsody in Blue,* and the conductor Paul Whiteman, whose band presented a pioneering jazz concert in New York City in 1922.

A SEARCH FOR VALUES

In letters, the arts, and learning there was a seeking for values that would be something more than the advertising man's paeans to mass production

Louis Armstrong's Hot Five, about 1927: Johnny St. Cyr, banjo; Kid Ory, trombone; Louis Armstrong, trumpet; Johnny Dodds, clarinet; Lillian Armstrong, piano (NATIONAL ARCHIVES)

cultures, as expressed in Bruce Barton's *The Man Nobody Knows.* This seeking is the reason so many of the younger writers were rejecting the popular values of the United States for those of Europe, which did not seem to them as yet caught in the new commercial maelstrom. Others were trying to interpret the new society with the psychoanalytical approach suggested by Freud or the economic determinism stemming from Marx.

Among ministers, publicists, philosophers, and economists seeking to interpret the new order, there was some confusion. The fundamentalist ministers went on much as before, although in some quarters they were subjected to ridicule in 1925 when their champion, Bryan, matched wits with the agnostic Clarence Darrow in the famous Scopes trial involving a Tennessee law forbidding the teaching of evolution. Ministers to the middle class who earlier had so exuberantly preached the social gospel or the great crusade in Europe had been beaten down in 1919 when they took up the cause of the striking steelworkers. Many businessmen were ready to adopt paternalistic policies and label them "Christian industrialism," but they denounced the militant social gospel as Bolshevism. Ministers further lost their hold on their following as middle-class reac-

George Gershwin (NATIONAL ARCHIVES)

tion spread against two of the causes in which they had been so deeply involved—the war in Europe and prohibition. Many ministers tended, consequently, to concentrate upon the building of fine churches and the development of a sophisticated theology embracing the new psychological concepts.

Many of the most popular publicists were negative in their view of government. Mencken and Irving Babbitt launched some of their most scathing attacks against the American democratic system. Lippmann, who had been deeply involved in the New Nationalism and the New Freedom, became aloof and brilliantly analytical in his observation of American society. The Socialist candidate for President in 1928, Norman Thomas, remarked: "The old reformer has become the Tired Radical and his sons and daughters drink at the fountain of the *American Mercury.*"

Nevertheless, some of the most influential philosophers and social scientists continued to write in modified progressive terms. Dewey, at the peak of his influence, was expounding a socialized pragmatism: man through science and technology could develop an organized social intelligence that could plan a rational and fruitful future society. The aged Thorstein Veblen was placing a similar faith in science: the engineers in contrast to the businessmen could bring forth an economic utopia. This doctrine, carried to its ultimate conclusion, engendered the technocracy movement of the early thirties. Other economists would not go this far, but some of them accepted Veblen's emphasis upon craftsmen and technicians, who, unlike businessmen, would not raise prices and restrict markets. Around them could develop an economy of still greater abundance. Agricultural economists, who were thinking in opposite terms of restriction, also looked forward to an age of social and economic planning.

Charles A. Beard was disseminating some of these ideas among a wider group of readers. In his and Mary Beard's *Rise of American Civilization* (1927), expressing mild economic determinism and emphasizing social and cultural factors, he did much to perpetuate progressive thinking among the new generation of intellectuals. Vernon L. Parrington's *Main Currents of American Thought* (1927), tracing the same themes in literature, helped create a Jeffersonian cult. Writing on a popular level, Claude Bowers developed similar ideas. Franklin D. Roosevelt, reviewing Bowers' *Jefferson and Hamilton* in 1925, commented: "Hamiltons we have today. Is a Jefferson on the horizon?"

twelve

President Hoover and the Great Depression

To many Americans a simple and effective way of perpetuating the Coolidge prosperity after 1928 seemed to be to put the "Great Engineer," Herbert Hoover, in the White House. His policies as Secretary of Commerce apparently guaranteed an indefinite continuation of businessmen's government and of boom without bust. Hoover himself shared this faith. In his acceptance address in August 1928 he proclaimed: "We in America today are nearer to the final triumph over poverty than ever before in the history of any land." He backed his assertion with so many statistics that it seemed irrefutable. "Given a chance to go forward with the policies of the last eight years," he promised, "we shall soon with the help of God be in sight of the day when poverty will be vanished from this nation." Yet fifteen months later the stock market crashed and sent the nation careening down into the blackest depression in its history. Hoover applied all the techniques and skills he had perfected during the years of prosperity and in desperation turned to new methods. All was to no avail.

RUM, ROMANISM, AND PROSPERITY: 1928 ELECTION

No one could have guessed in 1928 that businessmen's government would so soon be in ill repute. When President Coolidge had announced the previous summer, "I do not choose to run," a scramble had begun for the Republican nomination as a prize sure to bring four if not eight years in the White House. Hoover won the nomination easily. Second place on the ticket went to a senator from Kansas, Charles Curtis, most notable because he was partly of Indian ancestry and had spent part of his boyhood with Indian relatives.

Among Democrats the experienced politicians were still almost as badly divided as in 1924, but they saw no reason to turn their convention

161

into another brawl when their candidate had no chance of winning against Republican prosperity. Even those who were ardently dry and Protestant raised no barrier against the wet, Roman Catholic governor of New York, Alfred E. Smith. He was nominated to run on a platform not much more positive than that of the Republicans. It did, however, include a plank offering farmers the McNary-Haugen plan. More important, Smith promised to relax the Volstead Act for enforcing the Eighteenth Amendment. This brought prohibition to the forefront of the campaign. There was little except that and religion to campaign about.

Both Hoover and Smith were self-made men and proud of it. Hoover's path, from an Iowa farm through Stanford University, had been marked by a phenomenally successful rise as a business and government executive. Smith's path led from the East Side of New York through the Fulton Fish Market and the Tammany hierarchy to the governorship of New York. There he had demonstrated a consummate political and administrative skill. He had reorganized the state government, fought to build schools, parks, and parkways, and struggled for public development of the great power sites.

In the campaign Hoover stressed prosperity, which was popularly translated into the notion of a chicken in every pot and two cars in every garage. Smith evoked more enthusiastic loyalty and venomous hatred than any other candidate since Bryan. Millions of the urban masses, mostly of immigrant and Catholic background themselves, saw in Smith

Secretary Hoover the day he was nominated for President (NATIONAL ARCHIVES)

their spokesman, their great hero. Millions of Protestants in the rural South, where belief in prohibition was strong and the Ku Klux Klan boisterous in its anti-Catholicism, looked upon him as a threat to their way of life. Fiery crosses greeted him near Oklahoma City, where he courageously denounced the Klan. But his cause was hopeless. The Republican landslide exceeded expectations, as Hoover received a popular vote of 21 million to 15 million for Smith.

THE WALL STREET CRASH

President Hoover, the prophet of permanent prosperity, had been in office scarcely six months when the Great Depression began. It was touched off by a collapse of the stock market. For several years stock prices had been rising so rapidly that they ceased to have much relation to the actual earning power of corporations. The New York Stock Exchange had become for many speculators a great national gambling casino, where everyone won almost all the time. By the summer of 1929, however, there were many disquieting signs that the prosperity, so long gone for the farmers, was coming to an end for businessmen also. Construction had passed its peak and was declining rapidly; automobiles were filling dealers' garages; business inventories of all kinds were three times larger than a year before; freight carloadings, industrial production, and wholesale prices were all slipping downward.

On October 21, 1929, the stock market dropped sharply, and two days

Alfred E. Smith (NATIONAL ARCHIVES)

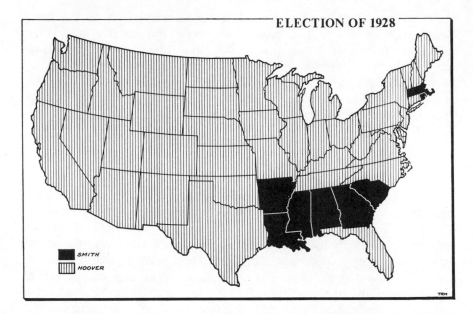

ELECTION OF 1928

SMITH
HOOVER

later the big crash began. Temporarily, J. P. Morgan and Company and other big bankers managed to stave off disaster, but on October 29 their efforts failed. That day 16 million shares were sold. Total losses for the month reached $16 billion. For two weeks more the market continued to drop, until stocks had lost over 40 percent in value.

The stock market collapse, though not the cause of the depression, precipitated it by replacing the inflationary spiral with a deflationary one even harder to stop. It brought to an end a decade of business optimism and opened one of almost unquenchable pessimism. Bewildered businessmen saw their only hope in retrenchment, and the more they retrenched, the worse conditions became.

For years afterward, economists, businessmen, and political leaders debated the causes of the depression. Certainly there had been serious defects in the economy of the 1920s. As production rose, too little of the profits went to farmers, others producers of raw materials, or workers. Too much went into the building of new industrial plants. So long as the expansion of capital facilities continued, new investments stimulated the economy, but the investments created more plant space than could be profitably used. By 1929 factories were pouring out more goods than consumers could purchase. This did not mean that Americans would not have consumed more had they had more income, for even in 1929 only one family in six had an automobile, only one in five a fixed bathtub or electricity, and only one in ten a telephone.

Government had played the wrong role in the economic system during the twenties. Taxes, by sparing the rich, had added to the inequality of incomes. High tariffs had discouraged foreign trade; large exports could have continued only so long as Americans kept on lending abroad. Fail-

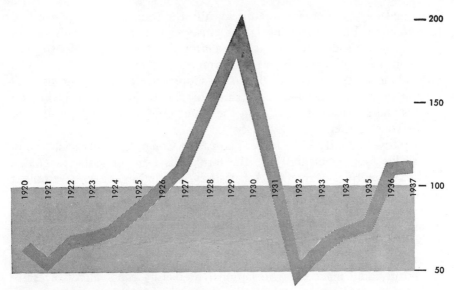

Prices of Common Stocks, 1920–1937

ure to break up or regulate big business had encouraged concentration and resulted in rigidly high prices. Nothing had been done to check speculation or supervise the securities market, and nothing effective had been done to restore the buying power of farmers.

THE HOOVER PROGRAM

In the view of critics a generation later, the government continued to make mistakes in facing the depression. It concentrated upon balancing the budget and maintaining the gold standard, both of which were deflationary, at a time when the country was already suffering from too much deflation. Blame for these policies should not fall solely upon President Hoover. They were the ancient formulas for the conduct of government during a depression; they were urged upon the President by leaders of both parties and of business and by experts in economics.

Actually, President Hoover was far more energetic and imaginative than any previous American President in trying to combat the depression. His Secretary of the Treasury, Mellon, was a "leave-it-alone liquidationist" who thought a thoroughgoing cycle of bankruptcy and deflation would be healthful. Hoover did not agree. He determined that the government should intervene positively but in a very limited way, seeking the voluntary cooperation of business and labor.

First, to restore confidence, Hoover declared: "The fundamental business of this country, that is, production and distribution of commodities, is on a sound and prosperous basis." Most of the business leaders echoed him. Next, he held a number of highly publicized meetings of business, farm, and labor leaders in an effort to rally the country to adopt a voluntary program. Businessmen pledged themselves not to cut payrolls or production; labor leaders, not to ask for better wages or hours. Hoover also announced a significant tax cut and arranged for the Federal Reserve to provide increased bank credit. He asked Congress for an increase of $423 million in public works—a huge sum for the period—and called upon mayors and governors to engage in the "energetic yet prudent pursuit" of public construction.

Already, in April 1929, Hoover had called Congress into special session to provide farm relief and raise the tariff. His farm program, embodied in the Agricultural Marketing Act of 1929, set up large-scale government machinery to aid the farmer. The program, as Hoover insisted, was voluntary and did not include any of the price-fixing schemes for which farm organizations were lobbying. It encouraged the voluntary combination of farmers to help themselves under government auspices. A farm Board of eight members administered a revolving fund of $500 million, from which the board could make loans to national marketing cooperatives or establish corporations to buy surpluses and thus raise prices.

Within six months the depression precipitated farm prices toward new lows. Until the summer of 1931 the Wheat Stabilization Corporation and the Cotton Stabilization Corporation were able to keep prices a bit above world levels. By 1932 their funds were spent, their warehouses full, and grain prices at the lowest point since the founding of the American colonies. The Farm Board had operated on too small a scale, and it had lacked power to limit production. When President Hoover later called for voluntary reduction of the wheat crop, acreage dropped only 1 percent in Kansas. The Farm Board experiment thus underscored the futility of a voluntary crop-control program and prepared the way for a more drastic measure.

Congress, taking President Hoover's advice to raise agricultural tariffs, prepared an overall measure, the Hawley-Smoot bill, which contained 75 increases on farm products and 925 on manufactured goods. It raised the average duty from the 26 percent of the Fordney-McCumber Act to a new high of 50 percent. By the time it was ready for the President's signature in the spring of 1930, a thousand members of the American Economic Association had signed a petition urging him to veto it as an unwise piece of economic nationalism. He ignored such warnings and signed the measure. Other nations in reprisal placed new restrictions on American goods. In a time of world depression, rampant economic nationalism was perhaps inevitable, but it was unfortunate that the United States led the way.

The worsening depression gave Democrats a political issue. In the fall of 1930 they won a bare majority in the House of Representatives and, with the aid of Republican progressives, took effective control of the Senate. From this point on, Congress began seriously to harass Hoover, demanding that he move from voluntary measures to large-scale federal relief and spending. He refused to budge. By the spring of 1931 conditions seemed to be improving, and Hoover and others thought the worst

AVERAGE ANNUAL PERCENTAGE RATES ON DUTIABLE GOODS

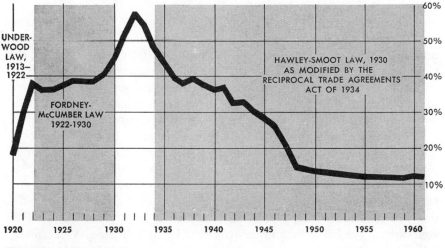

The Tariff, 1920–1961

was over. But the American economy took another downturn in consequence of a European financial panic. By May 1931 the largest bank in Austria had collapsed, and the disaster threatened to wreck the banking and monetary systems of Germany and other nations of Europe.

To avert a domino effect President Hoover proposed a one-year moratorium on reparations and war-debt payments, but France destroyed much of the good effect through her delay in accepting the plan. By September, England and most other nations of the world had gone off the gold standard. The crisis in Western Europe caused European gold to be withdrawn from American banks, and European holdings of American securities to be dumped on the market. As other nations devalued their currencies in going off the gold standard, American trade with them declined disastrously.

By December 1931, when Congress met, conditions were so frightening that President Hoover abandoned his reliance upon voluntary measures and proposed direct governmental action of an unprecedented kind to combat the depression. In January 1932 Congress created a giant loan agency, the Reconstruction Finance Corporation (RFC), which during 1932 loaned $1.5 billion, mostly to banks, railroads, and other businesses. Hoover, trying to parry criticism that he had set up a bread line for big business, asserted that his purpose was to stop deflation and thus increase employment, mainly by helping relatively small companies. Congress also provided for banks, together with further capital for existing loan banks, to help prevent mortgage foreclosures.

On the issues of very large-scale public works and direct relief for the unemployed, the President clashed bitterly with Republican progressives and Democrats in Congress. In July 1932 he vetoed their bill as being impractical and dangerous; he felt that direct relief was a state and local responsibility. Subsequently, he signed a bill he himself had recommended, authorizing the RFC to lend $300 million for relief and another $1.5 billion for self-liquidating public works.

Hoover believed that, while people must not go cold and hungry, feeding them was a voluntary and local responsibility. "If we start appropriations of this character," he had declared, "we have not only impaired something infinitely valuable in the life of the American people but have struck at the roots of self-government." It was hard for desperate people to appreciate such niceties of thought. Hoover, who had been one of the most popular of American heroes, became the scapegoat for the depression.

To some observers the 1928 election had seemed to be a great national referendum in favor of prohibition, yet prohibition was not to last much longer than prosperity. Though Hoover had referred to it as a "noble experiment," enforcement was breaking down so badly that Congress stiffened the penalties for violating the Volstead Act and authorized the new President to appoint a National Law Enforcement Commission. This commission, headed by a former Attorney General, George Wickersham, ultimately reported in 1931 that prohibition was not only unenforced but virtually unenforceable.

Rampant gangsterism and the open flouting of the law by millions of otherwise respectable citizens convinced many thoughtful Americans that prohibition was not worth its price in lawlessness. With the coming of the depression, some well-to-do people, already banded into antiprohibition organizations, redoubled their efforts in the hope that repeal would bring lower income taxes and greater prosperity. In February 1933 Congress submitted to the states the Twenty-first Amendment, repealing prohibition; by December it had been ratified, and the experiment was at an end.

DEEPENING DESPAIR

As the depression deepened, there were surprisingly few signs of social disorder or outbursts of violence within the United States. Communists agitated, won a few converts among intellectual leaders, but made almost no impact upon the masses.

The chain reaction of unemployment slowly spread from 1930 into 1933. At first those in marginal or poorer jobs were hit hardest, as those who had been in better jobs moved downward. In time millions who had never been unemployed for any length of time were jobless and unable to find work of any kind. They were bewildered, for they had been brought up in the sturdy tradition of self-reliance and had accepted the doctrine of rugged individualism—that opportunities were limitless if only one had the ambition and energy to take advantage of them. Now these people were humiliated and baffled at not being able to provide for themselves and their families. As they remained idle for months and then years, they were in danger of losing their skills as well as their morale. Physical and moral erosion threatened.

Care of the unemployed had always been a responsibility primarily of

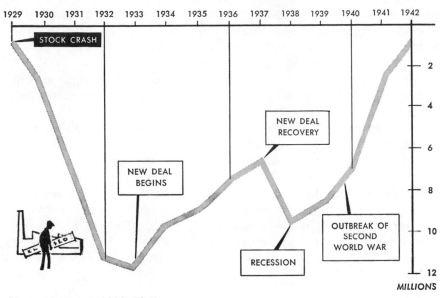

Unemployment, 1929–1942

private charity, and for several years the President and governors exhorted citizens to contribute to the Red Cross or to emergency funds. But the task soon became far too great for private charity to handle. By 1931 the Red Cross could provide only seventy-five cents a week to feed each hungry family in southern Illinois.

Although several European nations had maintained unemployment insurance programs for decades, not a single state in the United States enacted such a law until January 1932, when Wisconsin passed one. Even as the distress grew, many magazines and newspapers proclaimed that any permanent system of direct unemployment relief like the British dole would bankrupt the government and undermine the moral fiber of the recipients. Not until September 1931 did the New York legislature at the insistence of Governor Franklin D. Roosevelt establish the first relief organization of any state, the Temporary Emergency Relief Administration, which became the model for other states and the prototype of the later federal relief agency.

To some of the unemployed who had recently moved to cities, the solution seemed to be to return to the farm; the migration away from farms was now reversed. But farm prices fell so low that once again, on parts of the plains, farmers burned corn to keep warm. A rancher sold seven lambs in the Denver livestock market and, after paying commissions and fees, received a check for seventy-five cents. In a railroad diner two lamb chops cost the same amount. Prices of manufactured goods were relatively so high that it took ten bushels of wheat to buy a cheap pair of shoes. In drought areas farmers lacked even sufficient food.

Some bewildered farmers around Sioux City, Iowa, in 1932 embargoed milk bound for the city because they were receiving two cents a quart and it retailed for eight cents. Many more Iowa farmers participated in Milo Reno's militant Farmers' Holiday Association to block all farm products from the market until prices rose.

Through the summer of 1932 about 12,000 to 14,000 unemployed veterans congregated in Washington to demonstrate for the immediate payments of their bonus for wartime service, not due until 1945. For weeks they lived in squalor in abandoned tenements and in shanties on the mud flats of the Anacostia River. After Congress failed to pass a bonus bill, about half of them, discouraged, went home. The continued presence of the rest alarmed Hoover and many Washingtonians. After a riot the President called upon the army to oust the veterans. Under the personal command of General Douglas MacArthur, with tanks, gas masks, and fixed bayonets, the army did so. "That was a bad looking mob," MacArthur declared, expressing the alarm of conservatives. "It was animated by the essence of revolution."

WORLD DEPRESSION SHAPES FOREIGN POLICY

In foreign affairs as in domestic matters the depression and its repercussions were the dominant theme. With regard to Latin America, Hoover continued the movement that under his successor became the Good Neighbor policy. Before his inauguration he toured much of the hemisphere, promoting good will; during his administration he prepared for the removal of marines from Haiti and finally withdrew them from Nicaragua. He refused to intervene in Cuba, which was restless under a dictatorship. Throughout Latin America as depression toppled about half the regimes, he recognized de facto rulers without questioning the means by which they had come into power. Even when several countries defaulted on their obligations in October 1931, he did not press them to pay or threaten to seize their custom houses.

With reference to Europe, policy became increasingly concerned with economic conditions as the depression deepened. The moratorium on war-debt and reparations payments, begun in June 1931, aided Europe temporarily. Secretary of State Henry L. Stimson wished it to lead to a general cancellation of these obligations but could not convince the President, who considered them sacred. Soon Germany ceased reparations payments, and nations owing money to the United States, except for Finland, began to default or make mere token payments. Before the end of the Hoover administration, at least at one point—relations with Japan—the depression threatened the President's major foreign policy objective, the pursuit of peace.

With regard to the Far East, policies were aimed at safeguarding American rights while preserving peace. As unstable conditions in China continued throughout the 1920s, the United States could do little to protect China from the encroachments of strong nations. As Russia became stronger, she built up her forces in eastern Siberia, and in 1929, when China tried to oust her from northern Manchuria, Russia fought an undeclared war to retain her foothold. Stimson tried to invoke the Kellogg-Briand Pact, which outlawed war, and to bring about mediation; he failed, demonstrating the weakness of the pact.

Japanese military leaders, feeling that their treaty rights in southern Manchuria were being threatened by both the Russians and the Chinese Nationalists under Chiang Kai-shek, wrested the initiative from the Japanese foreign office in a manner little short of mutiny. In September 1931 they launched a large-scale military campaign in Manchuria at a time when the United States and Great Britain were preoccupied with the monetary crisis. For several weeks Stimson was moderate, in the hope that the civilians in the Japanese cabinet could regain control; the British were even less disposed to pursue a strong policy. The Japanese foreign office engaged in conciliatory talk but was unable to alter events as the army plunged deeper into Manchuria. By January 2, 1932, the conquest was complete.

As early as October 1931, Stimson had felt that the United States might have to cooperate with the League of Nations in imposing economic sanctions against Japan even though these might lead to war. Hoover strongly opposed such action and, in cabinet meetings, discouraged Stimson by referring to the Washington treaties and the Kellogg-Briand Pact as scraps of paper. He learned from the British that they too opposed sanctions. Hoover was willing to allow Stimson to exert moral suasion against the Japanese, and he suggested that the Secretary of State apply the doctrine of nonrecognition against territorial changes brought by force of arms. Stimson did so on January 7, 1932.

The American people were eager to see the United States assume moral leadership—and nothing more—against aggression. Their ideal was international disarmament, not policing. Hoover himself took the same view.

After the Geneva Conference of 1927 had failed to extend quotas to destroyers, cruisers, and submarines, the United States had threatened to begin a substantial building program. Hoover, fearing a naval race, called a conference, which opened in London in January 1930. There the United States, Great Britain, and Japan agreed not to build the capital ships authorized under the Washington treaty, and even to scrap some existing ships. They also agreed to ratios on smaller ships, to continue until 1936.

The United States participated vigorously in the World Disarmament Conference that opened under League sponsorship at Geneva in February 1932. With the Japanese attacking Shanghai and Hitler daily winning new converts to his militaristic Nazi movement in Germany, the French firmly demanded an international army and compulsory arbitration rather than disarmament. In June 1932 Hoover tried to break the deadlock with a proposal to abolish immediately all offensive weapons, such as bombing planes and tanks, and to cut all land and naval forces approximately 30 percent. Despite much enthusiasm for the proposal, nothing came of it. Along with depression, the world faced the threat of dictatorships and wars.

PROTEST AT THE POLLS: 1932

Even in these years of extreme despair, Americans were ready to turn to the ballot box. In 1932 Republicans meeting at Chicago renominated Hoover in a spirit far from jubilant; they had little illusion about the outcome of the election. The Democrats, assembling later in an excited, expectant mood, saw almost certain victory after twelve years out of power. Almost anyone they nominated would certainly be elected.

Well over a majority of the Democratic delegates were pledged to vote for Governor Franklin D. Roosevelt of New York. Roosevelt had been working astutely for the nomination for years. To a considerable degree he bridged the gulf between the urban and rural Democrats. He was ready to emphasize economic issues and ignore the earlier divisions over prohibition and religion.

Breaking precedent, Roosevelt flew immediately to Chicago to deliver his acceptance address before the convention. He endorsed the Democratic platform, which except for a promise of prohibition repeal was not much bolder than that of the Republicans. He declared: "I pledge you, I pledge myself, to a new deal for the American people." Thus the Roosevelt program acquired a name before the electorate had more than the haziest notion what it might embody.

Nor did the voters learn much during the campaign, for Roosevelt shrewdly confined himself to warm generalities that would offend few and yet would bring him the enormous vote of protest against Hoover. Through Roosevelt's speeches ran many of the old progressive themes, together with new suggestions of economic planning. An able team, largely of university professors under the leadership of Raymond Moley, helped devise policies and draft speeches for him. Newspapermen dubbed his group of advisers the "brain trust." At the Commonwealth Club in San Francisco, Roosevelt broke furthest from the past by insisting that the government must assist business in developing a well-regulated economic system. Everyone, he said, had a right to a comfortable living; the nation's industrial and agricultural mechanism could produce more than enough. If need be, to achieve this end, government must police irresponsible economic power. Roosevelt felt he was doing no more than restating the objectives of Jefferson and Wilson in terms of the complexities of the thirties when he proposed that the government should act as a regulator for the common good within the existing economic system. So far as Roosevelt explained the New Deal during the campaign, this was its essence.

President Hoover, tired and grim, took to the road in October to warn the populace that without his program things might be infinitely worse. His speeches, though earnest, were dull and dreary in both style and delivery compared with Roosevelt's breezy, optimistic performances. Hoover was the last of the Presidents to scorn the aid of speech writers.

Some voters, disappointed because they could detect little difference between Roosevelt's program and Hoover's, turned to Norman Thomas and the Socialists or to William Z. Foster and the Communists. Yet, even in this year of despair, the Socialists polled only 882,000 votes, and the Communists only 103,000. Roosevelt received 22,822,000 popular votes (57.4 percent), Hoover 15,762,000 (39.7 percent). The Democrats carried both houses of Congress by top-heavy majorities. Roosevelt had won an overwhelming mandate—but for what?

Actually, there had been discernible differences between the two candidates and their programs—besides the obvious difference that Hoover was a worn, discredited President, whereas Roosevelt was a buoyant candidate. Hoover had seen the depression as world-wide in origin and development; rather inconsistently he was ready to combat it internationally through currency stabilization and, nationally, through raising the tariff still higher if necessary. Roosevelt chose to regard the depression as domestic, specifically Republican, in origin. During the campaign, Hoover had forced him to equivocate on the old Democratic low-tariff position. Roosevelt was ready (as both his record as governor and his speeches indicated) to move toward economic nationalism. But he agreed with Hoover on the need for government thrift and a balanced budget.

THE INTERREGNUM OF 1932–1933

President Hoover faced an agonizing four months before Roosevelt would take office on March 4: the Twentieth (Lame Duck) Amendment to end this long carry-over of a defeated President and Congress was not ratified until February 1933. There had been a brief economic upswing in the spring months of 1932, reaching a peak in July. (Economists later ascribed this to Hoover's own brief plunge into deficit financing through public works

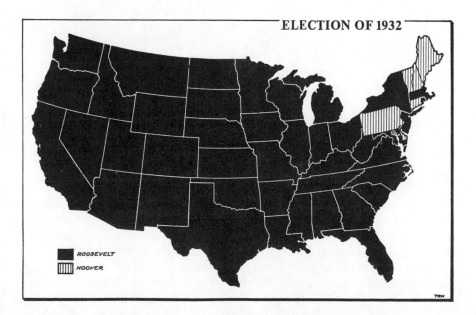

ELECTION OF 1932

ROOSEVELT
HOOVER

spending and RFC loans.) Hoover felt that he was bringing an end to the depression and that only the threat of unsettling measures from Roosevelt was preventing continued recovery. Hence, in a series of interchanges with Roosevelt during the winter of 1932–1933, he tried to bind the President-elect to economic orthodoxy.

Hoover favored the reestablishment of an international gold standard. He hoped that the United States and other nations would agree to this at an economic and monetary conference that was scheduled to meet in London after Roosevelt's inauguration. But Roosevelt would make no commitment.

By February 1933 an acute banking crisis had developed. Bank resources and deposits had been declining at an alarming rate. In the previous three years 5,000 banks had failed, and now one after another was collapsing as depositors lined up to withdraw their deposits. To stop the run on the banks governors began proclaiming banking holidays in their states. By March 4 banking was at a halt or drastically restricted in all states but one.

President Hoover wrote a letter to Roosevelt, charging that the crisis was caused by "steadily degenerating confidence" in the President-elect, and calling upon him to give prompt public assurance that there would be no tinkering with the currency, no heavy borrowing, no unbalancing of the budget. Roosevelt had not the slightest intention of adopting Hoover's views. In any event, on March 4, President Hoover, glum and exhausted, left office with the problem of the depression still unsolved. Could Roosevelt and the New Deal do better?

thirteen
Experimenting with a New Deal

In a period of one hundred days following the inauguration of Franklin D. Roosevelt on March 4, 1933, the Congress embarked on one of the largest and most remarkable legislative programs in American history. As the White House sent one bill after another to the Capitol for action, the government for the first time tried to utilize its full powers to pull the nation out of the depression. The direction of the recovery program was not new—indeed, President Hoover had already tried to persuade business and agriculture to head along the same path voluntarily. The Roosevelt program still emphasized voluntarism but provided far stronger positive incentives and negative penalties. It was based on the principles of progressivism and the techniques of the agencies of World War I. But in breadth and scale the early New Deal went well beyond Hoover's tentative measures and anything else previously known in peacetime. Under the first Roosevelt the government had begun to assume a significant role in the economy; under the second Roosevelt it took command in time of crisis.

FDR TAKES COMMAND

When Roosevelt was inaugurated, most of the nation's banks were closed. At least 13 million people were unemployed, some of them so close to starvation that they were scrabbling for food scraps in garbage dumps. Millions of farmers were on the brink of foreclosure; many others had fallen over the brink.

In his inaugural address President Roosevelt spoke with vigor and confidence. "This great Nation will endure as it has endured, will revive and will prosper," he declared. "So, first of all, let me assert my firm belief that the only thing we have to fear is fear itself." Somehow these words, although they said nothing new, helped inspire the American people. From their depths of helplessness they were ready for the moment to be commanded, and in Roosevelt they saw someone ready to take strong leadership. Such leadership he promised. If Congress did not act, he announced, he would ask for "broad executive power to wage a war against the emergency, as great as the power that would be given to me if we were in fact invaded by a foreign foe."

Few other Presidents have been better trained for the White House. Roosevelt had served in the New York State senate, been wartime Assistant Secretary of the Navy, and had been twice elected governor of New York. He was skilled in both legislative and administrative techniques as well as in practical politics. As a youth, he had spent much time in Europe and maintained a continuing interest in foreign affairs. Roosevelt's ideology was progressive, influenced by his wife's uncle, Theodore Roosevelt, whom he admired, and his former chief, Woodrow Wilson, whom he revered.

President and Mrs. Roosevelt returning to the White House from the inauguration, 1941 (TENSCHERT PHOTO © ANKERS CAPITOL PHOTOGRAPHERS, WASHINGTON, D.C.)

Neither the new President nor his advisers were clear-cut in their thinking. What was important was that Roosevelt, while basically rooted in the older economics and the social-justice tradition of the progressives, was ready to experiment. His program would be flexible, not doctrinaire; the new economic theories would grow from it, not it from the theories. When one of the brain trusters warned of perils ahead, Roosevelt declared: "There is nothing to do but meet every day's troubles as they come." This was his political pragmatism, and out of it grew the New Deal economic policies.

With the banking crisis at its height, he might well have taken drastic steps such as nationalization of the banks. But he seemed bent above all upon restoring the confidence of businessmen. His initial program differed little from what they had been advocating. He met the banking crisis in a manner pleasing to the banking community. He issued a proclamation on March 6, 1933, closing all banks and stopping transactions or exports in gold for four days until Congress could meet in special session. On March 9 he sent in a conservative bill that would bolster the stronger banks. It authorized the Federal Reserve System to issue notes against their assets and the Reconstruction Finance Corporation to make them loans. The bill dealt a death blow to weaker banks; inspectors would deny them licenses to reopen. It stopped the ebb of gold from the Treasury and the country by prohibiting hoarding and exportation. In effect, the country went off the gold standard (officially, it did so April 19, 1933). Congress passed the bill within four hours of its introduction. In the House, a rolled-up newspaper substituted for it, since there had not been time to print copies.

On March 12, in the first of his "fireside chats" over the radio, the President, speaking in a warm, intimate manner, told the American people that the crisis was over. "I can assure you," he declared, "that it is safer to keep your money in a reopened bank than under the mattress." And so indeed it was; by his legislation and his confident leadership, Roosevelt had averted the threat to banks and the capitalist system. Three-fourths of the banks in the Federal Reserve System reopened within the next three days, and a billion dollars in hoarded currency and gold flowed back into them within a month. Practically all unsafe banks were now out of business; there were very few new failures in the years that followed.

On the morning after the passage of the Emergency Banking Act, Roosevelt further reassured business by sending Congress an economy bill, to balance the budget by cutting salaries of government employees and pensions of veterans as much as 15 percent. This, Roosevelt declared, was the only way to avoid a billion-dollar deficit. This bill too passed almost instantly, although with such fierce opposition from veterans' organizations that it carried the House only with Republican votes. Pressure from veterans soon led Congress to rescind the pension cuts over Roosevelt's veto, but the President drastically slashed the regular expenditures of the government.

On March 13, 1933, Roosevelt proposed legalizing beer that had a 3.2

percent alcoholic content, pending repeal of the prohibition amendment. This, he felt, would stimulate recovery and bring in needed taxes. (It also rescued millions of law violators from the rigors of home brew and gangster-made beer.)

Thus far, except for the gold clause in the Emergency Banking Act, the program of the new administration might have been that of a Hoover with a smile. It restored the confidence of bankers and businessmen, the stock market going up 15 percent. But this was anticipatory of the real recovery to follow; for the moment nothing had been improved but the confidence of the American nation.

TENTATIVE BEGINNINGS

During his first hundred days in office, keeping Congress in special session, Roosevelt put through a series of laws and began to take steps that led him away from the "sound" position—so reassuring to bankers and other businessmen—that he originally had assumed.

Emergency Relief

The first step was to feed the millions of hungry unemployed Americans. While Roosevelt subscribed to his predecessor's maxim that relief was primarily the task of states and communities, he proposed that the federal government provide grants rather than loans to states. Congress established the Federal Emergency Relief Administration and appropriated an initial half-billion dollars for it. Roosevelt appointed the director of the New York State relief agency, Harry Hopkins, whom he hardly knew as yet, to run the federal program. Hopkins was a dedicated social worker with a lively tongue and a keen sense of professional ethics. He ardently believed in work relief rather than direct relief, but in the spring of 1933 everyone hoped recovery was at hand so that relief would be needed only for a few months.

But recovery lagged, and some new way had to be found to care for the unemployed through the winter of 1933–1934. Relief administrator Hopkins persuaded the President to establish a temporary work relief program, the Civil Works Administration. Between November and April it put 4 million people to work at emergency projects. Sometimes it was make-work like leaf raking, to which critics applied an old Texas term, "boondoggling." Some of the projects, despite lack of funds for materials and tools, made substantial improvements. The output was of secondary importance; the work raised the morale of the unemployed and increased their buying power by $950 million. The purchasing power thus injected into the economy was probably responsible for the wavering recovery, as the index of production rose from 71 in November 1933 to 86 in May 1934. But soon Roosevelt capitulated to fierce conservative criticism and liquidated the program.

Congress also created an organization that reflected Roosevelt's keen interest in preserving natural as well as human resources, the Civilian Conservation Corps (CCC). It received a grant of $300 million to enroll 250,000 young men from relief families and 50,000 veterans and woodsmen, to work at reforestation and flood control. Ultimately, the CCC enrolled 500,000 young men, but this was only a fraction of the unemployed youths in the nation.

Mortgage relief was a pressing need of millions of farm owners and homeowners. Roosevelt quickly consolidated all farm credit organizations into a new Farm Credit Administration. Congress voted such large additional funds for it that within two years it had refinanced one-fifth of all farm mortgages in the United States. The Frazier-Lemke Farm-Bankruptcy Act of 1933 enabled some farmers to regain their farms even after the foreclosure of mortgages. Unfortunately, these measures came too late to save all farmers; by 1934 a quarter of them for one reason or another had lost their property. A comparable Home Owners' Loan Corporation, established in June 1933, in a three-year period loaned $3 billion to refinance the mortgages of over a million distressed householders. Altogether it carried about one-sixth of the nation's urban mortgage burden. A year later, Congress established a Federal Housing Administration to insure mortgages for new construction and home repairs—more properly a recovery than a relief agency. All these mortgage agencies not only rescued mortgage holders but also eased the burden on banks and insurance companies, thus filling a recovery function.

Under the New Deal the Reconstruction Finance Corporation continued to function as the key loan agency for relief to business. The Democratic Congress inveighed against the RFC policy of making large loans only to big businesses and not to individuals. Congress therefore broadened the RFC's lending power so that it could, and indeed did, also lend to

Farm Defaults and Foreclosures, 1929–1945

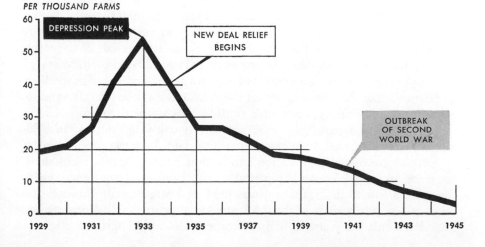

PER THOUSAND FARMS

DEPRESSION PEAK

NEW DEAL RELIEF BEGINS

OUTBREAK OF SECOND WORLD WAR

small businesses. Under the conservative management of a shrewd Texan, Jesse Jones, it continued to make most of its loans to large enterprises, including banks, and to governmental units, on sound security and with a high percentage of ultimate repayment.

The First AAA

The Agricultural Adjustment Administration (AAA), created in May 1933, marked the triumphant conclusion of the farmers' long struggle to get government aid for raising farm prices. Henceforth, the farmers, who continued to be a declining fraction of the whole population, received preferential treatment from the government.

Roosevelt was mainly interested in the relatively substantial farmers, such as the 300,000 who even in 1933 were paying dues of $10 a year or more to the Farm Bureau Federation. These and the Grange members desired a program to limit crops. Poorer members of other farm organizations like the Farmers' Union and the National Farmers' Holiday Association opposed production cuts, seeking instead direct relief and, above all, inflation. Roosevelt hoped to develop a program that would fit the Farm Bureau formula and yet would not drive poorer farmers into new revolt. He let the various farm organization leaders devise their own plan. Fifty of them met in Washington early in March 1933 and drafted an omnibus bill that contained scraps and reworkings of most of the old schemes. It provided for a "domestic-allotment" system. Producers of seven basic commodities (wheat, cotton, corn, hogs, rice, tobacco, and milk and dairy products) were to receive benefit payments if they cut acreage or production. Funds for these payments would come from a tax upon the processing of commodities—for example, a tax on the milling of wheat. The tax would be added to the price of the flour or other product, and so it would be passed on to the consumer, who would thus indirectly pay the farmer for growing less. Farm prices were to be brought up to "parity," that is, a level that would provide the same price relationship of farm products to manufactured goods as during the period 1909–1914.

Because the 1933 farm season was well under way when the AAA began operations, large-scale destruction was necessary to cut surpluses. Six million pigs and 220,000 sows about to farrow were slaughtered. Nine-tenths of their weight was inedible and processed into fertilizer, but they nevertheless provided 100 million pounds of pork for needy families. Bad weather so drastically cut the wheat crop that the AAA did not have to intervene to reduce it. Cotton farmers ploughed under a quarter of their crop—but it was the poorest quarter, and they so intensively cultivated the rest that 30 million acres produced more than 36 million had done the previous year.

Despite continued high cotton production, a short textile boom sent the price up from 5.5 cents per pound to 10.6 cents in the summer. Then the price began to sag again and was held to 9.6 cents only through another device. A subsidiary of the AAA, the Commodity Credit Corporation, loaned 10 cents per pound to cotton farmers who would agree to take additional land out of production the next year. Since the loan was in excess of the market value of cotton, the government in effect was buying the crop at a premium price in return for the promise of drastic cuts in production. In this way cotton farmers received double the cash in 1933 that they had in 1931.

Farmers in other crop-reduction programs did not fare as well, although a corn producer too could obtain commodity loans in the fall of 1933. Drought more than crop limitations reduced the output of wheat, corn, and hogs. Rising prices of manufactured goods canceled out most of the farmers' gain in real income. Yet on the whole his relative position improved somewhat.

The AAA actually hurt many of the farmers on the least productive farms, especially in the cotton belt. At times the AAA indirectly dispossessed them because planters, in reducing their acreage, sometimes evicted tenants and fired field hands. Unintentionally, the AAA stimulated the great migration away from sharecropper cabins, at a time when city jobs no

Father and son walking in the face of a dust storm, Cimarron County, Oklahoma (LIBRARY OF CONGRESS)

longer awaited the migrants. Rapid mechanization of farms and destructive wind storms on the Great Plains gave the great migration its impetus.

The NRA

Hard-pressed businessmen sought measures providing for government stabilization of business. Since 1931 leaders of the United States Chamber of Commerce and others had been urging an antideflation scheme that involved price fixing through trade associations. This plan would have necessitated suspension of the antitrust laws. President Hoover, who earlier had given strong support to the trade association movement, indignantly opposed price-fixing schemes. His Attorney General forced five leading trade associations to dissolve, and the Federal Trade Commission compelled revision of the trade association codes for sixty-two industries.

In the spring of 1933 businessmen sought from Roosevelt what Hoover had refused them. Many of them also demanded government enforcement of their agreements in order to raise prices and stabilize production. The New Deal was ready to give them what they wanted if they would accept wages-and-hours regulation and other concessions for labor. As a consequence of such an arrangement, prices and wages would go up. Consumers' buying power might lag and thus defeat the scheme. Therefore, the New Dealers drafting the great recovery bill added another ingredient for which there was much pressure: a large-scale public works spending program to prime the economic pump. This was the genesis of the National Industrial Recovery Act, which passed Congress in June 1933.

A new era of government alliance with business for the common good

Adjustment of Various Industries to the Depression

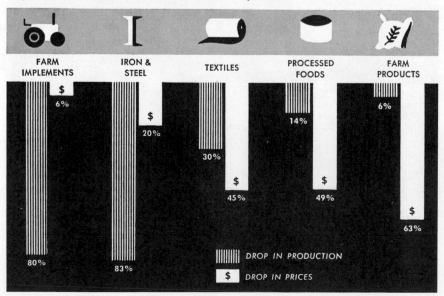

seemed to be opening. As he signed the act, Roosevelt called it "the most important and far-reaching legislation ever enacted by the American Congress." On the same day, the President appointed as administrator of the National Recovery Administration (NRA) the volatile, colorful General Hugh S. Johnson, who pictured himself as a kind of benign dictator presiding over the economy.

The President turned over the $3.3 billion for public works to Secretary of the Interior Harold L. Ickes, who slowly and methodically began to gather plans for projects, checking each carefully to make sure it would be really worthwhile. The need was for heavy spending in the next few months, but it was four years before Ickes' Public Works Administration pumped appreciable amounts of money into the economy.

President Roosevelt and NRA administrator Johnson called upon an excited nation to accept an interim blanket code, providing minimum wages of thirty cents or forty cents an hour, maximum working hours of thirty-five or forty per week, and the abolition of child labor. Employers who agreed with the code were to display the NRA blue-eagle symbol; consumers who cooperated were to sign pledges that they would buy only from blue-eagle establishments. In much the spirit of 1917, the nation participated in NRA parades and rallies. As Johnson began negotiating codes with big industries, recovery seemed really imminent.

By the beginning of September 1933, specific codes for most of the big industries were in operation. In the drafting of the codes, Johnson had tried to serve as arbiter to balance the conflicting interests of business, labor, and the consumer. All three were represented at the bargaining table and received some degree of protection. Nevertheless, the real power in drawing up the regulations went to the businessmen themselves, to the leaders within each industry. They flocked to Washington and in the urgency of the moment rewrote their old trade association agreements into

The NRA Eagle "—an Amerindian ideograph of unmeasured antiquity." (NATIONAL ARCHIVES)

new NRA codes. These codes often contained provisions that were difficult for small units in the industry to maintain. Most of them provided for limiting production and, though often in disguised form, for price fixing.

Production, after a sharp rise, skidded downward during the fall of 1933, from an index figure of 101 in July to 71 in November, even as prices began to creep upward. The brave words and great NRA demonstrations of the spring and summer had not brought recovery. The New Deal honeymoon was over, and as General Johnson had predicted, the dead cats began to fly.

In the spring of 1934 a National Recovery Review Board under a famous iconoclastic lawyer, Clarence Darrow, reported that the NRA was dominated by big business; he hinted that what was needed was socialism. In the ensuing storm of vituperation between Johnson and Darrow, the NRA lost still more prestige.

A case involving the National Recovery Administration finally reached the Supreme Court. The constitutional basis for the NRA was the power of Congress to regulate commerce among the states, but the test case involved alleged code violations by the Schechter brothers, who were operating a wholesale poultry business confined to one locality, Brooklyn. Among the

The N.R.A. Eagle: Jolting "Old Man Depression" in 1933 (LEFT, BY TALBURT FOR THE NEW YORK World-Telegram) *and, in 1935, nailed to the wall by the Supreme Court* (BY FITZPATRICK FOR THE ST. LOUIS Post-Dispatch)

charges against them were the selling of poor-quality poultry and the unfair treatment of employees. The Court (1935) unanimously held that the Schechters were not engaged in interstate commerce and that Congress had unconstitutionally delegated legislative power to the President to draft the codes.

The "sick chicken" decision outraged Roosevelt. Seeing in it a threat to the whole New Deal, he lashed out at the judges for thinking in terms of the horse-and-buggy era. Actually, the decision proved to be more a blessing than a catastrophe for the New Deal, since it ended the decrepit NRA code system with its tacit suspension of the antitrust laws. "It has been an awful headache," Roosevelt confessed privately.

TVA and Conservation

Increasingly, New Dealers turned their attention to measures that would remedy conditions they felt had helped bring on the depression. Their indignation burned especially hot against the private power interests, which they felt had gulled investors and overcharged consumers. The spectacular collapse of the great Insull utility empire in the Midwest lent credence to their charges. Hence the first and most far-reaching of the New Deal reform measures was the creation of the Tennessee Valley Authority (TVA).

Through the twenties, millions of progressive Americans of both parties had shared the dream of Senator George Norris of Nebraska that the government might develop the nation's great water resources to provide cheap electric power. Millions of others accepted the educational program of the utilities companies, which spent $28 million to $35 million per year combating the idea of a national power program. The battle centered on the great dam that had been started at Muscle Shoals on the Tennessee River but had not been finished in time to provide nitrates during the war. Coolidge and the conservatives wished to sell it to Henry Ford for private development. Norris and his cohorts in Congress blocked them. Norris wished to make Muscle Shoals the center for developing the resources of the area and bringing abundance to millions of people living in poverty. His bill was vetoed by Coolidge and again by Hoover but was approved by Roosevelt in May 1933.

Basically, the TVA aimed to prevent the devastating floods that all too frequently had rolled down the rivers of the area and to provide cheap, plentiful electricity as a yardstick for the measurement of private rates. More than this, the project became a great experiment in regional planning and rehabilitation.

Under a three-member board of directors with wide powers, the TVA in the next twenty years improved five existing dams and constructed twenty new ones. It stopped floods in the largest heavy-rainfall region in the nation and, by holding back the water, provided an inland waterway system with a 9-foot channel 652 miles long, soon heavy with traffic. From water power, and increasingly from steam plants, the TVA became the greatest producer of electricity in the United States. It also manufactured

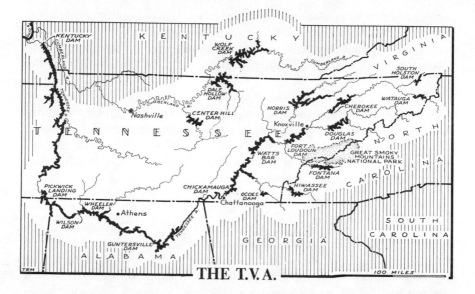

THE T.V.A.

low-cost phosphate fertilizers. It taught farmers how to use them, how to restore the fertility of their soil, and how to end erosion by means of contour plowing and reforestation. Although the TVA worked no miracles, it did bring a higher living standard to the farmers of the area. It brought new light industry and increased business. When World War II came, the new power plants provided indispensable electricity for the production of munitions, aluminum, and plutonium.

In its "yardstick" function TVA drove down the price of power in the area from 10 cents a kilowatt hour to 3 cents. Throughout the country, because of TVA and other pressures, the average residential rate dropped from 5.52 cents in 1933 to 3.67 cents in 1942. To private power companies the "yardstick" seemed grossly unfair, and they claimed that the TVA did not set its rates on the basis of true costs, including taxes. Its officials replied that its payments to local and state governments were comparable to the taxes assessed against private power companies.

Other great public power and irrigation developments were under way in the West during the same years. On the Colorado River, the Hoover Dam (begun during the Hoover administration) was finished in 1936, and on the Columbia River the Bonneville Dam was constructed in 1937 and the Grand Coulee Dam in 1942. In 1937 Norris proposed the creation of six additional regional authorities like the TVA; Congress failed to act, and the debate over public versus private development of power continued.

To combat drought conditions in the West Roosevelt in 1934 by executive order set aside $15 million to build a "shelter belt" of trees on the Great Plains to break the wind, collect moisture, and harbor wildlife. Critics scoffed, but somehow the trees grew where no one had believed they would. A Soil Erosion Service (later Soil Conservation Service), using much Civilian Conservation Corps manpower, was active, especially in the West. Homesteading on the range, which meant dry farming under almost insuperable difficulties, came to an end with the passage of the Taylor Grazing Act of 1934, which withdrew overgrazed land and set regulations for the use of public range land.

Money and Banking

Much of the New Deal was aimed at raising prices as a means of stimulating recovery. One way was to cut down production, as the AAA tried to do for agriculture and the NRA for industry. Another way was to put money into circulation through government spending, as was done in the relief programs (though recovery was not the primary aim of these). Still another way—at least in theory—was to manipulate the currency so as to increase the money supply.

By the summer of 1933 Roosevelt was ready to follow the reasoning of two Cornell University agricultural economists, who contended that if the price of gold were raised, the prices of other commodities would rise in rough proportion. The government needed only to purchase quantities of gold and cut the gold content of the dollar (as authorized by Congress). When financially orthodox Treasury officials refused to make the purchases, Roosevelt turned to the head of the Farm Credit Administration, Henry Morgenthau, Jr., who began buying gold every day along with wheat, corn, and oats. Soon Morgenthau was made Secretary of the Treasury.

The silver-purchase program had much the same object as the gold-purchase program. From the seven silver-producing states with their fourteen senators came strong pressure, reminiscent of that of the Populist era, culminating in the Silver Purchase Act of 1934. This measure nearly tripled the price of silver at home. It also sent up the world silver price and wrought havoc in nations whose currencies were on a silver standard. It did little or nothing to raise prices in the United States.

Roosevelt explained to a critical congressman: "I have always favored sound money, and do now, but it is 'too darned sound' when it takes so much of farm products to buy a dollar." In January 1934 he fixed the gold content of the dollar at 59.06 percent of the former amount. The resort to managed currency created new precedents for government action and thus, like the income tax a generation earlier, helped bring about an important change in the relationship of government and the economy. But it had little immediate effect upon recovery.

Through other legislation the government acquired new powers over the banks, including the power to manage the supply of bank credit through increased control over the Federal Reserve System. In June 1933 Roosevelt signed the Glass-Steagall Act, aimed at curbing speculation by banks. This also established the Federal Deposit Insurance Corporation (FDIC), which he had not favored. The FDIC guaranteed small deposits up to $2,500 and functioned so successfully that the guarantee was raised by successive stages, eventually reaching $15,000. It was a longer task to work out a comprehensive overhauling and strengthening of the Federal Reserve System to remedy the defects that had appeared during the depression. This was accomplished through the Banking Act of 1935, which established a seven-member board of governors with direct power over interest rates. By lowering the rates, the board could encourage borrowing from banks, and this would ordinarily have an inflationary (price-raising) effect.

To protect investors further Congress passed the so-called Truth in Securities Act of 1933, requiring corporations floating new securities to register them with the Federal Trade Commission and to provide full and accurate information on them. In June 1934 Congress went further and established the Securities and Exchange Commission to police the stock markets. Wall Streeters protested, but their complaints lost some of their effect when a former head of the New York Stock Exchange was sentenced to Sing Sing for larceny.

In many other areas as well reform measures were enacted or were in the making in 1934: the Communications Act, establishing the Federal Communications Commission to regulate radio, telegraph, and cable operations; the Air Mail Act, establishing tight controls in the awarding of contracts; and the Railroad Retirement Act, providing pensions for workers. Most significant of all, Roosevelt had appointed a Committee on Economic Security to develop an overall plan for national social security.

fourteen
The New Deal Shifts Toward Reform

By 1935 the New Deal was outgrowing the moderate premises of the Progressive era and was emphasizing massive government intervention on behalf of the underprivileged. President Roosevelt still wished to maintain a balanced program providing for the welfare of each of the economic and political groups in the country, but realities were forcing him to shift toward reform as he became the champion of the emerging political coalition of farmers, laborers, and millions of poor people.

In part, Roosevelt changed because he felt that large business had defected, that it had betrayed his recovery program and was fighting politically to destroy the New Deal. He had to counteract the threat of this opposition, numerically not frightening but carrying with it powerful means of influencing voters' opinion. Aligned against him were some 70 percent of the newspaper publishers and most of the large contributors of campaign funds. Roosevelt's quite human reaction was to regard this opposition as reckless and unprincipled and to force reform upon it for its own good.

Far more important was the threat from the left, and it was this that was mainly responsible for the gradual shift in the New Deal. In undermining this threat, Roosevelt's political pragmatism combined with his humanitarian inclinations to carry him along the road to reform even further than the progressives had dared venture, toward positive government action on behalf of the general welfare. "We have not weeded out the overprivileged," he told Congress in January 1935, "and we have not effectively lifted up the underprivileged." To do so became the goal of the New Deal.

THE PRESSURE OF POLITICS

Through 1934 Roosevelt was still trying to hold the support of businessmen and bankers. As late as October he told the American Bankers' Association: "The time is ripe for an alliance of all forces intent upon the business of recovery. In such an alliance will be found business and banking, agriculture and industry, and labor and capital. What an all-American team that would be!" There was little chance of it. In August 1934 conservative businessmen and self-styled Jeffersonian Democrats founded the American Liberty League to fight for free enterprise, states' rights, the open shop, and an end to New Deal bureaucracy.

As the congressional elections of 1934 approached, conservatives within the Liberty League and without campaigned against the New Deal on the grounds that it was destroying the Constitution and driving the country toward bankruptcy. All they succeeded in doing was to drive the dispossessed millions closer to the New Deal. Instead of losing ground to the Republican party—which would have been normal in a midterm election—the Democrats gained an additional ten seats in the Senate and also in the House.

Throughout the nation leaders arose who promised much to those despairing people whom the New Deal had not yet rescued. An elderly physician in California, Dr. Francis E. Townsend, attracted a following of 5 million destitute old people with his plan to obtain a federal pension of $200 per month for everyone over sixty. This would have cost nearly half the national income. The Townsendites claimed, however, that since the pensions would have had to be spent within the month, "the velocity of money" would have ended the depression. The immediate realities of the movement were that its promoters raised nearly a million dollars in two years and commanded a formidable bloc of votes.

Among restless people in Northern cities, Father Charles Coughlin's politico-religious broadcasts attracted a wide following. Starting with a mixture of papal encyclicals and Populism, he at first supported, then went far beyond, Roosevelt. Coughlin advocated silver inflation and nationalization of banks, utilities, and natural resources. Ultimately, in 1938 he founded the antidemocratic, anti-Semitic Christian Front. In January 1935 he was able to demonstrate his power by inspiring an avalanche of letters and telegrams to senators protesting against the World Court. His program was vague, but the discontent he was able to tap was concrete.

From the South, Senator Huey P. Long of Louisiana succeeded in launching a far more telling assault upon the New Deal. A skillful politician, he built a powerful organization in Louisiana and a rapidly growing following that spilled out first into neighboring states, then by 1935 into the Midwest, the Pacific Coast, and indeed every part of the country. Within Louisiana he had delighted his poverty-stricken supporters by immobilizing their traditional enemies through his strong-armed techniques. Within the state he built bridges, roads, hospitals, and a modern educational system. It was an era of dictators in Europe, and it was easy to assail the self-styled Louisiana Kingfish with ambitions to be a *Führer*, although his techniques were the time-honored ones of the American political boss. Ambitious to become President, he lured the masses by offering them more than Roosevelt. His "Share Our Wealth" program promised through confiscatory taxes on great fortunes to provide every family with what in those depression years seemed in itself a fortune: an income of $2,500 per year and a homestead worth $5,000. Even in Iowa, farmers guffawed when he called the Secretary of Agriculture "Lord Corn Wallace." The New Dealers' political tactician, Postmaster General James A. Farley, estimated in the spring of 1935 that Long could poll 3 or 4 million votes on a third-party ticket and possibly could throw the 1936 election to the Republicans.

The "thunder from the left" was so ominous early in 1935 that many despairing New Dealers, chafing at Roosevelt's apparent inertia, predicted defeat in 1936. Roosevelt, who never liked to explain his tactics, remarked confidentially that he had no intention of engaging in public debate with the leaders of the "lunatic fringe." Rather, he quietly went about stealing their thunder with the reform programs the New Dealers had long been planning.

THE WORKERS' WELFARE

Frances Perkins, the first woman cabinet member, had accepted the office of Labor Secretary only with Roosevelt's pledge that he would support a social security program. For several years she and a group of New Dealers sought to win converts in the cabinet, in Congress, and throughout the country to their view that social insurance would not only aid the unemployed but also help prevent future depressions.

The Social Security Act of 1935 provided two types of assistance for the aged. Those who were destitute could receive federal aid up to $15 per month, depending upon the matching sums that the states provided. Those who were working could receive upon retirement annuities provided from taxes upon their earnings and their employers' payrolls. The 1935 law specified payments, to begin in 1942, ranging from $10 to $85 per month, and excluded wide categories of workers from the program—but it was a beginning. The act also provided for unemployment insurance, aid for the blind and crippled, and assistance for dependent mothers and children—all such funds to be administered by the states in keeping with minimum federal standards. A Social Security Board supervised the entire system.

Social Security could not immediately help those already unemployed in 1935; to aid them, Congress in April voted $5 billion to supplant direct relief with the Works Progress Administration (WPA). Work relief was more expensive but was essential to prevent the moral erosion and, if possible, to save the skills of the unemployed.

The WPA under Hopkins did much to "help men keep their chins up and their hands in." It enrolled an average of 2.1 million workers between 1935 and 1941 on a wide variety of projects. Since the WPA workers were, theoretically at least, the least employable segment of the working force and since almost all WPA money went for wages rather than tools and materials, its undertakings could not compare in efficiency with private construction projects. Many people tended to forget this and regard WPA as a politically inspired paradise for loafers. Nevertheless, WPA built nearly 600 airports and built or rebuilt 110,000 public buildings, more than a half-million miles of roads and streets, over 100,000 bridges, a half-million sewers, and over a million privies. In the realm of art, music, and the theater it gave opportunities to a remarkable proportion of the nation's talented people; its writers, for example, produced a useful set of state guidebooks.

The National Youth Administration, established in June 1935, as a kind of "junior WPA," aided young people between sixteen and twenty-five, seven-eighths of who received student aid in schools and colleges.

Meanwhile, improved living quarters were being provided for working-class families. From the outset in June 1933, the Public Works Administration (PWA—not the same as WPA), through an Emergency Housing Division, began federal sponsorship of public housing. It cleared some of the nation's most notorious slum blocks, replacing them with about 50 developments containing almost 22,000 family units. The rent was an average of $26 per month, too high during these years for many previous slum dwellers to meet. Congress in 1937 finally passed Senator Wagner's bill creating the United States Housing Authority, which with $500 million (later in 1941 increased to $1.6 billion) took over and expanded the housing program to 511 projects with 161,000 units intended for the truly poor.

A NEW DEAL FOR WOMEN AND MINORITIES

Women, who were discriminated against when the depression led to cuts in the working force, made some gains during the New Deal. Numbers of women lost their jobs on the grounds that they were married and presumably did not need them; teachers and government workers especially suf-

Harry Hopkins (NATIONAL ARCHIVES)

fered. Large numbers of women who did hold jobs were not much better off; they were paid so much less than men—sometimes not enough to live upon. They gained wages-and-hours protection through New Deal legislation, but married women continued to suffer.

The New Deal brought more women into significant federal positions than ever before. Roosevelt had made heavy use of women as campaigners, and after his election, Mary Dewson, head of the Women's Division of the Democratic National Committee, together with Eleanor Roosevelt, the President's wife, and Secretary Perkins, saw to it that women received substantial numbers of appointments.

The black experience during the New Deal was comparable. Not only were blacks the last hired and first fired, but whites losing jobs ousted blacks from their traditional menial employment. Northern blacks earned so little that business in black ghettos like that of Cleveland came almost to a standstill.

Because the depression was so crushing, the blacks benefited proportionately well from the relatively meager benefits they received. The NRA and the AAA may have harmed blacks more than they helped, and black youths had difficulty in enrolling in the CCC, but for the first time since the Reconstruction years large numbers of blacks received direct federal assistance. The money they received from relief and WPA employment, the small-crop benefit checks, and the third of federal housing units they received—all combined to help the blacks again to obtain a toehold in the economy.

The New Deal did less for black civil rights. Although President Roose-

Black cotton pickers—Ben Shahn (LIBRARY OF CONGRESS)

velt sympathized with the drive for federal antilynching legislation, he feared Southern filibusters against it in the Senate would also block New Deal legislation. He gave only indirect support.

Roosevelt did appoint so many blacks to important administrative and advisory positions that they formed what was called a black cabinet. The number of black federal employees increased from 50,000 in 1933 to 200,000 in 1946, and segregation against them in federal facilities greatly diminished. President Roosevelt declared at Howard University in 1936: "Among American citizens, there should be no forgotten man and no forgotten race." Northern blacks responded by leaving the party of Lincoln and voting overwhelmingly for that of the New Deal.

Among Spanish-speaking Americans there were less gains in Washington, but they too participated in New Deal programs. Young Lyndon B. Johnson as head of the National Youth Administration in Texas saw to it that Mexican Americans as well as blacks shared in its benefits.

For American Indians there was a turn away from the program of the 1920s to assimilate them as rapidly as possible. The Indian Reorganization Act of 1934 ended distribution of tribal lands and returned to the Indians freedom to govern themselves through their tribes and to revive their own culture and religion. Numerous New Deal agencies gave aid to the Indians as they did to other Americans in distress. The Soil Conservation Service, mentioned earlier in Chapter 13, tried to show the Navajos how to improve the grass on their rangelands through fencing it to prevent overgrazing and through stopping erosion by employing Indian crews on relief wages to fill in gullies and build check dams. The Department of the Interior still retained much power over Indian finances, but the morale of many Indians improved as they slowly took advantage of their new opportunities.

"I have worked hard all my life and all I have now is my broken body." Mexican laborer, Imperial Valley, Calif.—Dorothea Lang (LIBRARY OF CONGRESS)

Navajo working on a check dam
(SOIL CONSERVATION SERVICE)

ENCOURAGING UNIONS

For those fortunate enough to be employed, Roosevelt preferred a paternal-istic program of wages-and-hours guarantees and Social Security benefits. Union leaders wanted to use collective bargaining to gain these advantages for their workers, so that they would look to the unions, not to the govern-ment.

Labor leaders had gained much of what they wanted just before the advent of the New Deal, with the passage in 1932 of the Norris-LaGuardia Act. This prohibited the courts from issuing injunctions against most ordinary collective-bargaining practices, and it made unenforceable any yellow-dog contracts—that is, pledges from employees that they would not join unions. The Norris-LaGuardia Act stopped federal courts from interfering on behalf of employers in struggles with employees. It left management and the unions free to bring economic pressure upon each other as best they could in collective-bargaining procedures.

In the depression years, however, employers were usually stronger than unions. Besides, strikes could interfere with economic recovery. Hence in 1933 Section 7a of the National Industrial Recovery Act affirmed the right of labor to bargain collectively and led to the establishment of a govern-ment agency—the National Labor Board—to settle disputes arising under Section 7a. The relatively weak board was at first favorable to employers.

While Roosevelt had always maintained cordial relations with labor leaders, he was little inclined to give them firm collective-bargaining guar-

antees in place of the weak Section 7a in the National Industrial Recovery
Act. Congress, under the leadership of Senator Robert F. Wagner, felt dif-
ferently. In May 1935 the Senate passed Wagner's bill, providing strong
government protection for the unions. Roosevelt, bowing to the inevitable,
signed the measure. What he had reluctantly accepted became one of the
mainstays of the New Deal. The Wagner Act, passed at a time when unions
were relatively weak, outlawed a number of the "unfair practices" by
which management had been bludgeoning them and created a powerful
National Labor Relations Board to police the employers. Militant Labor
thus obtained the governmental backing essential to a drive to unionize
the great mass-production industries.

Even before the adoption of the Wagner Act, union membership had
risen from a depression low of less than 3 million to 4.2 million. A group
of leaders of industrial unions (which offered membership to everyone
within an industry) had chafed over the conservatism of the craft unions
(which took in only those working at a given trade). In 1934 men like the
head of the United Mine Workers, John L. Lewis, and the leaders of the
two great garment unions, Sidney Hillman of the Amalgamated Clothing
Workers and David Dubinsky of the International Ladies' Garment Workers, had forced President William Green of the AFL and the craft unionists to agree to charter new industrial unions in the big unorganized
industries.

In 1935 organization of these industries began. It led to violent opposition not only from the corporations but also from the AFL craft unions,
which feared they would be submerged by the new giant unions. Jurisdic-
tional fights led to a schism between the AFL leadership and the industrial

*Workers balloting at a National Labor Relations Board election, Ford Plant,
1941* (LIBRARY OF CONGRESS)

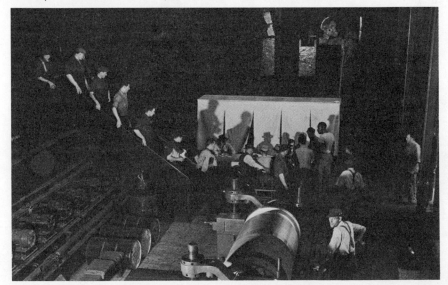

unionists, who formed a Committee for Industrial Organization (within the AFL) in November 1935. Industrial warfare followed, as both the AFL and the CIO mounted great rival organizational drives.

President Roosevelt and a few industrial leaders favored industrial unionism. Gerald Swope of General Electric told Roosevelt that his company could not conceivably negotiate with a large number of craft unions but might find advantages in contracting with a single industrial union. Generally, however, in the spring of 1936 the point was still far off when big business could see advantages in big labor. Vigorous young organizers had to battle it out, often by physical force, with "loyal" strong-arm squads, occasionally with the police, and sometimes with rival organizers. The great difference between this and earlier periods of labor warfare was the aid the federal government provided unions through the National Labor Relations Board.

Through 1936 the United Automobile Workers gained recruits despite vigorous company opposition. There was good reason, for in 1934, at about the time the organizing drive began, nearly half of the auto workers were receiving less than $1,000 per year. General Motors alone, in an effort to keep down union organization, spent almost $1 million on private detectives between 1934 and 1936. In the first two months of 1937, workers closed seventeen General Motors plants through the new device of the sit-down strike, the workers staying by their machinery inside the plants. General Motors soon recognized the UAW, and other automobile com-

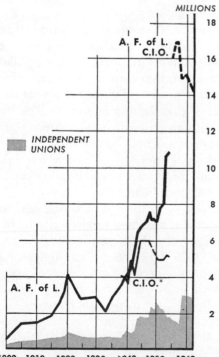

Organized Labor, 1900–1956

*C.I.O. figures not available for 1948-1950.

panies gradually did the same. Rubber and other industries were similarly organized. Newspapers saw in the sit-down strikes a menace to private property, and much of the public became thoroughly alarmed.

Bloody warfare in the steel industry heightened the alarm. In 1936 the CIO voted a $500,000 fund to organize the industry and began its great onslaught, winning tens of thousands of workers from company unions. United States Steel chose to capitulate rather than face a long strike just as prosperity seemed to be returning. In March 1937, to the amazement of the nation, one of the company's subsidiaries signed a contract with the Steel Workers' Organizing Committee. For the first time "Big Steel" was unionized. But three of the "Little Steel" companies, under the leadership of Tom Girdler of Republic Steel, resisted furiously. At the Republic plant in South Chicago on Memorial Day, 1937, the police killed ten strikers. Republic Steel, according to the prolabor La Follette committee, was the largest purchaser of tear gas and sickening gas in the United States; Youngstown Sheet and Tube Company owned an arsenal of over a thousand weapons. The Republic strikers lost completely, to the relief of middle-class Americans who, like the newspapers they read, blamed the strife upon the unions and the New Deal.

Yet organized labor continued to grow. By 1941 union membership totaled about 9.5 million.

MORE FOR FARMERS

In January 1936 the Supreme Court held that it was unconstitutional for the AAA to regulate farm production or to impose a tax for such a purpose. Congress hastily passed a law (the Soil Conservation and Domestic Allotment Act) to meet the Court's objections and yet continue the crop-reduction effort. Under the new law, Congress appropriated money to pay farmers for conserving the soil by leaving part of their land uncultivated. The law provided that landlords must share with their tenants and sharecroppers the payments for withdrawing land from production. Nevertheless, in 1937, while the average plantation operator was grossing $8,328, of which $833 came from the soil conservation program, the average tenant family received only $385, of which $27 came from the government.

Agricultural interests pressed for a new AAA to cope with an enormous threatened surplus. The end of the drought, increased mechanization, and other improvements like the rapid spread of hybrid corn in the Midwest outmoded the crop controls of the 1936 legislation. The Agricultural Adjustment Act of 1938—the "second AAA"—provided a number of devices to cut back production: soil conservation payments, marketing quotas, export subsidies, and crop loans. Surpluses of five nonperishable commodities upon which farmers received federal loans would be stored under government seal until need in lean years, thus creating what Secretary Wallace termed an "ever normal granary." The surpluses so stored were to be of vital aid in feeding allies during the war years. The 1938 act also established

Strip and contour farming in Georgia (U.S. DEPARTMENT OF AGRICULTURE PHOTO)

a Surplus Marketing Administration to channel surpluses to needy persons and provide food for school lunches.

To improve the condition of the poorer farmers, those on submarginal soil, the government undertook to resettle them on better land. The Resettlement Administration (1935) and its successor, the Farm Security Administration (1937), made short-term loans for rehabilitation and long-term loans for purchasing farms but succeeded in moving only a few thousand farm families.

The more fortunate farmers were benefited by the Rural Electrification Administration, which was established in 1935 to extend power lines to farms through cooperatives. Since its activities also stimulated private power companies to extend into the country, it was effective both directly and indirectly. Power lines had reached only 4 percent of the farms in 1925; they reached 25 percent by 1940.

LESS FOR BIG BUSINESS

After the NRA had been declared unconstitutional, parts of the law were reenacted piecemeal and with alterations to form a "little NRA." As early as February 1935, in response to the Supreme Court's invalidation of legislation to prevent the overproduction of oil, Congress passed the Connally Act prohibiting the shipment of "hot oil" (oil produced in excess of state limitations) in interstate commerce. The Guffey Act of August 1935 virtually reenacted the NRA bituminous-coal code, fixing prices, limiting production, and protecting labor. When the Supreme Court threw out the new coal-control law in 1936, Congress passed the second Guffey Act of 1937. Roosevelt feared a wages-and-hours law would be unconstitutional,

A *sharecropper's family*, 1936 (LIBRARY OF CONGRESS)

but he signed the Walsh-Healey Act of August 1936, setting minimum wages and maximum hours for work done on federal contracts. In order to protect small retailers, the Robinson-Patman Act of 1936 prohibited wholesalers or manufacturers from giving preferential discounts or rebates to chain stores or other large buyers; the Miller-Tydings Act of 1937 fortified state "fair trade" price-fixing laws.

As yet, Roosevelt did not resort to vigorous use of the antitrust laws, but he advocated tightening the regulation of big business. In March 1935 he recommended passage of an act to prohibit after five years the pyramiding of utility holding companies, which had led to flagrant abuses in the 1920s. In the 1930s thirteen companies still controlled three-fourths of the nation's electric power. They fought desperately through the summer of 1935 against what they viewed as a threatened "death sentence." One company alone spent $700,000 lobbying against the measure. In the Holding Company Act of 1935 the companies gained a partial victory; it permitted two strata of holding companies above the operating companies.

Between 1935 and 1940 Congress passed a series of other laws stiffening federal regulation. These strengthened the Federal Power Commission, brought trucks and carriers on inland waterways under the supervision of the Interstate Commerce Commission, created a new Maritime Commission to subsidize and regulate a merchant fleet, and set up a Civil Aeronautics Authority (later Board) to regulate airlines.

One of the most effective ways to regulate was to tax, and in 1935

Roosevelt proposed democratizing the federal tax structure by placing far higher levies upon big corporations and wealthy people. He pointed out that a person receiving $6,000 per year paid twice as high a tax as one receiving $4,000, yet the tax upon a $5 million income was only about five times as high as on $1 million. Conservative newspapers immediately attacked this proposal as a "soak the rich" tax scheme, but it passed Congress. It wiped away the last vestiges of Secretary Mellon's influence on tax policy, as it established the highest peacetime rates in history at the top: a maximum 75 percent income tax, 70 percent estate tax, and 15 percent corporate income tax. It was an important step toward the redistribution of American income.

Big business seemed to have grown bigger through New Deal inadvertence. The NRA relaxation of the antitrust laws had given it an opportunity to thrive at the expense of smaller business. In the two years after the end of the codes, the Attorney General initiated even fewer antitrust suits than during the NRA period.

Then, in April 1938, the President sent Congress a message vehemently denouncing the unjustifiable concentration of economic power. Less than 5 percent of all corporations in 1935 owned 87 percent of all the assets, he declared. This was leading to such a serious maldistribution of income, he pointed out, that in 1935–1936 the upper 1.5 percent of the population had a share of the national income as great as the 47 percent at the bottom —and these had less than $1,000 per year per family. The remedy, Roosevelt proposed, was to study economic concentration and enact more modern antitrust laws to cope with the newer techniques of monopoly. In response, Congress established the Temporary National Economic Committee under the chairmanship of Senator O'Mahoney. It conducted lengthy public hearings and published thirty-nine volumes of reports and forty-three scientific monographs by the end of 1941. By that time the national attention was entirely engrossed elsewhere; legislation never followed.

Meanwhile, in 1938 Roosevelt launched an immediate trust-busting program through Thurman Arnold, whom he appointed head of the Antitrust Division of the Department of Justice. Arnold, who felt there was nothing wrong with existing legislation, made new and sophisticated use of the Sherman and Clayton acts as he undertook 215 major investigations and 92 test cases.

Well before Roosevelt reached this point, by 1937, the conservative opposition in Congress was beginning to thwart his reform thrust.

fifteen
The Limits of Reform

In 1936 Roosevelt was at the zenith of his popularity and power. But soon he was to run into stronger political opposition than ever, and by 1938 he was to turn his attention from domestic reform to foreign policy and military defense.

MANDATE FROM THE PEOPLE

Roosevelt's vigorous reform program, enacted in its main outlines by 1936, made him a sure winner in the election of that year. Many millions felt that their personal lot had been improved by the New Deal. The violent attacks upon it from the right and the cries of anguish over such measures as the "soak the rich" taxes convinced them even more that Roosevelt was their friend. Despite the misgivings of many conservatives within the party, the Democratic convention in 1936 renominated him by acclamation. His control was so complete that he even obtained abrogation of the two-thirds rule through which minorities had often hamstrung conventions.

As for the Republicans, they nominated their strongest candidate. Ignoring former President Hoover and the right wing, which was crying calamity, they chose a one-time Bull Mooser who had never strayed far from the 1912 Progressive position. This was the competent governor of Kansas, Alf M. Landon. His running mate was another Bull Mooser who had moved well to the right, the Chicago publisher Frank Knox. The Republican platform promised to do most of what the New Deal was undertaking—but more competently, constitutionally, and without running a deficit. Landon's dry voice could not match Roosevelt's radio eloquence, and Landon was further handicapped because, though he was a moderate, he had to try to hold the militant Republican right.

The election demonstrated the extent to which the New Deal depended upon a coalition of farmers, union members, and the poor. The unions

Alf M. Landon (NATIONAL AR-
CHIVES)

were the heaviest Democratic campaign contributors, providing $1 million.
The "lunatic fringe" coalition against Roosevelt stirred hardly a ripple.
Huey Long had been assassinated the year before; the Union party candi-
date was "Liberty Bell" William Lemke—who was "cracked," said wise-
acres. His ticket polled only 890,000 votes; the Socialists, 190,000; the
Communists, under 80,000.

A preelection postal card poll by the *Literary Digest* had indicated that
Landon would win by a big margin. How could it be so wrong? The names
and addresses of those polled were taken from old telephone directories. A
majority of people who could afford telephones and had not been forced
to move favored Landon. In the election he received 16,680,000 popular
votes, compared with 27,477,000 for Roosevelt, and got the electoral votes
of only Maine and Vermont.

In the campaign Roosevelt had challenged his right-wing opponents—
economic royalists he called them—and now he had not only received an
overwhelming endorsement for himself, but he had carried with him many
congressmen pledged to his support. Nevertheless, those economic royalists
would still have the upper hand as long as the Supreme Court continued
to check New Deal laws. He felt he had a mandate from the people to do
something about the obstructionist Court.

STORM OVER THE COURT

Foes of the Coal Act, the Holding Company Act, the National Labor
Relations Act, and the Social Security Act were openly flouting these laws,
confident that the Supreme Court would disallow them as it had already
done the NRA and the first AAA. The Court, through its narrow interpretation of the federal power over commerce and taxation and its broad in-

terpretation of freedom of contract in the Fourteenth Amendment, seemed to have created an economic no man's land within which neither the federal nor the state governments could act.

Critics of the Court had been urging passage of some kind of constitutional amendment to provide the federal government with more extensive economic powers. Roosevelt's opinion (which subsequent Supreme Court decisions were to sustain) was that the Constitution granted adequate powers. All that was wrong was the Court's antiquated interpretation, he felt, but the four or five justices firmly opposed to the New Deal enjoyed excellent health and showed no signs of resigning. Consequently, Roosevelt decided to propose adding to the Supreme Court—and to lower federal courts—new justices (presumably sharing his viewpoint) to match superannuated ones.

At this point Roosevelt's political sixth sense deserted him and, instead of presenting his proposal frankly and firmly in terms of its economic implications, he enclosed it in a larger scheme. Without informing congressional leaders in advance, in February 1937 he sent a surprise message proposing a needed general overhauling of the federal court system and the appointment of as many as six new Supreme Court justices. His nearest approach to frankness was a statement that the addition of younger blood would revitalize the courts and help them meet the needs and facts of an ever-changing world.

There was no real question about the constitutionality of Roosevelt's proposal, since Congress had from time to time changed the number of justices on the Supreme Court. Nevertheless, the plan aroused a great furor throughout the country. Many thoughtful people who had supported Roosevelt in 1936 heeded the warning of conservatives that, through such constitutional shortcuts, dictators came into power. Within Congress the controversy cut across party lines. Some Democrats fought against the "packing" of the Court, while the Republican progressive Senator Robert M. La Follette, Jr., supported the President. La Follette declared that the Court had already been "packed" for years "in the cause of Reaction and Laissez-Faire."

Some of the old-line Democratic leaders, especially from the South, had gone along with the New Deal mainly because of party loyalty and pressure from their constituents. Now that much of the electorate was turning against the administration, these conservatives broke loose. They joined with the bulk of the Republicans to form a new conservative coalition in Congress. Roosevelt fought back by using every device of party discipline to round up votes in Congress. He might have succeeded in obtaining at least a compromise measure, had not the Supreme Court itself eliminated the necessity for one.

The justices—including Louis D. Brandeis, the oldest and most liberal—had been indignant over charges that they were too old to handle the business of the Court. Chief Justice Charles Evans Hughes even wrote a letter insisting that they were not falling behind in their work. Four of them, far to the right, were of no disposition to take a broader view of the Constitution. Three of them took a more progressive if not a New Deal view. Chief Justice Hughes on occasion voted with them, while Justice Owen J. Roberts more often voted with the conservative four.

Just before the President sent his court plan to Congress, Roberts joined with Hughes and the three more liberal justices in the case of *West Coast Hotel* v. *Parrish* to validate, by a 5-to-4 decision, a state minimum wage law. This reversed a 5-to-4 decision of the previous year invalidating a similar law. "You may have saved the country," Hughes jubilantly told Roberts. The decision was announced on March 29, 1937. Two weeks later, the Court, again 5 to 4, upheld the Wagner Act, and in May, the Social Security Act. Since there no longer seemed to be any pressing need for judicial reform, the new conservative alliance in Congress easily dealt Roosevelt a personal defeat by voting down his court plan. At the same time, the shift of the Supreme Court's interpretation of the Constitution was a significant victory for Roosevelt and the New Deal.

Almost at once the older justices began retiring, and Roosevelt replaced them one by one with his appointees. In the next decade the Roosevelt Court rewrote large sections of constitutional law. The new justices sharply divided among themselves, but usually upon technical matters. In the main they interpreted the commerce and tax clauses so broadly and the Fourteenth Amendment so narrowly that there remained few restrictions upon economic regulation by either the federal or the state governments. For several years the judges tended to restrict governments in their interference with organized labor, but by the end of a decade, labor too was subject to firm restraints. Thus almost all constitutional impediments to government regulation of the economic system were removed.

RECOVERY AND RECESSION

A sharp recession developed in the fall of 1937. It came just as many economists were fearing that an inflationary boom might get out of hand. There had been a remarkable recovery. The national income, which had dropped from $82 billion in 1929 to $40 billion in 1932, was back up to nearly $72 billion. Yet there were still 7.5 million unemployed and nearly 4.5 million families on relief. And there had been no upsurge of capital investment and business expansion as in the 1920s.

Recovery had come because of the enormous sums spent on work relief, the gradual momentum of the public works program, the loans to farmers, and the payment in 1936 (over Roosevelt's veto) of the veterans' bonus. All this government spending had powerfully stimulated the economy. Out of this experience emerged new economic theories, centering upon the concept that the government could help pull the nation out of a depression by liberal expenditures. As a corollary, the government could help curb inflationary booms by means of restrictive policies. These new economic theories came to be known as Keynesianism, after the famed British economist John Maynard Keynes.

In 1937 Roosevelt as much as his Republican opponents abhorred a deficit and worried about the mounting national debt, which had risen to $30 billion. He actually feared another disastrous crash like that of 1929. Acting in terms of the older economics, he had the Federal Reserve tighten credit even though the upswing had been sound rather than speculative. More important, he tried to balance the budget by drastically reducing government spending. Between January and August 1937 he cut the WPA in half, sending 1.5 million workers on unpaid "vacation."

And since, with the ending of the drought, a huge farm surplus was again imminent, produce prices fell sharply. The fragile new boom collapsed and sent the economy plummeting. The index of production dropped from 117 in August 1937 to 76 in May 1938; 4 million additional workers were thrown out of employment. It seemed like 1932 all over again.

In October 1937 the President called Congress into special session to renew heavy public spending and to reform the "selfish interests" he blamed for the recession. Congress passed an emergency appropriation of $5 billion; the public works and work relief programs once again poured these large sums into the economy, and by June 1938 recovery was under way. The "spending school" had scored a point, and the government seemed to have assumed a new role in warding off threatened economic disaster.

Thus the New Deal entered into its final stage of reform, combining what was as new as Keynesianism with what was as old as progressivism. The trend had been toward big business, and now big government had come with the active intervention of the New Deal in so many aspects of the economy. The number of civilian government employees swelled from 588,000 in 1931 to 1,370,000 in 1941.

Since questions of constitutionality no longer seriously interfered after the changes in the Supreme Court, New Dealers fought the Fair Labor Standards Act through Congress in 1938. This established a minimum wage of twenty-five cents an hour (to be raised gradually to forty cents by 1945) and a maximum work week of forty-four hours (to be lowered to forty) for most laborers, excepting agricultural, domestic, and maritime workers. It also forbade employment of children under sixteen in most areas except agriculture. Low though these standards were, they raised the pay of 300,000 workers and shortened the workweek for 1.3 million. In subsequent years the standards were raised repeatedly, and the scope of the law was broadened to include additional categories of workers.

Roosevelt worried about the strong negative power that the conservative coalition was developing in Congress. In many states the Democratic party was under the leadership of conservatives. Postmaster General Farley, in charge of patronage, had done little to aid New Dealers who tried to challenge this leadership. In 1938 Roosevelt intervened in several pri-

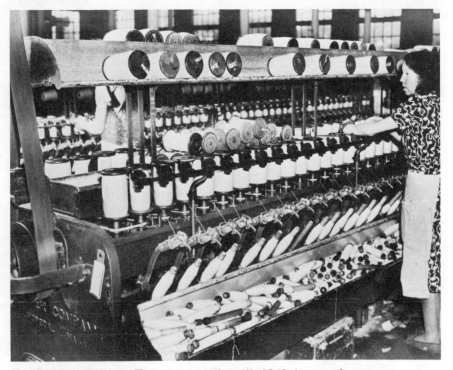

Tending spindles in a Tennessee textile mill, 1940 (WOMEN'S BUREAU, U.S. DE-
PARTMENT OF LABOR)

maries, mostly in the South, to try to defeat powerful conservative Democrats who headed congressional committees. Since these people had strong
organizations behind them and the New Deal candidates were relatively
unknown, the conservatives won in almost every contest. The 1938 elections reflected the degree to which the prestige of Roosevelt and the New
Deal was waning. The Republicans gained eighty seats in the House and
seven in the Senate. Together with the conservative Democrats, the
Republicans could dominate Congress.

By the end of 1938 the New Deal was close to its limits. The threat
of a second world war was beginning to overshadow even the most critical
domestic problems. The President could drive Congress with its Southern committee chairmen in the direction of strong defense legislation
and a vigorous foreign policy only if he conciliated them by abandoning
reform.

CULTURE IN THE DEPRESSION

Both the depression and the government's efforts to combat it left a mark
on the cultural life of the time. Unemployment left many people with

unaccustomed leisure time, which they used either to protest against or to escape from unpleasant realities. The federal government became a patron and promoter of culture on a scale it had never attempted before.

Even before the establishment of the Federal Art Project, which eventually enrolled 5,000 persons, the government had aided artists through an earlier relief project and the commissioning of extensive murals for new public buildings. Some of these artists expressed leftist themes comparable to those of the highly popular Mexican muralists. Many turned their attention, sometimes satirically, to the American scene. This was the heyday of Grant Wood, with his patterned Iowa landscapes and austere rural portraits, and of Thomas Hart Benton, who with dramatic sympathy portrayed sharecroppers and blacks. In sculpture, responding to the new government aid and the resurgent nationalism, Gutzon Borglum finished the enormous heads of Washington, Jefferson, Lincoln, and Theodore Roosevelt, which were carved on a rocky mountainside in the Black Hills. Altogether, thousands of artists and sculptors worked during the depression years; never before had America possessed so many who were competent and promising.

Appreciation of the arts took a strong upturn, partly through art classes sponsored by the Federal Art Project, partly through the opening of new art museums. In 1941 the National Art Gallery in Washington opened, displaying collections of European art valued at $35 million, the gift of Andrew W. Mellon. Samuel H. Kress added 400 Italian paintings. More people than ever before visited galleries and bought reproductions of the old masters and of the French impressionists, especially Vincent Van Gogh.

Although jazz more than held its own, interest in classical music increased. The Federal Music Project employed 15,000 persons. They

Grant Wood (NATIONAL ARCHIVES)

"American Gothic" by Grant Wood (THE ART INSTITUTE OF CHICAGO)

brought concerts to 100 million people and gave free music lessons to over a half-million pupils, most of whom could have afforded neither concerts nor lessons. Much of the music they played was that of American composers, such as Roy Harris' Third Symphony, and Aaron Copland's *Music for the Theatre*. Through new high-quality radio receivers and recordings, many additional millions listened to fine music, especially the symphony broadcasts conducted by Arturo Toscanini and the Metropolitan Opera performances. In 1940 listeners contributed over $300,000 to help "save the Met." Many millions more mourned the death in 1937 of young George Gershwin, composer of *Porgy and Bess* and *Rhapsody in Blue*. To the great mass of Americans, music still meant either sweet pop-

Thomas Hart Benton (NATIONAL ARCHIVES)

ular songs played by bands like Guy Lombardo's or jazz like Benny Goodman's, which came surging back into favor in 1934.

After depression and competition from motion pictures had thrown most actors and old vaudeville performers out of employment, the Federal Theater Project found employment for 12,500 of them. It brought performances to millions who had never previously seen a stage production. Some of these were highly successful as entertainment, some were of an advanced experimental nature, and some were so far to the left that they kindled the wrath of Congress, which killed the project in 1939. Many of the Broadway playwrights, impervious to congressional hostility, also took a critical look at social problems, as did Lillian Hellman in *The Little Foxes*. Robert E. Sherwood, who illustrated another trend, stopped writing light comedies and dramatized the impotence of the intellectual (*The Petrified Forest*, 1936) and the menace of war (*Idiot's Delight*, 1936). Later, in the pressure of world events he reversed themes, and glorified the intellectual fighting totalitarian aggression (*There Shall Be No Night*, 1940). Meanwhile, Thornton Wilder wrote *Our Town* (1938) and Eugene O'Neill, who in 1936 won a Nobel Prize, labored quietly on a long-continuing cycle of plays.

Novelists likewise divided into those who, like William Faulkner, seemed to be largely unaffected by the era, and others like Ernest Hemingway, who paralleled Sherwood's cycle from 1929 (*A Farewell to Arms*) to 1940 (*For Whom the Bell Tolls*). Thomas Wolfe richly and poetically portrayed the world swirling around him in his *Of Time and the River*

(1935) and his posthumous *You Can't Go Home Again* (1940). Many other novelists turned out proletarian themes from Marxist molds. John Steinbeck sentimentalized his suffering protagonists in his best-selling novel about the Oklahoman trek to California, *The Grapes of Wrath* (1939). The lure of romantic escape and the bargain of the sheer bulk helped make best sellers of Hervey Allen's *Anthony Adverse* (1933) and Margaret Mitchell's *Gone with the Wind* (1936).

Reading was one of the most inexpensive pursuits of the depression years, and although libraries suffered from slashed funds, book circulation increased considerably. Depression likewise cut the cost of radios and enlarged the size of audiences. In 1929, 12 million families owned radios; by 1940, 28 million families, comprising 86 percent of the population, owned them. This in part explains why Roosevelt, the master of the radio "fireside chat," campaigned so successfully with at least 70 percent of the metropolitan newspaper circulation opposing him. A radio serial, *Amos and Andy*, was so popular that Huey Long took the name of one of its characters, the Kingfish, as his sobriquet. Motion-picture audiences dropped one-third early in the depression, then by 1939 boomed to a yearly box-office average of $25 per family. Like radio serials, motion pictures

Drought refugees stalled on the highway, New Mexico, 1937 (LIBRARY OF CONGRESS)

dispensed mostly escapist themes—because of the vigor of the Catholic-led Legion of Decency, founded in 1934, it was a less sexy escape than in the twenties. Theaters also dispensed two movies rather than one and offered giveaways of a wide variety in order to bolster the box office. As yet, the coming threat to the movies, television, was still in the engineering laboratory—a curiosity exhibited at the New York World's Fair of 1939. It was too expensive for commercial development during the depression.

EDUCATION AND THE PROFESSIONS

The two depression factors of lack of funds and excess of leisure time also operated in education. It was estimated in 1935 that one-third of the unemployed were young people. Many went to school for lack of an alternative, and high school enrollment increased by one-third between 1929 and 1935. In spite of this, economy-minded chambers of commerce and citizens' committees led a drive for cuts so deep that they carved out educational sinew along with the fat. Colleges and universities dropped in enrollment until 1935, then more than recuperated but continued to suffer budgetary crises. Vocational education was strongly emphasized on both the high school and the college levels. Serious students explored social and economic questions so energetically that frightened civic and patriotic organizations warned that "pinks" were taking over the educational systems.

Alarmists feared that pinks were taking over the churches also, for ministers responded as enthusiastically to the new demands for human welfare as they once had responded to the social gospel. Of 20,000 ministers polled in 1934, nearly one-third favored socialism, and three-fifths, a "drastically reformed capitalism." The main intellectual current among ministers was toward neoorthodoxy. Reinhold Niebuhr, without disavowing political and social liberalism, found powerful psychological pressures driving human beings toward sin, from which they could be rescued only by faith, that is, submission to God.

Though the depression seriously cut funds for medical research, the thirties were another decade of advance in medical knowledge. Ironically, by 1935, when the American Medical Association was warning that 20 million people were suffering malnutrition or were close to it, highly publicized discoveries in vitamin research were leading the well fed to consume a variety of vitamin-fortified foods and to swallow vitamin pills in quantities second only to laxatives. Sulfa drugs, typhus vaccine, blood plasma, and the "artificial lung" all came into use. Life expectancy increased from fifty-six years in 1920 to sixty-four in 1940, but malnutrition, illness, and sometimes lack of good medical care wrought a heavy toll during the depression. Army medical examiners rejected almost half of the first 2 million young men Selective Service called up in 1940–1941.

Yet doctors were ill paid (even in 1929 half of them netted less than

$3,000) and were idle much of the time. When some relief units and the Farm Security Administration offered medical aid to the destitute, the demand was overwhelming. Senator Wagner in 1938 introduced a national health bill, but it met stern opposition from the American Medical Association. Voluntary group health and hospitalization plans spread rapidly in some sixty cities and gained 3 million or more subscribers.

While scientists suffered temporary cuts in research funds, university budgets and industrial resources for research were back at a peak level by 1936; federal expenditures, by 1940. Thus the decade was one of increasing scientific investigation. The need for reorganization and reinvigoration of some of the government's scientific agencies led to the creation in 1933 of a Science Advisory Board, which futilely tried to obtain a New Deal for science. In 1935 the National Resources Committee (succeeding several similar planning agencies) took over the problem and prepared a study, *Research—A National Resource* (1940). The way was being prepared for centralized scientific planning in the future.

The thirties were years of marked scientific achievement in both basic and applied research in many fields. A series of discoveries by individuals of many nationalities opened the way to the possibility of nuclear fission. In 1931 Harold C. Urey of Columbia discovered a heavy isotope of hydrogen—deuterium—which, combined with oxygen atoms, formed heavy water. Bombardment of deuterium atoms by various types of atom smashers brought new knowledge about the nature of the atom, knowledge that could lead to revolutionary applications. Science, a neglected stepchild of the New Deal, was to become the nation's savior in time of war.

sixteen
America Faces the World Crisis

When the Roosevelt administration first took office, the threat of a second world war already darkened distant horizons. Gradually, through the thirties the threat became more and more immediate, until most Americans came to feel there was little likelihood war would be avoided. At the same time, they and their President were determined that the United States should not become involved. There was no question most people wished the nation to remain a neutral bystander, but there was no certainty that the United States could avoid being pulled into the vortex of the world crisis.

SEEKING FRIENDS AND CUSTOMERS

President Roosevelt inherited from the Hoover administration the questions of war-debt settlements, disarmament, and currency stabilization. He did not share Hoover's view that the proper settlement of these was a key to recovery. In April 1934 he signed an act sponsored by Senator Hiram Johnson, forbidding private loans to any defaulting nations; from then on all war-debt payments, except those from Finland, stopped altogether. Meanwhile, the United States continued to assert a strong moral position to try to bring about substantial disarmament. But Hitler was bent upon rearming, not disarming, and in October he withdrew from both the Geneva Conference and the League of Nations. A new arms race was under way.

In the same months that hopes for an arms settlement collapsed, so did those for international economic stabilization, and the blame this time was assessed against Roosevelt. He had agreed to cooperate in the World Economic Conference, which President Hoover had called to meet in London in June 1933. He gave vague assurances to the representatives of eleven countries who visited him in advance that he favored currency stabilization, which he announced on May 16 was essential to "establish order in place of the present chaos." This was the policy under which Secretary of State Cordell Hull, a firm believer in international economic cooperation, and the American delegation went to London. After their arrival President Roosevelt changed his mind, deciding that currency stabilization would be disadvantageous until the dollar had fallen to a competitive position on the world market. Whatever chance of agreement there had been disappeared when Roosevelt on July 3, 1933, cabled Hull a "bombshell message" disavowing currency stabilization.

The hope of stimulating foreign trade led Roosevelt to recognize Soviet Russia in November 1933. Since the revolution of November 1917 the Russian government had gone unrecognized while a number of irritating questions between the two nations continued to fester. Americans, hungry for what they unrealistically dreamed would be a substantial Russian trade, were eager for recognition. The Russians had even stronger motives for obtaining recognition, for they were afraid of being attacked by Japan. Maxim Litvinov, the Russian foreign minister, after discussions with Roosevelt at the White House, agreed that Russia would end her propaganda activities in the United States, guarantee religious freedom and protection in the courts to Americans resident in Russia, and negotiate a settlement of debts and claims.

By January 1934 Roosevelt was ready to listen seriously to Hull's homilies on the necessity of lowering tariff barriers in order to improve foreign trade. With Roosevelt's support, Congress (in June 1934) passed Hull's cherished program, the Reciprocal Trade Agreements Act. It authorized the administration to negotiate agreements, lowering tariffs by as much as 50 percent on specified goods coming in from individual nations in return for their reducing tariffs on American goods.

The immediate effect of the reciprocal trade agreements is difficult to estimate. During the depression years, they were drafted carefully to admit only products not competitive with American industry and agriculture. By 1939 Hull had negotiated agreements with twenty-one countries, ranging from Cuba to the United Kingdom. These lowered the tariff an estimated 29 percent, at the same time that they gained concessions for American exporters, especially growers of cotton and tobacco. By the end of 1938 American exports to the sixteen nations with which the United States then had trade agreements had increased nearly 40 percent.

At the Inter-American Conference at Montevideo in December 1933, Hull won such acclaim with his proposals for reciprocity that President Roosevelt gave him full support upon his return home. To small nations like Cuba, dependent upon exports to the United States, reciprocity seemed a way out of the depression. While Hull offered economic succor, he reiterated to the people of Latin America at Montevideo (and Roosevelt said the same thing in Washington) that the United States was opposed to armed intervention in Latin America. Hull even signed a convention declaring: "No state has the right to intervene in the internal or external affairs of another."

Thus Hull took the United States a step further than the Hoover administration, which had unofficially disavowed the Theodore Roosevelt Corollary to the Monroe Doctrine but had reserved the right to intervene in self-defense. This seemed to be the American policy, as late as the summer of 1933, when revolution exploded in Cuba. Sumner Welles, one of the chief drafters of the new Latin American policy, was sent into Cuba to offer the "good offices" of the United States. Welles helped bring pacification without calling in the marines. In 1934, when a more conservative government came into power in Cuba, the United States gave up its right of intervention under the Platt Amendment. It also withdrew the last marines from Haiti and negotiated a treaty (not ratified until 1939) relaxing the restrictions upon Panama.

The new Good Neighbor policy of nonintervention received a severe testing in 1938 when Mexico expropriated all foreign oil holdings, including property valued by its American owners at $200 million. The United States conceded the right of expropriation but at first contended that the price the Mexicans wished to pay was so trivial as to be confiscation. In 1942, after years of involved controversy, a commission evaluated the property at $24 million, and the State Department then told the protesting oil companies that they must accept the settlement or receive nothing. This renunciation of the right to intervene for the purpose of protecting American property in Latin America was a reversal of dollar diplomacy. In encouraging trade, the new policy was of immediate benefit. It came to be even more valuable in promoting mutual defense, as the threat of war in Europe increased.

As for the Philippines, primarily the depression and secondarily isolationism brought them the long-sought but economically dubious blessing of independence. American producers of sugar, fats, and oils were determined to push their Filipino competitors outside the tariff wall. Isolationists were also eager to drop this dangerous Far Eastern military commitment. The Tydings-McDuffie Act of 1934 thrust upon the Philippines complete independence rather than the dominion status they sought. In 1935 the Philippines entered upon a transitional commonwealth period; on July 4, 1946, they became a fully independent republic. The United States was demonstrating that it was trying to rid itself of possessions rather than seize new ones.

At the London Naval Conference of 1935 the Japanese withdrew after they failed to obtain equality with the Americans and British in place of the 5:5:3 ratio, and thus the way was opened for competitive naval building. The United States soon turned to building the fleet with which it was later to fight the opening battles of a Pacific war.

LEGISLATING NEUTRALITY

With the breakdown of the naval status quo and the threatened aggressions in both Asia and Europe, most Americans felt that at all costs they must stay out of impending wars. Many leaders of the peace movement—dedicated Wilsonians and advocates of the League—had become disgusted with the League's inability to stop Japanese aggression. They reasoned that internationalism had failed to maintain the peace. Others, taking an economic-determinist view of wars, concluded that Wall Streeters and munitions makers, along with Wilson's legalistic insistence upon outmoded neutral rights on the high seas, had trapped the nation into World War I. Senate investigators, under the progressive Republican Gerald P. Nye of North Dakota, revealed exorbitant wartime profits and tax evasion and claimed that bankers had sought war to rescue their loans to the Allies. President Roosevelt, himself impressed by the Nye investigation, privately wrote his regret that Bryan had left the State Department in 1915.

The Nye Committee findings and similar sensational popular writings convinced a large part of the public that entrance into World War I had been a frightful mistake. The way to avoid its repetition seemed to be to legislate against the supposed causes. As Mussolini openly prepared to conquer Ethiopia in 1935, Americans feared that a general European war might develop. They felt that the way to avoid involvement was not to participate in strong deterring pressure against Italy, since Mussolini might strike back. Rather, it was to isolate the nation by means of neutrality laws.

President Roosevelt also favored legislation, but he desired, as Hull had proposed in 1933, a law that would enable the President to embargo war supplies to the aggressor and allow their sale to the victim. But Congress passed a neutrality act providing a mandatory embargo against both aggressor and victim and empowering the President to warn American citizens that they might travel on vessels of belligerents only at their own risk. This first Neutrality Act of 1935, a temporary measure, was renewed in 1936 and again, with even stronger provisions, in 1937.

When the attack upon Ethiopia came, in October 1935, the League branded Italy an aggressor and voted sanctions against her. Britain and France made gestures against Italy but showed no inclination toward determined action. Hull imposed a "moral embargo" upon oil. Mussolini easily conquered his African empire and then withdrew from the League. In October 1936 he joined with Hitler to form a new Rome-Berlin axis.

All this seemed to strengthen the determination of the American people to stay out of war. The new public opinion polls (based on samplings of only 1,500 to 3,500 people, with a probable error of 4 to 6 percent) indicated top-heavy opinion against involvement. A typical poll in November 1935, after the attack on Ethiopia, queried: "If one foreign nation insists upon attacking another, should the United States join with other nations to compel it to stop?" The answer was: yes, 28 percent; no, 67 percent; no opinion, 5 percent.

This anti-involvement sentiment continued to be the mood of the nation when a new danger arose in July 1936, as General Francisco Franco and the Falangists (modeled after the Fascists) revolted against the republican government in Spain. Hitler and Mussolini sided with Franco;

Russia, France, and, to a lesser extent, Great Britain favored the Loyalists. To prevent the Spanish Civil War from spreading into a general European conflict, Britain and France agreed to send no aid to either side. Roosevelt, trying to cooperate with France and Britain, persuaded Congress to apply the existing Neutrality Act to civil as well as international wars. The result was that the United States and other Western nations denied assistance to republican Spain. The republican government came to depend increasingly upon Russia for what little help it received. As for Franco, he received massive aid from Mussolini and Hitler, and ultimately crushed the Loyalists.

American feelings became inflamed over the invasion of Ethiopia and the Spanish Civil War, but President Roosevelt voiced the majority attitude in August 1936, a month after the outbreak of the war in Spain, when he asserted: "We shun political commitments which might entangle us in foreign wars; we avoid connection with the political activities of the League of Nations. . . . We are not isolationists except in so far as we seek to isolate ourselves completely from war."

FACING JAPAN AND GERMANY

A great Japanese drive into the five northern provinces of China began in the summer of 1937. At first the State Department pursued a middle-of-the-road policy, favoring neither country. Japan avoided declaring war, and President Roosevelt did not invoke the Neutrality Act. Private American ships at their own risk could carry arms and munitions to both belligerents. The administration's purpose was to help the Chinese, who needed American supplies more than the Japanese did.

By October 1937 the administration was ready to take a firm position against Japan. The British proposed a joint arms embargo, which seemed to involve no great risk. At this time and during the next four years, the consensus of the experts was that Japan was a mediocre military power. Hull persuaded Roosevelt to make a statement to counteract isolationism. The President, speaking in Chicago, declared: "The peace-loving nations must make a concerted effort in opposition to those violations of treaties and those ignorings of humane instincts which today are creating a state of international anarchy, international instability from which there is no escape through mere isolation or neutrality." War, he asserted, was a contagion that must be quarantined by the international community.

There is evidence that Roosevelt had in mind nothing more drastic than a collective breaking off of diplomatic relations, that he did not favor economic or military sanctions. Immediate press reaction and White House mail was favorable, but within a few days, as the Chicago *Tribune* and Hearst press continued to draw sinister implications from the "quarantine" speech, it plunged the nation, as the *Tribune* reported, into a "hurricane of war fright." This set Roosevelt back in his thinking. In November 1937 he sent a delegate to an international conference in Brussels to consider the Japanese aggression—but instructed him neither to take the lead nor to be a tail to the British kite.

Japan had no need to fear economic or military reprisals from the United States. On December 12, 1937, young Japanese aviators bombed and sank the United States gunboat *Panay* on the Yangtze River. The aviators claimed they bombed it in error, but visibility was excellent and an American flag was painted on the deck. As at the sinking of the *Maine* in 1898, a wave of excitement swept the country, but this time it was fear that the nation might become involved in war. The United States quickly accepted the profuse Japanese apologies and offers of indemnity.

At the end of 1938, as the Japanese supplanted the Open Door with their so-called New Order in East Asia, they were making conditions almost untenable for Americans in China. But the threat of war in Europe overshadowed the Asian impasse.

The traditional American isolationism, as exemplified by Hearst editorials and the speeches of several senators, implied strict nonintervention in Europe but a considerably more active role in Asia—no sanctions but an insistence upon the Open Door in China. Within the Western Hemisphere these isolationists were ready to give the President almost a free hand toward both Canada and Latin America. Indeed, there were no more devout exponents of the Monroe Doctrine than they.

Roosevelt took full advantage of these feelings to inaugurate, within the hemisphere, policies that he could later apply across the Atlantic and the Pacific. In December 1936 he traveled to Buenos Aires to put his personal prestige behind a pact to enlarge the Monroe Doctrine into a mutual security agreement. Henceforth, if any outside power threatened the American republics, instead of the United States acting unilaterally, they would all consult together for their own protection. The understanding covered disputes among the republics themselves but was specifically aimed at meeting the threat of the Axis. It provided that the members would consult "in the event of an international war outside America which might menace the peace of the American Republics." In December 1938, with war in Europe imminent, the republics, at a meeting in Lima, Peru, established a means of consultation. Roosevelt also extended hemispheric security to the north when he issued a declaration of solidarity with Canada in August 1938.

By 1938 Hitler had rebuilt such a strong German army and air force that he was ready to embark upon a course of intimidation and conquest. In March he proclaimed union with Austria and paraded triumphantly through Vienna. This union put western Czechoslovakia into the jaws of a German vise. Hitler began tightening it with demands on behalf of the minority of 3.5 million Germans in Czechoslovakia. In September 1938 he brought Europe to the brink of war with his demands for the cession of the Sudeten area in which the minority lived. The Czechs, who had a strong army, were ready to fight rather than submit, but the people of other Western nations, appalled at the threat of another world conflict, were eager for a settlement on almost any terms. Roosevelt joined in the pleas to Hitler for a peaceful solution. At Munich on September 29 the French and the British signed a pact with Hitler granting his demands in Czechoslovakia. "This is the last territorial claim I have to make in Europe," he declared.

Within a few weeks the once strong Czechoslovakia was whittled down to impotence. In March 1939 Hitler took over the remaining areas as German protectorates, thus demonstrating the worthlessness of his Munich pledge. In April he began harassing Poland. The British and French, seeing clearly that appeasement had failed, gave firm pledges to Poland and to other threatened nations. They made half-hearted gestures toward Russia, which had been left out of the Munich settlement, but Stalin signed a nonaggression pact with Hitler in August. The pact freed Hitler to attack Poland if he could not frighten that country into submission. Poland stood firm, and Germany invaded her territory on September 1, 1939. Great Britain and France, true to their pledges, declared war on Germany on September 3. World War II had begun.

AIDING THE ALLIES

With the outbreak of war Roosevelt issued a neutrality proclamation pointedly different from Wilson's 1914 plea for Americans to be impartial in thought as well as action. "This nation will remain a neutral nation," Roosevelt stated, "but I cannot ask that every American remain neutral in thought as well."

Promptly, Roosevelt called Congress into special session and, despite a heated debate, was able to muster the votes for a revision of the Neutrality Act. The 1939 measure still prohibited American ships from entering the war zones, but it allowed belligerents to purchase arms on a "cash-and-carry" basis. Had Britain and France been able to defeat Hitler with this limited assistance, Roosevelt probably would have been satisfied with it. Indeed, after the quick Nazi overrunning of Poland, overoptimistic American publicists during the quiet winter of 1939–1940 asserted that the Allies were calling Hitler's bluff and, after a long and boring blockade on sea and land, would triumph. During these months of the "phony war," American indignation flared hottest over the Russian invasion of Finland. The administration applied a tight "moral embargo" on shipments of munitions to Russia but went no further.

Optimistic illusions about Hitler's weakness turned into panic in the spring of 1940 when the Nazis invaded Denmark and Norway, then swept across the Netherlands and Belgium deep into France. On May 16 Roosevelt asked Congress for an additional billion dollars for defense expenditures and obtained it quickly. On the premise that the United States must build great air armadas to hold off the Nazis, he set a goal of at least 50,000 airplanes a year.

On June 10, 1940, Mussolini joined the Germans by attacking France. Roosevelt that evening asserted: "The hand that held the dagger has struck it into the back of its neighbor." And, with France tottering from the German onslaught, he proclaimed that the United States would "extend to the opponents of force the material resources of this nation." He was taking the United States from a status of neutrality to one of non-belligerency on the side of the democracies.

Twelve days later France fell, and in all western Europe only the shattered remnants of the British army that had been retrieved from Dunkirk opposed the Nazis. Already the new prime minister, Winston Churchill, was showering Roosevelt with requests for destroyers and arms of all kinds to help the British man their bastion. The odds against the British were heavy, but Roosevelt made the bold and dangerous decision to "scrape the bottom of the barrel" and make it possible for the British to buy all available war materials. As the Germans, preparing for an invasion, began to bomb Britain from the air, Roosevelt gave Britain fifty overage destroyers in return for ninety-nine-year leases on eight bases to be located on British possessions ranging from Newfoundland to British Guiana in the Western Hemisphere. The "destroyer deal" was, as Churchill later wrote, "a decidedly unneutral act." Roosevelt also turned back to the factories government-purchased war planes to be resold to Britain. In September 1940 he gave an indication that aid would not be confined indefinitely to materials alone when he pushed through Congress the Burke-Wadsworth bill, which inaugurated the first peacetime conscription in American history.

Roosevelt threw the resources of the United States behind the British as completely as Congress would let him. He did so with the feeling that an Axis victory would mean disaster to the nation. A large part of the public suddenly seemed to agree. In March 1940 only 43 percent of those polled thought a German victory would be a threat to the United States; by July, 69 percent did. In May 1940 only 35 percent favored aid to Britain at the risk of American involvement; four months later, 60 percent did. Yet as late as November 1941 only 20 percent of those polled favored a declaration of war against Germany. Roosevelt and the American public seemed to share incompatible aims. They wished to bring about the defeat of the Axis without involving the United States in a shooting war. Sometime in the next eighteen months Roosevelt probably came to feel that complete entrance into the war was desirable; the public never did.

"INTERVENTION" OR "ISOLATION"?

The whole country was drawn into a great debate on the issue of neutrality as against all-out aid to the Allies. With a rather careless use of words on both sides, the advocates of neutrality called their opponents interventionists, and the advocates of all-out aid responded with the term "isolationists."

William Allen White, the Kansas editor, headed the Committee to Defend America by Aiding the Allies, often called the White Committee.

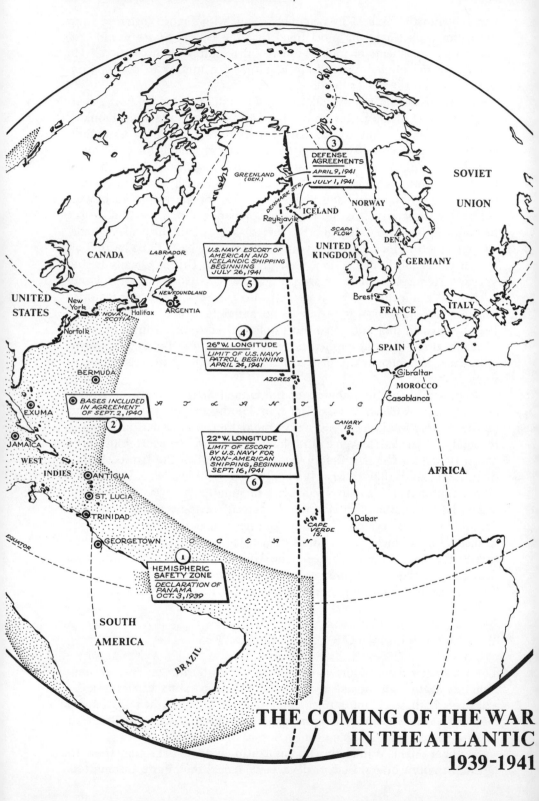

DEFENSE
AGREEMENTS
APRIL 9, 1941
JULY 1, 1941

U.S. NAVY ESCORT OF
AMERICAN AND
ICELANDIC SHIPPING
BEGINNING
JULY 26, 1941

26° W. LONGITUDE
LIMIT OF U.S. NAVY
PATROL BEGINNING
APRIL 24, 1941

BASES INCLUDED
IN AGREEMENT
OF SEPT. 2, 1940

22° W. LONGITUDE
LIMIT OF ESCORT
BY U.S. NAVY FOR
NON-AMERICAN
SHIPPING, BEGINNING
SEPT. 16, 1941

HEMISPHERIC
SAFETY ZONE
DECLARATION OF
PANAMA
OCT. 3, 1939

GREENLAND
(DEN.)

DENMARK STR.

ICELAND

Reykjavik

SOVIET

UNION

NORWAY

SCAPA
FLOW

DEN.

UNITED
KINGDOM

GERMANY

CANADA

LABRADOR

NEWFOUNDLAND

ARGENTIA

Brest

FRANCE

ITALY

UNITED

STATES

New
York

NOVA
SCOTIA

Halifax

Norfolk

SPAIN

Gibraltar

MOROCCO

Casablanca

BERMUDA

AZORES

A   T   L   A   N   T   I   C

EXUMA

CANARY
IS.

JAMAICA

WEST

INDIES

ANTIGUA

AFRICA

ST. LUCIA

TRINIDAD

Dakar

GEORGETOWN

O   C   E   A   N

CAPE
VERDE
IS.

EQUATOR

SOUTH

AMERICA

BRAZIL

THE COMING OF THE WAR
IN THE ATLANTIC
1939-1941

The Red Cross flew bandages and dressings to Europe both before and after the United States entered the war (AMERICAN RED CROSS)

White himself (like a large percentage of Americans) favored merely aid, but a minority wanted to go further and declare war. In April 1941 this group founded the Fight for Freedom Committee. On the anti-involvement side, a Yale student, R. Douglas Stuart, Jr., organized an America First Committee under the chairmanship of a leading Chicago business- man, General Robert E. Wood. It drew upon the oratorical talent of the aviation hero Charles Lindbergh, General Hugh Johnson, and Senators Nye and Wheeler. It won the editorial support of the Hearst and other large newspapers. It appealed to a considerable segment of patriotic Amer- icans, and inevitably it also attracted a small fringe of pro-Nazi, anti- Semitic, and American Fascist fanatics. The debate was bitter, and through the summer and fall of 1940 it was complicated by a presiden- tial election.

The Republicans met at Philadelphia in June, at the time of the col- lapse of France. National defense suddenly became the most important issue. Roosevelt underscored this and stole headlines from the Republican convention by appointing to his cabinet two of the most distinguished Re- publicans. He made the elder statesman Henry L. Stimson the Secretary of War, and the 1936 vice-presidential candidate and sharp critic of the New Deal, Frank Knox, the Secretary of the Navy.

The chagrined Republicans at Philadelphia promptly read Stimson and Knox out of the party but could not ignore the defense issue. They suc- cumbed to the grass-roots pressure, which had been built up through a careful advertising campaign, and nominated a young internationalist, Wendell Willkie. This was a startling blow to the isolationist majority among the Republican politicians, but it provided them with a tousle- haired, personable candidate who could win hysterical devotion from the amateur party workers. Both the platform and the candidate pledged that

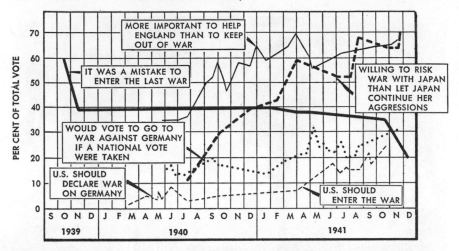

Public Opinion about Intervention, 1939–1941 (REPRODUCED BY PERMISSION
OF PROFESSOR HADLEY CANTRIL AND THE PUBLIC OPINION RESEARCH PROJECT
OF PRINCETON UNIVERSITY)

the nation would be kept out of war but would aid peoples fighting for
liberty.

By the time the Democrats met in mid-July, it was a foregone conclusion that they would renominate Roosevelt. He was even able to force
the Democratic politicians to swallow his choice for Vice President, Secretary of Agriculture Henry A. Wallace, who was considered an advanced
New Dealer.

Willkie embarked upon an appealing but slightly amateurish campaign, whistle stopping so vigorously that he nearly lost his voice, denouncing the bad management of the New Deal rather than its basic program, and always referring to his opponent as "the third-term candidate"
(no President had ever run for a third term before). Numerous right-
wing Democrats and even some early New Dealers like Moley and General Johnson supported him. John L. Lewis threatened to resign as president of the CIO if Willkie was not elected—a possibility that did not
seem to frighten organized labor.

Roosevelt, a wily old campaigner, tried to give the appearance of not
campaigning at all. Defense problems were so acute, he insisted, that he
had to spend his time touring army bases, munitions plants, and shipyards. He followed routes that somehow took him through innumerable cities, where he cheerily greeted quantities of voters.

Foreign policy was paramount. On this both Willkie and Roosevelt
had much the same views. Willkie approved of the destroyer-bases agreement. Both made fervent antiwar statements to placate the isolationists.
Willkie declared that if Roosevelt's promise to stay out of a foreign war
was no better than his pledge to balance the budget, the boys were "already almost on the transports." This was an effective campaign issue that
cut into Roosevelt's support. In Boston, Roosevelt (making the mental

Wendell Willkie (NATIONAL AR-
CHIVES)

reservation that any attack upon the United States would not be a foreign war) picked up the challenge in words the isolationists were to mock incessantly: "I have said this before, but I shall say it again and again and again: Your boys are not going to be sent into any foreign wars."

A large part of the vote of those opposing aid to the Allies went to Willkie. Those favoring vigorous aid or even intervention (including many who fervently opposed New Deal domestic policies) voted for Roosevelt. They preferred Roosevelt's sure leadership to Willkie's inexperience. It was a relatively close vote: 27,244,000 for Roosevelt, and 22,305,000 for Willkie; 449 electoral votes to 82. The combined third-party vote was less than 200,000. Within a few weeks Willkie was on his way to Britain with a letter from Roosevelt to Churchill in his pocket.

ARSENAL OF DEMOCRACY

By mid-December, the British had so nearly exhausted their financial resources that they had practically stopped making new contracts, yet Churchill warned Roosevelt that their needs would increase tenfold in the future. The Neutrality Act of 1939 and the Johnson Act of 1934 forbade American loans; a request for repeal would have reawakened the old ill feelings about unpaid war debts. Roosevelt, cruising in the Caribbean after the election, thought of a formula. The United States, "to eliminate the dollar sign," should lend goods rather than money, while serving as an "arsenal of democracy."

A Lend-Lease bill went into the congressional hopper at the right

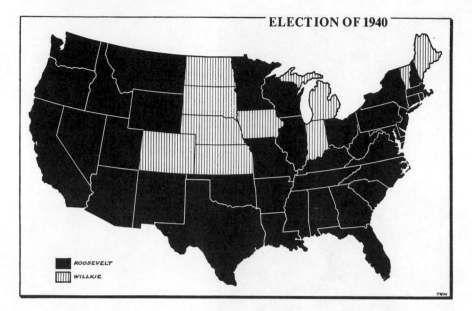

moment to bear a significant number: it became House Resolution No. 1776. After fierce debate, the bill went through Congress by a wide margin and was signed by the President in March 1941. It empowered him to spend an initial $7 billion—a sum as large as all the controversial loans of World War I.

Lend-Lease formally committed the United States to the policy the President had been following since the fall of France, the policy of pouring aid into Great Britain to help her withstand the German onslaught. Since Lend-Lease shipments had to cross the Atlantic to be of aid, the United States acquired a vital interest in keeping the Atlantic sea lanes open against the formidable wolf packs of German submarines, which in the spring of 1941 were destroying a half-million tons of shipping a month, twice as much as could be replaced. The President did not dare to convoy vessels openly to Britain as Secretary Stimson urged; isolationists in Congress were too powerful. Instead, he fell back upon the advice of "hemispheric defense." The American republics had proclaimed an Atlantic neutrality zone in 1939; in 1941 Roosevelt extended it far to the east, almost to Iceland, and ordered the navy to patrol the area and give warning of aggressors. This meant radioing to the British naval and air forces the location of Nazi submarines. The United States occupied Greenland in April 1941 and began escorting convoys as far as Iceland in July.

In secret, the United States had gone even further, for in the spring of 1941 American and British officers in Washington reached agreement on the strategy to be followed if the United States should enter the war. President Roosevelt demonstrated publicly in August 1941 how close he had come to carrying the United States from nonbelligerency to cobelligerency with Britain when he met with Prime Minister Churchill off the coast of Newfoundland. Roosevelt refused to make military commitments

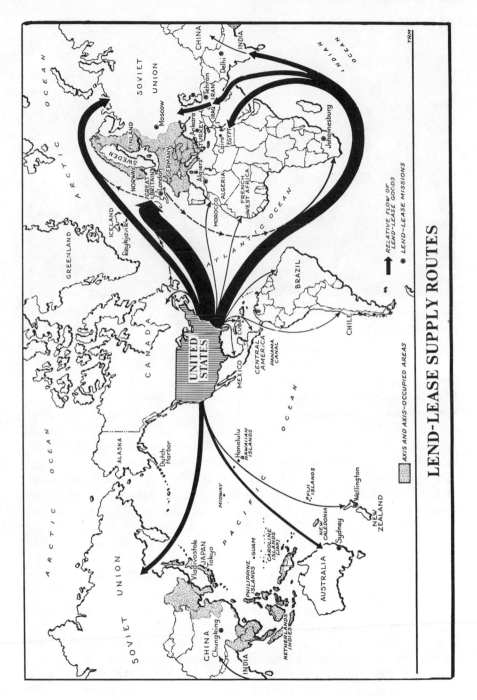

LEND-LEASE SUPPLY ROUTES

Lend-Lease supplies for Russia being unloaded on the Persian Gulf (NATIONAL ARCHIVES)

but did join Churchill in signing a press release on mutual war aims—the Atlantic Charter. As Churchill later pointed out, Roosevelt, representing a nation not at war, subscribed to a document that referred to "the final destruction of the Nazi tyranny" as a war aim.

In June 1941 Hitler unleashed against Russia a surprise attack so powerful that American military leaders predicted that Russia would collapse in a few weeks or months. The Russians fell back before the deep Nazi invasion but continued to fight, and in September Roosevelt, again gambling, extended Lend-Lease to them. This made it even more imperative to patrol the seas effectively.

The German answer was to strike back with submarines. In May 1941 they sank the American ship *Robin Moor* off the coast of Brazil. The Nazis replied to protests by saying: "Germany will continue to sink every ship with contraband for Britain whatever its name." In September a submarine attacked but failed to hit the destroyer *Greer*, which was radioing the submarine's position to the British. President Roosevelt, who did not know or at least did not reveal what the *Greer* was doing, issued orders to the navy to "shoot on sight." In October another destroyer was hit, and the *Reuben James* was sunk. Congress voted legislation to arm merchantmen and allow them to sail to belligerent ports. Naval war with the Nazis was under way.

The Chief of Naval Operations, Admiral Harold R. Stark, wrote in his diary that Hitler "has every excuse in the world to declare war on us now, if he were of a mind to." But Hitler was not, and war came from the Pacific, not the Atlantic.

PEARL HARBOR

The Japanese saw in the European crisis an unparalleled opportunity to extend their empire. In the summer of 1939 they forced from Great Britain concessions that demonstrated their intentions. The United States promptly took a most serious step and gave the requisite six months' notice to terminate its 1911 commercial treaty with Japan. Beginning in January 1940 the United States was free to cut off its shipments of oil, scrap iron, and other raw materials.

The United States was determined to restrain Japan, even at the risk of a war. More was at stake than tin, rubber, and other vital raw materials. In September 1940 Japan signed a defensive alliance with Germany and Italy (the Tripartite Pact); any further Japanese thrusts would damage the world status quo to which the State Department was committed. The administration policy toward Japan was inseparably interrelated with and subordinate to that policy toward Germany.

Under the Export Control Act, by the fall of 1940 the United States had placed an embargo upon aviation gasoline and almost all raw materials with military potential, including scrap iron and steel. Already war was close. The Japanese government of Prince Konoye wished to conciliate the United States if it could do so without serious concessions. Negotiations began in the spring of 1941 and dragged on into December. At first the Japanese informally suggested rather generous proposals, but by May they were making formal ones that were unacceptable: the United States should ask Chiang Kai-shek to make peace on Japan's terms, should restore normal trade with Japan, and should help Japan procure natural resources in Southeast Asia.

The German attack upon Russia relieved the Japanese of one of their greatest worries, since they thought they no longer needed to fear interference from Siberia. They decided to move into southern Indochina and Thailand. The United States had broken the Japanese code and, through intercepted messages, knew this was probably a prelude to attacks upon Singapore and the Dutch East Indies. At the end of July 1941, when the Japanese occupied southern Indochina, the United States, acting firmly with the British and the Dutch, froze Japanese assets in their respective countries, so that the Japanese could not convert these assets into cash. This put the Japanese into such a desperate plight that they would either have to abandon their aggressions or attack British or Dutch East Indian possessions to get needed supplies.

Since the Japanese naval leaders wished to avoid a war they feared they might lose, the Japanese cabinet sought a compromise. Konoye requested a personal meeting with Roosevelt at which Konoye was ready to make some concessions. (Simultaneously, Japan prepared for war in case agreement could not be reached.) Roosevelt was enthusiastic, since Konoye was ready to promise that Japan would not expand further southward and would not attack the United States in the event of war with Germany. Hull was becoming discouraged because he feared Konoye could not bind

The magazine of the U.S.S. Shaw *exploding during the Japanese raid on Pearl Harbor* (OFFICIAL U.S. NAVY PHOTO)

the Supreme Command. On Hull's advice, Roosevelt refused to meet Konoye without specific advance commitments about China, and these Konoye would not give.

Roosevelt and Hull seemed to make the foolish error of thinking Japan was bluffing when she was not. Instead of granting limited concessions that would have strengthened the Japanese moderates and postponed or avoided a war that the United States was in no position to fight in 1941, the American policy makers took an adamant moralistic position that played into the hands of the Japanese extremists. The Japanese made an even more grievous miscalculation by provoking a war that few of their leaders were sure they could win.

Each nation refused to budge on the question of China. On November 20, 1941, Japan offered a modus vivendi (temporary settlement) highly favorable to herself. Hull rejected it and replied in the basic American terms, insisting that Japan get out of China. He not only knew Japan would not accept these terms but knew also, through intercepted Japanese messages, that she had made her last offer and that after November 29 things would happen automatically. "I have washed my hands of the Japanese situation," Hull told Stimson on November 27, "and it is now in the hands of you and Knox, the Army and Navy."

The United States knew that Japan was on the move and that war was imminent. A large Japanese convoy was moving southward through the China Sea. The administration thought an attack upon American territory unlikely. The commanders in Hawaii were routinely warned. Negligence there and in Washington, not diabolical plotting as was later charged, led to disaster ahead. Meanwhile, on November 25, a Japanese naval task force had sailed eastward from the Kuriles.

At 7:55 on Sunday morning, December 7, 1941, the first wave of Japanese airplanes hit the United States naval base at Pearl Harbor, Hawaii; a second wave came an hour later. The attacks were successful beyond Japan's greatest expectations. Within two hours the planes destroyed or severely damaged 8 battleships, 3 light cruisers, 4 miscellaneous vessels, 188 airplanes, and important shore installations. There were 3,435 casualties. The Japanese task force withdrew without being detected, having lost 29 airplanes, 5 midget submarines, and fewer than 100 men. In the first strike the United States was rendered almost impotent in the Pacific, but the bitterly wrangling nation was suddenly unified for the global war into which it had been precipitated.

seventeen
Outproducing the Axis

In the grim days following the attack on Pearl Harbor, the United States, along with its allies, seemed powerless before the onslaught of Japan, Germany, and Italy. Yet experts, comparing the potential war production of the United States with that of the Axis, never lost their optimism. They were sure that it was only a question of time before the United States could pour such weight of armaments into the struggle that the tide would turn.

The American nation was united in the task of producing these armaments and training the men to fight with them. On the Monday after the debacle at Pearl Harbor, millions of Americans listened at their radios as President Roosevelt grimly addressed Congress: "Yesterday, December 7, 1941—a date which will live in infamy—the United States of America was suddenly and deliberately attacked by the naval and air forces of the Empire of Japan." Within four hours the Senate unanimously and the House 388 to 1 voted for a war resolution against Japan. Three days later Germany and Italy declared war on the United States, and on the same day, December 11, Congress reciprocated without a dissenting vote.

Total war (the enlistment of all the people and resources of a nation in the effort) made the planning of industrial production as vital as military strategy. The Industrial Mobilization Plan of 1939 had stated:

> War is no longer simply a battle between armed forces in the field—it is a struggle in which each side strives to bring to bear against the enemy the coordinated power of every individual and of every material resource at its command. The conflict extends from the soldier in the front line to the citizen in the remotest hamlet in the rear.

MOBILIZING FOR DEFENSE

At the time of the Munich crisis in 1938, Roosevelt had ordered the armed forces to modernize their production plan. Just before the outbreak of war in Europe, he authorized the War and Navy departments to appoint a civilian advisory committee to survey the 1939 plan. This was the War Resources Board, made up of five leaders of big business together with the presidents of the Massachusetts Institute of Technology and the Brookings Institution and an army colonel. At this point politics began. The unfortunate use of the word "war" rather than "defense" in the title frightened the public, especially after the invasion of Poland, when even the existence of such a body seemed a move toward involvement. The firmly anti–New Deal attitude of the board pained Roosevelt. He speedily disbanded the War Resources Board and submitted to the pressures against substituting any new defense agencies.

With the collapse of France in the late spring of 1940, however, Roosevelt could delay mobilization no longer. At the time of Pearl Harbor, the United States still had small amounts of armaments because so much had been shipped to Great Britain and because so many of the plants had only recently begun production. The new productive capacity was remarkably large. Despite errors and chaotic conditions, the United States was producing more combat munitions than any of the belligerents—indeed almost as much as Germany and Japan combined. Airplane production was up to a rate of almost 25,000 per year. The armed forces already had inducted and were training 2 million men. This mobilization was only a fraction of what was soon to come, for a large-scale construction of factories and training camps was under way. While the nation during the debate over neutrality had not built its defenses with the smoothness and speed that critics demanded, it had achieved a substantial degree of preparedness.

The Japanese attack on Pearl Harbor created almost as much chaos indirectly in American war production as it did directly in the fleet in the Pacific. The war agencies in Washington began ordering tremendous quantities—indeed far too much—of everything.

The problem of restoring some order to war production, then raising it to astronomical totals, was a joint one. The armed forces, the Maritime Commission, and other procurement agencies did the ordering. The War Production Board (WPB) tried to control the size of the procurement program and to allocate materials between the armed forces and the civilians. The WPB was thus trying to control the entire economy and inevitably was coming into collision with the armed forces over the size and nature of war orders as opposed to what was to be reserved for civilians. Internecine conflict among the agencies and personality clashes among the administrators were unavoidable.

Out of the confusion a pattern gradually emerged. The first step, oddly enough, was to cut back the building of plants, although at times this created a furor throughout a region, as when the Higgins Shipyards in New Orleans were abandoned. After the middle of 1942 the amount of new construction being started declined sharply; in another six months the larger part of the war plants and military facilities had been built.

The second step was to coordinate the various phases of the war-pro-

The mushrooming of war plants: Two pictures taken in the same spot in 1941 (top) and 1942 indicate the speed of construction of the Morgantown, West Virginia, ordnance plant (DU PONT)

duction program. As late as the summer of 1942, bottlenecks were halting some assembly lines. The vital shipbuilding program had to be cut back because of scarcities of raw materials like steel plate and glass and of components like valves, turbines, and engines. The WPB eventually broke most of the bottlenecks through the Controlled Materials Plan, which established a balanced production of finished products and allocated precise quantities of raw materials to each manufacturer.

The shortage of rubber became so critical in 1942 that it required special attention. After the WPB failed to solve the problem, Roosevelt appointed a committee under Bernard Baruch to make a special report. This recommended sharp restrictions upon the use of motor vehicles, including a national speed limit of thirty-five miles per hour, and immediate construction of enormous synthetic rubber plants. Roosevelt ordered the restrictions and appointed a Rubber Director in the WPB, William M. Jeffers, president of the Union Pacific Railroad, to construct the plants. By the end of 1943 the synthetic rubber industry was producing one-third again as much rubber as the country had normally used before the war.

An indispensable adjunct of the war agencies was the Senate War Investigating Committee, headed by Harry S Truman, previously little known. The senators consciously patterned it after the Committee on the Conduct of the War of the Civil War period but avoided the pitfalls of their predecessors by ruling out questions of military policy. Instead, they ferreted out incompetence and corruption in the war-production and military-construction programs: outrageous expense in building army camps, improper inspection of airplane engines, a quixotic scheme to build an Arctic pipeline, and the like. The Truman Committee uncovered and stopped hundreds of millions of dollars of waste. In the wartime expenditure of $400 billion there was amazingly little corruption.

By the beginning of 1944 factories had turned out what seemed to be needed to win the war. The output was double that of all Axis countries combined. Cutbacks began but were haphazard and ill planned, and when the armed forces met reverses, some turned out to have been premature. With the cutbacks came pressure for a resumption of the manufacture of civilian durable goods. The military leaders staunchly opposed this.

War needs even at their peak took only about one-third of American production. While manufacture of goods such as automobiles, most electrical appliances, and nondefense housing had come to a halt in 1942, production of food, clothing, and repair and maintenance goods was continued or even slightly increased.

TRANSPORTING THE SUPPLIES

As war production grew, the problem of transporting the supplies within the country and overseas became acute. Inside the United States the Office of Defense Transportation, established in December 1941, coordinated

Final assembly of airplanes in a California aircraft plant (NATIONAL ARCHIVES)

all forms of transport—railroads, trucking, airlines, inland waterways, and pipelines. In contrast to the system in World War I, railroads remained under private control but functioned effectively, carrying double the traffic of 1939 with only 10 percent more locomotives and 20 percent more freight cars. Since they could not, however, transport sufficient oil to the East when German submarines began attacking coastal tankers in 1942, the government authorized construction of the Big Inch pipeline from Texas to eastern Pennsylvania.

Transporting troops and supplies overseas required one of the most spectacular construction programs of all. The Germans had sunk more than 12 million tons of shipping by 1942. To replace it the United States Maritime Commission had to abandon its program of building fast, efficient ships requiring scarce turbines, valves, and electrical equipment. As early as July 1940, Admiral Emory S. Land, head of the commission, and William Knudsen recommended to Roosevelt mass production of a freighter that, while slow (sailing only eleven knots), would be simple to construct and would not require scarce components. By using the existing designs for an old-fashioned British tramp steamer with a reciprocating engine and steam winches, they saved six months in starting production. This "ugly duckling" was the Liberty ship. After a slow beginning, builders substituted welding for riveting and applied prefabrication and subassembly techniques in constructing it. In 1941 construction of a Liberty ship required an average of 355 days; by the end of 1942 the time had been cut to 56 days, and one of Henry J. Kaiser's companies completed one in 14 days. During 1942 alone, 8 million tons of shipping were built; by 1945 the United States had over 36 million tons of ships afloat.

SCIENTISTS AGAINST THE AXIS

The most revolutionary changes for the future came out of laboratories, as scientists pooled their skill in a race against those of the Axis—above all the Germans—to turn the basic knowledge that was available to all into decisive weapons of war. Between the two wars, while the United States had neglected military research and development, Germany had sprinted far ahead, except in the field of radar. In the 1920s the Naval Research Laboratory in Washington had discovered the principle of radar by bouncing back a radio beam directed at a ship on the Potomac. The British had developed radar most highly, and it was their salvation during the air blitz of 1940–1941.

Other potential weapons were in the offing that could have meant Nazi victory in the war had the Germans developed them first. (This was one of the reasons why the armed forces had decided to concentrate upon defeating Germany first.) The only way in which American scientists could catch up seemed to be through teamwork. The German threat brought the creation of a government scientific agency such as the New Deal had failed to produce. A leading scientist, Vannevar Bush, persuaded Roosevelt to create a committee for scientific research in June 1940. A year later, under the direction of Bush, it became the Office of Scientific Research and Development, which mobilized scientists with such effectiveness that in some areas they outstripped their German opponents.

The Americans and the British developed superior radar, which not only detected enemy airplanes and ships but helped direct shells against them. In these shells, by 1943, were radio-directed proximity fuses that detonated the shells as they neared their targets. American rocket research produced weapons that enormously increased the fire power of airplanes, ships, and tanks. But the Americans still lagged behind the Germans, who before the end of the war were blasting London with enormous V-1 and V-2 rockets. The Germans also built the first jet airplanes and snorkel submarines, which would have been an even more serious menace if they had come into full production.

There was a danger, little publicized, that Germany might develop an atomic weapon. In the summer of 1939 a physicist, Enrico Fermi, and a mathematician, Albert Einstein, got word to Roosevelt that German physicists had achieved atomic fission in uranium; what had long been theoretically possible had been accomplished. Next might come a bomb. Roosevelt authorized a small research project, and a race in the dark against the Nazis began.

In December 1942 physicists produced a controlled chain reaction in an atomic pile at the University of Chicago. The problem then became the enormous technical one of achieving this release of power in a bomb. Through the Manhattan District of the Army Engineer Corps the government secretly poured nearly $2 billion into one project for producing fissionable plutonium and into another, under the supervision of J. Robert Oppenheimer, for building a bomb. This was an enormous and frightening

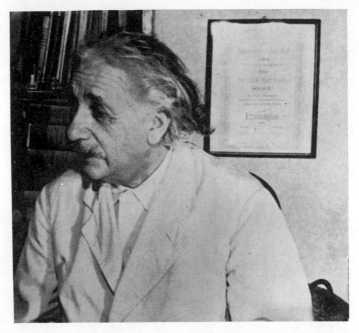

Albert Einstein working on a war project (NATIONAL ARCHIVES)

gamble, against the hazards that the device might not work and that the enemy might succeed first. Only after the war did the United States discover that the Germans were far from developing a usable atomic device. On July 16, 1945, after the end of the war in Europe, the first A-bomb was exploded, on a tower in New Mexico, producing the most blinding flash of light ever seen on earth and then a huge billowing mushroom cloud.

THE AMERICAN PEOPLE IN WARTIME

No American could escape the impact of the war effort. Everybody was affected—and most people very deeply—by war jobs, wages, prices, rationing and other controls, taxes, and propaganda. The nation, after grappling for years with the problem of millions of unemployed, found itself hard pressed for sufficient people to swell the fighting forces, man the war plants, till the fields, and keep the domestic economy functioning. There were periodic demands for national service legislation or a labor draft, but unions were so vehemently opposed that no such measure ever passed the Senate. The relatively weak War Manpower Commission tried to coerce workers into remaining at defense jobs at the risk of being drafted, but the war came to an end without any tight allocation of manpower comparable to that of materials. The armed forces had first call upon men through Selective Service, which had been in operation since the fall of 1940. Altogether, draft boards registered 31 million men. Including volunteers, over 15 million men and women served in the armed forces during the war. Nevertheless, the working force jumped from 46.5 million to over 53 million as the 7 million unemployed and many previously considered unemployable, the very young and the elderly, and several million women found jobs. The number of civilian employees of the federal government trebled.

This mobilization of manpower entailed the greatest reshuffling of population within such a short time in the entire history of the nation; altogether 27.3 million people moved during the war. It also meant a heavy weight of wartime tension on American families. With the return of prosperity and the impending departure of soldiers, both marriage and birth rates rose. In 1942 and 1943 about 3 million children were born each year, compared with 2 million a year before the war. But young wives and moth ers fared badly in crowded housing near defense plants or army bases or, after husbands had been shipped overseas, back home with parents. Draft boards deferred fathers as long as possible, but more than 1 million were ultimately inducted. More than 2.5 million wives were separated from their husbands because of the war. The divorce rate increased slowly. Because men in the armed forces could not be divorced without their consent and because many estranged wives stayed married in order to continue receiv-

Women unloading a boxcar in Cleveland, Ohio (WOMEN'S BUREAU, U.S. DEPARTMENT OF LABOR)

Welfare poster at Patterson Field, Dayton, Ohio (WOMEN'S BUREAU, U.S. DEPARTMENT OF LABOR)

ing allotment checks, a heavy backlog was built for postwar divorce courts.

When mothers were forced to work, children often suffered neglect or were upset over the change. Court cases involving juvenile delinquency, especially among children from eight to fourteen, and among girls, the "bobbysoxers," increased 56 percent. Even among the nondelinquents, a serious price had to be paid at the time and later for the disruption of more American families for a longer period of time than ever before.

As adolescents found jobs, the percentage of those between fourteen and nineteen who attended school dropped from 62 in 1940 to 56 in 1944. Teachers also left for the armed forces or better-paying war jobs. Universities kept functioning through military research projects and training programs.

The great migration to war plants was stripping the agricultural South of underprivileged whites and blacks alike, as 5 million people moved within the South and another 1.6 million left the area completely. In the South this exodus led to the false rumor among outraged white homemakers that the departing black domestics had formed "Eleanor Clubs," named after Eleanor Roosevelt, to "get a white woman in every kitchen by 1943." In the North it led to explosive tension when blacks, enjoying their new freedom, were jostled in crowded streetcars against indignant whites newly migrated from the South. A serious riot, in which twenty-five blacks and nine whites were killed, shook Detroit in June 1943. New York narrowly averted a similar disaster. At the very time when the United States was fighting a war against the racist doctrines of Hitler, many whites became resentful over the rapid gains blacks were making.

In June 1941, after the head of the Pullman porters' union, A. Philip Randolph, had threatened a march on Washington, President Roosevelt established the Fair Employment Practices Committee. It worked diligently throughout the war against discrimination in employment. By 1944, 2 million blacks were at work in the war industry, and many previous barriers to economic opportunities for blacks were permanently cracked.

Not everyone shared in the new prosperity. Government economists reported in 1943 that 10 million families still received less than the $1,675 per year requisite for a minimum standard of living. Most Americans, however, were relatively more affluent than they had been. The living standard of working people advanced rapidly. This was due less to wage increases than to payment of time and a half for overtime beyond 40 hours. The average workweek lengthened from 40.6 hours in 1941 to 45.2 in 1944. As living costs rose (on a 1935–1939 base of 100) from 100.4 in 1940 to 128.4 in 1945, gross weekly wages went up from $25.20 to $43.39. Workingwomen and children created social problems, but they also brought additional prosperity to millions of families.

Men, women, whites, and blacks at a lunch counter in a Chicago factory (WOMEN'S BUREAU, U.S. DEPARTMENT OF LABOR)

RESTRAINING LABOR UNIONS

Labor unions rapidly grew in strength during the war, and their unpopularity among Americans of the middle and upper classes increased. Union membership rose with the rise in the working force, from about 10.5 million workers in 1941 to over 13 million in 1945. Keeping these workers satisfied was no easy matter. The administration was determined to prevent strikes and to restrain the formidable pressure of the labor unions from forcing wages, and thus all prices, upward. President Roosevelt followed the procedure of World War I by establishing a National Defense Mediation Board (March 1941) made up of representatives of management, labor, and the public. In November 1941 it broke down when the CIO members resigned over the refusal of the board to recommend a union shop (that is, one in which all new workers hired must join the union) in coal mines. In January 1942 Roosevelt replaced it with the National War Labor Board, similarly constituted but much stronger. This board could set wages, hours, and working conditions, and through the war powers of the President it could enforce these in a final extremity by government seizure and operation of plants.

On the union-shop question, which was creating much hostility between management and labor, the board arrived at a compromise, the "maintenance-of-membership" clause. Nonmembers hired into a war plant did not have to join a union, but members had to remain in it, and the union remained the bargaining agent for the duration of the contract. Pressure for wage increases, which might contribute to inflation, was more serious. The board hit upon a solution in ruling upon the Little Steel cases in July 1942. Taking January 1, 1941, as the base date when workers had received a standard wage, it recognized a 15-percent rise in the cost-of-living index since then. Consequently, it felt that a proportionate increase for steelworkers would be equitable. The Little Steel formula, except for those receiving substandard wages (like some textile workers), served thereafter as a wage ceiling.

Despite the no-strike pledges of the major unions, there were nearly 15,000 work stoppages during the war, involving the loss of more than 36 million man-days. These stoppages involved only one-ninth of 1 percent of the working time (though they indirectly caused more damage than this). When Lewis' United Mine Workers defied the government in their strike against the Little Steel formula in May 1943, Congress reacted by passing over Roosevelt's veto the Smith-Connally or War Labor Disputes Act (June 1943). This act required unions to wait thirty days before striking and empowered the President to seize a struck war plant.

PRICE CONTROLS, WAR FINANCE

At the beginning of the war, with a two-year supply of wheat, cotton, and corn stored in Secretary Wallace's ever-normal granary, there seemed no danger of food shortages in the United States. But within six months after Pearl Harbor, scarcities of many kinds began to develop. The United States felt the increased demand of the armed forces and its allies and the reduction of supplies due to the loss of fibers and oils from Southeast Asia. By 1942 meat production was half again that of depression years, but American consumers with their increased buying power were eager to buy even more. Consumer income in 1943 was 65 percent above depression levels, and much of it was in the pockets of people who had not eaten adequately for years.

A food administrator did exist, Chester Davis, but he resigned in protest when his views (and those of the American Farm Bureau Federation) did not prevail; his successor was Marvin Jones. Neither man had the dictatorial powers to provide the scarce supplies and manpower that the dominant farm bloc in Congress would have liked to bestow upon agricultural producers. Rather, farmers had to depend upon whatever the WPB would allocate to them and upon a generous draft-exemption program they obtained from Congress. They also received legislation raising the ceiling on commodity prices to 110 percent of parity. Since this came into conflict with the anti-inflation efforts of the administration, a dogged struggle developed between the President and the congressional farm bloc over farm prices. Neither side won entirely.

Pressures from business, farmers, and labor, combined with the scarcity of consumer goods and the burgeoning of buying power, created an almost irresistible trend toward inflation. During the defense period, the Office of Price Administration (OPA), under a vigorous New Dealer, Leon Henderson, lacked real coercive power and failed to halt inflation. Between the invasion of Poland and the attack on Pearl Harbor, prices of twenty-eight basic commodities rose by nearly one-fourth. Immediately thereafter, pressures became so acute that prices went up 2 percent per month. Soon Congress hastily passed a bill authorizing only selective price fixing and setting ceilings with a preferential trap door for agriculture.

In April 1942 the OPA issued a General Maximum Price Regulation that froze prices of consumer goods, and of rents in defense areas only, at their March 1942 level. But the rise of uncontrolled farm prices toward 110 percent of parity forced an upward revision of food prices. This gave ammunition to the labor unions' barrage against fixed wages. In October 1942 Congress, grudgingly responding to the President's demand, passed the Anti-inflation Act. Under its authority, Roosevelt immediately froze agricultural prices, wages, salaries, and rents throughout the country.

In July 1943 Roosevelt appointed a former advertising executive with remarkable administrative talents, Chester Bowles, to head the OPA. With a small enforcement staff, Bowles braved general unpopularity to hold the increase in living costs during the next two years to 1.4 percent. Altogether, the price level went up less than 29 percent from 1939 to the end of the war, compared with 63 percent between 1914 and the armistice.

Consumers nonetheless suffered numerous irritations and discomforts. The OPA, through unpaid local volunteers manning 5,600 price and ra-

I PAY NO MORE THAN TOP LEGAL PRICES

I ACCEPT NO RATIONED GOODS WITHOUT GIVING UP RATION STAMPS

The Home Front Pledge: The OPA urged housewives to put this sticker in their windows

tioning boards, administered the rationing of canned goods, coffee, sugar, meat, butter and other fats, shoes, tires, gasoline, and fuel oil. The OPA could not, however, control deterioration of quality. Black-marketing and overcharging grew in proportions far beyond OPA policing capacity; in 1943 Congress slashed the funds of the enforcement division.

One of the most important inflationary controls was the sale of war bonds and stamps to channel off some of the excess purchasing power, which for the single year 1945 mounted to nearly $60 billion. Throughout most of the war, personal incomes were at least one-third greater than the available civilian goods and services. The Treasury Department, through eight war bond drives and its payroll deduction plans, but with few of the lurid or coercive touches of World War I, sold $40 billion worth of series "E" bonds to small investors and $60 billion more to individuals and corporate entities other than banks.

Had this been the total of government loans, the effect would have been to quell inflation, but the Treasury had to borrow $87.5 billion more from Federal Reserve and commercial banks. Since in effect the banks created new credits that the government then spent, the result was to inflate bank credits and money in circulation by over $100 billion.

Taxes did much more to drain off surplus purchasing power. The government raised 41 percent of its war costs through taxation, compared with 33 percent during World War I. The Revenue Act of 1942, which Roosevelt hailed as "the greatest tax bill in American history," levied a 94-percent tax on the highest incomes; the President had suggested that no one should net more than $25,000 per year during the war. Also, for the first time, the income tax fell upon those in lower-income brackets. To simplify payment for these new millions Congress enacted a withholding system of payroll deductions in 1943. Corporation taxes reached a maximum of 40 percent on the largest incomes. In addition, excess profits were subject to a 90-percent tax, reclaiming for the government a large part of the return from war contracts. However, these taxes could be rebated to companies to aid them in reconversion (changing back to peacetime production), a provision of future significance. In effect, the government taxed away a large part of the profits of corporations, then returned it later when it was needed. Heavy excise taxes on transportation, communication, luxuries, and amusements completed the levies.

Between 1941 and 1945 the government raised $138 billion through taxation—nearly a $100 billion of it from income and excess profits taxes. Those in the top 5 percent of the income scale suffered a serious relative economic loss, as their share of disposable income dropped from 26 percent in 1940 to 16 percent in 1944. Few persons or corporations were able to make fortunes out of the war, and a considerable amount of economic leveling—upward more than downward—had taken place. Despite the heavy taxation, by the end of the war consumers possessed an estimated $129 billion in liquid savings.

From 1941 to 1945 the federal government spent twice as much as the total appropriations from the creation of the government to 1941, and ten times as much as the cost of World War I—a total of $321 billion. The national debt rose from $49 billion in 1941 to $259 billion in 1945, yet the black warnings of national bankruptcy that had punctuated the New Deal years all but disappeared.

INFORMATION AND MISINFORMATION

As an incentive for winning the war, advertisers presented a vision of a postwar America in which every husband would have a chrome-trimmed car and every wife a gleaming kitchen filled with wonder-working gadgets. President Roosevelt promised even more. "In the future days, which we seek to make secure," he told the people (January 1941), "we look forward to a world founded upon four essential freedoms." These were freedom of speech and worship and freedom from want and fear. They were for the postwar future, not necessarily for the wartime present.

Persons Paying Personal Income Tax, 1939 and 1942

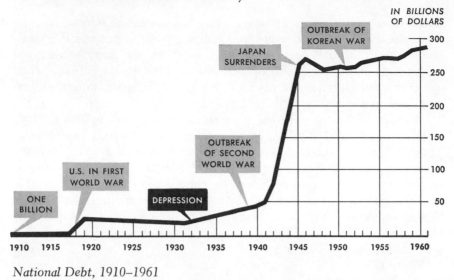

National Debt, 1910–1961

From Pearl Harbor on, there was the suspicion that through the Office of Censorship, almost immediately established under a competent Associated Press executive, Byron Price, the government was withholding information not because it was vital to the enemy but because it would be damaging to public opinion of the armed forces. Diligent newspapermen, aided by Price, exerted pressure on the armed forces to make censorship an instrument for security, rather than for the concealment of incompetence. Newspapers following Office of Censorship rules censored themselves to withhold local news that might be of value to the enemy.

The overlapping and conflict among government information agencies led to the establishment in June 1942 of the Office of War Information (OWI) under a shrewd news commentator, Elmer Davis. Although the OWI consolidated four previous organizations, it coordinated rather than assumed the information function of domestic war agencies.

The OWI aroused the misgivings of Congress, partly because of internal feuding and the mass resignation of the pamphlet writers, but mainly because conservatives objected to several of the OWI pamphlets: one on the dangers of inflation, another on blacks in the war, and another on the need for high taxes. A fourth pamphlet, intended only for overseas distribution, a cartoon biography of Roosevelt, especially worried antiadministration congressmen. They feared that the OWI might promote New Dealish policies and the 1944 candidacy of Roosevelt. In 1943 Congress cut funds for the domestic branch of the OWI so drastically that it had to stop producing propaganda.

Overseas, the OWI carried on a program employing 8,400 persons by V-E (Victory in Europe) Day. Through Voice of America broadcasts begun in 1941 and propaganda of many kinds, it presented an idealistic view of American war aims and aspirations for a peaceful postwar world. As the symbol of this idealism it dramatized Roosevelt. By the end of the

"Welders" by Ben Shahn, rejected as a poster by the O.W.I., and widely used by the CIO Political Action Committee (COLLECTION MUSEUM OF MODERN ART)

war, he was more of a hero overseas than at home, and American aims appeared more idealistic abroad than in the United States.

The war produced less hatred and vindictiveness at home than had World War I. The energy that had gone into crude vigilantism in the earlier war now went into serving as air-raid wardens and doing similar duties for the Office of Civilian Defense. People continued to eat hamburgers and sauerkraut and listen to Wagner. They demonstrated little animosity toward Americans of German background and practically none toward Italians. A few Nazi agents and American Fascists were jailed, but the most ambitious effort to punish them, a sedition trial of twenty-eight, ended in a mistrial after the defendants' lawyers had engaged in long weeks of delaying tactics. A few papers like Father Coughlin's *Social Justice* were barred from the mails. But Socialists went unpunished, and religious conscientious objectors who were willing to register went to Civilian Public Service camps rather than to prison.

FATE OF JAPANESE AMERICANS

In sad contrast to this moderation, the frenzy of public fury turned toward the Japanese. The fighting in the Pacific developed a fierce savagery, reflected in the public anger within the United States. On the Pacific Coast, hatred of Americans of Japanese background became extreme. Wild stories circulated about sabotage at Pearl Harbor and plots to aid a Japanese landing on the California coast—later proved completely untrue. Under public pressure, Roosevelt, in February 1942, authorized the army to remove all people of Japanese ancestry from the West Coast. Some

117,000 people, two-thirds of them United States citizens, were abruptly herded behind barbed wire, and later shipped into ten relocation centers in wild and disagreeable areas. They suffered the financial loss of at least 40 percent of their possessions and for several years were barred from lucrative employment. Yet Japanese Americans in Hawaii were left unmolested without incident throughout the war. There were 17,600 Japanese Americans in the armed forces. Their units, especially in Italy, established outstanding records for bravery under fire.

The Supreme Court in 1944 validated the evacuation and, in other decisions as well, upheld military control over civilians. In time of war or national emergency, United States citizens apparently could expect no court protection of their civil rights from military or executive authority. In this way the war had led to a threat to the civil rights of all Americans. During the war, no price seemed too great to pay to win security from the Axis, and restrictions upon the freedom of the individual seemed to be part of the bill.

The United States won the battle of production, even though the economic mobilization fell short of being total and efficient. It succeeded

Japanese-Americans being evacuated from the Pacific Coast (NATIONAL ARCHIVES)

only because of the larger resources and industry of the United States and because its organization was more effective than that of Germany and Japan. Because of the huge production, the United States could sustain serious losses of supplies at sea yet provide arms for its allies and supply the troops abundantly. Germans were almost incredulous at the abundance of munitions that enabled American troops advancing in France to spray trees with machine-gun bullets to drive out snipers. Heavy war production built a margin for victory and helped make that victory less costly in American lives.

eighteen
Fighting a Global War

The bombs dropped on Pearl Harbor blasted out of existence the old America living in an illusion of isolation, and the United States found itself not only fighting a global war but also having to assume an irrevocable position of open leadership among the world's nations. A minority, who earlier had been isolationists, were ready to interpret the war solely as American retaliation for a Japanese attack. The vast majority, even most of those who had opposed entrance, recognized that the nation would never again be able to retreat to the comfortable dream of isolation within the bounds of the Western Hemisphere.

The United States did not fight, as it had during World War I, as a nation gingerly "associated" with the Allies. Rather, it took the initiative in drafting and signing, on January 1, 1942, a Declaration by United Nations, setting forth the war aims of the Atlantic Charter, committing its full resources, both military and economic, to the prosecution of the war and pledging itself to cooperate with other signators and not to make a separate peace with the enemies. In effect, it was taking the lead in establishing a grand alliance, the United Nations, among the twenty-six signatory powers and the twenty more that signed before the war was over. From this beginning the United States, as it grew in military strength, took an ever more dominant lead in international diplomacy.

In war strategy, too, the United States played a determining part, very different from its 1917–1918 experience. From the outset it took the lead in the Pacific, making the war there preponderantly an American one against the Japanese. At first it deferred to Great Britain in the European area but, as American strength grew, assumed forceful leadership there also.

The United States, Great Britain, Russia, and China formed the Big Four. China did not determine global policy; Russia made her own decisions, influenced only slightly by American and British proposals. The grand alliance was, therefore, basically a close and rather smooth-working entente between the United States and Great Britain, with the British Commonwealth, the Fighting French under General Charles de Gaulle, and some of the lesser powers all contributing vigorously. The powerful Russians were associated with these countries in fighting a common enemy but were semi-isolated and suspicious. They made constant demands for Lend-Lease (and received $11 billion worth of vital supplies). They also insisted incessantly that the Western powers open a second front in France. But they participated in no combined strategic planning and seldom divulged their own plans or their knowledge of the Germans.

Postwar considerations influenced the British more than the United States in war planning. Prime Minister Churchill seemed at times to be more concerned with bringing the war to a satisfactory conclusion; President Roosevelt with bringing it to a speedy end. Roosevelt idealistically hoped to supersede power politics in time with a workable international organization. At times Churchill shared his enthusiasm; at times he pessimistically fell back on older thinking. Thus, inevitably, diplomatic problems were closely intertwined with the military during the four years of American participation, and even before the end of the war the shape of the new world was emerging.

THE AMERICAN MILITARY ORGANIZATION

In December 1941 neither the army nor the navy seemed very well prepared for the enormous tasks ahead, and Pearl Harbor had not improved confidence in their commands. Enormous industrial production alone could not win the war. The military must know what to order, and where and how to use it, on a scale they had not envisaged in their prewar establishments. The navy possessed 300 combat ships—and it was a truism that navies usually fought wars with the ships they had when hostilities commenced—but at the close of the war it had 1,167 major ships and was only employing one of the prewar vessels in the final attacks on Japan.

The army in July 1939 had officially nine infantry divisions but actually only the equivalent of about three and one-half at half strength. Nor could it organize tactical units larger than a division. By mid-1941 it had twenty-nine infantry and cavalry divisions at nearly full strength, organized into four field armies—still fewer than one-half million men. The army air force, nominally under the army but in practice almost independent, had only 22,000 officers and men and 2,400 aircraft in 1939.

There was little hint of what was to come. The most important of the war plans, "Orange," devised to go into effect in case of conflict with Japan, had presumed primarily a naval war, with the army mobilizing over a million men. By 1940 the more comprehensive "Rainbow" plans superseded these; by December 1941 a substantial mobilization was under way, though it was still far short of wartime totals.

Vast increases in personnel and equipment forced rapid changes in planning and organization. General George C. Marshall, Chief of Staff of the Army, reorganized the army high command in March 1942. That same month, Admiral Ernest J. King, a clear-headed hard driver, became Chief of Naval Operations. Together with General H. H. Arnold of the army air force, these men met with a personal representative of the President, Admiral William D. Leahy, to constitute the Joint Chiefs of Staff. They functioned as the overall command and represented the United States in combined planning with the British or occasional negotiations with the Russians.

Over the Joint Chiefs of Staff was the commander in chief, President Roosevelt, who bore responsibility for the conduct of the war. Personally, and through assistants like Harry Hopkins and cabinet members, he coordinated the war planning of the Joint Chiefs with war production and manpower and with foreign policy. The War Plans Division of the Army General Staff had pointed out that civilians should decide the "what" of national policies and the professional soldiers the "how." Roosevelt, who had always zealously guarded civilian control even in the Navy Department and the War Department, followed this course throughout the war. He depended heavily upon the advice of the Joint Chiefs of Staff and, once major policy had been decided, seldom interfered with their strategy.

The first of the great policy decisions had come in 1940, when the Americans decided that, even if Japan entered the war, their primary goal would be to defeat Germany with her superior military force, war production, and weapons development. The United States confirmed this priority in the initial wartime conference with the British at the end of December 1941. This decision did not mean neglecting the war against Japan. By August 1941, when the build-up, especially of airplanes, was under way in the Philippines, and later when General Douglas MacArthur received orders to fight, the strategy was shifting to a two-front war. The war against Germany was to be offensive, while that against Japan was to be defensive. It was difficult to hold to this policy as the Japanese tide in the Pacific swelled far beyond the bounds that the most pessimistic planners had anticipated. For Roosevelt, furious over Japanese treachery, and for the navy, primarily responsible in the Pacific, it was not an easy deci-

Expansion of U.S. Armed Forces, 1941–1945

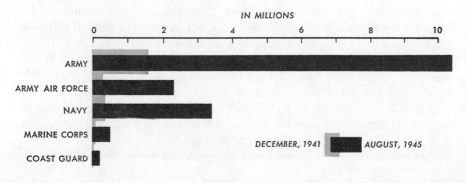

IN MILLIONS

ARMY
ARMY AIR FORCE
NAVY
MARINE CORPS
COAST GUARD

DECEMBER, 1941   AUGUST, 1945

sion to maintain. General MacArthur, the panic-stricken public on the Pacific Coast, and most Americans elsewhere clamored for prompt and stern action against the Japanese.

During the first chaotic months of shocking reverses, the armed forces allotted their men and supplies piecemeal to try to meet each new Axis threat. Top strategists emphatically warned that such dissipation of effort might lead to defeat. No one was more insistent than Dwight D. Eisenhower, who had been brought to Washington after Pearl Harbor as a Far Eastern expert and who by the spring of 1942 was head of the Operations Planning Division under General Marshall. In emphatic memoranda Eisenhower hammered away at the need to build up men and supplies in Europe for the invasion of North Africa that Roosevelt and Churchill had decided upon in their December 1941 meeting. Because of his vigor and his important role in developing an invasion plan, Eisenhower became the logical man to send to Britain (in June 1942) as commanding general in the European theater.

ON THE DEFENSIVE: 1941–1942

While the United States was building and equipping its fighting forces, it had to depend upon the Russians and the British to hold back the Germans as best they could. During the discouraging first six months of American participation, the American forces had to stand perilously on

WACs washing their mess kits (NATIONAL ARCHIVES)

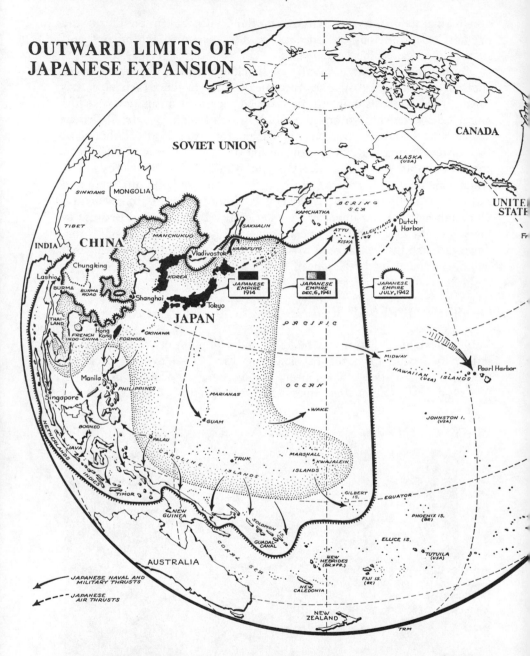

OUTWARD LIMITS OF JAPANESE EXPANSION

the defensive in both the Atlantic and the Pacific. There even seemed danger of a breakthrough in Egypt and the Caucasus that might enable the Germans and Japanese to join forces in the Middle East or India.

Ten hours after the strike at Pearl Harbor, Japanese airplanes hit the airfields at Manila, destroying half the American bombers and two-thirds of the fighter planes. That same day the Japanese sank two British warships off Malaya, the only Allied warships in the Far East. Three days later

Guam fell; then, in the weeks that followed, Wake Island and Hong Kong. The great British fortress of Singapore in Malaya surrendered in February 1942, the Dutch East Indies in March, and Burma in April. In the Philippines on May 6 the exhausted Filipino and American troops, having made brave withdrawals to the Bataan peninsula and the island of Corregidor in Manila Bay, ran down the last American flag in the Far East.

Only one weak outpost, Port Moresby in southern New Guinea, stood as a bulwark against the invasion of Australia. It seemed likely to fall, but there containment began through the efforts, on land, of Australian and American troops and, on the sea, of American aircraft carriers. In the Battle of Coral Sea on May 6–7, 1942, the Americans turned back Japanese invasion forces threatening Port Moresby. Under General MacArthur, who had escaped from the Philippines, American and Australian troops began clearing the Japanese from New Guinea.

After the Battle of Coral Sea, the navy, having intercepted Japanese messages, knew the next move and rushed every available plane and vessel into the central Pacific. Near Midway Island, June 3–6, 1942, these forces inflicted heavy damage on a Japanese invasion fleet and headed off a drive to capture the island and neutralize Hawaii. The United States had achieved its goal of containment in the Pacific, and as men and supplies could be spared from the operations against the Nazis, it could assume the offensive against Japan.

In the Atlantic during the early months of 1942, the Nazis tried by

Japanese airplanes attacking the carrier Yorktown, *Battle of Midway* (OFFICIAL U.S. NAVY PHOTO)

means of submarines to confine the Americans to the Western Hemisphere. By mid-January the Germans had moved so many submarines to the Atlantic coast, where at night they torpedoed tankers silhouetted against the lights of cities, that they created a critical oil shortage. Against convoys bound for Europe they made attacks with devastating success. In the first eleven months they sank over 8 million tons of shipping—1.2 million tons more than the Allies had meanwhile built—and threatened to delay indefinitely the large-scale shipment of supplies and men to Europe. Gradually, the United States countered by developing effective anti-submarine vessels, air patrols, detecting devices, and weapons.

The submarines made it difficult to send assistance to the British and Russians in the summer of 1942, when they needed it most. The German *Afrika Corps* raced to El Alamein, only seventy-five miles from Alexandria, Egypt, threatening the Suez Canal and the Middle East. At the same time, German armies in Russia were plunging toward the Caucasus. In May the Russian foreign minister, Vyacheslav Molotov, visited Washington to demand an immediate second front that would divert at least forty German divisions from Russia; the alternative might be Russian collapse. Roosevelt promised to do everything possible to divert the Germans by invading France. But Churchill arrived the next month, when the Germans were threatening Egypt, and he strongly urged an invasion of North Africa instead.

Merchant Ships Sunk by German Submarines, 1941–1943

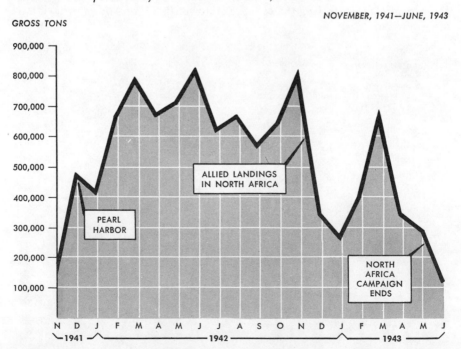

GROSS TONS   NOVEMBER, 1941–JUNE, 1943

Welcoming Molotov, 1942: (left to right) Chief of Staff George C. Marshall, Secretary of State Hull, Chief of Naval Operations Ernest J. King, Foreign Commissar V. M. Molotov, Ambassador Maxim Litvinoff (NATIONAL ARCHIVES)

THE MEDITERRANEAN OFFENSIVE

The overwhelming losses in the August 1942 raid on Dieppe, France, undertaken by experienced Canadian troops, indicated the wisdom of making the first American landing on a relatively unprotected flank. Through advance negotiations with officials of the Vichy government of defeated France, the Americans hoped to make a bloodless landing in French North Africa. At the end of October 1942 the British opened a counteroffensive at El Alamein that sent the *Afrika Corps* reeling back. On November 8 Anglo-American forces landed at Oran, Algiers, and Casablanca, Morocco, with some bungling and gratifyingly few losses. They met determined Vichy French resistance only at Casablanca.

Admiral Jean Darlan, earlier one of the most notorious collaborators with the Nazis, signed an armistice with the Allies on November 12. He ordered a cease-fire and promised the aid of 50,000 French colonial troops. Outraged American liberals protested against the deal with the Vichyites as opposed to the French resistance forces under General Charles de Gaulle. The critics quieted somewhat a few weeks later when Darlan was assassinated. Unsavory though it was to idealists, the Vichy gamble probably saved lives and speeded the liberation of North Africa.

The Germans tried to counter the invasion by ferrying troops from Sicily into Tunisia at the rate of a thousand a day. Early in 1943 the *Afrika Corps,* which had retreated westward across Tripoli, joined them and threw the full weight of its armor against the green American troops. The Americans lost heavily but with the aid of the British held on to their bases and gained in experience. Allied air power and the British navy so seriously harassed the Axis supply line from Sicily that Germany decided not to make a major stand in Tunisia. From March into May the British army in the east and the armies in the west under Eisenhower gradually closed a vise on the German and Italian troops. On May 12, 1943, the last Axis troops in North Africa surrendered. The Mediterranean had been reopened, and the Americans had learned lessons that would be useful in the successful invasion of France.

That invasion, despite the continued clamoring of the Russians, was not to take place immediately. The fighting in Tunisia had tied up too large a part of the Allied combat resources for too long. Nazi submarines were still taking too heavy a toll of the Allies' inadequate shipping. Some of the ships and production had to be diverted to the antisubmarine war and others to the prosecution of the Pacific campaigns. Also, the planners in London had come to recognize that an enormous build-up was necessary for a successful cross-Channel invasion. Fortunately for the Allies, the tide turned for the Russians also during the winter of 1942–1943, when they successfully held the Germans at Stalingrad in the Ukraine, eliminating an army of 250,000 men.

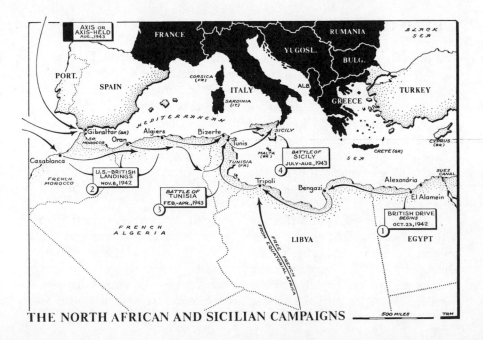

THE NORTH AFRICAN AND SICILIAN CAMPAIGNS

As early as mid-January 1943, Roosevelt and Churchill and their staffs, while conferring at Casablanca, looked ahead to the next move. This was to be an invasion of Sicily, even though General Marshall feared it might delay the invasion of France. Churchill argued persuasively that the operation in Sicily might knock Italy out of the war and lead the Germans to tie up many divisions in defense of Italy and the Balkans.

On the night of July 9, 1943, American and British armies landed in the extreme southeast of Sicily, where defenses were comparatively light. The Americans made grievous errors, the worst being to shoot down twenty-three planeloads of their own paratroops, but learned from their mistakes. In thirty-eight days the Allies conquered the island and looked toward the Italian mainland. Mussolini now fell from power, to be replaced by the pro-Allied Marshal Pietro Badoglio. At once Badoglio opened complicated negotiations to switch Italy to the side of the United Nations. As the negotiations went on, the Nazis moved eight strong divisions into northern Italy, concentrated other troops near Rome, and turned the country into an occupied defense bastion.

A limited but long and punishing campaign opened on the Italian peninsula on September 3, 1943. It started with the greatest optimism, for that same day the Italian government signed an armistice agreement, and the Allies quickly seized bases and airfields in southern Italy. But the Nazi defenders fought so fiercely from hillside fortifications that by early 1944 they had stopped the slow and deliberately moving Allies at Monte Cassino. When the Allies tried to break behind the line by landing at Anzio, south of Rome, they were almost thrown back into the sea. With relatively few divisions the Nazis were tying down the Allies while concentrating their main effort upon Russia. Finally, in May 1944, the Allies captured Monte Cassino, pressed on from the Anzio beachhead, and on June 4 captured Rome, just before the cross-Channel invasion of France began.

THE LIBERATION OF EUROPE

In the fall of 1943 Germany was already reeling under the incessant blows from the growing Allied air power. Great Britain had begun her mass bombing of German industrial centers in the late spring of 1942 with a thousand-plane night raid on Cologne. In August the Americans made their first experimental daytime raids on the Continent. Bombing almost around the clock began on a gigantic scale in February 1944. One of the objects of these bombing raids was to draw German fighter planes into battle. By the end of the war the Americans were flying over 7,000 bombers and 6,000 fighters in Europe, had dropped nearly a million and one-half tons of bombs, and had lost nearly 10,000 bombers. British figures were similar. Especially in the last year of the war, the bombing drastically cut production and impeded transportation. As early as the winter of 1944 it

THE ITALIAN CAMPAIGN 150 MILES

had so seriously demoralized the German people that 77 percent of them already regarded the war as lost.

The bombing attacks, first upon the aviation industry, then upon transportation, did much to clear the way for the invasion in the late spring. By May 1944 the *Luftwaffe* was incapable of beating off the Allied air cover for an invasion. As D-Day (invasion day) approached, the invasion was postponed from the beginning of May until early June despite the likelihood of worsening weather, in order to obtain an additional month's production of special landing craft. A sudden storm delayed the operation for a day, but on the morning of June 6, 1944, the invasion came, not at the narrowest part of the English Channel, where the Nazis expected it, but along sixty miles of the Cotentin peninsula on the Normandy coast. While airplanes and battleships offshore incessantly bombarded the Nazi defenses, 4,000 vessels, stretching as far as the eye could see, brought in troops and supplies.

Within two weeks after the initial landings, the Allies had put ashore a million men and the equipment for them. They also had captured Cherbourg, only to find that the Germans had blocked its harbor so skillfully that it could not be used until August.

Well into July, the Allies fought mile by mile through the Normandy

Ninth Air Force P-47 hitting German ammunition truck (OFFICIAL U.S. AIR FORCE PHOTO)

The Invasion of Normandy (OFFICIAL U.S. COAST GUARD PHOTO)

hedgerows. The breakthrough came on July 25, 1944, when General Omar Bradley's First Army, using its armor as cavalry had been used in earlier wars, smashed the German lines in an enormous sweep southward, then eastward. The invasion on the Mediterranean coast, beginning on August 15, quickly seized new ports (also seriously blocked) and opened new supply lines for the Allies. On August 25 French forces rode into Paris, jammed with cheering throngs. By mid-September the Allied armies had driven the Germans from almost all of France and Belgium, including the port of Antwerp, and had come to a halt against a firm line of German defenses.

Cold weather, rain, and floods aided the Germans. In December they struck with desperate fury along fifty miles of front in the Ardennes Forest, driving fifty-five miles toward Antwerp before they were stopped (in the "Battle of the Bulge") at Bastogne.

While the Allies were fighting their way through France to the Westwall (German defense line) and up the Italian peninsula, the Russian armies had been sweeping westward into central Europe and the Balkans. The Russian armies advanced more rapidly than had been expected and, in late January 1945, launched an offensive of over 150 divisions toward the Oder River, far inside Germany.

After liquidating the German thrust into the Ardennes, which had almost exhausted the Nazi fighting capacity, the Allied armies pushed on to the Rhine. The Americans captured Cologne on the west bank March

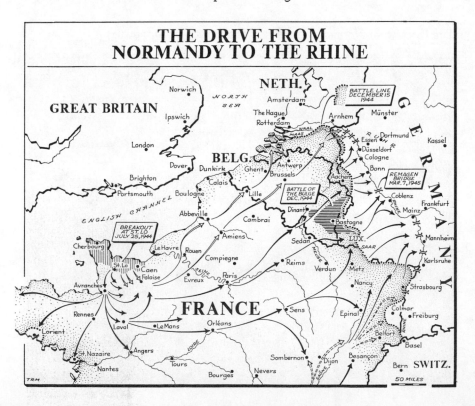

THE DRIVE FROM NORMANDY TO THE RHINE

6, 1945, and on the next day, through remarkable luck, captured a bridge across the Rhine at Remagen. Troops poured across it. By the end of March the last great drives were under way as the British commander Montgomery with a million troops pushed across the north while Bradley's army, sweeping through central Germany, completed the encirclement and trapping of 300,000 German soldiers in the Ruhr. Russian troops were about to mount a spring offensive only thirty-five miles from Berlin.

There were fears that the Nazis were preparing for a last stand in an Alpine redoubt centering on Berchtesgaden on the Austrian border. In fact, however, the German western front had been demolished. The only real questions were where the Americans would drive next and where they would join the Russians. The Americans, capable of moving much farther eastward than had been anticipated, could have beaten the Russians to Berlin and Prague. This would have cost American lives but would have reaped political gain in Europe. General Eisenhower decided, instead, to send American troops to capture the Alpine redoubt and then halt along the Elbe River in central Germany to meet the Russians.

On May 8, 1945, the remaining German forces surrendered unconditionally, and V-E Day arrived amid monster celebrations in western Europe and in the United States. The rejoicing was tempered only by the knowledge of the continuing war against Japan.

THE PACIFIC OFFENSIVE

The offensive strategy against the Japanese involved amphibious warfare of a type that the marine corps had been developing since the early 1920s. In the Pacific these new tactics came to be so perfected that troops were able to cross and seize vigorously defended beaches when the United States could not by-pass them and immobilize advanced Japanese strong points. The American strategy was, whenever feasible, "Hit 'em where they ain't."

The southern Solomon Islands to the east of New Guinea were being developed as a Japanese base for air raids against American communications with Australia. In August 1942 the navy and marines opened an offensive against three of these islands, Gavutu, Tulagi, and Guadalcanal. Around and on Guadalcanal a struggle of unprecedented ferocity developed as the American and Japanese navies battled for control in a series of large-scale engagements. By the time the struggle was over, the United States and its allies had lost heavily in cruisers, carriers, and destroyers but had sunk forty-seven Japanese vessels. The Japanese navy had lost its offensive strength and thereafter concentrated upon defensive operations.

During the months when the great naval battles had been going against the United States, the Americans had gained control of the air and thus were able to sustain the marines, and subsequently the army, in their precarious jungle onslaught. By February 1943 Guadalcanal

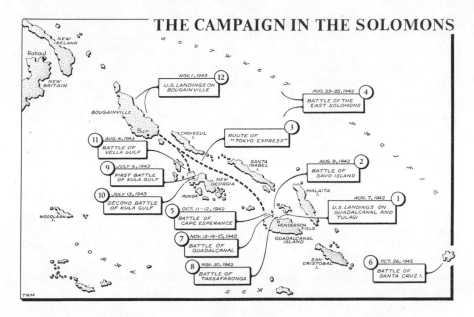

THE CAMPAIGN IN THE SOLOMONS

had been won. Through the year the island hopping continued all around the enormous Japanese-held perimeter: in the South Pacific through the northern Solomons to New Georgia, and in November to Bougainville; in the central Pacific, also in November, the marine landing on Makin and the bloody assault on Tarawa in the Gilberts; in the northern Pacific, the inexpert reconquest of Kiska and Attu in the Aleutians.

Victories in the Marshall Islands in February 1944 cracked the

The top admirals: Admiral King, Secretary of the Navy James V. Forrestal, Admiral Halsey, and Admiral Nimitz (NATIONAL ARCHIVES)

Japanese outer perimeter, and before the month was out the navy had plunged far within it to wreck the bastion at Truk and raid Saipan in the Mariana Islands. American submarines were increasingly harassing Japanese shipping, and thus hampering the economy. In 1943 the Americans sank 284 ships; in 1944 they sank 492—necessitating by summer a cut of nearly a quarter in skimpy Japanese food rations and creating a crucial gasoline shortage. The inner empire of Japan was coming under relentless siege.

Meanwhile, in 1942, the Japanese forced General Joseph H. Stilwell out of Burma and brought their troops as far west at the mountains bordering on India. China was so isolated that the United States could send in meager supplies only through an aerial ferry over the "hump" of the Himalayas. On the return trip, the planes brought Chinese troops for Stilwell to train and arm. Through 1943, Stilwell with Chinese, Indian, and a few American troops fought back through northern Burma, constructing a road and parallel pipeline across the rugged mountains into Yunnan province, China. The Ledo or Stilwell Road was not open until the fall of 1944, but meanwhile the Air Transport Command managed to fly in sufficient supplies to enable the Fourteenth Air Force (before Pearl Harbor, the "Flying Tigers") to harass the Japanese. The command undertook a still larger task when B-29 bombers struck the Yawata steel mills in Japan from Chinese bases (June 1944). The Japanese retaliated in the next few months by overrunning the bases from which the bombers operated and clearing the coastal area so that they could bring supplies northward from Southeast Asia by rail or road. They drove so far into

THE BURMA CAMPAIGN

the interior that they threatened the Chinese terminus of the Ledo Road, and perhaps even the center of government at Chungking.

The great Japanese offensive precipitated a long-simmering crisis in Chinese-American affairs, centering upon the relations between General Stilwell and Chiang Kai-shek. Stilwell was indignant because Chiang was using many of his troops to maintain an armed frontier against the Chinese Communists and would not deploy them against the Japanese.

OFFENSIVES AGAINST JAPAN

In order to bolster Chiang adequately the United States would have had to send such substantial immediate support that the campaigns against Germany and directly against Japan would probably have been slowed down or postponed.

During 1944, Japan came under heavy blockade from the sea and bombardment from the air. American submarines firing torpedoes and laying mines continued to make heavy inroads in the dwindling Japanese merchant marine.

In mid-June an enormous American armada struck the heavily fortified Mariana Islands, quickly but expensively capturing Tinian, Guam, and Saipan, 1,350 miles from Tokyo. These were among the bloodiest operations of the war. In September the Americans landed on the western Carolines. The way was being prepared for the return to the Philippines. For weeks in advance navy craft swept the central Pacific, and airplanes ranged over the Philippines and Formosa. Finally, on October 20 General MacArthur's troops landed on Leyte Island in the Philippines. The Japanese, threatened with being fatally cut off from their new empire in Southeast Asia, threw their remaining fleets against the invaders in three major encounters—together comprising the decisive Battle of Leyte Gulf, the largest naval engagement in history—and lost almost all their remaining sea power.

ATOMIC TRIUMPH OVER JAPAN

With remarkable speed but grievous losses the American forces cut still deeper into the Japanese empire during the early months of 1945. While fighting continued in the Philippines, the marines landed in February on the tiny volcanic island of Iwo Jima, only 750 miles from Tokyo. The Americans needed Iwo Jima to provide fighter cover for Japan-bound bombers and a landing place for crippled ones. The Japanese defended the island so grimly that the marines suffered over 20,000 casualties. It was the bloodiest battle in the history of the marine corps.

The battle for Okinawa, an island sixty-five miles long, beginning on April 1, 1945, was even bloodier. This island lies 370 miles south of Japan, and its conquest clearly would be a prelude to an invasion of the main islands. On land and from the air, the Japanese fought with literally a suicidal fury. Week after week they sent *kamikaze* suicide planes against the American and British ships, losing 3,500 of them but inflicting great damage. Ashore at night, Japanese troops launched equally desperate attacks on the American lines. The United States and its allies suffered nearly 50,000 casualties on land and afloat before the battle came to an end in late June 1945. The Japanese lost 110,000 killed and 7,800 prisoners.

This same kind of bitter fighting seemed to await the Americans when they invaded Japan—if indeed they should ever have to invade. There were signs that the Japanese might surrender, for they had almost

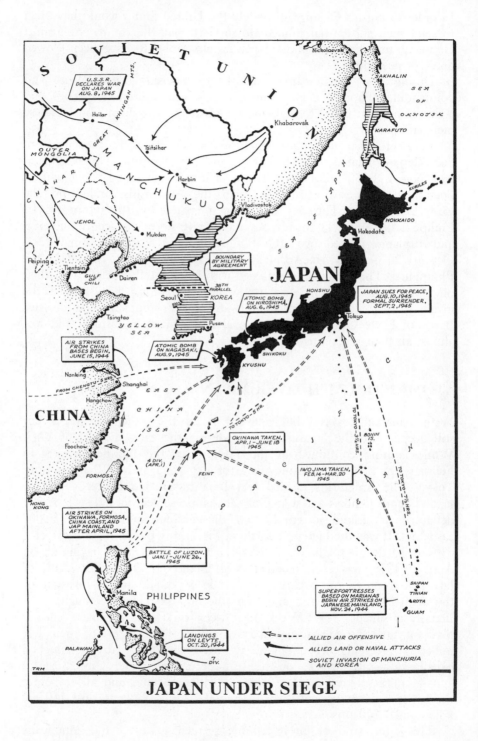

JAPAN UNDER SIEGE

The mushroom cloud over Nagasaki, August 9, 1945 (OFFICIAL U.S. AIR FORCE PHOTO)

no ships and few airplanes with which to fight. In July 1945 American warships stood offshore with impunity and shelled industrial targets, most of which were already in ruins from the heavy bombing attacks. Long since, moderate Japanese leaders had regarded the war as lost. Upon the invasion of Okinawa, the emperor appointed a new premier and instructed him to sue for peace. The premier could not persuade the army leaders to lay down their arms, but nevertheless he, and in early summer the emperor himself, tried to obtain mediation through Russia.

Apparently the Russians were determined, at their own time, to enter the war. But the atomic bomb rather than Russian intervention was to be decisive in bringing the war to an end. At a meeting of Allied leaders in Potsdam, Germany, in mid-July 1945, President Harry S Truman (who had succeeded Roosevelt) received word that the first atomic test was successful. He and Prime Minister Clement Attlee (who had succeeded Churchill) issued the Potsdam Declaration urging the Japanese to surrender or face utter devastation. The Japanese premier wished to accept the ultimatum, but the army leaders would not surrender. President Truman had set August 3 as the deadline; when it passed and the Japanese continued to fight, he ordered an atomic bomb to be dropped on one of four previously selected Japanese cities.

On August 6, 1945, a B-29 dropped an atomic bomb on Hiroshima, destroying most of the hitherto undamaged city, and killing 80,000 people (according to American estimates) or 200,000 (according to the Japanese). Even after the horror of Hiroshima, the Japanese army remained adamant. Russia declared war on Japan as of August 9. That same

Hiroshima, Japan, October 1945 (NATIONAL ARCHIVES)

day, the air force dropped a second atomic bomb, on Nagasaki. This was the final blow. After frantic negotiations, on August 14 the Japanese government agreed to give up. On September 2, 1945, aboard the battleship *Missouri* in Tokyo Bay, the articles of surrender were signed.

World War II was at an end. All together, some 14 million men under arms had been killed, and countless millions of civilians had died. In comparison, about 322,000 Americans had been killed or were missing; total United States casualties were about 1,120,000. Despite this frightful expenditure in lives and an astronomical cost in material resources, the American people faced a future made uncertain and perilous by the tensions with the Russians and the threat of future atomic wars.

nineteen
Victory Without Peace

Only the imminent threat of Axis victory had forced an uneasy and unsatisfactory form of cooperation between Russia and its Western allies, Great Britain and the United States. As the threat began to lift in 1943, it became increasingly difficult to keep the alliance cemented and to plan for a postwar world in which a decent peace could be maintained.

THE DANGEROUS ALLIANCE

The difference between British and American strategy—the British opposing a cross-Channel invasion and preferring campaigns in southern and eastern Europe—affected the two nations' dealings with the Russians. To a certain extent the United States seemed nearer to the Russians in insisting with them upon an early invasion of France. Roosevelt seemed at times to take a middle position between Stalin and Churchill.

As the Nazi tide receded, the postwar patterns began to emerge throughout eastern Europe, as they were already doing in Italy. Firm political agreements were necessary if these areas were not to fall entirely under Russian hegemony, just as firm military plans were essential to the achievement of final victory.

At Casablanca, Morocco, in January 1943, after previous consultation with Churchill, Roosevelt announced the doctrine of unconditional surrender by the Axis. What Roosevelt seemed to desire was to avoid the kind of negotiations that had marred the 1918 armistice, causing bickerings among the Allies at the time and German misunderstandings afterward. As the war progressed, it became clear that the unconditional-surrender doctrine left the United Nations free to state to the Axis powers the peace terms the latter might expect. Roosevelt and Churchill both emphasized that the phrase did not mean, as the Nazi propagandists charged, that extremely severe terms would be imposed. Yet, after the war, some historians charged that the unconditional-surrender doctrine seriously discouraged the anti-Nazi German underground movement, stiffened the Nazi will to fight, and thus lengthened the war.

In October 1943 Secretary Hull, although he was seventy-two and in precarious health, flew to Moscow to confer with the British and Russian foreign ministers. His faith in Wilsonian idealism almost limitless, Hull returned from Moscow elated because the Russians had agreed to a Declaration of Four Nations on General Security. (China was the fourth nation.) This was a pledge to continue the united action of war "for the organization and maintenance of peace and security" and to create, as soon as practicable, a general international organization.

With an air of optimism Roosevelt and Churchill traveled eastward in November 1943 for a long-awaited meeting with Stalin at Teheran, Iran. On the way they stopped at Cairo to confer with Chiang Kai-shek and to prepare a statement (released after the Teheran conference) drawing a map for the postwar Far East. They proposed stripping Japan of her empire in order to restore Manchuria, the Pescadores, and Formosa to China and to create in due course a free and independent Korea. Japan was to lose, in addition, all other territory she had acquired since 1914.

At Teheran, Roosevelt undertook to establish a friendly, intimate relationship with Stalin of the kind he enjoyed with Churchill. Stalin reaffirmed his intention to bring Russia into the Pacific war soon after hostilities had ended in Europe, and expressed his satisfaction with the Cairo communiqué on Japan. In a cordial way the three leaders discussed the means, through an international organization, of keeping

Stalin, Roosevelt, and Churchill at Teheran (NATIONAL ARCHIVES)

Germany from ever again becoming a menace. Stalin wished Russia to retain the areas she had seized in her period of collaboration with Germany, including eastern Poland as far as the so-called Curzon line proposed in 1919. Roosevelt and Churchill agreed to the Polish boundary.

Roosevelt and Churchill seem not to have recognized realistically the nature of the peace that was being foreshadowed at Teheran. In the general rejoicing over the apparent accord among the Big Three and in their assumption that Russia would be content within her new boundaries, they overlooked the appraisal that one of the American participants at Teheran wrote a few days later: "The result would be that the Soviet Union would be the only important military and political force on the continent of Europe. The rest of Europe would be reduced to military and political impotence."

It was unrealistic to expect, as Roosevelt apparently did, that the Russians would forbear from exploiting the great European and Asian power vacuums that the defeat of Germany and Japan would create. This miscalculation led the United States into a tragic triumph—a victory without peace.

THE YALTA CONFERENCE

Churchill's mood fluctuated with the ebb and flow of Russian good will. Upon leaving Moscow, after a visit in the fall of 1944, he wrote Stalin: "This memorable meeting . . . has shown that there are no matters that cannot be adjusted between us when we meet together in frank and intimate discussion." By January 1945 he was so badly disillusioned that he wrote Roosevelt concerning the forthcoming Yalta meeting: "This may well be a fateful Conference, coming at a moment when the Great Allies are so divided and the shadow of the war lengthens out before us. At the present time I think the end of this war may well prove to be more disappointing than was the last." Such was the bleak and unpromising setting for the great conference at Yalta in the Crimea (February 1945).

At that time American forces were having to reduce Germany mile by mile; there seemed no reason to think Japan would be different. General MacArthur insisted on the necessity for Russian aid, taking the position that otherwise the United States would have to fight a series of difficult and expensive campaigns to overcome the Japanese in Manchuria. Consequently, the Joint Chiefs did not revise their timetable calling for the defeat of Japan eighteen months after German surrender, and they continued to regard Russian aid as indispensable. Roosevelt expressed to Stalin his hope that Japan could be bombed into submission without invasion—but the Americans could not count upon it.

These were the limitations upon the Americans in their bargaining at Yalta. In return for Stalin's reiterated promise to enter the Far Eastern

war two or three months after German surrender, Roosevelt and Churchill promised him the Kurile Islands north of Japan and the restoration
of "the former rights of Russia" lost in the Russo-Japanese War. This
meant the return of southern Sakhalin Island, the return of a lease on
Port Arthur as a naval base and internationalizing of the port of Dairen,
Manchuria (in both instances with recognition of Russia's preeminent
interests), and joint operation with China of the Chinese Eastern and
South Machurian railroads feeding into the ports. China was to retain
sovereignty over Manchuria, but Roosevelt did not clarify what "preeminent interests" meant. (For many months these clauses remained
secret because Russia was still at peace with Japan.)

In its disposition of central European questions, the Yalta conference for the most part ratified previous decisions. Germany was to be
divided into zones of occupation previously agreed upon. Since Berlin
was to be deep in the Russian zone, the Americans and British proposed
an accord providing freedom of transit into Berlin. The Russians held
back, and in the general spirit of amity at Yalta, the matter was postponed. At the time, the Russian demands for heavy reparations in the
form of German factories, goods, and labor seemed far more important.
The British tried to scale down the Russian demand for $20 billion in
such reparations, of which Russia was to obtain half. This would so strip
and starve the Germans, Churchill pointed out, that the United States
and Great Britain would have to feed them. Consequently, he and
Roosevelt agreed to the Russian figure only as a basis for discussion by
a reparations commission. Already, in the light of reality, the West had
left far behind the Morgenthau plan (initialed by Roosevelt and Church-

The final meeting at Yalta (NATIONAL ARCHIVES)

ill at Quebec in October 1944) for the pastoralization of Germany, that is, to wipe out its industries.

One of the touchiest questions was what would constitute a democratic government for Poland, a matter over which Russia and the West had negotiated for months. The Russians did not wish to allow the Polish government in exile in London or the Polish underground to assume any substantial share of power with a government the Russians had established at Lublin. At the beginning of August 1944, as the Red army drove within ten miles of Warsaw, the underground in the city arose against the Germans. The Russians halted, ignored the revolt, and despite the strong pleas of the United States and Great Britain, stood by while the Polish patriots were annihilated in sixty-three days of fighting. The Russian explanation was military exigency, but the situation seemed to show the type of government Stalin was determined to establish in Poland.

At Yalta the West managed to obtain Stalin's agreement that the Lublin (Communist) government should be broadened to include democratic leaders from Poland and abroad. What the percentage should be was not specified. Subsequently, the new government should hold "free and unfettered elections as soon as possible on the basis of universal suffrage and secret ballot." As for the Polish boundary, it was to follow the Curzon line in the east, and the Poles were to receive territorial compensation in the north and west.

For the rest of liberated or defeated Europe, the Big Three agreed to establish interim governments "broadly representative of all democratic elements" and to provide for free elections that would create "governments responsible to the will of the people."

In years after the war, disappointed Americans harshly criticized the Yalta agreements, especially for their violations of the Atlantic Charter. The morality of the Far Eastern arrangements is open to challenge. Their purpose was to obtain Russian aid, which top military leaders thought would shorten the war against Japan and perhaps prevent a million American casualties. The terms promised nothing to Stalin that he could not have taken anyway. The morality of the European arrangements (except perhaps for the ethnic dislocations wrought by the new Polish boundaries) would have been defensible if the terms had received their customary Western interpretation. Roosevelt may be most severely criticized for not insisting at every point upon absolutely clear, sharply defined agreements that could receive only one interpretation in Russia—the interpretation as understood by the West. This was especially true of the question of entry into Berlin. Experience with the Russians long before Yalta had pointed to the need for precise understandings.

Roosevelt was careless in this respect because he pinned his hopes upon the good faith of the Russians and their willingness to enter into and actively participate in an international organization for the preservation of the peace.

THE UN ORGANIZATION

A few months before war broke out in Europe—and long before the attack at Pearl Harbor—Secretary Hull had taken the first step toward proposing a new international organization in which the United States would participate. In January 1940 he appointed an Advisory Committee on Problems of Foreign Relations. Its membership was composed of congressmen from both parties and distinguished experts from within and without the State Department. Several private organizations like the Council on Foreign Relations also prepared numerous studies for the State Department.

President Roosevelt, determined to avoid Wilson's failure, encouraged Hull to include Republicans in the planning for the peace. However, Roosevelt did not consult Congress before making his most famous statements of war aims: Senator Robert A. Taft asserted in 1943 that he did not believe "we went to war to establish the 'four freedoms' or any other freedom throughout the world," nor "for the purposes set forth in the Atlantic Charter." The administration, to counter this kind of resentment, included prominent Republicans in at least sketchy briefings on wartime diplomacy and let them participate more fully in postwar planning of many kinds. In this way it won their support. In 1943 four senators, two Republican and two Democratic, none of whom were serving on the Foreign Relations Committee, introduced a resolution calling for American leadership in establishing a United Nations organization. Public-opinon polls indicated a general enthusiasm for the resolution; the Senate passed a similar declaration 85 to 5. Senator Arthur H. Vandenberg of Michigan, previously one of the most forthright isolationists, assumed Republican leadership in helping mold a "bipartisan" foreign policy. He thus gained for himself and the Republican party new power and stature.

The Big Four powers, conferring in the summer and fall of 1944 at Dumbarton Oaks, a Harvard-owned estate in Washington, drafted tentative outlines for a new international organization. These were the starting points for the drafting of a United Nations charter at a conference of fifty nations in San Francisco, opening April 25, 1945. Roosevelt had appointed a bipartisan delegation headed by his new Secretary of State, Edward R. Stettinius, Jr. One of its most effective members was Senator Vandenberg, who helped to wrest concessions from the Russians at San Francisco and to win the votes of reluctant Republicans for ratification in the Senate.

Basically, the charter of the United Nations was a refurbishing of the old Wilsonian League Covenant with the former American objections removed through giving a veto to each of the five main powers. The Americans and British, as well as the Russians, had insisted upon the veto as a seemingly necessary protection of their sovereignty. The American delegates, led by Vandenberg, succeeded in obtaining for the

The United States representative signing the United Nations Charter: (left to right) President Truman, Secretary of State Stettinius, Senator Tom Connally, Senator Vandenburg, Harold Stassen (NATIONAL ARCHIVES)

small nations in the General Assembly freedom to discuss and make recommendations—in effect creating "a town meeting of the world."

The Senate quickly ratified the charter (July 1945) by a vote of 80 to 2, in remarkable contrast to the slow and painful defeat it had administered to American membership in the League of Nations. But the great and growing gulf between Russia and the West destined the United Nations to be, like its predecessor, the League, a town meeting for international discussion or a sounding board for national views, rather than the forerunner of a world government.

A FOURTH TERM FOR FDR

With "bipartisanship" prevailing, there had been no serious disagreement between Democrats and Republicans on the issues of peace planning. But in regard to domestic questions there had been politics as usual. Indeed, despite all the platitudinous pleas to put aside politics in the interest of national unity, the struggles became even more virulent during the war.

Conservatives saw in the war an opportunity to eradicate hated remnants of the New Deal; some liberals regarded it as an opportunity to bring Wilson's ideas to fruition, and even go beyond them to establish a global New Deal. Every one of the great pressure groups in the country fought to maintain or improve its relative position; spokesmen for large business and small, farmers and labor, jockeyed for positions in Washington. The tenor of Congress continued to be conservative, and it was sensitive as always to the demands of organized constituents. Throughout the war, key committee chairmen who were leaders of the conservative coalition dominated Congress and forced their will upon Roosevelt. Through the election of 1942, as the United States and its allies suffered unparalleled military disasters and the war administration in Washington seemed to compound confusion, the criticism rose to a crescendo. In the election the Republicans gained forty-seven seats in the House and ten in the Senate. Within both parties the trend was to the right.

Roosevelt, in order to get crucial congressional support in prosecuting the war and planning the peace, continued to accept the sacrifice of New Deal measures. At a press conference in 1943 he announced that "Dr. Win-the-War" had replaced "Dr. New Deal."

Dissatisfaction with wartime regimentation and smoldering resentments still glowing from the prewar debate over intervention seemed to give the Republicans an opportunity in 1944. They had seen auguries of a national shift toward the right in the congressional election of 1942. In their vigorous young candidate, Governor Thomas E. Dewey of New York, who ran with Governor John W. Bricker of Ohio, they seemed to have an answer to Roosevelt and the aging New Dealers.

As for Roosevelt, it was a foregone conclusion that he would be nominated for a fourth term if he so desired. There was none of the suspense that had preceded the third-term nomination. Rather, since he was visibly aging, unwell, and thinning so that his clothes ill fit him, there was much speculation over his choice for the vice-presidential nominee. During the war, Vice President Wallace was the hero of most advanced New Dealers and much of the CIO membership. But he was

As a wartime Presidential candidate, Governor Thomas E. Dewey inspects a medium tank (NATIONAL ARCHIVES)

sneered at by party bosses and some Southern Democrats as a visionary who wished to extend the New Deal to the entire globe, to bring "a quart of milk for every Hottentot." They rallied behind James M. Byrnes of South Carolina, who had been functioning ably as the unofficial assistant president—but Byrnes was unacceptable to organized labor. Out of the skirmishing among the rival factions within the Democratic party came Roosevelt's proposal of a compromise candidate acceptable to most of them, Senator Harry S Truman of Missouri. Truman had won newspaper approval as chairman of the Senate War Investigating Committee, was a consistent New Dealer in his voting record, and was from a Border State. He was popular in the Senate.

In keeping with the bipartisan spirit, Republican and Democratic leaders had arranged for practically identical planks on foreign policy, thus eliminating it as an issue in the campaign. Dewey had a good chance to make it an issue when he got word that American intelligence had broken the Japanese code before Pearl Harbor. With this information he could have charged that the Roosevelt administration knew—or should have known—of the coming Japanese attack. But an envoy from General Marshall dissuaded Dewey from using the information, which if made public would have caused the Japanese to change their code (American intelligence was still exploiting it) and thus would have disadvantaged United States forces fighting in the Pacific. Even without this issue, the election promised to be close—partly because the vote was likely to be small, and presumably a light vote would aid the Republicans.

The possibility was like an injection of adrenalin into Roosevelt. At the end of September 1944, addressing a raucously appreciative audience of Teamsters Union members, he was at his sardonic best. He followed this triumph with a strenuous campaign in Chicago and throughout the East. This he climaxed with a day-long drive in an open car through New York City in a soaking rain.

Roosevelt's seeming capacity to serve four more years, his international leadership, and his promise to return to the New Deal after the war were a winning combination. Organized labor, working through the CIO Political Action Committee, brought out the workers' votes. Roosevelt defeated Dewey by a margin of 432 electoral votes to 99, and a popular vote of 25,602,000 to 22,006,000. The Democrats lost one seat in the Senate, but gained twenty in the House. The Democratic victory seemed to mean a revival of the New Deal at home, and the campaign promises of both parties indicated that the United States would continue to take a lead in international affairs.

But Roosevelt lived to see neither the triumph in war nor the tragedy of peace. Already his vigor was draining away, and he could ill afford the exertions of the campaign or those of the grueling trip to Yalta. Addressing Congress on his return, he was very tired and for the first time he made public reference to his paralyzed legs and his heavy steel braces as he remained seated and spoke optimistically of the Yalta agreement—which he said contained no secret provisions. Suddenly, on the afternoon of

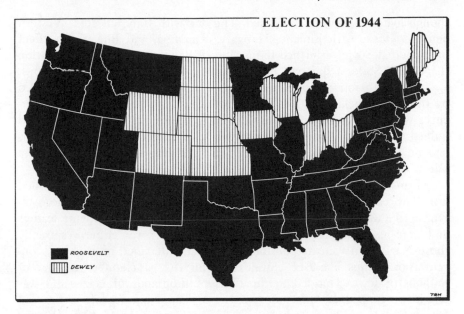

ELECTION OF 1944

ROOSEVELT

DEWEY

April 12, 1945, he died of a cerebral hemorrhage at his private retreat in Warm Springs, Georgia.

TRUMAN TAKES OVER

Through no fault of his own, President Truman was unbriefed and poorly prepared for the task of concluding the war and making the peace. No one doubted his sincerity when he remarked to reporters the day after he had suddenly taken his oath of office: "I felt like the moon, the stars, and all the planets had fallen on me. I've got the most terribly responsible job a man ever had."

During the first phase of his relations with the Russians, Truman was moderately firm but tried to give the Soviet government no cause for protest. He was chagrined when in May 1945 the Foreign Economic Administration enforced his order ending Lend-Lease so precipitately as to call back some ships at sea. The British were the most hard hit, but Stalin complained most bitterly.

At the Potsdam conference (July 1945) Truman could secure few satisfactory agreements on questions involving occupied and liberated countries. Despite the failure at Potsdam, Truman's Secretary of State, James F. Byrnes, continued in a conciliatory fashion to seek accommodation with the Russians.

The Potsdam conferees provided for a Council of Foreign Ministers to draft treaties with Italy and the former Axis satellites. During a tedious and depressing round of meetings of the council in London, Moscow, Paris, and New York (between September 1945 and December 1946), relations between the West and Russia steadily deteriorated, though five treaties were concluded. The one with Italy reflected Western demands; those with Finland, Hungary, Rumania, and Bulgaria in effect incorporated Soviet armistice terms. By ratifying the three latter treaties, the United States acquiesced in the Russian domination of these nations.

In Berlin a four-power Allied Control Council began sessions marked by the same blocking and delaying tactics that made other joint conferences with the Russians so dismal. The Western nations had visualized unified controls for Germany to prevent her resurgence. But the Russians had no interest in a Germany reunified in a manner acceptable to the West. Germany was to remain split indefinitely.

Meanwhile, in occupied Germany and Japan the United States pursued firm but conflicting policies compounded of harshness and idealism. During the war, the American people had come to hate the enemy leaders and were insistent that they be punished for their war crimes, especially those Nazis who were responsible for the maintenance of frightful concentration camps like Buchenwald and for the gas-chamber murder of millions of Jews. This led to the trials of thousands of Nazis and war criminals, capped by that of twenty-two key Nazi leaders before an International Military Tribunal at Nuremberg in 1945–1946. Eleven were sentenced to death.

There was also a sweeping purge of Japan, and a trial was held for twenty-five former top Japanese military and civil officials. Seven of them, including two premiers, were executed. The dangerous precedent seemed to be established, as Churchill pointed out, that "the leaders of a nation defeated in war shall be put to death by the victors."

At first the Americans seemed bent on the pastoralization as well as reform of conquered Germany. They banned all industry directly or indirectly contributing to German war potential, including even the construction of seagoing ships, drastically cut steel and chemical production, destroyed munition plants, and allowed the dismantling of some factories for shipment to the Russians. They disbanded cartels and encouraged only agriculture and peaceful domestic industries. Along with this, they wished to foster American-style democracy in place of the repudiated nazism. These economic policies, coming at a time when so much of German housing and industry was rubble, and when several million exiles were making their way from eastern Germany and from Czechoslovakia, reduced western Germany to a living standard not much better than that of a giant relief camp. The army undertook to feed the German people between 1945 and 1948 at a subsistence level of 950–1,550 calories per day.

Even this near-starvation diet cost the British and Americans nearly one-half billion dollars per year. The Russians were adding further to the economic burden by taking out of their zone (and from the western zones to the extent agreed at Potsdam) reparations totaling $1.5 to $3 billion dollars per year. They were siphoning out of Germany more than the Americans and British could pump in.

In Japan American occupation policy suffered fewer obstacles and profited from the initial errors in Germany. During the first critical weeks,

General MacArthur, the Supeme Commander for the Allied Powers (SCAP), set up an overwhelmingly American occupation, based on a directive radioed him from Washington on August 29, 1945. Truman refused Stalin's demand that Russians occupy part of the northern Japanese island, Hokkaido. The irritated Russians had a voice but no real power on an eleven-country Far Eastern Commission in Washington and on a four-power Allied Council to advise MacArthur in Tokyo.

The American occupation authorities in Japan acted rapidly to demilitarize and democratize the country. From the outset they recognized that Japan must be left with a healthy economy, but in practice—by limiting the nation's war potential—they reduced Japan like Germany to a relief state.

As tensions with the Soviet Union slowly developed, Americans became disillusioned over the consequences of World War II. They came to realize that the victory of the grand alliance had brought no real peace to the world.

twenty
The Menace of Cold War

The months after the final defeat of Germany and Japan brought the beginnings of a new titanic struggle with the Soviet Union, a conflict beginning with relatively minor tensions and mounting to the recurring threat of a new all-out war. Americans were psychologically as unprepared for this crisis as they had been for Pearl Harbor. As it continued with endless variations during the years that followed, it created more difficult problems and posed a more serious menace to the United States than had even the Axis onslaught. The cold war, as it came to be called, split most of the world into two power blocs. The maintenance of world stability came to depend upon a difficult and tenuous balance of power, not, as the United States had planned, upon an international organization.

DEMOBILIZATION AND REORGANIZATION

In the face of growing menaces in Europe and Asia, the United States speedily dismantled its army, air force, and navy. At the end of the war, there was a popular demand to "bring the boys back." In April 1945 President Truman announced that almost 7 million men had been released from the army—"the most remarkable demobilization in the history of the world, or 'disintegration,' if you want to call it that." He proposed a system of universal military training, but Congress did no more between 1946 and 1948 than to pass limited Selective Service measures. The gradual whittling of the armed forces continued, until by the spring of 1950 the army was down to 600,000 men and the ceiling on defense expenditures, to $13 billion. Lacking land armies, the United States sought to balance the Soviet power with atomic bombs and an air force that could deliver them.

Since September 1945 the administration had been ready to negotiate an agreement with Russia that would "control and limit the use of the atomic bomb as an instrument of war" and "direct and encourage the development of atomic power for peaceful and humanitarian purposes." Great Britain and Canada joined with the United States in proposing international control of atomic energy. The UN Assembly responded by creating the UN Atomic Energy Commission (January 1946), to which the American member, Bernard Baruch, submitted a plan. This proposed a thoroughgoing system of control and inspection of atomic-energy development through a UN agency. When the system became effective, the United States would liquidate its stockpile and join in an international ban on atomic bombs.

The Russians refused to accept the Baruch plan for international inspection and control of atomic development; instead, they constantly and vociferously demanded that the United States unilaterally destroy its atom bombs. Through their widespread propaganda the Russians tried to marshal world indignation against the United States while they rushed ahead with their own research on atomic weapons. American scientists and military leaders, not aware as yet of the successful Russian espionage and underrating Russian scientific and technical proficiency, predicted that it would be many years before the Soviet Union could produce a successful bomb.

Meanwhile, Congress lengthily debated the domestic control of American atomic energy. Democrats wished to vest control in civilians; Senator Vandenberg and the Republicans urged giving it to the heads of the armed forces. A compromise was reached in the Atomic Energy Act of 1946. This created a five-man civilian Atomic Energy Commission (AEC) with complete control over the research and the development of fissionable materials; linked to it was a Military Liaison Committee.

Under the protection of an atomic umbrella, military leaders indulged in the luxury of a vigorous and prolonged controversy over unification of the various armed forces. This measure, proposed to bring greater efficiency and effectiveness, led instead to heightened rivalry, as the generals pushed for it and the admirals feared for the loss of the marine corps and the relative weakening of the navy. Both sides brought the utmost pressure upon Congress. Finally, the National Security Act (July 1947) provided for a secretary of defense to preside over separate Departments of the Army, Navy, and Air Force, with the Joint Chiefs of Staff serving as advisers to him and to the President. To coordinate diplomacy and military planning, the 1947 act also provided for a National Security Council to consist of the President, certain cabinet members, and other advisers on foreign and military policy. This control was to be served by two other new agencies, a National Security Resources Board and a Central Intelligence Agency (CIA).

Within the reorganized Pentagon Building the old rivalries continued. Indeed, through the creation of a separate air force there now appeared to be three competing services where there had been only two before. The first Secretary of Defense, James V. Forrestal, exhausted by the struggle to make unification effective, resigned in 1949 and committed suicide.

His successor, Louis A. Johnson, became embroiled in a violent quarrel over cancellation of construction of a huge new aircraft carrier, a quarrel culminating in the resignation of the Secretary of the Navy and the replacement of the Chief of Naval Operations. This crisis led to amendments to the National Security Act, forcing greater unification, and formally establishing a Department of Defense.

CONTAINMENT OF COMMUNISM

Even while the United States was rapidly demobilizing, President Truman became concerned over the military containment of Communist expansion. As early as January 1946, concerned over Russian delay in withdrawing troops from Iran and over Russian threats against Turkey, he wrote his Secretary of State: "Unless Russia is faced with an iron fist and strong language another war is in the making."

Truman faced a peculiarly difficult task in trying to convince the American public that a truly deep and serious rift was developing between the Soviet Union and the West. For too many war years they had listened to publicists ranging from that advanced New Dealer Henry Wallace to the Republican president of the United States Chamber of Commerce, Eric Johnston, praising the Russians and picturing Stalin as a sympathetic figure. Many had come to imagine him as a benign, pipe-smoking sage, "good old Uncle Joe." In addition, idealists had too long placed all their hopes upon the "one world" of which Wendell Willkie had preached so eloquently.

Not even the revered Churchill could shift American opinion. In March 1946, through Truman's arrangement, Churchill, speaking at Westminster College in Fulton, Missouri, proclaimed a grim warning:

> From Stettin in the Baltic to Trieste in the Adriatic an iron curtain has descended across the Continent. . . . I do not believe that Soviet Russia desires war. What they desire is the fruits of war and the indefinite expansion of their power and doctrines. . . . From what I have seen of our Russian friends and allies during the war, I am convinced that there is nothing they admire so much as strength, and there is nothing for which they have less respect than for weakness, especially military weakness.

A new Truman policy for countering Communist aggression began to unfold in the spring of 1947. Already George F. Kennan, counselor of the American embassy in Moscow, was warning the administration that it faced "a political force committed fanatically to the belief that with the U.S. there can be no permanent *modus vivendi*." The only answer, Kennan wrote anonymously in the July 1947 issue of *Foreign Affairs*, must be "a long-term, patient but firm and vigilant containment of Russian expansive tendencies."

Russian pressure on Turkey and support of Communist guerrilla forces in Greece emphasized the immediacy of the Soviet threat. The British had been aiding the Greek government but could no longer carry the burden. Unless Stalin were contained quickly, he might achieve the centuries-old Russian prize of the straits leading from the Black Sea into the Mediterranean. Russia already controlled Albania on the Adriatic.

On March 12, 1947, President Truman appeared before Congress to request $400 million to bolster the armed forces of Greece and Turkey and to enunciate the doctrine that came to bear his name: "I believe that it must be the policy of the United States to support free peoples who are resisting attempted subjugation by armed minorities or by outside pressures." Senator Vandenberg again supported him, and the Republican Congress voted the Greek-Turkish Aid Act. The initial military aid and subsequent appropriations eased Russian pressure upon Turkey and by the fall of 1949 brought to an end the long civil war against Communists in Greece.

Military aid was not enough. The Truman Doctrine logically led to a program of economic reconstruction to bolster the stability of Europe and help eradicate the misery out of which the Communist parties in western European countries were gaining recruits. In April 1947 Secretary of State George C. Marshall returned from the Conference of Foreign Ministers in Moscow convinced that the Russians were interested only in profiting from the economic plight of Europe, not in ameliorating it. The solution, he and President Truman agreed, lay in State Department plans to aid European nations that were willing to cooperate with each other in rebuilding their economies. Speaking at the Harvard University commencement in June 1947, Secretary Marshall offered aid to all those European nations (including Russia) who would join in drafting a program for recovery.

Russia denounced the Marshall Plan as American imperialism and intimidated the satellites and Finland and Czechoslovakia into staying away from the planning conference. Germany had no government, and Spain was not invited. Sixteen other nations of Europe joined a Committee of European Economic Cooperation, which in September 1947 presented specifications for reconstruction to create a self-sufficient Europe by 1951. Opposition formed in Congress, but it was embarrassed from the start by possessing as unwelcome allies the American Communists, and in February 1948 it was overwhelmed by a shocked and aroused public opinion when Czech Communists seized power in Prague. Congress in April established the Economic Cooperation Administration (ECA). It cut the administration's request but did vote an initial $4 billion.

Altogether over a three-year period the United States spent $12 billion through the ECA. This helped to stimulate a remarkable recovery in Europe. By the end of 1950 industrial production was up 64 percent, economic activity was well above prewar levels, and Communist strength among voters in most areas was dwindling.

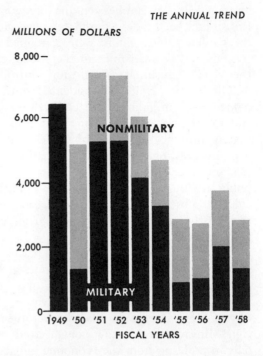

THE ANNUAL TREND

MILLIONS OF DOLLARS

U.S. Foreign Aid, 1949–1958

FISCAL YEARS

THE NORTH ATLANTIC ALLIANCE

In his inaugural address, January 20, 1949, President Truman challenged the nation to come to the aid of the "more than half the people of the world" who were "living in conditions approaching misery." Point Four of his foreign-policy proposals was a plan for aiding them through technical assistance and the fostering of capital investment. The Point Four or Technical Cooperation program began in 1950 with an appropriation of only $35 million, but spent $400 million in the next three years.

Soviet leaders reacted vigorously against the American efforts for world economic recovery. They had organized their own Warsaw Alliance of nine satellite nations (September 1947) to combat "American imperialism." Through a new Cominform (Communist Information Bureau) they sought to eradicate traces of nonconformity throughout eastern Europe. Their greatest triumph was the successful coup in democratic Czechoslovakia in February 1948. Because it was as horrifying to western Europeans as it was to Americans, it helped unify the Western world against the Communist countries. Later in the year, the pressure of Stalin and the Cominform on Marshal Tito provoked him to pull Communist Yugoslavia out of their orbit and with American aid to embark upon an independent course between Russia and the West. In western Europe, Communist parties tried to thwart the Marshall Plan, especially by calling out on strike the unions they controlled in Italy and France. Despite the strikes, progress continued.

Meanwhile, the United States moved with the British and the rather reluctant French toward the creation of a self-governing, economically strong West Germany. The culmination came on June 7, 1948, when they announced plans for a new federal West German government with sovereignty over domestic matters and full membership in the European Recovery Program. They also reformed the currency to stop the inflationary flood of marks from the Soviet zone, which was hampering recovery.

The Russians retaliated. Taking advantage of a lack of a written guarantee of land transit across the Soviet zone, they clamped a tight blockade around the western sectors of Berlin. The object was to force the Western powers to abandon either Berlin or the proposed West German republic. President Truman, unwilling to risk war by ordering in armed convoys by land, ordered the supplying of Berlin by increasing on a massive scale the airlift begun in April. By the time bad weather hampered flights in the late fall, adequate stockpiles had been established in Berlin. Through the winter and into the spring of 1949, the airlift continued. It was a remarkable demonstration to Europeans—especially to the Germans —of what the Americans and British could achieve. Altogether, they flew over 277,000 flights to bring in nearly 2.5 million tons of food, fuel, and other supplies to maintain 2 million people. They carried in more than had previously been brought by train.

In the spring of 1949 the Russians backed down and ended the blockade. In October 1949 the German Federal Republic came into existence at Bonn in West Germany, and the Soviets established a German Democratic Republic for East Germany.

Russian intransigence led to the consolidation of the Western countries into a new grand alliance. The North Atlantic Treaty was signed April 4, 1949, by twelve nations, and subsequently also by Greece and

The Berlin Airlift (OFFICIAL U.S. AIR FORCE PHOTO)

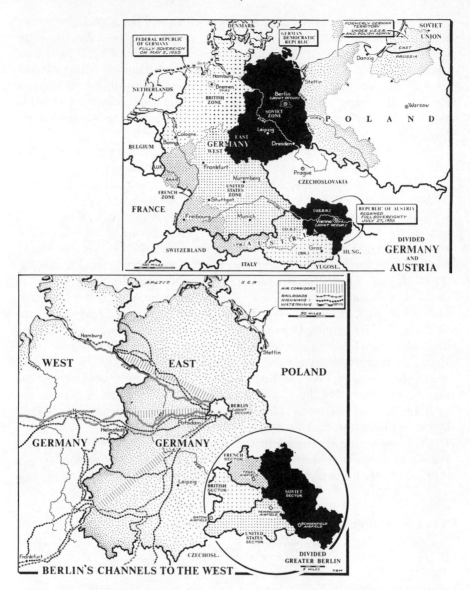

Turkey. It declared that an armed attack against one would be considered an attack upon all and provided for the creation of joint military forces. Under it the signatory powers established the North Atlantic Treaty Organization (NATO) to construct a defense force that, while not equal to that of the Russians, would be large enough to make an attack highly costly.

The United States began to shift from economic to military aid as the Mutual Defense Act of 1949 appropriated an initial billion dollars for armaments for the signatories. The governing body of NATO, the North Atlantic Council, established military headquarters near Paris early in 1951 under the supreme command of General Eisenhower. This was

SHAPE (Supreme Headquarters, Allied Powers in Europe). The number of divisions and airplanes under NATO command began gradually to grow, but while its power was still relatively feeble, its chief significance was the commitment that the United States had made with the nations of western Europe to stand firm against Russian threats.

That these threats were not to be taken lightly became even clearer on September 23, 1949, when President Truman issued a press statement: "We have evidence that within recent weeks an atomic explosion occurred in the U.S.S.R." The years of relative safety for the American people were already at an end.

CHINA TURNS RED

While the United States was struggling to contain the Soviet Union in Europe between 1947 and 1949, the Chinese Communists were destroying the armies of Chiang Kai-shek. To prevent civil war and to effect a coalition government the Truman administration in December 1945 had sent General Marshall to China. At first he obtained a cease-fire and encouraging signs of accommodation, but irreconcilable differences kept apart the two Chinese governments—the *Kuomintang* (Nationalists) and the Communists. Finally, in January 1947, Marshall returned to Washington disgusted with both governments and all factions except a handful of powerless *Kuomintang* liberals.

Full-scale war broke out. Although the Nationalist armies were larger and better equipped, they soon began to fall back before the better trained, more vigorous Communist forces. As the inept Chiang government failed both on the fighting front and at home, where inflation and inefficiency were rampant, it was plunging toward defeat.

President Truman now sent General Wedemeyer, who had been Chiang's chief of staff, to investigate. Wedemeyer warned that Communist control of China would imperil American interests, since the Communists were in fact closely tied to the Soviet Union. He believed that the United States could rescue Chiang only by sending 10,000 army officers and other advisers to introduce reforms, together with massive matériel support.

Truman did not request large-scale aid for Chiang, and for this omission critics subsequently castigated him. But to do so might have interfered with the program of containment in Europe; it would have been unpopular and, in any event, would probably have been too late. Truman did ask Congress to provide $570 million; in April 1948 it voted $400 million, of which China could spend only $125 million for military supplies. Basically, the administration decided, as Secretary Marshall made clear, that the United States could not salvage the Nationalist government so that it would be "capable of reestablishing and then maintaining its control throughout all of China." The collapse was rapid, and it came through lack of morale rather than shortages of arms and supplies.

In October 1948 the Communists seized Mukden, Manchuria, and as Nationalist troops surrendered or defected, the Reds swept on with captured American arms into central and southern China. At the end of 1949 Chiang and the Nationalists fled to Formosa. All of China was under the new People's Republic, which ruthlessly consolidated its strength by liquidating several million dissidents, harrying out American businessmen, teachers, and missionaries, and proclaiming its propaganda to all of East Asia.

Though Great Britain and some of the western European nations recognized the new government of Red China, the United States refused to do so and blocked its entry into the United Nations. Also, beginning in 1947, the American government introduced new policies in Japan to strengthen that nation in a manner similar to the rebuilding of Germany.

The American occupation in Japan brought a democratization of the government, extension of rights to women and underprivileged groups, expansion of the educational system (from a starting point as high as the goal of educational reform in China), land reform that was as drastic as that in China, a curbing of the power of the monopolistic *zaibatsu* industrial system, and an improvement in the status of labor. In Japan, more than anywhere else in Asia, the United States helped develop a dynamic alternative to communism. In 1949, to stimulate Japanese recovery the United States ended its reparations and stopped the dismantling of industrial combinations.

Negotiation of a Japanese peace treaty began in 1950 through the skilled offices of a Republican, John Foster Dulles, whom Truman appointed to undertake the task. Aside from the fact that it stripped Japan of all her recent conquests, it was a generous treaty, a "peace of reconciliation," as Dulles called it. By recognizing the right of the sovereign Japanese nation to self-defense, it opened the way to rearmament. Thanks partly to its negotiation by a Republican, the treaty easily received Senate ratification and went into effect in 1952. A security treaty, signed at the same time, permitted the United States to maintain armed forces in Japan. Two years later, a mutual-defense-assistance pact provided for Japanese rearmament with American aid, but the building of armed forces proceeded slowly. Disarmament had been one of MacArthur's most cherished reforms, and the American-imposed Japanese constitution had banned war forever. This encouraged such a strong pacifist sentiment that as late as 1957 only 100,000 Japanese had joined the armed forces. The task of defending Japan continued to rest largely with the United States.

Several nations to the south that had suffered either invasion or the threat of invasion during the war viewed with some concern the rebuilding of Japan as a military power. To reassure them the United States in 1951 signed a security treaty with the Philippines and the ANZUS pact with Australia and New Zealand.

While rebuilding Japan, the Truman administration refused to capitulate to the demands of the so-called China Lobby for military and naval aid to Chiang on Formosa, which might have led the nation into a war against Red China. On the contrary, the State Department issued a white paper (1949) charging the Nationalists with responsibility for their debacle. In January 1950 Secretary of State Dean Acheson publicly outlined a Pacific defense perimeter that did not include Formosa or Korea. If these areas were attacked, he declared, the people invaded must rely upon themselves to resist "and then upon the commitments of the entire civilized world under the charter of the United Nations."

Within a few months East Asia became the focal point of American foreign policy as the cold war turned hot in Korea.

DEFENDING SOUTH KOREA

During the hectic days at the end of the war in the Pacific, the United States had hastily proposed that Americans accept the surrender of the Japanese in the lower half of Korea, up to the 38th parallel and that the Russians do the same in the northern half. At the moment the arrangement was useful to the United States. Afterward, however, the Russians were willing to accept a reunited Korea only if it were Communist dominated.

The 38th parallel became more and more an impenetrable barrier. To the north of it the Communists developed a "peoples' government" with a strong aggressive army. To the south the United Nations held elections that led to a government under the ardently nationalistic Dr. Syngman Rhee, long an exile in the United States. Rhee would have liked to extend his government to the north, but the United States provided the South Korean army only with relatively light defensive weapons. Consequently, when the United States withdrew its forces from below the 38th parallel in June 1949, South Korea was left militarily weaker than its even more aggressive northern twin.

On June 24, 1950, the North Koreans acted swiftly, launching a full-scale invasion that caught the South Koreans and Americans completely by surprise. Almost immediately, President Truman and Congress re-

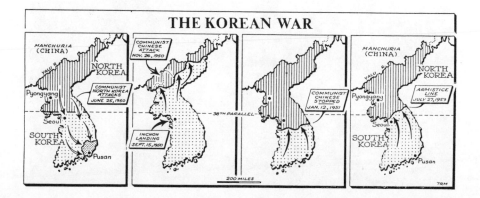

THE KOREAN WAR

versed the policy of withdrawal from the Asiatic mainland. Truman brought the question of the invasion before the UN Security Council. It could act more quickly than the Assembly, and at the moment the Russians were boycotting it and hence had no representative present to vote a paralyzing veto. The Council on June 25 passed an American resolution demanding that the North Koreans withdraw behind the 38th parallel and two days later called upon members of the United Nations to "furnish such assistance to the Republic of Korea as may be necessary to repel the armed attack." Truman on June 27 sent United States air and sea forces to the aid of the South Koreans; on June 30 he ordered ground forces into Korea and sent the Seventh Fleet to act as a barrier between the Chinese mainland and Formosa.

The Council of the United Nations on July 7, 1950, requested those nations providing troops to place them under a unified command headed by the United States. Truman appointed General MacArthur commander in chief. Some fifteen nations besides the United States and the Republic of Korea provided troops, but these never comprised more than 9 percent of the total fighting force. The United States sent about 48 percent; South Korea mustered 43 percent. What was officially a UN "police action" came to most Americans to seem a war on the part of the United States.

General MacArthur, who at first could draw upon only four understrength divisions in Japan, rushed in troop units piecemeal to slow the rapidly advancing North Koreans as they rushed southward past Seoul,

U.S.S. Missouri *bombarding North Korean installations* (OFFICIAL U.S. NAVY PHOTO)

threatening to envelop the entire tip of the peninsula. By thus sacrificing themselves, these forces gave MacArthur an opportunity to build stable defenses around the port of Pusan in the extreme southeast. When the North Koreans struck there in force early in August, strong army and marine reinforcements fresh from the United States hurled them back at each point of assault. As men and supplies poured into Pusan, marine officers devised a bold plan of attack that General MacArthur reluctantly accepted. Rather than try to push the North Koreans back mile by mile, on September 15, 1950, while the UN troops around Pusan opened a sharp counteroffensive, he launched an amphibious assault far behind the North Korean lines at Inchon, near Seoul. It caught the Communists almost completely unprepared. The UN troops quickly recaptured Seoul; within two weeks the North Korean armies, disrupted and demoralized, were fleeing as best they could to north of the 38th parallel.

RETREAT FROM NORTH KOREA

Amid jubilation the United States and the United Nations had to make new decisions. Should they capitalize upon their spectacular victory and move into North Korea? The premier of Red China on October 1 warned that the Chinese would "not allow seeing their neighbors being invaded by imperialists." A few days later, he announced the Chinese would send troops and dispatched a warning to the United Nations through India. These threats worried American strategists, but there was a possibility that China was bluffing, and there was the probability that the North Koreans, unless pursued, would recoup their strength and strike new blows.

The Joint Chiefs of Staff on September 27, 1950, ordered MacArthur to destroy the North Korean armed forces, but under no circumstances to cross the borders of China or Russia. The UN Assembly gave its sanction to the project on October 7, reiterating its aim to create "a unified, independent and democratic Korea." Two days later, the UN forces poured across the 38th parallel toward the Yalu River, which marked the boundary with Manchuria.

For several weeks the advance into northern Korea went well. On October 19, the capital, Pyongyang, fell, and parachutists landed thirty miles beyond to trap much of the remaining North Korean army. Then, on October 26, a Chinese Communist soldier was captured; four days later, fourteen more were taken. By November 4, eight Chinese divisions had been identified, and Russian-made MIG fighter planes had briefly engaged the UN air force.

General MacArthur issued a special communiqué warning that "a new and fresh army now faces us," and he excoriated the Chinese for their international lawlessness in intervening without notice and "massing a great concentration of possible reinforcing divisions with adequate supply behind the privileged sanctuary of the adjacent Manchurian border."

Fighter pilots on their way to combat, April 1953 (U.S. AIR FORCE PHOTO)

Both in his private communications to the Joint Chiefs of Staff and in the encouragement he gave to pressure groups in the United States, MacArthur engaged in a vigorous campaign for permission to bomb this "privileged sanctuary." Truman refused to allow all-out military action against China, because, he later explained, "if for no other reason . . . it was a gigantic booby trap."

In the two weeks after they first sighted Chinese troops, the UN forces marched into a serious trap. The Chinese suddenly appeared in overwhelming numbers, stalled MacArthur's offensive, and hurled back advance units. Through December 1950, in bitter weather, the outnumbered Eighth Army and X Corps fought a heroic withdrawal from North Korea. The United Nations tried to negotiate peace with the Chinese, but the Communists, as they swept below the 38th parallel and recaptured Seoul, set impossibly stiff terms. In March 1951 the Eighth Army counterattacked, for a second and final time capturing Seoul and recrossing the 38th parallel. Truman was ready again to seek a negotiated peace.

General MacArthur, far from ready to accept the position of his commander in chief, repeatedly made public his eagerness to win total victory in Korea at the risk of full involvement in war with China. On March 20, 1951, he communicated his views to the Republican minority leader

Eighth Army fighting Chinese Communists, February 1951 (U.S. ARMY PHOTO)

in the House of Representatives, Joseph W. Martin, concluding: "There is no substitute for victory."

Truman clung to his thesis that, in the great struggle against communism, western Europe with its concentration of heavy industry, not industrially weak Asia, was the main potential battlefield. He could not have won the support of western European partners in the United Nations for a more militant policy in Asia. He would not accept the arguments of the Asia-firsters that the United States should undertake unilateral action—"go it alone."

MacArthur thus emerged as a major figure in American politics, trying to reverse the administration policies. Five days after Representative Martin released MacArthur's letter to the press, Truman, on April 11, 1951, relieved MacArthur of his commands. A groundswell of outrage swept the United States; a Gallup poll reported that 69 percent of those interviewed favored the general, only 29 percent the President. MacArthur upon his return was greeted hysterically wherever he appeared; millions watched their television sets as he addressed Congress.

Truman's policy of fighting a limited war of containment continued to baffle and exasperate a considerable part of the American people. It went against the American tradition of total victory. It was difficult to explain to the public or to the soldiers fighting endlessly through the rice paddies and over the hilltops of Korea.

In June 1951 the Russian delegate to the United Nations hinted that settlement was possible. Armistice negotiations began on July 10, 1951,

General MacArthur addressing Congress (U.S. ARMY PHOTO)

near the 38th parallel, and continued for many weary months at Panmunjom. They came to revolve around the difficult questions of locating the cease-fire line, enforcing the armistice, and repatriating prisoners of war. By the spring of 1952, agreements had been reached upon all but the last question. Finally, in October 1952 the negotiations were recessed. By then the nation was in the midst of a presidential campaign, and though there was no large-scale fighting in Korea, the interminable negotiations, endless skirmishing, and ever-growing casualties had worn out the patience of the American people.

twenty-one
The Truman Era

Against the melancholy backdrop of permanent crisis in international affairs, Americans after 1945 settled into a life of precarious prosperity at home. They had, in the words of a political slogan, never had it so good, but because of foreign threats and domestic strains they were never sure how long prosperity would last. At first there were the tensions and problems of reconversion to face, and, for a generation that had known more than a decade of depression, the fears that the economy would collapse. But it was a boom era. Problems at many points were the reverse of those of the prewar years: inadequate rather than surplus production, inflation rather than deflation, and shortages of workers and of housing, automobiles, and almost every sort of consumer durable goods.

Some of the prewar problems came to the forefront in more acute form. This was especially true of civil rights questions. Some problems were new and especially troublesome, above all the fear that the menace from without was matched by subversion within. Other domestic questions seemed less exciting and important than they had before the war. During its first two years, the Truman administration drifted toward the right amid considerable uncertainty and confusion, then by 1948 moved more firmly toward what came to be known as the Fair Deal program. President Truman was able to translate his program into law only with tedious difficulty, yet actually many of the New Deal advances were consolidated and became commonplace. Some new measures were incorporated into the program. What resulted was neither progressivism nor a continuation of the New Deal; rather, it was the gradual, pragmatic development of a new American society and polity.

Truman, as the architect of the new program, superficially at least was in marked contrast to his predecessor, Roosevelt. During much of his nearly eight years in the White House, he was an underrated President. He was of such unspectacular background and average appearance that it was easy to dismiss him as a person having no unusual qualifications or talents. Many people who had regarded Roosevelt as the patron of the common man looked upon Truman as being himself the common man.

Although Truman had been chosen for the vice presidency because of his moderate, middle-of-the-road background, immediately after the war he aligned himself with the more liberal wing of the Democratic party. At the same time, he surrounded himself with predominantly conservative cabinet members and advisers who often worked against these policies and in favor of rapid abandonment of wartime economic controls. Truman seldom interfered with these cabinet members—individuals like Secretary of the Treasury John Snyder and Secretary of Agriculture Clinton Anderson. Consequently, they together with the conservative coalition in Congress took the nation along a rightward course.

RECONVERSION AND INFLATION

On September 6, 1945, only four days after the Japanese surrender ceremonies, Truman sent to Congress a twenty-one-point domestic program outlining the Fair Deal. He called for the expansion of Social Security, the raising of the legal minimum wage from forty to sixty-five cents an hour, a full-employment bill, a permanent Fair Employment Practices Act, public housing and slum clearance, long-range planning for the protection of natural resources and the building of public works (like TVA), and government promotion of scientific research. Within ten weeks he sent additional recommendations to Congress for federal aid to education, for health insurance and prepaid medical care, and for the St. Lawrence Seaway project.

Congress acted upon several of Truman's recommendations. The Maximum Employment Act became law in 1946. It established a three-member Council of Economic Advisers to aid the President and issue an annual economic report. Although the experts frequently disagreed, they became an integral part of the governmental machinery. They did much to accustom the public to the new Keynesian economics that had been emerging during the New Deal and the war.

Congressional conservatives tried to steer Congress and the public away from the Fair Deal program by concentrating upon the reconversion of industry to peacetime production. Truman himself recommended, first, speedily removing all possible controls that would hamper reconversion and, second, preventing increases in prices, rents, and wages. The two aims could easily conflict.

After Germany surrendered, cutbacks in war orders began, and after Japan capitulated, $35 billion in contracts was suddenly canceled. The WPB soon dropped controls, except on commodities that were still very scarce. Congress passed a new revenue bill cutting taxes nearly $6 billion. The War Assets Administration, established in January 1946, sold several hundred war plants, mostly to the corporations that had been operating them, and disposed of mountains of surplus, some of which enabled veterans with priorities to start small businesses. Members of the armed forces, who were being demobilized at an unparalleled pace, found their problems of readjustment to civilian life eased by the Servicemen's Readjustment Act of 1944 (the GI Bill of Rights), which provided them with further education and training, or aid while unemployed or starting in business or farming.

Industry changed back to civilian production with more speed and less economic dislocation than had been expected. The gloomy forecasts of 8 million unemployed did not materialize. By the end of November 1945, peacetime employment was up to the end-of-the-war total, and 93 percent of the war plants had been reconverted.

The expected glut of surplus goods did not materialize either. Instead, acute problems of scarcity arose. Shortages ranged from automobiles and appliances to men's suits, nylon stockings, and beef. Consumers commanded some $129 billion or more in savings and billions more in credit with which to back their demands. Added to these were the needs of the rest of the world. Against such pressures, it was impossible for the Office of Price Administration to hold prices down to the 1941–1942 level.

If prices were to be checked, wages must be also, and if wages were to be held down, so must prices be. It was a vicious circle. By January 1946 workers had gone on strike in a number of the nation's critical industries— steel, automobiles, electrical manufacturing, and others. When Philip Murray demanded a twenty-five-cents-an-hour increase for the United Steelworkers to bring them up to their wartime take-home pay, President Benjamin F. Fairless of United States Steel, acting as spokesman for the industry, refused unless the government would allow a $7-per-ton increase in the price of steel. President Truman announced that labor was entitled to the 33 percent that living costs had gone up since January 1941. The Wage Stabilization Board must approve the increase; but if it cut profits below the prewar level, the companies might obtain corresponding price increases. Ultimately, there was a steel settlement allowing raises of 18½ cents an

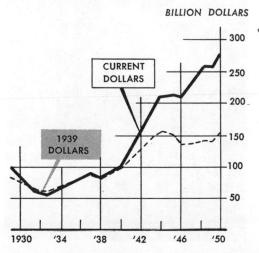

BILLION DOLLARS

Gross National Product, 1929–1950

hour and $5 per ton. Throughout industry the "bulge" led to a round of similar raises in wages and prices.

In April 1946 John L. Lewis precipitated a fresh crisis. He demanded that the bituminous coal workers receive, even before wage increases, drastic improvement in safety rules and substantial contributions to a health and welfare fund. Refusing White House suggestions of compromise, he led out 400,000 miners. Within six weeks, as coal supplies dwindled, much of the nation's industrial production had to be cut back. In mid-May Lewis allowed his workers back for twelve days' mining; in the interim a railroad strike threatened. Truman, by broadcasting a warning that the army would run the railroads, managed to avert a new walkout. The government took over the coal mines and provided the workers with most of what Lewis had demanded.

While unions were going on strike for higher wages, businessmen and farmers were exerting almost equal pressure upon Congress to obtain higher prices. Controls, they argued, were preventing full production, encouraging a black market, and robbing producers of a fair profit. After long debate, Congress passed a circumscribed price-control bill on June 27, 1946, just three days before the existing act was to expire. Truman unexpectedly vetoed the bill as "a sure formula for inflation," and most price controls expired.

During the first sixteen days of July 1946, the index of prices of twenty-eight basic commodities jumped 25 percent, compared with 13 percent

John L. Lewis (NATIONAL ARCHIVES)

during the previous three years. On the first day of free trade at the Chicago stockyards, prime beef jumped from $18 to $22 per hundred weight. As prices soared, stock raisers, who had been holding back their cattle, rushed them to market. Congress quickly passed a new price-control bill only slightly stronger than the vetoed one, and on July 25 Truman signed it. The decontrol board it created studied meat prices, decided they were unreasonable, and ordered prices rolled back to the old levels. Stockmen once again held back cattle until they could force abandonment of controls; angry consumers chafed in near-empty butcher shops.

For several weeks Truman stood firm, but as public discontent focused on the Democratic party, politicians already fearful of the worst in the congressional elections of 1946 persuaded him to relent. On October 14 he announced the immediate ending of meat controls. Meat came back, but like many other commodities, with new price tags so high that the old black-market price seemed to have become the new legal standard. Millions of consumers on small, inflexible salaries or pensions were hurt. Real earnings dropped 12 percent below those of July 1945.

"HAD ENOUGH?"

All that the Republicans needed in the fall of 1946 was the slogan, "Had Enough? Vote Republican." They captured both houses of Congress, controlling the House 246 to 188, and the Senate, 51 to 45.

Truman, accepting the returns as a mandate to liquidate regulations, dropped almost all remaining controls on wages and prices and on the channeling of construction into low-cost homes. Congress continued rent control to March 1, 1948, but allowed rents to go up 15 percent. Retail prices moved upward 3 percent per month, canceling the gains organized

"Weather Clear, Track Fast" by D. R. Fitzpatrick, for the St. Louis Post-Dispatch

labor had won in the spring of 1946. Unions fought for and obtained a second round of increases in 1947, and in 1948 as prices still went upward, a third round. The spiral of inflation was creeping upward relentlessly. Workers and others in modest circumstances began to notice that it was taking place under a Republican Congress whose spokesmen had asserted that laissez faire would cure the nation's ills.

The Chairman of the House Appropriations Committee, John Taber, proclaimed that he would apply a "meat-axe to government frills." He did so. Congress refused to appropriate funds for public housing, even of the moderate kind championed by Taft. It would not aid education or extend Social Security; it slashed budget allowances for reclamation and power projects in the West. It passed a tax bill that, as Truman pointed out in vetoing it, reduced the taxes of families receiving $2,400 or less by only 3 percent, but those of families receiving $100,000 or more, from 48 to 65 percent.

One of the few noncontroversial domestic achievements of this Congress was authorization of a commission on reorganization of the executive departments. Truman appointed former President Hoover chairman of the commission. Congress already had voted to improve its own procedures and to reorganize its committees, cutting those in the House from forty-eight to nineteen and in the Senate from thirty-three to fifteen.

The principal positive handiwork of the Eightieth Congress was a new basic labor law to supplant the pro-labor Wagner Act of 1935. The Taft-Hartley Labor-Management Relations Act loosened some of the previous restrictions upon employers and added several prohibitions against the unions. It also provided for "cooling-off" periods before unions could strike. Truman stingingly vetoed it on June 20, 1947. That same day Republicans and Southern Democrats in the House overrode his veto; the Senate followed three days later. In practice, the Taft-Hartley Act did not cripple organized labor, partly because of the skill of labor leaders and because of Truman's appointment to the National Labor Relations Board of members sympathetic toward labor. But the law did emphatically turn most of organized labor against the Republicans and back to the support of Truman.

TRUMAN BEATS DEWEY

When the Republicans met in Philadelphia (June 1948) to nominate a presidential candidate, they rejected Senator Robert A. Taft, the vigorous leader of the Eightieth Congress. Though the idol of many businessmen, Taft was hampered by his prewar isolationism and his lack of glamor as a campaigner. The Republicans again nominated Governor Thomas E. Dewey, who favored the new role of the United States in world affairs, and whose stand on domestic issues came closer to the Fair Deal than to the Republican record in Congress. His running mate was Governor Earl Warren of California, who was even more liberal. Their platform was a promise to continue all the things the Democrats had established but to do them more efficiently and cheaply.

It seemed a winning ticket and program, especially since the Democratic party suffered from two schisms. A faction to the left followed Henry A. Wallace out of the party. Wallace ran on a "Progressive" ticket to fight for thoroughgoing reform at home and more friendly relations with Communists overseas. Around him rallied a sprinkling of Americans who felt that the Truman domestic policies were too slow and ineffective and who feared that the foreign policies would lead to a third world war. Around him also rallied the American Communists and fellow travelers (sympathizers).

Despairing Democratic liberals organized as Americans for Democratic Action, sought some more glamorous candidate than Truman. The one candidate they could be sure would win votes by the million, General Eisenhower, rejected their overtures. At their convention (July 1948) the Democrats gloomily accepted the inevitable, the nomination of Truman. Certain of defeat, the liberals salvaged what they could by fighting through a platform containing a strong civil rights plank that proposed federal legislation to prevent discrimination in employment, penalize lynchers, and outlaw poll taxes. This platform was expected to help Northern and city Democrats in their local and state elections.

But it drove Southern Democrats, already angered by Truman's espousal of a strong civil rights program, into open revolt. Waving Confederate flags, a number of them met at Birmingham, Alabama (July 1948), to form the States Rights' Democratic Party and nominate Governor J. Strom Thurmond of South Carolina. They captured the party organization in Alabama, Louisiana, Mississippi, and South Carolina.

The defections on both the left and the right seemed to leave Truman in a pathetically hopeless position; all the public opinion polls showed him trailing far behind. Governor Dewey, campaigning in a cold and formal way, aroused as little animosity as possible and seemed to be delivering previews of his inaugural. Instead of campaigning against the impeccable Dewey, who stood for much the same in domestic and foreign policy, Truman launched his attack at the Republican Congress. Because he felt the press was giving a hostile impression of his administration, Truman embarked upon a strenuous personal tour of the United States, traveling 31,700 miles to speak 356 times directly to the American people. In this "whistle stop" tour, he spoke only a few times from manuscripts, preferring his far more effective, rather blunt extemporaneous style. To all those groups who could be convinced they had a grievance against the Republican Congress, he appealed effectively, winning the strong support of organized labor, disgruntled farmers, and Northern blacks.

On Election Day, to the amazement of everyone but himself, Truman defeated Dewey, 24,106,000 to 21,969,000 in the popular vote and 304 to 189 in the electoral vote. Thurmond's Dixiecrat ticket received 1,169,000 popular and 38 electoral votes. Wallace polled only 1,156,000. The Demo-

President Harry S Truman (UNITED PRESS PHOTO)

crats also regained both houses of Congress by a margin of ninety-three seats in the House and twelve in the Senate.

THE STRUGGLE FOR THE FAIR DEAL

President Truman, in his January 1949 message to Congress, called upon it to enact the Fair Deal. At times the Democratic Eighty-first Congress

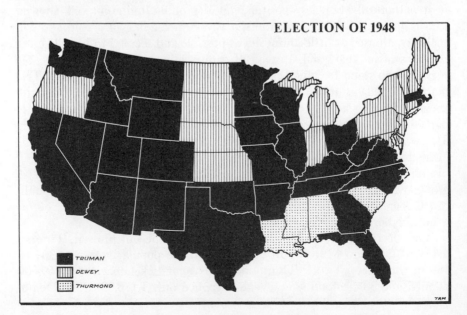

ELECTION OF 1948

TRUMAN
DEWEY
THURMOND

seemed much like its Republican predecessor, since again Southern Democrats allied themselves with Republicans to block some legislation. Truman obtained less than the program he felt a majority of the voters had approved at the polls but more than during his first years in office.

Congress raised the minimum wage under the Fair Labor Standards Act to seventy-five cents an hour. It also voted amendments to the Social Security Act, increasing the benefits to retired workers by three quarters and extending coverage to 10 million additional people.

For minorities Truman continued to press his civil rights program upon Congress. Southerners, through the threat of filibuster, were able to prevent action in the Senate. In March 1950 Senate supporters of Fair Employment Practices legislation were twelve votes short of the requisite two-thirds majority to vote closure of debate. Truman as early as 1948 through administrative orders began to attack segregation within the government and in the armed forces and to provide positive aid to minorities. Congress did vote the Displaced Persons Act of 1950, liberalizing the 1948 legislation, which Truman had denounced as discriminatory against Catholics and Jews because its quotas were unfavorable to people from southern and eastern Europe. It increased the number of persons to be admitted from 205,000 to 415,000—but even this latter figure was a total, not a yearly number.

The new Congress also strongly implemented some of the New Deal reforms. The National Housing Act of 1949 provided for the construction over the succeeding six years of 810,000 housing units for lower-income families, together with a subsidy for forty years to bridge the gap between costs and the rents the tenants could afford to pay. It also provided grants for slum clearance and rural housing. It voted increased appropriations for power development and reclamation in the West, for TVA, and for the Farmers Home Administration (which carried on the rehabilitation work of the earlier Resettlement Administration and Farm Security Administration). In contrast, the Fair Deal health-insurance program went down to crashing defeat under the vigorous opposition of the American Medical Association, which raised $3 million to combat it. Federal aid for education failed because of dissension over whether aid should go to parochial schools.

Altogether, the congressional votes for Fair Deal measures, together with the public support of Congress in these actions, seemed to indicate that the earlier reforms that had been questioned by the Eightieth Congress were indeed ones that the American people did not wish to reverse. Right-wing Republicans basically failed in their challenge to the Democrats on domestic policy as they had also on foreign policy. But in the question of loyalty they found a successful issue.

LOYALTY IN A FRIGHTENED NATION

In the disappointing months and years after the war, as the warm feelings toward the Soviet Union turned into apprehension and even alarm, the public became increasingly afraid that traitors within the government were betraying it to the Communists. As the Western world suffered setbacks from the Communists, it was easy to blame these disasters upon alleged Reds high in the councils of the government.

During the period of the New Deal and the war, there had been some Communists and Communist sympathizers in the government. At a time when the Russians and the Americans were allied, this seemed of little consequence, but in 1942 and 1943 President Roosevelt established loyalty checks. By 1946 the Soviet Union seemed more a potential enemy than an ally. The Canadian government discovered that at least twenty-three of its employees in positions of trust had turned over secrets, some of them concerning nuclear fission, to Russian spies. Several of the spy rings had operated across the boundary in the United States.

The federal government began extensive efforts to ferret out Communists. President Truman in November 1946 established a Temporary Commission on Employee Loyalty to recommend loyalty investigation systems and safeguards of fair hearings. This led, in March 1947, to the establishment of loyalty boards to undertake a sweeping investigation of all federal employees. In August 1950 Truman authorized the dismissal in sensitive departments of even those deemed no more than "bad security risks." By 1951 more than 3 million government employees had been cleared, over 2,000 had resigned, and 212 had been dismissed.

Against the recommendations of the Departments of Defense and Justice and of the Central Intelligence Agency, Congress overrode the President's veto and passed the McCarran Internal Security Act (September 1950). This did not outlaw Communist organizations but required them to publish their records. It barred Communists from employment in defense plants and denied them passports.

Already, in 1948, the Attorney General had obtained indictments against eleven key Communist leaders for violation of the Smith Act of 1940, which prohibited conspiring to teach the violent overthrow of the government. During their nine-month trial in 1949, the Communists engaged in elaborate harassing tactics, which further aroused the public against them. They were convicted. In the 1951 case of *Dennis* v. *United States*, the Supreme Court in a 6-to-2 decision rejected their appeal. Chief Justice Fred Vinson held that advocating or teaching revolution in the existing state of the world, or even conspiring to do so, fell within Justice Holmes' earlier definition of what was punishable—that it constituted a "clear and present danger." In dissenting, Justice Hugo Black remarked· "There is hope that in calmer times, when the present pressures, passions, and fears subside, this or some later court will restore the First Amendment liberties to the high preferred place where they belong in a free society."

While the Supreme Court was solemnly deciding that civil liberties must be circumscribed to protect the modern state, some less careful politicians were capitalizing upon the growing public hysteria over several spectacular cases. Above all, there was the case of Alger Hiss, in which these politicians seemed to put on trial and condemn a whole generation of liberal intellectuals. Hiss, a handsome and ambitious young man, had risen rapidly in the government during the 1930s to become a high-ranking official of the State Department. He was present as a clerk at the Yalta conference but in no way influenced policy there. In 1947 he resigned to head the Carnegie Endowment for International Peace. Whittaker Chambers, a self-avowed former Communist agent, had denounced Hiss as early as 1939, but because he provided no details and no supporting evidence, Chambers was ignored. In 1948 he repeated his accusations before the House Un-American Activities Committee. When Hiss sued him for slander, Chambers produced microfilms of classified State Department documents that Hiss allegedly had given him in 1937 and 1938.

Hiss was brought to trial for perjury (the statute of limitations prevented indictment for espionage). He called upon a number of the nation's most distinguished liberals to bear witness to his character. The first trial ended with a hung jury (July 1949); the second ended with conviction (January 1950).

More important in convincing Americans that a real Communist menace existed was the revelation, in February 1950, that a young British scientist, Dr. Klaus Fuchs, had turned over to Russian agents full details on the manufacture of atomic bombs. His confession led to the trial and ultimate execution of Julius and Ethel Rosenberg, Americans who were alleged to have been his accomplices—and who were hailed as martyrs by Communists throughout the world.

Among the politicians who capitalized upon the public's fears, none was more sensational in his rise than Senator Joseph McCarthy of Wisconsin. Already some other politicians were winning fame through crusading against communism. Representative Richard Nixon, who had helped keep the Hiss affair alive until Chambers produced the incriminating microfilms, was on his way to the Senate and a national reputation. McCarthy decided to exploit the same issue. In February 1950 he charged that a large number of Communists and people loyal to the Communist party were still shaping foreign policy in the State Department. When a subcommittee of the Senate Foreign Relations Committee took up his charges, they found not a single Communist or fellow traveler.

An excited public numbering many millions eagerly swallowed McCarthy's new claims as he went on from sensation to sensation more rapidly than his detractors could refute his unsubstantiated charges. Millions wanted to believe McCarthy when he attacked as Communists the "whole group of twisted-thinking New Dealers" who had "led America near to ruin at home and abroad." McCarthy was providing a troubled nation with a scapegoat and the Republican party with a winning issue.

A TROUBLED ELECTORATE

In 1950 the voters were disturbed by the charges of subversion, by the Communist victory in China, and by the Korean War. Many were led to believe that the events in China and Korea had resulted from a conspiracy in the State Department. When Hiss was convicted in January, his former acquaintance Secretary of State Dean Acheson declared that he would not turn his back on him; meaning, Acheson later explained, that he was following "Christ's words setting forth compassion as the highest of Christian duties." But Acheson's remark, together with Truman's early reference to the Hiss case as a red herring, served as Republican campaign texts. Representative Nixon declared: "Traitors in the high councils of our own government have made sure that the deck is stacked on the Soviet side of the diplomatic tables."

Bipartisanship in foreign policy disappeared as the Republicans pressed their issue. They did not capture Congress in November 1950, but they gained twenty-eight seats in the House and five in the Senate. Neo-isolationists, heartened by the election results and no longer restrained by Senator Vandenberg, who was fatally ill, opened a "great debate" in the Senate over foreign policy. They succeeded in passing a resolution (April 1951) restraining the President from sending troops to western Europe without congressional authorization.

Republicans undermined the Truman administration with charges of favor peddling and corruption, which implicated individuals in the White House though not the President himself. The President's military aide had received as a gift a $520 deep-freeze unit; the wife of an examiner of loans for the Reconstruction Finance Corporation (RFC) had acquired a $9,540 mink coat. These became the symbols of a moral malaise in Washington. Apparently go-betweens, in return for a 5-percent fee, could obtain contracts, arrange RFC loans, and take care of tax difficulties in the Bureau of Internal Revenue. Truman reorganized the RFC and reformed the Bureau of Internal Revenue and the Department of Justice, but much too slowly to satisfy his Republican critics.

As the election of 1952 approached, there was no indication that the majority of voters wished to reverse either Truman's foreign policy or his domestic program. They did want to "clean up the mess in Washington," and above all they wanted to see an end to the drawn-out, wearying Korean War.

EISENHOWER ELECTED

It was not surprising that in times so troubled the voters overwhelmingly turned to a successful and popular general who they felt could lead them to security in a frightening world. They turned not to MacArthur but to Eisenhower, who was closely linked to the military and foreign policies of the Roosevelt and Truman administrations.

Partly this was the logic of politics. The wing of the Republican party holding to the views of MacArthur was committed to Senator Robert Taft —but it was a minority within the party, even though it controlled the Republican National Committee. The majority (knowing they could count upon the votes of most of the minority) sought a candidate who could pull strong support from many who had favored the Democratic foreign and domestic policy. Consequently, they looked to Eisenhower—whom some liberal Democrats had sought to draft in 1948.

In the struggle for delegates, Eisenhower easily carried the East, and Taft the Midwest. Later, in a violent struggle on the floor of the convention, the Eisenhower forces won contested delegations and, with them, the nomination on the first ballot. Senator Nixon of California, who was acceptable to conservative Republicans, was nominated for the vice presidency. The platform was ambiguous enough to cover disagreements between the two wings of the party. Early in September Eisenhower went still further to mollify the Midwestern Republicans by conferring with Taft. He promised patronage to the Taft followers and avowed that the main issue of the campaign was "liberty against creeping socialization"—but he did not compromise on foreign policy. Later in Wisconsin he was conciliatory toward Senator McCarthy. Thus he was able to campaign with the diverse factions of the party unified behind him.

As for the Democrats, the Northern wing of the party was in control at the convention. President Truman had announced that he would not run again. The most vigorous campaigner in the primaries, Senator Estes Kefauver of Tennessee, won little support among party leaders; Vice President Alben Barkley was deserted by labor spokesmen, who declared that he was too old. So the Northern leaders drafted Governor Adlai E. Stevenson of Illinois, who had earlier declared that he would not run. His running

The Democratic nominees in 1952: Governor Adlai E. Stevenson and Senator John Sparkman (NATIONAL ARCHIVES)

mate was the liberal Senator John J. Sparkman of Alabama. The platform stated the positions of the Northern Democrats: endorsement of the Truman foreign policies, civil rights, repeal of the Taft-Hartley Act, and high price supports for farmers.

Stevenson began delivering speeches brilliant in their eloquence, clever in their wit, and startling in their candor. As he promised to "talk sense to the American people," he drew the hearty support of most intellectuals, whose critics derisively called them "eggheads." But Eisenhower appealed much more effectively to businessmen and the masses by promising to end their various frustrations.

Republican campaigners played upon the triple theme of "communism, corruption, and Korea." Speaking in Detroit on October 24, 1952, Eisenhower promised to bring the war to "an early and honorable end." To help do so he promised he would make a personal trip to Korea. The response at the polls was overwhelming: Eisenhower getting 33,936,000 votes to 27,315,000 for Stevenson. Despite Eisenhower's victory, the Republicans failed to gain complete control of Congress. They won a majority of eight seats in the House and only an even split in the Senate. The Republican candidate was far more popular than his party.

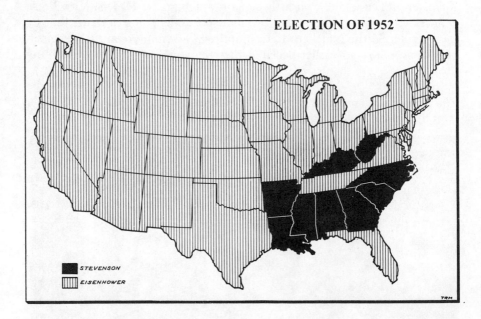

ELECTION OF 1952

STEVENSON
EISENHOWER

twenty-two
A Nuclear Balance of Terror

During the Eisenhower administration the perils and challenge of the clash between the Western democracies and the Communist world overshadowed all else. John Foster Dulles, the Republican expert in foreign policy, had criticized the Democratic program of "containment" as a passive one that left the initiative to the Communist side. Dulles proposed, instead, a program of "liberation" that would lead to a "roll-back" of Communist expansion. As Secretary of State in the Eisenhower administration, he continued to talk of new approaches. Yet the Eisenhower-Dulles policy was to be essentially a continuation of the Truman-Acheson policy.

A KOREAN ARMISTICE

Before his inauguration President-elect Eisenhower flew to Korea to talk to commanders about means of obtaining an honorable truce. In his inaugural he committed himself to a firm policy in Korea and elsewhere in the struggle against Communists.

Less than two months after Eisenhower took office, Stalin died. This opened the possibility of an end to the Korean War and perhaps some moderation of the cold war. When the new Soviet Premier, Georgi Malenkov, seemed conciliatory, the President called upon the Russians to show their good faith by signing an Austrian peace treaty and supporting an armistice in Korea. On July 27, 1953, an agreement was finally signed at Panmunjom. It provided for a cease-fire and withdrawal of both armies about a mile and one-half back of the existing battle line, which ran from coast to coast, from just below the 38th parallel in the west to thirty miles north of it in the east. A conference was to be held to seek peaceful reunification of Korea, but at the Geneva meeting (1954) no agreement was reached. The armistice turned into an uneasy and indefinite armed truce.

The Korean War had lasted more than three years and cost the United States alone 25,000 dead, 115,000 other casualties, and $22 billion. For Americans who liked to think in terms of total victory, it all seemed painfully inconclusive. The fighting had settled no problems in the Far East except to prevent the Communist conquest of South Korea.

"MASSIVE RETALIATION"

As Secretary of State from 1953 to 1959, Dulles gave the impression of formulating policy decisions on his own. A sturdy moralist, a skilled and stubborn advocate, and a tireless worker, he seemed to feel that he must participate personally in innumerable top-level negotiations all over the globe. Since as Secretary of State he flew 479,286 miles outside of the United States, his detractors liked to wisecrack that he was demonstrating an infinite capacity for taking planes. Assuming many of the normal functions of State Department officials, diplomats, and even the President, he dominated the making of foreign policy.

The Eisenhower administration had come into office firmly committed to existing collective security arrangements and a Europe-first priority. Nevertheless, it maintained a tenuous compromise with the ardently nationalistic Asia-first wing of the party. This group was exploiting at home the thesis that setbacks in Asia were due to internal subversion in the Truman administration, that Communist aggression in Asia must be met with military force, and that economic aid to remove the griev-

Secretary of State John Foster Dulles reporting to President Eisenhower and to the nation over television, May 17, 1955 (DEPARTMENT OF STATE)

ances the Communists were exploiting was a waste of money. The hero of the Asia-firsters was Chiang Kai-shek, and their special villain was Red China, which they insisted must be curbed or destroyed at all costs. Concurring with this group at some points were the business leaders dominant in the Eisenhower administration, who were determined that defense expenditures must fit within a balanced budget.

The pressures of these groups helped lead to crucial decisions in 1953. Again, as before the Korean War, a movement began to reduce the military establishment. At the same time, the Eisenhower administration wished to meet the Communist challenge in Indochina and elsewhere. The solution seemed to lie in a "new look" in defense policy, equally pleasing to the Secretaries of Defense, the Treasury, and State. This meant cutting the expensive army ground forces and basic scientific research. The United States would depend especially upon its thermonuclear weapons and their delivery by the air force. Popularized, this was the policy of "more bang for a buck."

A new diplomatic and strategic approach was necessary to make the "new look" in defense operate adequately. Secretary of the Treasury George M. Humphrey, looking at it from a standpoint of cost, asserted that the United States had "no business getting into little wars." If the nation had to intervene, he declared, "let's intervene decisively with all we have got or stay out." This was the economic basis for Secretary of State Dulles' proposal of "massive retaliation." The United States would depend less on local defense, he declared in an address on January 12, 1954, and depend more on "the deterrent of massive retaliatory power . . . a great capacity to retaliate instantly, by means and at times of our own choosing."

CHINA AND INDOCHINA

The Indochina crisis of 1954 offered the first test of the new approach. Under the leadership of Ho Chi Minh the people of Indochina, a French colony that had fallen to Japan in World War II, had been fighting for their independence—against the Japanese and then against the French. The end of the Korean War enabled the Chinese Reds to give indirect aid to the Indo-Chinese nationalists, who were largely Communists, at a time when the French were tottering on the edge of military disaster. In 1954 the rebels besieged an army of 12,000 Frenchmen and friendly Indo-Chinese in the frontier fortress of Dienbienphu. Already the United States was paying 70 percent of the French war costs, thus supporting colonialism as an alternative to communism. Now, it appeared, the United States would also have to send direct military aid if Dienbienphu and all of Indochina were not to fall under Communist control.

At a press conference President Eisenhower likened the nations in Southeast Asia to a row of dominoes. The moral was implicit; the first domino must not be allowed to fall. Many of Eisenhower's advisers

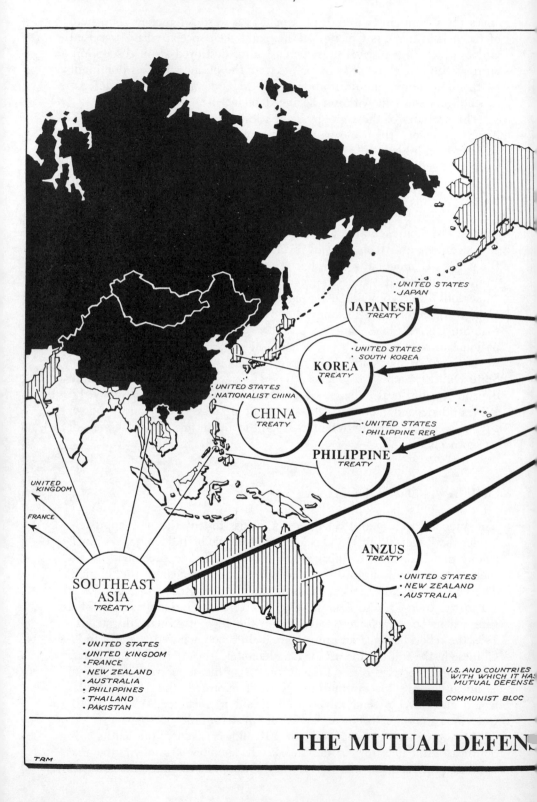

JAPANESE
TREATY
· UNITED STATES
· JAPAN

KOREA
TREATY
· UNITED STATES
· SOUTH KOREA

CHINA
TREATY
· UNITED STATES
· NATIONALIST CHINA

PHILIPPINE
TREATY
· UNITED STATES
· PHILIPPINE REP.

ANZUS
TREATY
· UNITED STATES
· NEW ZEALAND
· AUSTRALIA

SOUTHEAST
ASIA
TREATY
· UNITED STATES
· UNITED KINGDOM
· FRANCE
· NEW ZEALAND
· AUSTRALIA
· PHILIPPINES
· THAILAND
· PAKISTAN

UNITED KINGDOM

FRANCE

|||||| U.S. AND COUNTRIES
WITH WHICH IT HAS
MUTUAL DEFENSE

▮ COMMUNIST BLOC

THE MUTUAL DEFEN.

TRM

- UNITED STATES
- CANADA
- ICELAND
- NORWAY
- UNITED KINGDOM
- NETHERLANDS
- DENMARK
- BELGIUM
- LUXEMBOURG
- PORTUGAL
- FRANCE
- ITALY
- GREECE
- TURKEY
- WEST GERMANY

NORTH ATLANTIC TREATY

RIO TREATY

- UNITED STATES
- MEXICO
- CUBA
- HAITI
- DOMINICAN REP.
- HONDURAS
- GUATEMALA
- EL SALVADOR
- NICARAGUA
- COSTA RICA
- PANAMA
- COLOMBIA
- VENEZUELA
- ECUADOR
- PERU
- BRAZIL
- BOLIVIA
- PARAGUAY
- CHILE
- ARGENTINA
- URUGUAY

YSTEM IN THE 1950's

favored at least bombing the besieging army with carrier-based planes, but Dullies failed to gain support among allied nations. Congressional leaders had no stomach for an intervention that might soon involve more ground troops than the Korean War and in which the United States might have to fight alone. The United States did not intervene; there was no "massive retaliation." Dienbienphu fell on May 7, 1954. At a conference in Geneva, the United States, stripped of bargaining power (except for the threat of unilateral intervention), had to stand by, neither associating itself with negotiations with Red China nor approving the agreements of July 1954, which provided for a cease-fire and the partitioning of Indochina into three independent nations.

After the Geneva conference, Secretary Dulles succeeded in building a Southeast Asia Treaty Organization (SEATO) to serve as a counterpart of NATO and help contain communism. SEATO (established September 1954) was far less impressive, since the terms of the Geneva conference kept Nationalist China and nations of Indochina (Vietnam, Laos, and Cambodia) from participating. Several of the most important Asian states (India, Ceylon, Burma, and Indonesia) refused to join because they were committed to neutralism. This left only three nations of Southeast Asia—Pakistan, Thailand, and the Philippines—to join with the United States, Great Britain, France, Australia, and New Zealand. They drew up a pact, weaker than the North Atlantic Treaty, providing only that an attack upon one would be regarded as a threat to the others. SEATO opened the way for economic and military aid, but without the key nations of Southeast Asia participating, it remained a relatively ineffective organization.

The United States continued to function in Asia as best it could on a virtually unilateral basis. Trouble with Communist China developed over some offshore islands that Chiang continued to garrison—Quemoy and Matsu and the Tachen Islands. Occasionally, Chiang's air force attacked the Communists from them. Since the Mutual Defense Treaty with Chiang, signed at the end of 1954, did not include these islands, Red China in January 1955 began air attacks upon the Tachens and bombardment of Quemoy. Before invasion could follow, Congress granted Eisenhower rather indefinite emergency powers to aid Chiang. These sufficed to maintain a precarious status quo.

Intermittently, the Chinese Communists renewed their pressure upon Quemoy and Matsu. In August 1958 they began another serious bombardment. Secretary Dulles, although not always clear in what he said, implied repeatedly that the United States would help Chiang defend the islands. But the United States could not count upon the support of other Western nations if a large-scale struggle with Red China developed. The militant Chinese Communists in 1959 pressed on other borders. After crushing a revolt in Tibet, they pushed troops across several ill-defined frontiers into areas claimed by India. Of much more serious concern to the United States, they backed a Communist penetration deep into Laos, one of the nations of Indochina.

In the involved and unending struggle with Communist China, the American arsenal of atomic weapons was of relatively little effect even against a nation that as yet did not possess any. Against the Soviet Union, with its rapidly expanding nuclear strength, the threat of massive thermonuclear retaliation was still less effective.

OUR GERMAN ALLY

Fortunately, the United States and its allies did not depend upon nuclear power alone. The concept of NATO was embodied in its emblem of a sword and a shield. The sword stood for atomic weapons, the striking force, and the shield for conventional ground forces, to deter or withstand attack. During the Korean War, the United States began to rebuild its military establishment at home and gradually to pour funds into NATO to strengthen its defenses in terms of ground forces as well as atomic weapons.

Europeans worried over the slowness of the United States to provide arms and men, its failure (partly because of constitutional limitations) to commit itself clearly in advance to resist any armed attack on western European nations, and its desire to rearm Germany.

While the French were still afraid of the Germans, the Germans themselves were so war weary that it was difficult to persuade them to arm again. Between 1950 and 1954 they were able to win back step by step almost all their sovereignty in return for rearming.

To make the rearming of Germany acceptable to France, Great Britain promised in 1954 to keep four divisions and a tactical air force on the Continent as long as her allies wanted them. With this reassurance France agreed to a treaty that same month restoring full sovereignty to Germany (except for the stationing of allied troops in West Berlin until Germany was reunified). The West German army was to be limited to twelve divisions, which would be supplied to NATO. Germany promised not to seek reunification or extension of her boundaries through force and was prohibited from manufacturing nuclear, biological, or chemical weapons. Germany joined NATO and thus directly became a military ally of the United States. In 1957 she contributed her first forces—five divisions totaling 120,000 men.

THE GENEVA SPIRIT

After the death of Stalin in 1953, there were increasing signs that new Russian policies might lead to some enlargement of freedom behind the iron curtain and some relaxation of tensions with the Western powers. Russia extended a peace overture to Tito of Yugoslavia, returned a key base to Finland, recognized the Federal Republic of West Germany, and signed a peace treaty with Japan. Above all, the Soviet Union joined with the Western powers in signing a peace treaty with Austria, making it a neutral state, and terminating the long military occupation.

The softening of Soviet policy and the increase in international exchanges led to demands from Europeans, Asians, and even Americans for a conference among the heads of state—a "summit conference"—to consider means of easing international tensions. But the greatest single motive for such a meeting was the knowledge that both the United States and the Soviet Union were manufacturing hydrogen bombs of staggering destructive power.

In August 1953 the Russians had set off a hydrogen explosive. Eisenhower warned a few weeks later that the physical security of the United States had "almost totally disappeared before the long-range bomber and the destructive power of a single bomb." The meaning of this became dramatically clear in the spring of 1954 when the United States announced that it had exploded in the Pacific a bomb powerful enough to destroy or put out of commission all of New York City.

Against this background, the American people, after an initial wariness, became enthusiastic about the meeting of the heads of the United States, Great Britain, France, and Russia in Geneva (July 1955). Eisenhower, hopeful that he could wage "a war for peace," proposed at the meetings that the Russians and the United States exchange blueprints of their armed forces and permit inspection of their military installations from the air. He declared to Premier Nicolai A. Bulganin: "The United States will never take part in an aggressive war." Bulganin replied: "Mr. President, we believe that statement."

The affability of the Russians at Geneva immensely relieved the American people, who were hopeful for the moment that a real change of policy had come about. This "Geneva spirit," as newspapermen called it, led to a general feeling on the part of most Western nations that a nuclear war between the Soviet Union and the United States would not develop. Secretary Dulles declared, however, that the conference had avoided "creating an illusion that all was now so well that we could safely relax our efforts to build individual and collective self-defense." All proposals from both sides had been referred to a future foreign ministers' conference. Even before it met, several nations began to scale down their NATO contributions.

President Eisenhower upon his return from Geneva warned: "We must never be deluded into believing that one week of friendly, even fruitful negotiations can wholly eliminate a problem arising out of the wide gulf that separates East and West." The American public, less inclined to caution, greeted the President with unrestrained acclaim.

The subsequent foreign ministers' conference failed dismally to agree upon German unification, disarmament, or lowering of trade barriers. Even before it adjourned, the "Geneva spirit" rapidly evaporated throughout the West.

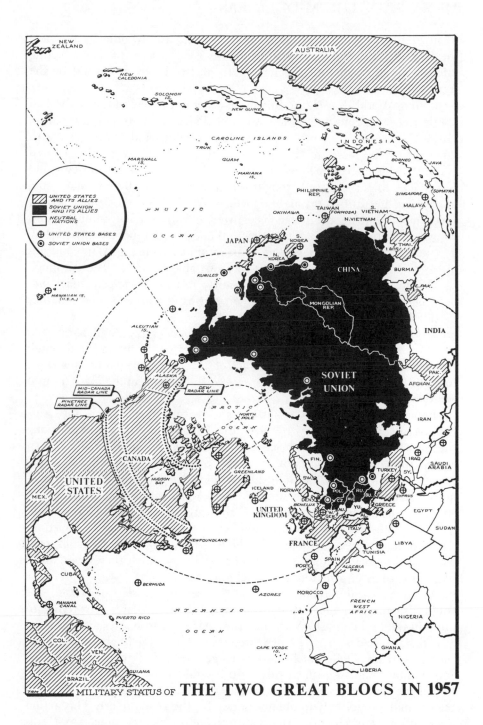

MILITARY STATUS OF **THE TWO GREAT BLOCS IN 1957**

MENACE IN THE MIDDLE EAST

Soon a new Russian drive was launched toward the Middle East, where the United States had long been deeply involved because of its conflicting interests in the people of the new state of Israel and in the oil of the Arab states.

During World War II, the British, in order not to offend the Arabs, had continued restrictions upon immigration to Palestine. Both political parties in the United States favored lifting these restrictions and creating a Jewish state. After the war, the British brought the problem to the United Nations, which recommended partitioning Palestine between Jews and Arabs. The Jews successfully fought off military attacks by the Arabs and, on the day the British mandate ended, May 14, 1948, proclaimed a new government. President Truman recognized it within a few minutes, thus ending UN proposals to put Palestine under a temporary trusteeship. The new nation, Israel, fought off armies from surrounding Arab countries until the United Nations established an unstable truce in 1949. Although the United States tried to promote amity, relations between Israel and its neighbors continued close to the point of explosion, and other quarrels in the Middle East persisted.

Gradually, the United States won over some of the Arab nations to the Western defense system. This country leased air bases from Saudi Arabia; and through the Baghdad Pact of 1955 Secretary Dulles managed to bring the northern bloc of Arab states—Iraq, Iran, and Pakistan—into the defense arrangement.

Dulles' diplomacy was less successful with Egypt, which for years had quarreled with the British over the Sudan and British bases along the Suez Canal. The United States tried to mediate; in 1954 the British agreed to remove their troops from the Suez area. After Gamal Abdel Nasser came to power, the State Department tried to woo him, although he proclaimed emphatic neutralist and Arab nationalist policies and strove for leadership of the entire Arab world. Secretary Dulles tried to win him with offers of economic aid—even the sum needed to construct the enormous Aswan dam on the Nile. Meanwhile, the Russians concluded a deal, made public in September 1955, by which they gave Nasser large quantities of armaments in exchange for cotton.

With sufficient Communist arms Nasser might destroy Israel. He could also threaten the security system the United States was trying to build in the Middle East. With the arms that went to Nasser and his close ally, Syria, would also go Russian experts to show Egyptians how to use them. Secretary Dulles met the challenge. Instead of continuing to be conciliatory toward Egypt, in July 1956 he suddenly withdrew his promise to provide funds for a dam. A week later Nasser retaliated by seizing the Suez Canal, purportedly to obtain money for the Nile project. This action gave him a stranglehold on the main oil line to Europe, since two-thirds of the proved oil reserves of the world were in the Middle East and four-fifths of the oil for western Europe flowed from there.

During the tedious months of negotiations with Nasser that followed, Great Britain, France, and Israel all came to feel that they were not obtaining as much support as they should from the United States. Meanwhile, the armed strength of Egypt was growing rapidly. On October 29, 1956, Israeli forces struck a preventive blow at Egypt. The next day the British and French intervened to drive the Egyptian forces from the Suez Canal zone. They were militarily successful, but not before the Egyptians had thoroughly blocked the canal. The United States led the United Nations in denouncing the military intervention; the Western alliances seemed in danger of dissolving; the Soviet Union threatened to send "volunteers" to the aid of Egypt. Under these pressures the British and French issued a cease-fire order on November 6. Another prolonged truce between Egypt and Israel began under the supervision of the United Nations.

The power vacuum in the Middle East in the weeks after the Suez cease-fire created new opportunities for the spread of communism. Once again the American public was alarmed and incensed, since coincident with the Suez crisis came brutal Soviet suppression of an uprising in Hungary. Because of the nuclear stalemate, the United States could not intervene in Hungary. It limited itself to fostering UN resolutions of censure and to admitting tens of thousands of refugees.

In the Middle East more positive action afterward seemed possible. The public was receptive when the President appeared before Congress on January 5, 1957, to enunciate what came to be called the Eisenhower Doctrine. He asked Congress to authorize military and economic aid "to secure and protect the territorial independence" of Middle Eastern nations "against overt armed aggression from any nation controlled by international communism." Congress authorized the President to use armed force as he deemed necessary and to spend $200 million on economic aid in the area.

As an instrument of pressure upon Egypt, the Eisenhower Doctrine was of little effect. Nasser reopened the Suez Canal on his own terms. In April 1957 American policy seemed more successful when the United States rushed its Sixth Fleet to the eastern Mediterranean to bolster the government of Jordan. Three other states, Saudi Arabia, Iraq, and Lebanon, seemed to give at least tacit support to the Eisenhower Doctrine.

Soviet penetration in the next few months, both through feeding Arab nationalism and through providing arms to Egypt, Syria, and Yemen, effectively countered the American policy. In August 1957 the Russians negotiated a $500-million arms-and-aid pact with Syria. In its aftermath, a pro-Soviet army clique seized power. Since the clique of course did not ask for American aid, the Eisenhower Doctrine was inoperative in Syria, but the State Department, declaring that Syria's neighbors were alarmed, sent them weapons. The strong tone of the United States led to an unfavorable reaction among the Arab nations, and they reaffirmed their solidarity.

Egypt and Syria, combining to form the United Arab Republic, continued to exert pressure on their neighbors. When a pro-Nasser clique took over Iraq (July 1958), it appeared that Lebanon and Jordan might also come under Nasser's domination. The pro-Western government of Lebanon requested aid against rebels, and the United States rushed in troops. At the same time Great Britain sent forces into Jordan. In the fall of 1958, when conditions became stabilized in Lebanon, the United States withdrew its troops. Iraq, however, continued to be a serious problem. Secretary Dulles, in order to balance its loss from the Baghdad Pact mutual-defense organization, announced that the United States would assume full partnership in the alliance. But the withdrawal of Iraq from the alliance did not lead that country into Nasser's United Arab Republic as expected. The elements favoring this course soon fell from power in Iraq, and the danger in 1959 and after seemed to be that the country would swing into the Communist bloc. Reacting against the Communist trend in Iraq, Nasser veered back toward the West, and the United States again began plying him with favors. Conditions were thus unstable and uncertain in much of the Middle East.

THE COMMUNISTS GAIN

The Eisenhower administration was hard pressed to contain the expansion of Communist power in the world, even without attempting the "roll-back" of which Dulles once had spoken. Indeed, before the end of the administration, the Communists appeared to be making further gains.

The Rocket Race

The onslaught of Communist ideology and power was especially frightening because of the apparent failure of the United States to keep pace with the Soviet Union in the development of intercontinental ballistic missiles, a failure that the Russians tried to exploit throughout the world. In early 1957 the United States had appeared to be abreast or ahead of the Soviet Union in the development of guided missiles with nuclear warheads. Because of the potential horror of these weapons, both nations seemed ready to reach disarmament agreements during seven months of discussions in 1957 at a meeting of the UN subcommittee in London. The United States insisted upon schemes of strict inspection, including proposals for aerial photography over strips of each other's territory. To this the Soviet Union would not agree.

Then, in August, the Soviet Union announced that it had successfully tested an intercontinental ballistic missile. In contrast, the United States had successfully tested only intermediate-range missiles that traveled from 1,500 to 3,000 miles. The Russian claims received sobering confirmation in October when Soviet scientists, using a rocket booster engine more powerful than any yet developed in the United States, launched the first successful satellite, the "sputnik."

Khrushchev, who in a series of bold moves had just consolidated his power in the Kremlin, now issued a series of strong statements. The intent of his "sputnik diplomacy" was clearly to shake the Western alliance and impress neutral nations. The reaction within the United States, especially when the first American attempt to launch a much smaller satellite failed, was more one of angry fear than of congratulations to the Russian scientists. Three months later the United States began launching its own, smaller satellites.

As an indication of his concern, President Eisenhower, although recuperating from a mild stroke, flew to Paris (December 1957) to lend strong moral support at a NATO conference. In January 1958 he devoted almost his entire annual message to Congress to the armaments crisis and to the need to surpass the Soviet Union in providing aid for developing countries. He called upon an acquiescent Congress for heavy additional expenditures to rush development and construction of long-range missiles and of submarines and cruisers that could launch missiles. The first task confronting the nation was "to ensure our safety through strength," he pointed out. "But we could make no more tragic mistake than merely to concentrate on military strength. For if we did only this, the future would hold nothing for the world but an age of terror."

Meanwhile, extensive nuclear testing after 1954 by both the United States and the Soviet Union, climaxed by the Russian explosion of several "dirty" bombs, greatly increased the fallout of radioactive isotopes. Throughout the world there was a fear of possible harmful effects. "Any dose, however small, produces some biological effect and . . . this effect is harmful," the Joint Congressional Committee on Atomic Energy granted in a 1959 report. If testing were to continue at the same rate over the next two generations, the report warned, the average concentration of radioactive strontium in the bones would be close to what scientists had estimated would be the maximum permissible body burden. This threat, well before 1959, was bringing popular pressure for the curtailing of nuclear tests.

In the spring of 1958 Khrushchev announced a unilateral abstention from nuclear tests by the Soviet Union. This left Eisenhower with the choice of two courses. He could follow the reasoning of most officials in the Defense Department, who held that nuclear weapons were the only way in which the United States could counter the enormous land armies of the Soviet Union and China—and continue tests. Or he could promise to stop tests on the condition that the Soviet Union would agree to adequate inspection.

He decided upon the latter course and announced that the United States and its allies would suspend tests for one year beginning October 31, 1958. The suspension would continue on a year-to-year basis, provided a proper system of control could be developed and substantial progress could be made on disarmament negotiations. The Soviet Union, proclaiming that this was a Western trick, announced that it would resume testing. Nevertheless, Eisenhower declared that for the time being the United

States would continue its suspension of tests as it sought some workable agreement with the Soviet Union. Representatives of the United States, Great Britain, and the Soviet Union met in Geneva and slowly, laboriously, tried to construct a regulatory treaty.

In 1959 Khrushchev made much propaganda use of the failure of the United States to catch up with Russia in astronautical feats. These feats obscured the fact that the "missile gap" between the two nations was not as great as had been feared two years earlier. The United States was successfully producing and testing its own missiles and developing plans for hiding and spreading the launching sites so that it would require ten times as many Russian missiles to destroy them. The success of the navy in constructing atomic-powered submarines that could launch missiles and in bringing the submarines up through the ice at the North Pole was a dramatic example of American achievement. The naval development of "Project Tepee," a radio-monitoring system that could detect any missile launchings anywhere in the world, was an indication of the technical advance of American defense.

If the Russians were to attack the United States, they could not expect their own cities to remain unscathed. The reverse held equally true—that American nuclear power would be incapable of destroying all the sites from which the Russians could launch missiles. The Congressional Joint Committee on Atomic Energy reported in August 1959 that an attack upon the United States, if it came, might kill 50 million people, seriously injure 20 million more, and destroy or render unusable for months half of the dwellings in the country. Crops would be contaminated and swept by fire. The only hopeful note was the assurance that bomb shelters for the entire population could reduce casualties by 25 or 30 percent.

Atomic-powered submarine U.S.S. Skate surfacing through the ice near the North Pole (U.S. NAVY PHOTO)

Friendly Overtures Fail

Suddenly, in November 1958, Khrushchev precipitated a new crisis over Berlin, where the West's position was, as always, vulnerable. He asserted that conditions had changed so markedly in Berlin since the end of the war that the occupation agreements no longer applied. In six months he proposed to sign a separate peace treaty with the government of East Germany, turning over to it all the Russian occupation functions in Berlin including control over the access routes that stretched 110 miles to West Germany.

The United States insisted that its treaty rights still held and undertook the twofold task of trying to maintain unity among its Western allies and of getting from the Soviet government concessions that would correspond to any that the United States might make. Neither task was easy. The Soviet Union made alternative proposals that were as unacceptable as the first demand had been, and Khrushchev manipulated the issue to try to force a summit meeting. The United States was not willing to go further than a foreign ministers' conference unless the Russians became more conciliatory. The Geneva sessions beginning in May 1959 were discouragingly unfruitful.

Meanwhile, the burden of conducting American foreign policy had shifted to a new Secretary of State, Christian Herter, when Dulles, dying of cancer, resigned in April 1959. Herter was a strong successor. He had capped his foreign-service record as a young man with a successful career in politics. But he did not continue the one-man determination of foreign policy that had distinguished Dulles. President Eisenhower now assumed a larger measure of responsibility, and this pointed toward new interchanges at the top with the Russians.

Exchanges at lower levels had been going on at an increasing rate since the Geneva thaw of 1955. One of its few positive effects had been personal and cultural interchanges of musicians, dancers, students, and delegations of all kinds, climaxed in the summer of 1959 by a visit to the United States of Anastas Mikoyan, a Soviet deputy premier, and to Russia of Vice President Nixon. The Russians demonstrated their wares at a fair in New York City, and the Americans at a corresponding fair in Moscow showed crowds of Russians the components of the high standard of living in the United States. While Nixon was at the fair, he engaged in informal debate with Khrushchev. The Russian press was for the most part hostile, but the crowds were friendly, and Khrushchev himself, while holding dogmatically to Soviet positions, seemed to demonstrate a keen interest in things American.

In August 1959 President Eisenhower announced that he would exchange visits with the Russian leader. The purpose in inviting Khrushchev, Eisenhower explained, was "to give him the opportunity to see what Americans are like" and "to give him, face to face, the basic convictions of our people on the major issues of the day." Khrushchev, during his travels in the United States, received on the whole a hearty welcome, despite the coldness of most American officials and the hostile demonstrations of certain groups, especially those sympathizing with the Hungarian rebels of 1956. He impressed Americans with his energy, toughness, and—except for a few petulant outbursts—good humor. Eisenhower, postponing his return visit, made tours of western Europe, southern Asia, and Latin America, to the cheers of enthusiastic crowds at almost every stop.

A second summit conference, to meet in Paris, was scheduled for May 1960. On May 1 an unarmed American U-2 plane was downed inside the Soviet Union. The American government at first denied, then acknowledged and attempted to justify the fact that the plane had been engaged in aerial reconnaissance of a kind the United States had been carrying on, systematically but secretly, for some time. At the Paris meeting, unsatisfied by Eisenhower's belated promise to discontinue flights over Russian territory, Khrushchev made the U-2 incident an occasion for denouncing Eisenhower and breaking up the conference.

Khrushchev also took back his invitation for Eisenhower to go to the Soviet Union. Eisenhower, having planned to stop in Japan on the way home from Russia, went ahead with arrangements for a Far Eastern trip in June. A new security pact, authorizing continued American bases in Japan, awaited ratification. Communist agitators now played upon the pacifism of the Japanese people, a pacifism that American occupation policies earlier had stimulated. In Tokyo mobs began wild demonstrations against the pact, against Premier Nobusuke Kishi, who sponsored it, and against the Eisenhower visit. At the last minute, after the President had reached as far as Manila, his Japan appearance was called off. The Kishi government managed to put the unpopular treaty into effect; but throughout the world the Eisenhower administration could scarcely avoid a serious loss to American prestige, which already had been weakened by the administration's handling of the spy-plane affair.

Disgruntled Neighbors

The incessant threats against areas close to the Communist perimeter so occupied the American government and people that they paid scant attention to an area of vital worth to the United States and of growing vulnerability to Communist influence—the area to the south. One of the minor ironies of this hectic age was the erosion of the Good Neighbor feeling between Latin American nations and the United States during the very years when this country was extending much of the Good Neighbor policy to Europe and Asia.

On paper there was no deterioration. Quite the contrary; the Latin American nations signed new pacts and received additional forms of aid. They all became members of the United Nations. In 1947, at a conference at Rio de Janeiro, they drafted an Inter-American Treaty of Reciprocal Assistance and the following year established an Organization of American States. The United States had abandoned the old unilateral Monroe Doctrine by entering into pacts and organizations providing

Preparing taped Voice of America programs for Japanese audiences (UNITED STATES INFORMATION AGENCY)

for mutual action whether in defense, settlement of disputes, or economic cooperation.

Yet the overwhelming military and economic power of the "colossus of the North" remained. Latin Americans were not pleased when the United States brought its prestige to bear against the totalitarian dictator of Argentina, Juan D. Perón, in 1946–1947, even though the pressure failed. They were not much more pleased when the United States successfully brought pressure against a pro-Communist regime in Guatemala in 1954. But in the late fifties, when many of the nations overthrew dictators, the more common complaint was that the United States had been too friendly toward despots, as in Venezuela, and not enthusiastic enough about rebels like Fidel Castro, who came into power in Cuba in 1959 and who thereafter devoted himself to denuciations of "Yankee imperialism."

Above all, the problems from which Latin American peoples were suffering were economic. After the close of World War II they could no longer sell raw materials from their farms and mines to the United States in such large quantities or at such favorable prices as before. The soaring costs of the American manufactured goods they imported further hurt them. At home they were undergoing a rapid industrial revolution, an accompanying social evolution, and an explosive population increase at the highest rate in the world, as much as 2.5 percent per year. Already their combined population had passed that of the United States. All these factors helped create acute internal problems.

Inevitably, the United States would have to be involved in the solution of economic questions because the hostility of neighbors to the south would be potentially ruinous and because the two areas had become increasingly interdependent economically. Trade with Latin America exceeded $8 billion a year by the end of the fifties and accounted for one-third of the imports and one-fourth of the exports of the United States. In Latin America 80 percent of the foreign capital was American; it had a book value of about $9.5 billion. (This figure was second only to the $13 billion invested in Canada, which was also unhappy about its economic relations with the United States.)

It seemed to Latin Americans that, despite these close economic ties, the United States was doing little specifically to help them solve their problems—to provide adequate capital for large-scale development, to stabilize raw materials at a profitable level, and to conquer inflation. They felt neglected as the American government poured billions into Europe and Asia while giving Latin America only a comparative pittance. Secretary Dulles was occupied elsewhere, and the Eisenhower administration, under the influence of two successive conservative secretaries of the Treasury, was cold to requests for government loans for development. The festering economic ills and other grievances that could easily be focused against the United States were ready made for the Communists. Exercising an influence out of proportion to their small numbers, they were active from Cuba to Guatemala and Argentina.

Despite riots and disorders, the Latin American discontent received little notice in the United States until May 1958, when Vice President Nixon was mobbed in Lima and Caracas. In the aftermath of the national shock, the State Department speeded changes in policy that were already slowly under way. This country helped Latin American nations negotiate export quota pacts among themselves to raise the price of coffee and some metals, and it expedited negotiations toward the establishment of a regional common market among the republics. When, in June 1958, the president of Brazil called for an Operation Pan-America to speed economic development, the American government agreed to furnish nearly half the capital for a new billion-dollar Inter-American Bank to make development loans. It also tried to improve public relations in a way Nixon had suggested by giving no more than a correct handshake to dictators but offering a warm embrace to democratic leaders.

The administration was increasing its attention to Latin America none too soon, since it was obvious that the well-disciplined, widely pervasive Communist activities throughout the area were receiving direction from Russia. Early in 1959 Latin American Communist leaders returned from attending the twenty-first party congress in Moscow and began the systematic denunciation of every point of the new United States program.

The full import of the Communist challenge to the south became clear in 1960. Fidel Castro, whose revolutionary accession to power had been cheered by Americans at the beginning of 1959, turned his administration increasingly to the left and indulged in shrill tirades against the United States. The Eisenhower administration, acting with restraint, was slow to retaliate economically until, in the summer of 1960, Castro systematically confiscated a billion dollars' worth of American property. At this point the United States stopped importing Cuban sugar at a subsidized price. Castro complained to the UN Security Council that the United States was engaging in economic aggression.

The Soviet leader Khrushchev proclaimed that the Monroe Doctrine was dead and that, if the United States were to intervene militarily, Soviet artillerymen could "support Cuba with rocket fire." In the fall of 1960 tension heightened as Castro tried to spread his revolution to neighboring republics. Eisenhower established a naval patrol to prevent an invasion of Guatemala or Nicaragua. At the same time, secretly, Americans were training an anti-Castro Cuban force at a camp in Guatemala. In January 1961 Castro ordered the staff of the United States embassy in Havana cut from eighty-seven to eleven. The United States then severed diplomatic relations with Cuba. Soviet influence clearly extended to within ninety miles of the United States.

twenty-three
Eisenhower Republicanism

In the prosperous but uncertain years of the early fifties, Americans above all else sought security in domestic as well as foreign policy. A majority of voters were more interested in preserving their economic gains than in adventuring toward new governmental programs or in retreating toward earlier dogmas. It was a nation moderate in its views that looked for its security to President Eisenhower. Throughout his presidency, Eisenhower took only brief excursions to the right or the left of his firm moderate principles.

BUSINESSMEN IN GOVERNMENT

Once in office, Eisenhower set up a businessmen's administration. To his cabinet he appointed one of the highest-paid corporation lawyers in the country (Secretary of State Dulles), the president of General Motors (Secretary of Defense Charles E. Wilson), the president of Mark Hanna's former firm M. A. Hanna and Company (Secretary of the Treasury George Humphrey), a New England manufacturer, two automobile distributors, a conservative specialist in farm marketing, and the wife of a wealthy Texas publisher (Mrs. Oveta Culp Hobby, who had been wartime commander of the WACS and who was named to head the Department of Health, Education, and Welfare when it came into existence in 1953). Something of an exception was the Secretary of Labor, Martin P. Durkin, the president of the plumbers' union, who had backed Adlai Stevenson in the 1952 campaign. "Eight millionaires and a plumber," the *New Republic* disrespectfully remarked. At the hearing on his appointment, Wilson played into the hands of Democratic critics by testifying that he had long assumed that "what was good for our country was good for General Motors, and vice versa." A few days later, Stevenson declared: "While the New Dealers have all left Washington to make way for the car dealers,

I hasten to say that I, for one, do not believe the story that the general welfare has become a subsidiary of General Motors."

Eisenhower's system of administering the government gave special importance to this cabinet made up preponderantly of businessmen. Borrowing from earlier army experience, he established his assistant, Sherman Adams, former governor of New Hampshire, as a kind of chief of staff, and from Adams down through the cabinet he extended a chain of command. Through the cabinet and through numerous new committees, administrators arrived at important policy decisions that they referred to the President, who relied heavily upon these recommendations.

"EISENHOWER PROSPERITY"

At the beginning of the new administration Secretary of the Treasury Humphrey undertook to restrict bank credit and thus prevent inflation. By the fall of 1953 the threat was one of deflation instead. When the economy slackened, Secretary Humphrey and the Federal Reserve Board reversed the scarce-money policies and eased credit. The Republican administration's first venture with the expedients of Keynesian economics (manipulating money and credit to control the business cycle) was a success. By the summer of 1955 the American economy was again booming.

In order to avoid strikes that might unsettle economic conditions, several large industries, led by the automobile manufacturers, made new concessions to organized labor. As early as 1948 Walter Reuther, the president of the United Automobile Workers, had obtained from General Motors, and later from other manufacturers, an "escalator clause" in contracts, providing for automatic increases or decreases in wages every three months as the consumer price index rose or fell. In 1955 he demanded from the Ford Motor Company a guaranteed annual wage. Ford compromised by agreeing that workers should receive 65 percent of their net weekly wages for the first four weeks they were unemployed, and 60 percent for the next twenty-two weeks. General Motors followed. A few months later, steelworkers received from the American Can Company and the Continental Can Company the first guarantee of an annual wage.

The round of wage raises continued through 1956. After a five-week strike, steelworkers won a substantial gain, and the United Mine Workers without a strike obtained a thirty-cents-an-hour increase. Factory workers' wages went up to approximately $80 per week. These wage increases, together with other factors, led to widespread wholesale price rises and a renewed threat of inflation.

In December 1955 the American Federation of Labor and the Congress of Industrial Organizations merged at the top into a new giant federation, the AFL-CIO. The powerful Teamsters' Brotherhood in 1957 became the focal point of a congressional investigation into labor racketeering. A Senate committee charged the president of the Teamsters, David Beck, with the misappropriation of over $320,000 in union funds. When Beck appeared before the committee, he refused to answer questions, invoking the constitutional protection of the Fifth Amendment against self-incrimination. Ultimately, the committee brought forth so much evidence against Beck that he declined to run for reelection as president of the Teamsters. But at their convention the Teamsters defiantly elected, as their new president, James Hoffa, also under attack by the committee. His election resulted in the eviction of the Teamsters, the largest union in the United States, from the AFL-CIO. The congressional investigation led to the Labor Reform Act of 1959, which was intended to promote honest elections of union officials, safeguard union funds, ban Communist leaders, and restrict boycotting and picketing.

The great staples piled up in surplus, and from 1948 to 1956, farm prices dropped one-third while the national income went up by one-half. In 1948 farmers received 8.9 percent of the national income; in 1956, only 4.1 percent. Farm population declined steadily, to 22,300,000 in 1956— only one-ninth of the nation. In that single year one out of every eleven of the farm population either moved to a city or was absorbed by an expanding city. While farm produce prices fell, consumer food prices continued to rise. Mainly this was because distribution costs were steadily going up. The farmer was caught in a squeeze, as prices for his produce slipped while prices of what he bought gradually increased.

As surpluses of such agricultural staples as wheat and cotton piled up, the government sought to bolster the prices through $8 billion worth of purchases. In 1954 President Eisenhower and Secretary of Agriculture Benson proposed a shift away from rigid price supports to a flexible sliding-scale program. The purpose was to cut government losses and end artificiality in production and distribution. The 1955 harvest was the first to be grown under the new flexible system, but already Democratic politicians were denouncing flexible supports as ones that could only "flex" downward. Seeking to win the farm vote, in 1956 they wrote a bill providing for high price supports and a subsidy for farmers who let land lie fallow. They thought they had put Eisenhower in an impossible position, and as they expected, he vetoed the bill. But in May 1956 he pulled out of the vetoed bill the provision for a "soil bank" of fallow land and threw it back at the congressional Democrats. In this form Congress passed the bill, and it became law. Under the 1956 program, farmers took 12.3 million acres out of production in return for payments of over $250 million.

In the realm of public power development, the administration demonstrated its friendliness toward private enterprise. Eisenhower in 1953 referred to expansion of the Tennessee Valley Authority as "creeping socialism." The administration sought to circumvent the TVA by contracting with the Dixon-Yates syndicate in 1954 to build a huge steam power plant on the banks of the Mississippi. The administration declared that the contract would save taxpayers an immediate $100 million in construction costs, but opponents pointed to the large profits that the syndicate would collect over many years. The power would cost the government $3.5 million per year more than TVA power. Ultimately, in 1955, when the city of Memphis, Tennessee, offered to build the plant, Eisenhower retreated to the principle of decentralization and canceled the Dixon-Yates contract.

The Eisenhower administration proposed federal "partnership" with local public or private enterprise in power construction. Secretary of the Interior McKay thus permitted a private power company to plan three small power dams in Hell's Canyon on the Snake River rather than obtain appropriations for one large federal multipurpose dam. In keeping with his feeling that development of resources should be decentralized, Eisenhower signed a bill turning over to states offshore oil lands along the Gulf of Mexico and the Pacific Coast.

While the Eisenhower administration moved toward the right, conciliating the Taft wing of the Republican party in Congress, the President retained the basic general welfare programs that had been enacted during the previous twenty years. He took a firm stand against so-called socialized medicine but proposed a public health-insurance program that would involve little more than limited underwriting of private insurance companies issuing health policies. Congress passed no health-insurance legislation, but in 1954 extended Social Security to 10 million more people and unemployment compensation to an additional 4 million. In 1956 Congress authorized a ten-year highway-building program for which it would allocate almost $25 billion.

This concept of the limited role of the federal government in providing for the general welfare was what Eisenhower referred to as "dynamic conservatism." It appealed to many members of Congress. During his first two years in office, when Congress was narrowly Republican, Eisenhower was supported more often than not by a coalition of liberal Republi-

Traffic interchange, Dallas, Texas (DEPARTMENT OF COMMERCE)

cans and Democrats. Of eighty-three key issues brought to a vote in the 1953 session of Congress, the administration won seventy-four but succeeded in fifty-eight of these only through Democratic support. After the elections of 1954 the Democrats controlled both the House and the Senate.

DECLINE OF McCARTHYISM

Among the politicians who, after the Communist victory in China, had encouraged and capitalized upon the American people's fear of communism, none, as we saw earlier, rose more sensationally than Senator McCarthy. He received so much attention that "McCarthyism" became a synonym for hysterical anticommunism. Only gradually after the Korean armistice was the nation relieved from the worst excesses of McCarthyism.

The hunt for subversives in the government, begun during the Truman years, was intensified early in the Eisenhower administration. Large numbers of employees resigned or were dismissed—a total of 2,200 according to an official report. But most of the serious security risks had already been removed in the Truman purge. A study of some 400 of the Eisenhower administration cases by the Fund for the Republic of the Ford Foundation indicated that in a majority of them the charges had been insupportable, and often reinstatement ultimately followed. In July 1955 the Congress established a bipartisan Commission on Government Security to reevaluate the security program.

Senator McCarthy himself plummeted from the national limelight to relative obscurity. His downfall followed his serious blunder in obliquely attacking President Eisenhower and directly assailing Secretary of the Army Robert Stevens, in January 1954. The attacks led to congressional hearings, which turned into a great national spectacle viewed by millions over television. Many people for the first time saw McCarthy in action, as for thirteen days he bullied and harried Secretary Stevens, evading issues through irrelevant countercharges and insinuations, and interrupting to object at every point. As the public watched, McCarthy seemed to change from a national hero into something of a villain, then into a low buffoon. In December 1954 the Senate voted 67 to 22 to condemn him for conduct unbecoming a senator. He no longer had much of a following when he died in May 1957.

Remnants of the attitudes that had made possible the rise of McCarthy remained. There was, for example, the case of a consultant to the Atomic Energy Commission (AEC), J. Robert Oppenheimer, who had directed the wartime laboratory at Los Alamos, New Mexico, that made the first atomic bomb. In 1950 he had opposed the development of a hydrogen bomb. The FBI in 1953 distributed to the White House and several government departments a report on Oppenheimer detailing his prewar associations with Communists. On order from Eisenhower, a "blank wall" was placed between Oppenheimer and government secrets, pending hearings. A three-man board voted 2 to 1 against granting him security clearance; the AEC ratified the decision 4 to 1. Scientists were bitterly split over the wisdom of the decision.

The Supreme Court, as a result of the appointments of the Republican President, seemed to be moving toward a more liberal rather than conservative policy. In one case in 1957 it ruled that the government could not use secret FBI evidence against a defendant unless it was made available to his lawyers. Congress quickly passed legislation safeguarding FBI files. In four other cases the Court protected individuals who were suspected of being subversive against undue encroachment by federal or state power. In 1958 the Court ruled 5 to 4 that the State Department, in the absence of an act of Congress, was exceeding its authority in refusing passports to persons who failed to file affidavits "with respect to present or past membership in the Communist party." These decisions attracted relatively little attention compared with the Supreme Court rulings on desegregation.

DESEGREGATION BEGINS

A series of cases before the Supreme Court breaking down bit by bit racial segregation in public schools had been pressed by the National Association for the Advancement of Colored People since the late 1930s. Their target was a Supreme Court decision of 1896, *Plessy* v. *Ferguson*, which had interpreted the Fourteenth Amendment clause requiring that states give "equal protection of the laws" to mean that separate but equal facilities should be furnished to blacks. Finally, the Supreme Court reversed this doctrine in the case of *Brown* v. *Board of Education of Topeka* in May 1954. Chief Justice Earl Warren (who had been appointed by President Eisenhower in 1953, after the death of Chief Justice Vinson) delivered the unanimous opinion of the Court: "We conclude that in the field of public education the doctrine of 'separate but equal' has no place. Separate educational facilities are inherently unequal." The Court called for the desegregation of schools "with all deliberate speed."

Some Southern and Border States resorted to every possible legal device to avoid mixed schools. Each September, mob action against integration in a few communities within the South attracted widespread attention throughout the world. By the fall of 1957, of some 3,000 biracial school districts in the South, a total of 684 had begun desegregation. Schools within these districts in large cities in the upper South or the border area, like Washington, Baltimore, Louisville, and St. Louis, opened quietly on an integrated basis. But 2,300 districts, including all those in the Deep South and in Virginia, remained racially separate. Some districts attempted desegregation on a very slow, "token" basis. One of these was Little Rock, Arkansas, where intervention by the governor and threats by a mob led Eisenhower to send federal troops to maintain order.

Pressure from growing blocs of black voters in the North, and from blacks rising in economic status in the South, helped bring other changes. Eisenhower completed the desegregation of the armed forces and tried to bring about greater integration in the government and the District of Columbia. "There must be no second-class citizens in this country," he wrote the black Representative Adam Clayton Powell. Representative Powell, ironically, was instrumental in killing Eisenhower's school-aid program of 1956, which provided for grants of $250 million a year for five years to match state funds. Powell succeeded in amending the bill to ban racial segregation; Southern segregationists aligned themselves with Northern conservatives to defeat the bill.

Congress in August 1957, after debating sixty-three days, passed a new civil rights law—the first since Reconstruction—to give federal protection to blacks wishing to vote. In eight Southern states with an adult black population of over 3,750,000, only 850,000, or 25 percent, were registered and still fewer went to the polls. In a 1955 election in Mississippi, only about 1 percent of the adult blacks had voted. The Civil Rights Act empowered the federal government to remove some of the obstacles that state and local officials were placing in the way of black registration and voting. Federal judges were authorized to enjoin state officials from refusing to register qualified persons. The judges could fine recalcitrant officials up to $300 and could sentence them to forty-five days in jail, without a jury trial.

With the Supreme Court ruling out school segregation and the Congress legislating for civil rights, it seemed that a "second Reconstruction" was beginning, one that would complete the task of emancipation left unfinished in 1877.

A SECOND TERM FOR "IKE"

In 1955 President Eisenhower was at the height of his popularity. Only the anti-third-term Twenty-second Amendment, ratified in 1951 as a belated slap at Roosevelt, seemed to bar his remaining in the White House as long as he chose. Apparently, his health was excellent, but while vacationing in Colorado, on the morning of September 24, he suffered a heart attack.

Eisenhower began to make a promising recovery, but no one expected him to run for another term. In June, stricken a second time, he was operated upon for ileitis. Although the operation was serious, Eisenhower's advisers never let the question arise whether or not he would continue as a candidate—and except among some Democrats it seemed a matter above debate. At the Republican convention in San Francisco at the end of August, Eisenhower and Vice President Nixon were renominated by acclamation. The proceedings seemed to some observers to reflect more the atmosphere of a coronation than a party convention. Regardless of Eisenhower's overwhelming popularity, Adlai Stevenson and Estes Kefauver fought vigorously for the Democratic nomination in state primary after primary. In the end Stevenson triumphed at the Democratic convention and Kefauver became the vice-presidential nominee.

It was a rather dull campaign. Stevenson sought an issue by proposing that the United States agree to end hydrogen-bomb tests. The average voter, relieved because the stalemate in nuclear weapons seemed to rule out a third world war, refused to worry about international affairs until actual shooting in the Suez area just before Election Day sent him to seek refuge with Eisenhower as commander in chief. Altogether, about 58 per-cent of the voters marked their ballots for Eisenhower, although he was sixty-six, the oldest man ever to be reelected to the presidency, and had suffered two serious illnesses in little more than a year past. He received more than 35 million votes to only 26 million for Stevenson and carried forty-one states. It was not much of a triumph for the Republican party. The prestige of the President pulled some Republican congressmen to narrow victories, but the Democrats continued to control both houses of Congress.

During Eisenhower's second administration, domestic policies were lit-tle changed. In 1957 Congress occupied itself largely with trying to slash the President's $71.8 billion budget, the largest in peacetime history. Even Secretary of the Treasury Humphrey (who resigned a few months later) joined in the onslaught against the "terrific" expenditures.

At the close of 1957 the nation skidded into the most serious recession since the war. By late spring of 1958 industrial production had dropped 14 percent below the level of a year earlier, and approximately 5 million workers were unemployed. Again the so-called built-in stabilizers of the economy, such as unemployment-insurance payments to those out of work, somewhat softened the blow of the recession.

As Republicans prepared for the congressional campaign of 1958, they

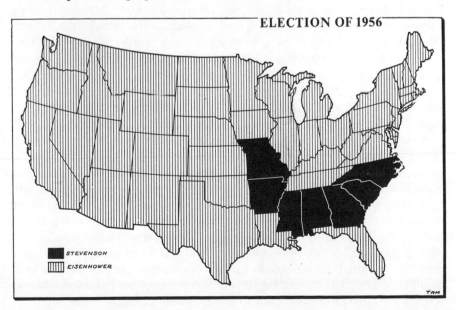

ELECTION OF 1956

STEVENSON
EISENHOWER

were handicapped by the persistence of economic trouble. Some of the more conservative Republican candidates, most notably Senate Minority Leader William Knowland, running for governor of California, centered their campaigns on attacks on organized labor. In some states they sought "right-to-work" laws to outlaw union shops (plants in which every employee hired must join the union). This onslaught, in most states, succeeded only in ensuring a large labor vote for Democratic candidates. The Republican party was also weakened by the revelation in the spring of 1958 that Sherman Adams, in effect Eisenhower's Chief of Staff, had received gifts from a New England textile manufacturer. Adams resigned in September, too late to benefit the party.

The result on November 4, 1958, was a Democratic landslide of impressive proportions. The Democrats won 13 additional seats in the Senate, giving them a 62 to 34 majority. They gained an added 47 seats in the House, providing a majority of 282 to 153—the largest margin since Roosevelt's 1936 victory.

The voter reaction in 1958 had slight effect upon the national administration in the two years that followed. President Eisenhower presented Congress in January 1959 with a $77 billion budget, which he promised would be in balance—a budget that Northern Democrats decried as not sufficiently large in an expanding economy and not providing the services the nation needed. At first the Democrats in Congress gave promise of pushing far beyond Eisenhower's limited requests. As prosperity returned in the spring of 1959, however, public opinion began to react to the incessant warnings of the President and of conservative publicists that budget balancing was the only way to avoid another ruinous round of inflation. Eisenhower, acting more vigorously than in previous years, was able to marshal much public support and congressional voting strength for his conservative course, and Speaker Sam Rayburn and Senate Majority Leader Lyndon B. Johnson were more disposed to compromise than to throw their large Democratic majorities against him. As a result, Eisenhower succeeded in keeping down expenditures for inexpensive public housing for families displaced from slums and for other social services. He also succeeded in ending the 1960 fiscal year with a billion-dollar surplus. In the following year he repeated the battle over the 1961 budget, which proposed expenditures of $70.8 billion and a surplus of $4.2 billion. But by the fall of 1960 the economy had again stalled into a recession; tax revenue declined, and the fiscal year ended with a serious deficit.

In his final State of the Union message, in January 1961, President Eisenhower granted that problems of recession and unemployment left little room for complacency. But he pointed out that during his eight years in office the inflationary spiral had all but ceased and that the nation's output of goods and services had increased 25 percent; the income of the average American family, 15 percent; and the real wages of workers, 20 percent. "In a united determination to keep this nation strong and free and to utilize our vast resources for the advancement of all mankind," he asserted, "we have carried America to unprecedented heights."

twenty-four

A New Thrust Toward Reform

The tragically brief administration of President John F. Kennedy, followed by the first years of the Lyndon B. Johnson presidency, set new themes for the nation. Kennedy's New Frontier and Johnson's Great Society programs were addressed to those problems that had become critical with the increasing urbanization and industrialization of the midcentury. A crusade to attain higher living standards and its explosive counterpart, an intense struggle for civil rights, led to fresh political debates concerning the future course of the federal Union.

KENNEDY OVER NIXON

The presidential election of 1960 was notable both for its remarkable closeness and for the relative sobriety with which the two major candidates addressed themselves to the issues.

Kennedy won the Democratic nomination only after a vigorous struggle in the primaries. A forty-three-year-old senator from Massachusetts and a Roman Catholic, he was thought to be handicapped by his youth and his religion. In the primaries he had to dispose of a fellow senator, Hubert Humphrey of Minnesota, who was considered more liberal than he. Then, at the convention in Los Angeles, he had to overcome the powerful opposition of Johnson of Texas, the Senate majority leader. In the 1930s Johnson had been one of the coterie of ardent New Dealers. By 1960, without entirely abandoning his earlier allegiances, he had become the most respected spokesman of the industrialized and conservative South. When Kennedy won the presidential nomination, he offered the vice-presidential nomination to Johnson, who accepted and campaigned energetically.

The Republican nomination went almost by default to Vice President Nixon, whom President Eisenhower favored. Nixon's only rival, Governor Nelson Rockefeller of New York, dropped out of the contest months before the primaries. Henry Cabot Lodge, ambassador to the United Nations, was nominated for Vice President.

Kennedy and Nixon represented the broad moderate position within their respective parties, though Kennedy was slightly to the left of center and Nixon slightly to the right. As Vice President, Nixon had enjoyed eight years on the front pages and had even argued with Khrushchev in Moscow. Thus he was able to offer a continuation of President Eisenhower's "peace and prosperity" and—though he was only four years older than Kennedy—mature leadership.

When Kennedy challenged Nixon to a series of television debates, Nixon's advisers thought Kennedy would be no match for their man, and they agreed to four joint appearances. In the first debate, however, everything went wrong for Nixon. Not yet recovered from an illness, he appeared tired, haggard, and heavy jowled, in contrast to Kennedy, who seemed relaxed, self-confident, and well informed—before an estimated 70 million television viewers. From then on, Kennedy seemed to take the lead from Nixon.

The business recession also hurt the Republicans. Nevertheless, in the closing days of the campaign, a vigorous Republican campaign drive, with the aid of President Eisenhower, brought a hairline decision at the polls. Out of 68,836,000 votes cast, Kennedy received 34,227,000, or 49.7 percent, and Nixon, 34,109,000, or 49.5 percent. (The remaining 502,000 votes were divided among thirteen minor candidates.)

Before the election Kennedy had hoped that on taking office he could push through Congress a legislative program as sweeping as that of Frank-

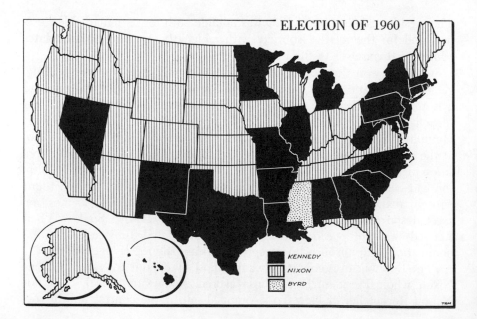

ELECTION OF 1960

KENNEDY
NIXON
BYRD

lin D. Roosevelt during the first hundred days of the New Deal. Kennedy did not abandon his reform plans, but the closeness of the decision led him to move with caution. Unlike the Eisenhower cabinet, which had predominantly represented business, the Kennedy cabinet balanced the economic and political as well as the regional interests in the nation. The most controversial of the appointments was that of Kennedy's thirty-five-year-old brother and campaign manager, Robert F. Kennedy, as Attorney General.

THE KENNEDY PROGRAM

President Kennedy—the youngest man, except for Theodore Roosevelt, ever to occupy the White House—sent a record number of messages, twenty-five, to the first session of the Eighty-seventh Congress. Some called for long-range national undertakings: economic recovery and growth, health care for the aged, federal aid for schools, conservation and use of natural resources, highway construction, housing and community development.

The existence of a Democratic majority in each house did not mean that Kennedy could count upon an easy enactment of his program, since many Democrats were conservative and frequently voted with the Republicans.

President John F. Kennedy and Vice President Lyndon B. Johnson reviewing the inaugural parade (JOHN F. KENNEDY LIBRARY)

By dint of persuasion and compromise he managed to obtain considerable legislation. An improvement in the minimum wage law provided considerably less coverage than Kennedy had wished, but it did bring an additional 3,624,000 workers under the law. It raised the minimum hourly pay rate, effective in several steps over two to four years, from $1 to $1.25. Another measure increased Social Security benefits substantially along the lines of the President's recommendations. The Housing Act of 1961 fully embodied his proposals, authorizing $4.9 billion in federal grants or loans over a four-year period for the preservation of open spaces in cities, the development of local mass-transit systems, and the construction of middle-income housing. Congressional conservatives dealt Kennedy two sharp setbacks when they defeated his bills to provide medical care for the aged and federal aid for school construction and teachers' salaries.

Kennedy obtained from Congress additional expenditures for unemployment compensation and aid to depressed areas—appropriations totaling $900 million. The only other large additions to the federal budget were $4 billion in defense spending to meet new challenges from the Soviet Union and large amounts of farm-crop subsidies that had to be paid by virtue of earlier legislation. These expenditures were sufficient to bring about, well before the end of 1961, a substantial economic recovery.

But employment improved only slightly; in a time of record prosperity over 5 percent of the working force had no jobs. Out of a total of approximately 4.4 million unemployed (as of March 1962) between 1 and 2 million were formerly connected with eight industries in which the total number of jobs had declined from 7.5 million to 5 million in the years since World War II. Among these industries were textiles, coal, automobiles, and aircraft. The Kennedy administration tried to eliminate such employment through the retraining of dismissed workers under the Manpower Training Bill and through the establishment of new industries in chronically depressed areas under the Area Redevelopment Act.

During his first two years in office, Kennedy emphasized that, because of the inflationary danger, the budget must be kept balanced. He also used his presidential power vigorously to try to prevent inflationary moves on the part of labor and industry. In the spring of 1962 he persuaded the United Steel Workers to accept a contract granting only small wage increases. When, almost immediately, United States Steel and most other companies unexpectedly announced 3.5-percent price increases, the President exploded with anger. During the three days that followed, he brought every variety of pressure he could muster, until the steel companies returned to their old prices. The cost to Kennedy was the hostility of the business community, which vented its anger upon him and blamed him for a stock-market drop a few weeks later. A year afterward, in the spring of 1963, when steel companies announced limited increases in prices, Kennedy commented only that the companies had shown some restraint; he hoped the steel union and steel users would do likewise.

By January 1963 Kennedy had become convinced that the only way to stimulate economic growth and to reduce unemployment was a bold tax cut. He proposed to Congress a reduction of $13.5 billion in income taxes over a period of three years.

Kennedy was also becoming convinced that the government must do more than it had done for blacks—to whose votes he owed his narrow victory in the 1960 election. Nearly a decade after the Supreme Court's historic decision against segregation, the equal rights movement was making little or no progress.

The National Association for the Advancement of Colored People (NAACP), which had led the cause, was still pressing lawsuits and seeking court orders, but more and more blacks were growing impatient with its methods and were embittered by white obstruction of the cause. Blacks began to form more militant organizations. A desperate minority of perhaps 200,000 joined the Black Muslims and, in a spirit reminiscent of the Garvey black nationalism of the 1920s, proclaimed black supremacy and demanded a complete separation of the races. Others continued to struggle for integration but turned to direct action through new organizations such as the Congress of Racial Equality (CORE) and the Southern Christian Leadership Conference (SCLC). The SCLC was led by an eloquent young Baptist minister, Dr. Martin Luther King, Jr., who had gained national and international fame as an advocate of passive resistance and, for his work, was to win the Nobel Peace Prize in 1964.

In the South, beginning in 1960, youthful blacks with some white sympathizers engaged in "sit-ins" to demand the right to eat in restaurants or at lunch counters or the right to use books in the main public libraries rather than in segregated branches. Blacks and whites went on "freedom rides" to desegregate interstate buses and terminals. Thousands engaging in mass demonstrations accepted arrest; on several occasions the jails of Southern cities were filled to overflowing. Demonstrations spread to the North in mass attacks against de facto segregation in schools and housing and against the exclusion of all but a handful of blacks from various kinds of employment. By the summer of 1963 the movement had reached such a peak that it was being proclaimed by news magazines as the "Negro revolution." More than 200,000 demonstrators (10 to 15 percent of them white) participated in a "March on Washington," converging on the Lincoln Memorial.

In areas where federal power could be invoked, those protesting against segregation received the support of the Kennedy administration. Attorney General Robert F. Kennedy mustered federal force behind the integration of interstate transportation, and the President sent troops to the University of Mississippi to protect a black student, James Meredith, Jr., who had been enrolled by order of a federal court. Throughout the South campaigns were under way to enroll black voters under the protection of the civil rights legislation of 1957. As pressure intensified in 1963, President Kennedy threw the prestige of his administration behind the most comprehensive civil rights bill ever presented to Congress.

"LET US CONTINUE"

In the fall of 1963, though congressional conservatives were blocking enactment of the two major bills in the New Frontier program, the civil rights and tax-cut measures, President Kennedy felt optimistic. He was looking ahead to the election of 1964, which most observers thought would result in his own reelection by a comfortable margin. He hoped that the election would bring to Washington a more liberal Congress.

To court Southern support Kennedy visited Florida and then Texas in November 1963. The Texas trip began well. On Friday, November 22, as he drove through the streets of Dallas, to the cheers of an enthusiastic crowd, the wife of Governor John Connally of Texas remarked to him: "You can't say that Dallas isn't friendly to you today." As Kennedy started to reply, he was hit in the neck by a bullet; another bullet struck the back of his head. His bleeding head cradled in the lap of his wife Jacqueline, he was rushed to a hospital.

An assassin, shooting three times in quick succession from a sixth-floor window, had killed President Kennedy and seriously wounded Governor Connally. Police arrested Lee Harvey Oswald, a self-styled Marxist who had once tried to expatriate himself in Russia, and charged him with the murder both of the President and a policeman. Piece after piece of circumstantial evidence seemed to tie Oswald to the murders, but through hours of questioning he continued to protest his innocence. Two days after the shooting, while he was in the Dallas city jail, on his way to be transferred to the county jail, he was himself murdered by a Dallas night-club operator, before an incredulous national television audience. Inevitably, rumors spread concerning the possibility that a ramifying plot lay behind Kennedy's assassination. In an effort to eliminate uncertainties, a presidential commission headed by Chief Justice Warren sifted through the evidence and several months later reported to the American people that Oswald had been a lone assassin. Not everyone accepted the conclusions of the Warren Commission, however. Kennedy's assassination remains a subject of speculation.

About two hours after the assassination, Vice President Lyndon B. Johnson was sworn in as the thirty-sixth President of the United States. When he addressed a joint session of Congress on November 27, President Johnson expressed his main theme in the words "let us continue." The most fitting memorial to Kennedy, he reminded Congress, would be the enactment of the civil rights and tax bills and, indeed, the whole agenda of the New Frontier.

The Eighty-eighth Congress responded and, in its 1964 session, enacted not only several vital measures of the New Frontier program but also one of President Johnson's own recommendations, an antipoverty bill. In getting the program adopted, the new President utilized to the utmost the formidable political skills he had perfected earlier as Senate majority leader. Not only did he conciliate and persuade congressional majorities, but he also built a great national following.

President Johnson takes the oath (WIDE WORLD PHOTOS)

From the outset Johnson assiduously courted businessmen. Most of them were Republicans, and the proposal of a tax cut deliberately creating a deficit in the budget at a time of prosperity went diametrically against their economic thinking. Nevertheless, after Congress passed the legislation early in 1964, the reduction of taxes seemed to stimulate an unprecedented continuation of prosperity and economic growth. By the beginning of 1965 the United States had experienced four years of boom without recession, a peacetime record since 1945. The rate of unemployment had dropped to about 5 percent for the first time in years.

To the delight of many businessmen, Johnson accompanied the lowering of taxes with the presentation of a federal budget smaller than they had anticipated for the 1965 fiscal year. Despite the overall cutback, he was able to increase expenditures on health, education, and welfare, through sharp limitation of the defense budget. While courting business, the administration remained on cordial terms with labor leaders. Workingmen and women shared in the boom as take-home pay rose 4 percent in 1964.

To aid those who were not sharing in the national prosperity Johnson in January 1964 called upon Congress to enact a thirteen-point program that would declare "unconditional war on poverty." In August 1964 the antipoverty bill was passed. It called for the establishment of VISTA, a volunteer corps of social workers, and for remedial education, vocational training, part-time employment for teen-agers and students, and federal grants to states or communities for local attacks on poverty. The initial budget was almost a billion dollars.

COMMITMENT TO EQUAL RIGHTS

Throughout the nation the problem of civil rights was closely related to that of poverty. A large proportion of the very poor were blacks, unable either South or North to obtain adequately paid, secure employment. In cities like New York, blacks (together with Puerto Ricans) filled a large number of badly paid service positions and jobs not requiring skill. The average Harlem family received $2,000 a year less in income than its white neighbors. Of the blacks (largely youths) 13 percent were unemployed, since the poorer jobs were the kind being most rapidly eliminated by automation. Either through discrimination or through lack of training, young people were barred from more highly skilled work. Many Northern blacks were crowded into substandard housing, and their children were enrolled in poor schools integrated in name only.

A number of young Northerners went to Mississippi in the summer of 1964 to enroll several thousand young blacks in "Freedom Schools" and to conduct drives registering blacks to vote. Three of the first civil rights workers to arrive disappeared; after some weeks the FBI found their bodies buried deep beneath an earthen dam.

As the struggle intensified, President Johnson threw his weight behind the comprehensive civil rights bill that Kennedy had presented to Congress. Bipartisan leadership in the Senate finally overcame Southern opposition. In June 1964, for the first time in history, the Senate voted to end a filibuster, so that the bill could be passed. The Civil Rights Act of 1964 strengthened earlier legislation to protect the voting rights of blacks and to expedite the desegregation of schools. It also prohibited discrimination in public accommodations and facilities and in private employment.

After the act went into effect, blacks ate with whites for the first time in some restaurants in the Deep South, stayed in some hotels and motels, sat in "white only" sections of motion-picture theaters, and swam in previously segregated swimming pools. Compliance was not universal, and several test cases challenging the constitutionality of the law were brought before federal courts.

In 1965 violence again erupted in the South, especially in Selma, Alabama, where masses of blacks and a few white sympathizers demonstrated in protest against registration procedures that kept blacks off the voting rolls. The state police brutally broke up a parade, and assassins (said to be Klansmen) murdered two white civil rights workers from the North. To protect the demonstrators, President Johnson called up the Alabama National Guard. He also persuaded Congress to pass a bill guaranteeing the right to vote in presidential, senatorial, and congressional elections. This law provided for federal registration of voters in those states where there were literacy or other special tests for registering and where fewer than one-half of the people of voting age actually went to the polls.

ONE MAN, ONE VOTE

Meanwhile, constitutional amendments and court decisions were affecting, actually or potentially, the political rights of many Americans, both black and white.

The Twenty-third Amendment (1961) gave the franchise in presidential elections to residents of the District of Columbia. Home rule for Washington, which had the highest percentage of blacks of any city in the country, continued to be withheld by Congress.

The Twenty-fourth Amendment (1964) gave symbolic, if not much practical, aid to black voters by providing that the right to vote in any primary or other federal election should not be abridged for failing to pay a poll tax. Most states in the Deep South were using methods other than the poll tax to try to disfranchise blacks.

An issue involving the rights of representation of a large part of the American electorate came before the Supreme Court in 1962, in a case involving the apportionment of legislative districts in Tennessee. Although the state constitution called for reapportionment every ten years, none had taken place since 1901, with the result that rural dominance in the legislature was out of all proportion to population. Moore County, with a population of 3,454, sent one legislator; Shelby County (Memphis), with 627,019 residents, sent only three. A vote in Moore County was worth more than sixty times as much as one in Shelby County. By a 6-to-2 decision, the Supreme Court gave the federal district court a mandate to order reapportionment if it found a violation of the Constitution. Similar inequities existed in a surprising number of other states; in all but six states, fewer than 40 percent of the population could elect a majority of the legislature. As a result of the Tennessee decision, many states quickly made some reapportionment of their legislative districts, either as a result of court action or as a means of forestalling it.

An even more important Supreme Court decision (in *Reynold* v. *Sims*, 1964) held that congressional districts within a state also must be substantially equal in population. The case before the court involved the congressional district containing the city of Atlanta, Georgia, a district that had a population of 820,000 as compared with the population of 270,000 in another Georgia district. Several state legislatures quietly initiated a counteraction by endorsing a constitutional amendment (proposed by the National Legislative Conference) that would negate federally enforced reapportionment. Within a few years thirty-three legislatures had approved it. If one more should act, Congress would be required, according to the Constitution, to call a national convention to consider submitting the proposal to the states for their ratification. The movement lost its chief congressional sponsor, however, when Senator Everett Dirksen of Illinois died in 1969.

JOHNSON DEFEATS GOLDWATER

As he took up and expanded the Kennedy program, President Johnson restated the objective as the creation of the Great Society. "For half a century we called upon unbounded invention and untiring industry to create an order of plenty for all our people," he declared in May 1964. "The challenge of the next half century is whether we have the wisdom to use that wealth to enrich and elevate our national life—and to advance the quality of American civilization." But Johnson himself was to jeopardize the Great Society program when, in 1965, he committed the country to large-scale war in faraway Vietnam.

In the presidential campaign of 1964 the moderate liberalism for which Johnson had spoken confronted extreme conservatism. During the years following the collapse of McCarthyism, militant conservatives in the United States had organized a number of action groups. The best known was the John Birch Society, whose founder, Robert Welch, called for the impeachment of Chief Justice Warren and seemed to suspect the loyalty of even President Eisenhower. Senator Barry Goldwater of Arizona, though not himself a member of the so-called radical right organizations, became the hero of most of these groups. In the Senate he had voted against tax reduction and against the antipoverty and civil rights bills.

At the Republican convention in San Francisco, the Goldwater forces were in complete command from the outset. They produced a platform conforming to their conservative philosophy and making no concessions to the moderate and liberal wings of the party. When Governor Rockefeller of New York tried to obtain a stronger civil rights plank, they hooted him down. Nor did Goldwater try to "balance the ticket" in his vice-presidential choice—Representative William E. Miller of New York stood staunchly to the right. Goldwater received tumultuous applause when, in his acceptance address, he declared: "I would remind you that extremism in the defense of liberty is no vice! And let me remind you also that moderation in the pursuit of justice is no virtue!"

As Senator Goldwater carried the Republican party far to the right, President Johnson tried to preempt not only the center of the road but also a wide strip to both the right and the left of it. Although he had been President for only nine months when the Democratic convention met at Atlantic City late in August 1964, he was firmly in control of his party. His main concern seemed to be to achieve as broad a consensus as possible in the platform. His supporters worked to minimize differences between the North and the South, especially over the seating of delegates. Delegates from Mississippi and Alabama were denied votes unless they pledged themselves to support the party's candidates in the November election, and most of them departed. Two votes were given to a black delegation representing the new Freedom Democratic party of Mississippi. In addition, the convention voted that in 1968 it would seat only those delegations that were chosen in a nondiscriminatory way.

The only drama in the convention concerned the question of whom President Johnson would ask the delegates to nominate for Vice President. Earlier he had eliminated one of the party's favorites, Attorney General Robert Kennedy, brother of the assassinated President. When Johnson, in person, revealed his choice to the convention, it was Senator Humphrey of Minnesota, identified with the liberal wing of the Democratic party.

Paradoxically, the campaign was one of the most hectic and yet one of the dullest ever to weary the electorate. In contrast to the comparatively precise debates of four years earlier, neither candidate ever went much beyond his acceptance speech. Yet each campaigned incessantly, often spanning the continent by jet in a day's appearances. Much of the Goldwater campaign centered upon charges of corruption and moral malaise in Washington. In mid-October, Johnson's chief White House aide was forced to resign because of personal scandal, but that same week the American people were even more startled by news of the precipitate removal of Khrushchev from the leadership of the U.S.S.R. New uncertainties abroad seemed to help drive the voters toward the President. Throughout the campaign Johnson was as wary of making specific, detailed promises as Eisenhower had been in 1956 and Roosevelt in 1936; his best strategy seemed to be merely to gather the votes against Goldwater.

And gather them he did. He received more votes, over 42 million, and a larger plurality than any other candidate in history. On election night he told the American people that he regarded the overwhelming victory as a "mandate for unity." It gave him and the Democratic majority in Congress an opportunity to move on toward what he had been describing as the Great Society, a society as free as it could be from poverty, prejudice, ignorance, and ugliness.

THE JOHNSON PROGRAM

When the Eighty-ninth Congress convened, Johnson presented to it comprehensive proposals to make a beginning toward his long-range goals. With unprecedented speed almost all of this far-ranging program became law. The overwhelmingly Democratic majorities in Congress, which had accompanied the landslide victory over Goldwater, were Johnson's to command.

Massive sustained federal aid to education at last began. Johnson succeeded in circumventing the impasse in Congress over the question of whether parochial schools should receive a share of federal funds. He called for grants for text and library books for students in both public and parochial schools—and significantly the grants were to be made on the

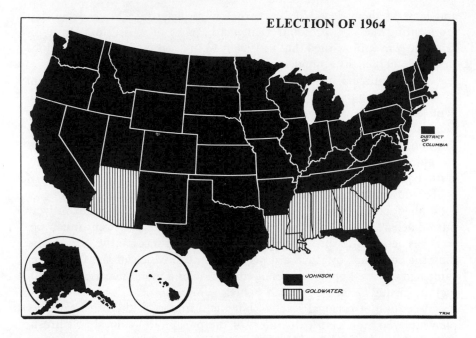

ELECTION OF 1964

DISTRICT OF COLUMBIA

JOHNSON
GOLDWATER

basis of the needs of individual students, not schools, a formula that the Supreme Court had approved when it applied to federal funds that were to provide milk or transportation to students. The Elementary and Secondary Education Act of 1965 and subsequent legislation gave aid to schools in both urban and rural areas in proportion to the number of poverty-stricken students in them. Federal funds purchased textbooks and library materials, financed special programs for adults and for the handicapped, and strengthened state educational agencies. Total federal expenditures in education and technical training rose from less than $5 billion in 1964 to more than $12 billion in 1967.

The establishment of Medicare for the 19 million Americans over sixty-five through the Medicare–Social Security Act of 1965 altered the lives of the elderly and had great impact upon American medicine. The debate over Medicare, which had been so bitter for twenty years, ended as the program went into effect. Expected resistance did not materialize. In the South, where hospitals had to accept desegregation in order to obtain funds, nearly nine-tenths of the hospitals complied. But numerous practical problems arose that made future adjustments likely. It was particularly difficult to institute the program in an era of rapidly rising costs. Objections to complicated paper work led more than one-half the nation's doctors to force patients to pay directly; patients were required to submit receipted bills for government reimbursement. The irritations were serious, but less important than the fact that large numbers of older Americans were receiving care that they could not previously have obtained or that would have exhausted their savings.

Rising costs also created problems for the Medicaid program, which was launched in 1968 to provide financial assistance to persons who were not old enough to qualify for Medicare but were too poor to pay their own medical bills. Under the Medicaid law each state was to set up its own plan, determining payments and standards of eligibility for them, and the federal government was to contribute from 50 to 80 percent of the expense. During the first year, however, the program cost the federal government more than ten times as much as had been expected. Congress and the state legislatures, therefore, changed their definition of the needy so as to make the benefits available to fewer people than had originally been covered.

Medicare and Medicaid were parts of the effort to eradicate the "pockets of poverty" within the prosperous nation. More than 9 million people classified as poor were receiving no aid from federal food programs, a Senate subcommittee learned. There was hunger in great cities, in Appalachia, the Deep South, the Southwest, and on Indian reservations. Yet over 5 million people were receiving aid through federal food programs; either they were given food or could purchase it with reduced-cost stamps. Many millions were receiving other types of relief.

The poverty program of Johnson, continuing and expanding that of Kennedy, approached the problem in numerous ways. By 1966 the Office of Economic Opportunity, established in 1964, had put about two-fifths of its budget into a variety of Community Action Programs. Another two-fifths went into youth programs—the Job Corps, Neighborhood Youth Corps, and College Work Study. Most of the remaining funds went into the Work Experience Program. VISTA served as a kind of Peace Corps at home.

While Social Security aided the considerable proportion of the poor who were aged, the Office of Economic Opportunity placed its emphasis upon helping the great numbers of poor among the young. The 1,000 core Community Action Programs were locally proposed and operated, in part by poor people themselves. Some of these programs not only gave poor people an opportunity to help themselves but gave them some feeling of political power. The job-training efforts, however, proved more expensive and less effective than had been predicted.

Especially among the urban black unemployed, the job-training programs were a disappointment. Although blacks began to penetrate the ranks of the white-collar workers, the total numbers were small. Nominally, union restrictions against them no longer existed, yet few could gain employment as skilled, highly paid construction workers. Industries that might have hired blacks were moving out of the cities, away from where they lived. The training programs could not easily provide the overall education and motivation that most of these unemployed blacks lacked. A New York black woman declared in despair, "We are being trained for the unemployed."

While starting his "war on poverty," Johnson was escalating his war in Vietnam. The enormous costs of the latter made it more and more difficult to pay for the former.

twenty-five_____
The Quality of American Life

By the late 1960s the quality of American life came sharply into question. The standard of living had risen spectacularly; yet millions still lived in misery. Millions still were being discriminated against because of their race or sex. By the middle of the 1970s it had become apparent that redress for these people could not come almost automatically through an ever-expanding population and economy. Rather, many resources were fast being depleted, and the environment was deteriorating. Acute problems to which there were no ready solutions faced the nation. How could it eradicate poverty, improve environments in both cities and the countryside, and better the living conditions of everyone? How could it attain equal opportunities for all Americans to enjoy that better quality of life?

THE CROWDING COUNTRY

"We have always assumed that progress and 'the good life' are connected with population growth," the President's Commission on Population Growth and the American Future reported in 1972. "If that were ever the case, it is not now. There is hardly any social problem confronting this nation whose solution would be easier if our population were larger."

In 1967 the demographic clock of the Census Bureau indicated that the population of the United States had passed the 200-million mark. In 1970 the census takers counted a total of 203,184,772. That was almost twice as large as it had been in 1920 and about 24 million larger than in 1960.

The rapid population growth after World War II belied the predictions of demographic experts who, on the basis of falling birth rates during the depression of the 1930s, had expected an early leveling-off. The baby boom of the 1950s caused pessimists to go to the opposite extreme. At the postwar rate of growth, some predicted, the population within 800 years would be so large that each American would have only one square foot of land to stand on. During the 1960s, however, the birth rate dropped even lower than it had been during the depression. By 1972 it was down to 2.11 children per woman. This was a "zero population growth" rate, one that could mean eventually (after two more generations of child-bearing women) just enough births to offset the number of deaths. Meanwhile, the birth rate might rise again, and so population predicting remained as uncertain as ever.

Immigration accounted for less than one-half million, or about 20 percent, of the population increase during the decade 1960–1970. The immigration act of 1965 eliminated the national-origins quota system, which had allowed only a certain percentage of each nationality to enter the country. The new law provided that, from 1969 on, there would be a ceiling of 120,000 on immigration from the Western Hemisphere and 170,000 from the rest of the world. The law allowed parents, spouses, and children of United States citizens to enter the country without regard to the overall limitations. Thereafter, the largest numbers of immigrants no longer came from Canada and the United Kingdom but from Italy and the Philippines. For the first time illegal immigration became a serious problem. Several million immigrants, mostly from the Americas, succeeded in evading restrictions and settled in the United States.

Mobility continued to characterize Americans, as it had always done. In 1970 more than one-fourth of the natives of the United States were living in a state other than the one they were born in (in 1850 the proportion had been about the same). During the 1960s, as during previous decades, the greatest interstate movement was to the Far West, especially to California, already the most populous state by 1960 and the home of nearly 20 million people in 1970. A reversal seemed under way in 1970, when, for the first time in a hundred years, as many people moved out of California as moved into it. From 1920 to 1960 so many blacks had left the South that the region lost more than it gained by migration, but during the 1960s it gained 1.8 million whites from the North while losing 1.4 million blacks to the North. As a whole, the black population grew 33 percent faster than the white during the decade and constituted about 11 percent of the nation's total population in 1970.

The flight from the farm continued, at an accelerating speed. In 1920 the people had been distributed about evenly between city and country. By 1970 the rural population had increased slightly, but the urban population had nearly tripled. The number of farms (and farmers) actually declined after 1935, from a peak of 6.8 million in that year to fewer than 3 million in 1970, and the figure was expected to be below 2 million by 1980. In 1970 about 63 million people were classified as rural (most of them nonfarm), about 62 million as strictly urban (living in cities proper), and 75 million as suburban.

RISE OF THE MEGALOPOLIS

During the decades after World War II, metropolitan areas expanded until they met and merged with one another. From north of Boston to south of Washington a single urban region—a megalopolis—was coming into being. Elsewhere, supercities of one kind or another were also taking form.

The proper governing of these areas was a problem. It was complicated by the escape of affluent whites from city jurisdictions and tax collectors to the suburbs and by the concentration of poor blacks in the inner cities. While the city governments needed more and more financial resources, the tax base was growing very slowly or actually shrinking.

Because individual metropolitan problems transcended city and sometimes state lines, special governmental authorities to deal with matters like harbor development or transit had come into existence. Together with traditional governments they led to a multiplicity of governmental agencies. Within the 212 standard metropolitan areas in the 1960s there were some 18,000 units of government, ranging from counties to school boards. There was little cooperation among them: most of these governments were ready to give little or no aid to the ailing cities. Many state, county, and suburban officials resisted the establishment of the federal Department of Housing and Urban Development, in 1965.

The problems with which metropolis and the merging megalopolis had to grapple were those long faced by city dwellers: improvement of housing, transportation, living conditions, educational and cultural opportunities, and above all the economic base for both the family and community; conversely, the elimination of pollution, blight, crime, and violence. The size of the new metropolitan areas made these problems far larger and sometimes more complex than in earlier generations.

Federally sponsored housing, which had originated three decades earlier in the New Deal era, together with the urban renewal programs developed after World War II, were good examples. Proponents of housing hoped through combining public and private funds to wipe out the blighted core of the metropolis; erect beautiful, modern structures; and in addition provide comfortable housing that families of varying incomes could afford. Much was achieved, but reality sometimes ran counter to the dream.

Federal aid in one form or another had helped make possible the vast growth of suburbia since 1945—and then the white exodus from cities into suburbs. By 1963, 5 million families owned houses built with Federal Housing Administration (FHA) aid; millions more lived in houses financed through the GI Bill of Rights. Federal guarantees had helped 27 million homeowners to borrow money for repairs. The government encouraged the deposit of money in savings and loan associations, which issued millions of mortgages, by insuring the deposits.

Simultaneously, with the growth of suburbs, attempts were made to rejuvenate decaying central cities through federal aid. Urban renewal projects were to transform slums into business and cultural areas and above all into attractive apartment complexes. The new buildings were expected to bring a fivefold increase in taxes, thus helping to solve urban financial problems.

A small beginning during the New Deal had involved federal clearing of slums and construction of public housing. From 1937 on, the federal government helped cities in the undertaking. The 1949 legislation provided for a bold departure. The federal government would help cities finance the purchase of slum land, which would then be sold to private entrepreneurs at reduced costs. Federal loans or mortgage insurance gave these builders a further profit incentive. Thus private enterprise would be persuaded to rebuild the cities.

For five years the program made little progress and thereafter seemed most effective in producing profits for the entrepreneurs. There were numerous complaints that it was the land where the poorest people (often blacks) lived that was being taken over and that these people seldom received adequate housing elsewhere at rents they could afford. Sometimes land was cleared and left idle for years while builders were sought. Sometimes the new construction was a complex of luxury apartments, as in the West End of Boston.

Beautification, cleanliness, and safety were also problems requiring community and even national action. Cities in an affluent society produced ever-increasing quantities of waste. Keeping streets and vacant lots clean was relatively simple compared with disposing of the innumerable tons of sewage, garbage, and trash. In 1920 the average person threw away less than 3 pounds of refuse per day; by the mid-1960s he was discarding 4.5 pounds. Household and industrial waste had turned many of the nation's rivers into huge sewers. Smoke and fumes from industries, automobiles, incinerators, and burning dumps created acute smog hazards in widespread areas.

Maintenance of safety was an old problem that each generation faced anew. In 1967 the President's Commission on Crime declared that there was far more crime than ever reported to the police—three times as many burglaries, half again as many robberies, double the number of assaults.

THE TRANSPORTATION HEADACHE

Increasingly, after World War II, older modes of conveyance deteriorated. Streetcars, which had taken over America in the early years of the twentieth century, almost completely disappeared, to be supplanted by buses or additional subways. Transit lines, unable to meet rising costs with revenues that failed to keep pace, faced bankruptcy. Municipally owned systems ran heavier and heavier deficits. Between 1955 and 1965 the number of riders on public transit lines declined 25 percent. Railroads, to cut losses, tried to drop commuter services. The number of passengers commuting by train declined 45 percent between 1929 and 1963 and continued to decline thereafter. City dwellers and suburbanites depended more and more upon automobiles, which were quicker and more convenient. But automobiles required six to forty-five times more space on highways per passenger than did buses, and multiple-unit rail cars were even more efficient.

While public transportation languished, the federal government helped subsidize the building of 6,000 miles of expressways. This forced the leveling of countless blocks of urban buildings (including a disproportionate amount of poor people's housing), and other buildings were leveled to provide parking lots. As a consequence, still more automobiles poured into the cities, compounding traffic problems and, during public transportation strikes, creating chaos. An opposite approach at both the local and federal levels was to try to improve public transit or even to develop new systems as, most spectacularly, in the San Francisco Bay region. In 1966 Congress created a new Department of Transportation.

National transportation problems were interrelated, as railroad passenger service rapidly declined and trucks became an increasingly important factor in carrying freight. The large-scale program of turnpike building that marked the first decade after World War II came to an end as thousands of miles of toll-free superhighways were built, beginning with the Interstate Highway Act of 1956, which set standards for the roads (no grade crossings, for example) and provided federal funds for 90 percent of the cost. For public transportation, Americans had to depend either upon buses or airlines.

By the mid-1950s airlines, which had been luxury transportation before World War II, were carrying over 30 million passengers per year. By the mid-1960s the figure had nearly quadrupled and was expected to double again within a decade. Especially along the northeast coast, the air lanes were so crowded that at the height of the evening rush, about 100 planes would be landing or about to land at the three major New York area airports, while another 250 private planes were also taking off or landing at these and smaller fields. Despite an occasional collision and numerous near collisions, the airlines were able to boast a remarkable safety record. But the congestion of people at the major airports worsened with the appearance, in 1970, of the "jumbo jet," carrying more than twice as many passengers as any previous airliner.

For the future, when airlines might not be able to meet the passenger demands along the northeast corridor between Washington and Boston, the federal government was fostering high-speed train service which it hoped ultimately would carry passengers at 160 miles an hour. The Metroliner, with a potential speed of 120 miles an hour, was operating between New York and Washington by 1969. There might be a future along a few congested routes for rail passenger service of this kind. In the early 1970s a government-owned corporation, Amtrak, was running passenger trains on a number of railroad lines and was attracting more and more riders, despite the handicap of poor roadbeds and rolling stock. The principal railroad companies of the Northeast were bankrupt or facing bankruptcy, however, and only massive federal aid could keep them in business.

THE COSTS OF ABUNDANCE

For the American people as a whole the quarter-century following World War II was a time of unprecedented enjoyment of material things. But abundance had its costs in the pollution of the environment and the depletion of natural resources. By the 1970s it had begun to appear that the age of plenty was about over and a new age of scarcity was at hand.

In the 1960s most Americans were still enjoying a living standard far higher than any they had previously known. Though the population had been growing, the output of goods and services had been growing much faster. Even allowing for the rise in prices and in taxes, the average person was better off than ever before. True, income continued to be very unevenly distributed, the top 5 percent of the people receiving 20 percent of the income. Some 40 percent of the people lived in what was considered "either poverty or deprivation" (which meant, as of 1960, having a family income of less than $6,000 a year). Yet workers were getting more pay for less work than in the past. With a forty-hour instead of a forty-four-hour week and with paid vacations, the average industrial employee enjoyed much more free time than his father or grandfather had in 1900. Workers could afford to spend a smaller proportion of their wages for food, clothing, and shelter and a larger proportion for automobiles, appliances, medical care, recreation, and other luxuries. Even among families classified as living in "poverty" (having an income of less than $4,000 a year), 60 percent owned automobiles in 1960. In 1964, 93 percent of the homes, including those of the poor as well as the rich, contained television sets.

The goods that came forth in such abundance were produced by industries the ownership and control of which were more and more highly concentrated. In 1960 the eighty-seven largest corporations held 26 percent of the total of corporate assets, and in 1970 they held 46 percent. During the 1960s, companies merged at a faster rate than ever, usually to form conglomerates. Many of these became "multinational" firms by acquiring subsidiaries in foreign countries. Corporations, "agribusinesses," took over a larger and larger share of agriculture in the United States, and the average size of farms increased as the number of farms declined.

While consumers enjoyed the bounty that industry provided, a growing number of them complained that too many of the products were useless, dangerous, falsely advertised, overpriced, defective, or lacking in durability. The complaints resulted in an accelerating movement for consumer protection. As early as the 1920s the Consumers Union had begun to test products and issue reports on them. In 1966 Ralph Nader emerged as a leading advocate of the new consumerism when he published a book, *Unsafe at Any Speed*, exposing the built-in hazards of many American cars. Nader started a number of consumer organizations to bring public pressure on both business and government. One of these organizations reported in *The Monopoly Makers* (1973) that federal regulatory agencies often conspired with the industries they were supposed to regulate.

Public services were less plentiful than commercial services and commodities. As population grew, the construction and maintenance of schools, hospitals, streets, sewers, public housing, and other community facilities fell behind the mounting needs. The times were characterized by private wealth and public poverty. That was the theme of John K. Galbraith's widely quoted book *The Affluent Society* (1958). "The line which divides our area of wealth from our area of poverty," Galbraith wrote, "is roughly that which divides privately produced and marketed goods and services from publicly rendered services." The contrast was symbolized by the picture he described of a prosperous middle-class family driving in an air-conditioned car over poorly paved and trash-littered streets and billboard-cluttered highways to lunch on "exquisitely packaged food from a portable ice box" at a picnic spot beside a polluted stream.

There seemed to be, in some material respects, a lowering of the quality of American life, and for much of this the population growth itself was responsible. The results of growth, as the sociologist Dennis H. Wrong pointed out, included "traffic jams, spreading urban and suburban blight, the overcrowding and destruction of beaches, parks, and other outdoor recreational facilities, water shortages, air pollution," and "deterioration in professional and social services resulting from shortages of trained personnel."

The worsening pollution of the environment resulted not only from population growth but, much more, from the great increase in factory output and from the development of new industrial processes and products. The production of synthetic fibers, for example, used more energy and hence directly or indirectly yielded more pollutants than the production of cotton or wool. Synthetic detergents, plastic materials, and aluminum cans were not biodegradable as were the objects for which they were substituted.

One of the worst offenders, with regard to air pollution, was the automobile. Motor vehicle registrations, which had amounted to only 8,000 in 1900, rose from 31 million in 1945 to 109 million in 1970. Thus the number of vehicles grew by more than 300 percent while the number of people was growing by about 50 percent. Many of the newer cars and trucks had more powerful, higher-compression engines than earlier models and gave poorer mileage while using high-test gasoline that contained a lead compound, an additional pollutant.

The befouling of air and water posed an immediate threat to human well-being and an ultimate threat to human existence. Environmentalists raised a demand for government action, and Congress responded with the Clean Air Acts of 1963, 1965, and 1970. These encouraged states and municipalities to set up their own programs for controlling pollution from stationary sources and required car manufacturers to see that vehicle emissions were drastically cut by 1975. Pittsburgh had long since set an example for other municipalities by starting, in 1941, a smoke-abatement program, which, by the 1950s, had changed the city from one of the smoggiest and grimiest to one of the cleanest. Most communities, however, were slow to act, though some of them experimented with methods of transforming waste into salable products—converting fly ash from incinerators into an ingredient for concrete, manufacturing fertilizer from garbage and sewage, and retrieving metal from dumps. Industrialists generally resisted the application of antipollution measures to their own industries, since such measures tended to raise production costs and lower profits.

The war effort of 1941–1945 had used up tremendous quantities of raw materials, and the ensuing production boom used up still larger quantities of resources, especially fossil fuel. After the war Americans turned more and more away from coal to oil and natural gas for generating electrical energy as well as for heating houses and other buildings. Manufacturers of plastics, synthetic fibers, and petrochemicals demanded increasing quantities of petroleum as a raw material. Drivers of cars, trucks, and buses added greatly to the demand, and the air force added further with its fueling of bombers in Vietnam.

Signs of an approaching energy crisis appeared in the United States as early as the mid-1960s, with the sudden failures of the electrical supply and the temporary blackouts and brownouts of New York City and other areas in the Northeast. The events of 1973–1974—the restrictions on oil exports by the Arabs and quadrupled price increases by the Arabs and other foreign producers—only made acute a condition that was already on the way to becoming chronic. For the indefinite future, Americans faced a recurring energy shortage. They could take little comfort in the probability that they would not be quite as bad off as the Europeans or the Japanese.

The United States still possessed considerable oil resources, already discovered or yet to be discovered, in addition to vast shale deposits that eventually could be made to yield petroleum. The country had enough coal in the ground to last for centuries. It also had the capacity to build additional atomic power plants. But the exploitation of petroleum, coal, or atomic fission endangered the environment in one way or another—through possible spills from drilling, damage to surroundings from oil transportation (as in the case of the Alaska pipeline to bring oil south from new Alaskan fields), destruction of mountains to get at shale, scarring of land by strip mining, pollution of air by the burning of low-grade coal, leakage of radioactive wastes from an atomic reactor, or some even more deadly accident with an atomic power plant.

In time the harnessing of the sun's rays might provide clean energy, but other resources would remain scarce in comparison with the abundant supplies of the past. Seemingly, as they advanced toward the twenty-first century, Americans would have to face the necessity of stabilizing

A pushcart man had easier going, as long lines of motorists waited for gasoline during the oil shortage of 1973 (UPI)

their population, limiting their industrial growth, and changing their way of life so as to consume less of material goods.

BLACK POWER

While the living standards of all Americans faced the prospect of decline, minorities were engaged in a vigorous struggle to obtain a fairer share of the national income and recognition of their civil rights. The black population, as was shown earlier, had been increasing more rapidly than the white population and had been shifting from the rural South to the cities throughout the nation, especially in the North. In 1910 only about a quarter of blacks lived in cities, and only one-tenth outside the South; by 1966, 69 percent were living in metropolitan areas; 45 percent were living outside the South. In several of the largest cities the proportion of blacks at least doubled between 1950 and 1968. Negroes constituted at least 30 percent of the population of seven of these cities and 66.6 percent of the population of Washington, D.C. A corresponding exodus of whites from the cities to the suburbs dramatically increased the areas of residential and school segregation in the black ghettos.

While urban blacks were sharing in the national prosperity, their proportional gains were decidedly less than those of the whites. Indeed, the gap between their incomes and those of whites was growing wider. Impatient urban blacks, disappointed at the meager return that cooperation seemed to have brought them, began increasingly to turn toward other possible solutions: black power, separatism, or even violence.

With increasing rapidity after 1964 the United States moved into a double crisis, compounded of rioting in the poverty-stricken black areas in Northern cities and escalation of the intervention in Vietnam into a major—but stalemated—military confrontation. Each crisis interacted with the other. White college and university students and Northern liberals shifted their efforts from the civil rights drive in the South to concentrate on protest against the Vietnam War. Blacks in the rural South, and even more in the urban North, increasingly sought to take their destiny into their own hands through their own organizations, independent of aid or funds from whites.

The gradual shift from white participation and leadership to black domination of civil rights organizations was one indication of the new mood. The Congress of Racial Equality (CORE), founded in 1941–1942, had long been the most interracial of the organizations, but by 1962 was predominantly black; after 1965 CORE allowed only black leadership in its chapters. At their height these organizations through direct action did succeed in obtaining some votes for blacks and political participation, even in Alabama and Mississippi. In the North they helped force open new, desirable employment opportunities for adequately educated blacks. But they could not change the inferior conditions under which most blacks suffered. Their failure helped stimulate feelings of separateness and militancy among black youth in the large cities.

Out of James Meredith's march southward from Memphis, Tennessee,

Leaders of the March on Washington, August 28, 1963. In front row: Rev. Martin Luther King, Roy Wilkins, and A. Phillip Randolph (UPI)

to Jackson, Mississippi, in June 1966 there grew the concept of black power. Politically, it meant separate action through which blocs of black voters would win control in Northern ghettos or the Southern black belt. Economically, it meant creating black business to serve blacks. CORE and SNCC (the Student Nonviolent Coordinating Committee) became associated with the concept of black power—of black separateness. In some respects black power seemed to critics to be retrogressive, a harking back to the proposals of Booker T. Washington; it seemed to propose a withdrawal comparable to that which white racists had been demanding. Black militants replied that blacks by themselves must attain economic and political parity with the white population before effective integration could take place.

On August 11, 1965, a black crowd had gathered in Watts, a Los Angeles suburb, to protest a traffic arrest; a policeman hit a bystander with his club, and several days of violence were touched off. Before the rioting was over, thirty-four people had been killed, hundreds wounded, and about $35 million in property destroyed. White Americans, hopeful that the civil rights movement was solving black problems, were shocked out of their optimism.

In the summer of 1966 there were forty-three outbreaks, with especially serious trouble in Chicago and Cleveland. In the summer of 1967 there were eight major riots. In the worst of these, at Detroit, forty-three persons (thirty-three blacks, and ten whites) were killed. On their television screens the people of the nation saw alarming scenes of arson, plunder, and military action. President Johnson, calling for law and order, warned also that the only genuine long-range solution must be an attack upon the conditions that were causing despair and violence. He appointed a group of distinguished citizens to a commission to investigate the disorders and recommend preventive measures for the future.

The report of the Commission on Civil Disorders, which appeared in the spring of 1968, deflated numerous wild stories: there had been few black snipers and no organized conspiracy instigating and directing the riots. The report pointed to the complexities of the problems facing the occupants of the black ghettos, and it recommended massive spending to erase these ghettos and the inequities their occupants suffered. "Only a commitment to national action on an unprecedented scale can shape a future compatible with the historic ideals of American society," the commission concluded. But Congress proceeded to cut rather than to increase spending for the alleviation of urban poverty.

In April 1968 the assassination of Dr. Martin Luther King, Jr., shocked the nation but did not alter the economizing mood of Congress. King, whose insistence upon Gandhi-like nonviolent techniques seemed old fashioned to black militants, was preparing to lead a protest march on behalf of striking garbage workers in Memphis, Tennessee. While standing on a motel balcony, he was struck by a sniper's bullet and died within a few minutes. King's death touched off the most widespread rioting the nation had yet undergone in the black areas of cities from coast to coast. Looting and arson were endemic; forty persons were killed. Washington was the worst hit, as fires gutted buildings within sight of the Capitol and the White House. Yet within the black districts, innumerable residents worked doggedly to end the disorders. Simultaneously, the nation mourned the assassinated leader, as King was given a funeral bringing together an assemblage of notables and receiving television coverage exceeded only by that of President Kennedy.

Within a week Congress responded by enacting the Civil Rights Act of 1968, which had been pending for two years. It outlawed racial discrimination in the sale and rental of four-fifths of all homes and apartments. But as poor people assembled in Washington a few weeks later in the campaign that King had been planning at the time of his death, Congress was still preoccupied with economy and little disposed to provide financial aid for them.

THE PAN-INDIAN MOVEMENT

The American Indian population, growing much faster than the population as a whole, nearly doubled during the twenty years after 1950. By 1970 the total had reached about 800,000, of whom more than one-half lived on or near reservations and most of the rest in cities. The population increase had come in spite of a lower-than-average life expectancy. Indeed, the descendants of the aborigines were, as a group, much worse off than other Americans, even those of African descent. Annual family income for Indians was $1,000 less than for blacks, and the unemployment rate for Indians was ten times the national rate. Suicides among Indian youth were a hundred times as frequent as among white youth.

Despite the 1924 grant of citizenship to all Indians, those on the reservations continued to be treated as "wards of the nation," with little or no control over their own affairs. They had been promised a New Deal in the Indian Reorganization Act of 1934, which had been expected to reverse the policy laid down in the Dawes Severalty Act of 1887. Presumably, the Bureau of Indian Affairs would no longer try to make white farmers out of Indians but, under the 1934 law, would encourage the revitalization of aboriginal culture and tribal government. Congress failed to provide sufficient funds, however, to help the Indians advance very far in the new direction. Then, in 1953, Congress reverted to the old policy of forcing the Indians to adopt the white man's ways. A congressional resolution of that year declared the intention of terminating federal relations with the tribes and leaving them on their own. Thereafter, relations with some tribes were terminated, among these the Menominee of Wisconsin, who saw their reservation converted into Menominee County. "Termination" led to further Indian impoverishment, both material and spiritual.

During the 1960s, more Indians than ever before joined in a movement to bring all the tribes together and redress their common wrongs. In 1961 more than 400 members of 67 different tribes gathered in Chicago and drew up a Declaration of Indian Purpose, which stressed the "right to choose our own way of life" and the "responsibility of preserving our precious heritage." In 1964, while Congress was considering the Economic Opportunity Bill, hundreds of Indians and white sympathizers assembled in Washington to urge Congress to include Indians in the antipoverty program. After black militants had proclaimed black power as their aim, a number of young, college-educated Indians adapted the slogan to their own use and began to speak of red power. Some repudiated the name "Indian"—which, as they pointed out, whites had mistakenly given them—and insisted on being called Native Americans (a term that anti-immigrant whites had applied to themselves more than a century earlier).

Congress included Indians in the coverage of the Economic Opportunity Act, and for a time many of the reservation dwellers were allowed to plan and carry out their own antipoverty programs. Except for this, neither the Kennedy nor the Johnson administration did much more than the Eisenhower administration had done to meet the Indians' needs and demands. Johnson failed to give effect to his words of 1968: "I propose a new goal for our Indian programs: a goal that ends the old debate about 'termination' of Indian programs and stresses self-determination; a goal that erases old attitudes of paternalism and promotes partnership self-help."

Frustrated Indians turned more and more to direct action, to confrontations with whites, to defiance of state and federal authority. In 1968 Indian fishermen, seeking to exercise old treaty rights of fishing on the Columbia River and in Puget Sound, clashed with officials of the state of Washington. In 1969 a group of Indians of various tribes, to dramatize the plight of their people, landed on Alcatraz Island, the site of an abandoned federal prison in San Francisco Bay, and claimed the place "by right of discovery." The frustrations of many Indians found witty as well as angry expression in the writings of Vine Deloria, Jr., a Sioux, who titled one of his books Custer Died for Your Sins (1969).

THE SPANISH-SPEAKING MINORITY

Much more numerous than the descendants of North American tribes were the people of Latin American origin, most of whom also had Indian ancestors and some of whom were at least partly of African descent. Numbering more than 9 million in 1970, the Spanish-speaking minority was, next to the American black minority, the largest in the country. The people of Puerto Rican background were concentrated mainly in New York, those of Cuban background mainly in Florida, and those of Mexican background mainly in California, Texas, and other states of the Southwest. The Mexican Americans, totaling almost 7 million, included legal immigrants from Mexico, illegal immigrants ("mojados" or "wetbacks"), and temporary workers ("braceros") brought in under labor contracts, as well as descendants of families who had been living in Mexican territory at the time it was incorporated into the United States.

The Spanish-speaking peoples had suffered from various forms of discrimination, though they had not been consigned to separate schools. To advance their interests many of them had joined organizations of one kind or another, but these were specialized or localized. During the 1960s, for the first time, large numbers of Mexican Americans were brought together in a broad, inclusive "Chicano" (from "Mexicano") movement.

Its outstanding hero was César Chávez, an Arizona-born California farm worker. Its main focus, for the time being, was a farm workers' strike that Chávez called in 1965 and soon converted into a nonviolent crusade for social justice. He enlisted the cooperation of college students, churchmen and women, and civil rights groups, including CORE and SNCC. To bring pressure on employers, who brought in strikebreakers, he appealed for a nationwide boycott of California table grapes. The boycott gained the support of millions of sympathizers throughout the country but received no assistance from the federal government, which increased its purchases of grapes to be sent to American troops in Vietnam. Chávez won a victory in 1970, when the growers of half of California's table grapes signed contracts with his union.

Governor Raul H. Castro of Arizona. Before becoming Governor, Castro had served as a federal judge and an ambassador. Born in Mexico, he came to the U.S. at the age of eleven

WOMEN'S RIGHTS

American women in general could hardly be called a minority, since 51 percent of the population was female; yet they suffered inequities comparable to those imposed upon minority groups, and women of these groups bore a double burden of discrimination.

True, more and more job opportunities were opening up for women, and an increasing proportion of them, including wives and mothers, were working outside the home (fewer than 25 percent of women over sixteen had been counted as part of the labor force in 1940; more than 43 percent were so counted in 1970). But women were paid much less than men, even for comparable work (in 1971 for men employed full time the median yearly pay was $9,630; for women it was $5,700). Women had fewer chances than men to make a professional or managerial career. In the mid-1960s women constituted only 7 percent of the nation's physicians and less than 4 percent of its lawyers, and the proportion of women managers or owners of businesses, already small, was actually declining. Women were being replaced by men in top positions in schools, libraries, and social work—which once had been considered women's fields.

In comparison with men, women were receiving too little education, but in comparison with their own career opportunities they were receiving too much. They composed a smaller percentage of the college population in the 1950s than in the 1920s and were granted a smaller percentage of college degrees in 1960 than in 1930. During the 1960s, they were earn-

Representative Barbara Jordan, before her election to Congress in 1972, was the first woman to serve as President of the Texas state senate

ing only one in three of all B.A.'s and M.A.'s and only one in ten of the Ph.D.'s. Yet the college graduates—like other, less well educated women—often were handicapped in getting and holding outside employment because they had to carry the extra burden of bearing and rearing children and keeping house. Women with higher education seemed especially to resent the "double standard" that all women confronted in practically every aspect of life.

Educated women of the middle class took the lead (as they had done in earlier feminist crusades) in the dozens of women's liberation movements that sprang forth in the 1960s. One of the most influential of the leaders was Betty Friedan, who in *The Feminine Mystique* (1963) denounced the American home as a "comfortable concentration camp" and called upon its inmates to free themselves. Friedan helped to found, in 1966, the most inclusive and effective of the new women's rights organizations, the National Organization for Women, or NOW. "There is no civil rights movement to speak for women, as there has been for Negroes and other victims of discrimination," the organizers of NOW declared, thus revealing that they, too, had been inspired, at least in part, by the example of the blacks. The organization's 1967 "bill of rights" demanded an Equal Rights Amendment to the Constitution—"Equality of Rights under the law shall not be denied or abridged by the

One distaff demonstrator goes all the way back into Biblical history to get a point across at a Women's Liberation Rally in New York (UPI)

United States on account of sex"—and Congress in 1970 approved the amendment and sent it to the states for ratification. NOW also called for enforcement of the 1964 Civil Rights Act, which prohibited discrimination in employment on account of sex as well as race, and "men wanted" and "women wanted" began to disappear from classified ads.

NOW disclaimed any "enmity toward men" and advocated a "self-respecting partnership" with them, but some of the other liberation groups practically declared a war of the sexes. The majority of American women, however, saw little need to support the feminist cause in any of its forms. A poll in 1970 put the question: "In your opinion, do women in the United States get as good a break as men?" Of the women replying, 65 percent said yes.

twenty-six

Kennedy, Johnson, and Confrontation

"We face a hostile ideology—global in scope, atheistic in character, ruthless in purpose, and insidious in method. Unhappily the danger it poses promises to be of indefinite duration." So said President Eisenhower in the farewell address he directed to the American people shortly before leaving office in 1961. "A vital element in keeping the peace is our military establishment. Our arms must be mighty, ready for instant action, so that no potential aggressor may be tempted to risk his own destruction."

While warning of dangers from outside, Eisenhower also drew attention to a possible threat arising within the nation. This was the threat of undue power accruing to the military-industrial complex that had developed to provide for the national defense. For the first time in their history the American people had in their midst, on a permanent basis, the "conjunction of an immense military establishment and a large arms industry." Supporting the industry and supported by it were certain labor unions and numerous scientific groups, many of these in universities that had government research contracts.

Under President Eisenhower's successors—Kennedy, Johnson, and Nixon—the United States continued to face a "hostile ideology" abroad. And the military-industrial complex continued to grow. It seemed to gain a greater and greater role in the determination of policy. How to provide for the national security while preserving and promoting individual freedom and opportunity—how to defend democracy without destroying it in the process—this was America's basic dilemma.

There was a ray of hope. The Soviet Union and the People's Republic of China were ancient enemies, with differences of interest too profound to be patched over indefinitely by the shared ideology of communism. By 1961, signs of serious conflict between the two countries had already begun to appear. If the conflict should worsen, one or both of the two Communist powers might be willing to seek or to accept improved relations with the United States. This prospect caused some Americans to look toward an eventual "détente," a relaxation of tensions in world politics. Actually, the most dangerous crisis between the United States and the Soviet Union was yet to come. By 1973, however, the achievement of some kind of détente seemed at last a real possibility.

KENNEDY DIVERSIFIES DEFENSE

In his inaugural address, President Kennedy had advised: "Let us never negotiate out of fear. But let us never fear to negotiate." During the next few years, as the Soviet Union and the United States faced one another over the issues of Berlin, Cuba, and nuclear testing, the spirit of negotiation was put to severe trials.

At the time Kennedy took office, the military establishment of the United States was spending half of the federal budget and nearly one-tenth of the gross national product; it was directly employing 3.5 million people. The incoming President and his new Secretary of Defense, Robert McNamara, were as determined as President Eisenhower had been in his farewell address that this vast establishment should protect but not dominate the American nation.

President Kennedy and Secretary McNamara built their plans upon the theory that the strength of thermonuclear weapons on the part of both the United States and Russia was sufficiently great to constitute a "mutual deterrent" against war. During the campaign of 1960, Kennedy had warned that the United States lagged behind the Soviet Union; soon after he took office, his Secretary of Defense reported that the missile gap, if there was one, favored the United States. This nation, possessing sufficient striking power to destroy the Soviet Union several times over, was committed to staying ahead of Russia in missile and nuclear development. The new administration speeded the placing of nuclear-armed missiles in underground sites and the building of nuclear-armed Polaris submarines to rove the seas. These retaliatory weapons would guarantee that if the United States suffered destruction, so would the attacking nation.

There was the assumption, however, that under the umbrella of the mutual deterrence of countering nuclear forces, the Communists would seek to gain new territories by subversion or by conventional warfare. Experts pointed to areas like South Vietnam to illustrate what they meant; nuclear deterrents were of no value there. So the President wished to develop forces expert in guerrilla and jungle warfare and equipped with special arms. A million American men were thus trained in "counterinsurgency." In addition, United States military missions aided other countries in establishing their own programs. During its first two years, the administration also committed more of its defense expenditures to increasing its conventional forces. It raised the number of army combat divisions from eleven to sixteen and air force tactical wings from sixteen to twenty-one.

Since the inception of the Truman Doctrine (1947) and the Marshall Plan (1948), the United States had depended on economic aid as well as military power to defend many areas of the world against communism. For both strategic and humanitarian reasons, President Eisenhower year after year requested and received huge appropriations for the mutual security program.

President Kennedy continued and in some ways elaborated upon the policy of financial assistance abroad. He established the Agency for International Development (AID) to coordinate various projects and to explore means of making them more effective. He sponsored the so-called Alliance for Progress, which was not really an alliance but a set of agreements between the United States and Latin American governments for cooperative undertakings in Latin America. He also brought about the establishment of the Peace Corps, which trained and sent abroad thousands of specialists, mostly young people, to work for two years in developing areas.

The returns from foreign aid were debatable. The most successful of the programs—and the least expensive—was probably the Peace Corps. The Alliance for Progress was criticized by businessmen in the United States on the grounds that the administration's demands for tax and land reforms, as prerequisites to aid, were frightening investors away from Latin America. The Alliance was opposed by businessmen and landowners in Latin America on the grounds that, by demanding reforms, the United States was encouraging communism. Foreign aid appeared to help in counteracting Russian influence in the emerging nations of Africa.

Heightening Tension

The Cuban dictator Fidel Castro was drawing closer to the Soviet Union, heaping invective upon the United States, and exporting "Fidelismo"

Peace Corps volunteers at work in Punjab, India, and Abidjan, Republic of Ivory Coast (PEACE CORPS)

Children in Venezuela greeted President Kennedy with a sign pleading for a new home (JOHN F. KENNEDY LIBRARY)

throughout Latin America. President Kennedy had declared: "Communist domination in this hemisphere can never be negotiated."

Once in office, Kennedy and his advisers faced the question of whether to go ahead with a project that the Eisenhower administration had begun. Under the direction of the Central Intelligence Agency, anti-Castro Cubans were secretly being trained and equipped in Central America for a landing in Cuba. They were intended to overthrow the Castro regime with the aid of discontented groups still on the island. Kennedy decided to authorize the invasion but refused to provide United States air support. On the morning of April 17, 1961, a force of about 2,000 rebels landed at the Bay of Pigs. No accompanying revolt, such as had been expected, took place in Cuba, and the invading rebels were left to the mercy of the Cuban army and air force. Within two days the beachhead was wiped out.

Throughout Latin America, and in many allied and neutral nations as well as Communist countries, the United States was the object of condemnation. This country reaped all the disadvantages and none of the potential advantages of the invasion attempt. Kennedy retorted on April 20: "We do not intend to abandon [Cuba] to the Communists." But Castro moved rapidly toward aligning Cuba fully with the Soviet Union, proclaiming that it was a "socialist" state.

In the somber aftermath of the Bay of Pigs fiasco, President Kennedy in June 1961 met Premier Khrushchev in Vienna for a frank interchange of views. It was not encouraging. According to reports, Kennedy told Khrushchev that Russia wanted to trade an apple for an orchard, but the United States did not do business that way.

An ominous sequel to the conference was renewed Russian pressure upon Berlin, bringing with it the serious threat of nuclear war. On June 15, 1961, Khrushchev, who was then back in the Soviet Union, set a deadline—the end of 1961—for the settlement of the Berlin issue. With or without the Western powers, he proposed to conclude a peace treaty with the East German government (the "German Democratic Republic"), which would then control access routes to West Berlin. As he well knew, the NATO powers did not possess conventional forces of sufficient strength to defend West Berlin and its access routes with any certainty of success. The defense of Berlin must rest upon the use of nuclear power, and Khrushchev acted as though he thought the United States would not risk the danger of world holocaust to defend Berlin.

What was pushing the Soviet Union toward this dangerous confrontation was the spectacular success of West Berlin as a "showcase of democracy" behind the iron curtain. East Germans could easily slip into West Berlin, though barbed wire and minefields prevented fugitives from crossing the rest of the border between Communist countries and western Europe. West Germany with its higher living standards and its demands for skilled workers and professionals was an irresistible lure to the poor, regimented East Germans.

Suddenly, before dawn on August 13, 1961, the East German government closed the border between East and West Berlin and in the next few days began erecting elaborate concrete block and barbed-wire barriers. East Germany was transformed into a vast concentration camp and West Berlin into a beleaguered island. Khrushchev had thus gained by a single act of force much that he had been seeking unsuccessfully at the conference table. The United States protested but was not ready to use armed force to destroy the new wall.

Fears of thermonuclear war ran so high throughout the United States that the nation faced seriously for the first time the problem of trying to construct fallout shelters sufficient to protect the entire population. There followed much controversy and some hysteria about shelters but little actual construction, despite the encouragement of the federal and state governments. Fears were intensified when the Soviet Union announced an extensive series of nuclear tests. During the autumn, Russia exploded approximately fifty nuclear devices, one with an estimated force of sixty-five megatons—3,000 times more powerful than the Hiroshima bomb. The series as a whole produced double the amount of fallout of all previous atomic tests. The United States, fearing it would fall behind in the nuclear competition, announced it would resume tests underground and in outer space.

President Kennedy, speaking in Berlin, declared: "Ich bin ein Berliner" (JOHN F. KENNEDY LIBRARY)

Cuba: The Missile Crisis

The Berlin crisis slowly subsided during the autumn of 1961, to be succeeded a year later by a new, more frightening encounter, this time in regard to Cuba. In mid-July 1962, shiploads of Russian technicians and equipment began arriving on the island. Photographic reconnaissance, which the United States was carrying out secretly around the periphery of Cuba, indicated, as Kennedy announced on September 4, that the armaments were solely defensive.

Refugees from Cuba brought reports, however, that Russia was also introducing offensive missiles into the island. Kennedy authorized photographic reconnaissance of all Cuba to ascertain if this was true. On October 14 a U-2 plane brought back incontrovertible evidence—photographs of new missile sites being rushed to completion. Why were the Russians engaged in this dangerous and expensive gamble? This was the first question Kennedy's advisers pondered as they began deliberations on October 16. The Russian move would more than redress the missile balance that had favored the United States. According to the London *Observer* (October 28, 1962): "Within a month, if the U.S. sat tight, Russia could get 200–300 missiles in position—enough, at least in theory, to knock out a large part of the U.S. retaliatory forces in a surprise 'preemptive' attack."

How could the United States counter the Russian move? One of the two main alternatives was to strike the bases from the air; the other was to blockade Cuba. The President and his advisers decided upon a "quarantine"—a blockade. Meanwhile, on October 18, Soviet Foreign Minister Gromyko called upon the President to assure him that Soviet assistance to Cuba was solely defensive.

On October 22 Kennedy was ready to act. Appearing on television, he presented the photographic evidence of the missile sites and announced

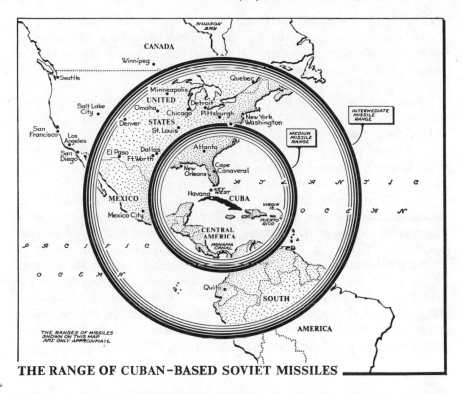

THE RANGE OF CUBAN–BASED SOVIET MISSILES

that the United States would establish a quarantine on all offensive weapons bound for Cuba.

Several days of acute tension followed as the United States instituted its naval and air blockade, uncertain what would happen if a Soviet vessel among the twenty-five bound for Cuba should refuse to stop and should be sunk. Some of the Soviet ships changed course or stopped. But low-flying Navy P-8U planes brought back evidence that work on the Soviet bases continued at top speed.

All week long the United States negotiated with the Soviet Union, and behind the stand of each side was the threat of nuclear force. The United States left no doubt that it was in earnest. The navy established a 2,100-mile ring about Cuba, employing 180 ships, including 8 aircraft carriers. The Strategic Air Command began "massive airborne" alerts on October 22, keeping quantities of its heavy nuclear-armed B-52 bombers in the air at all times. Behind these were 156 intercontinental ballistic missiles in combat readiness and a fleet of Polaris submarines. Soviet miscalculation could bring a holocaust.

Late on the evening of October 26, Kennedy received a long, rambling letter from Khrushchev in which he compared the United States and the Soviet Union to two men tugging on a rope, pulling a knot tighter and tighter until it could be cut only by a sword. In effect, the letter said that if Kennedy would cease tugging on his end, Khrushchev would do likewise. The letter seemed to imply that the Soviet Union would remove the missile bases provided the United States would promise not to invade Cuba. The next morning Moscow radio broadcast quite a different proposal from Khrushchev's—that the Soviet Union would dismantle the bases in Cuba if the United States would withdraw its missile bases from Turkey.

Time was running out for the United States, and meanwhile in Cuba antiaircraft fire had downed one American plane and menaced others. Under these tense conditions Kennedy decided to accept Khrushchev's first offer and to ignore the second: if Khrushchev would remove the missiles, Kennedy proposed, the United States would end the blockade and not invade Cuba. The next day, October 27, Khrushchev accepted.

Though an armed clash had been avoided, trouble over Cuba by no means had been brought to an end. The Soviet Union did indeed remove the missiles and dismantle the bases, but Castro refused to allow on-the-spot inspection. Thousands of Soviet technicians remained, and although President Kennedy pressured Khrushchev to remove them, their return to Russia was slow. Cuban refugee groups, bewildered and angered by the no-invasion pledge, engaged in plots of their own against Castro and were resentful when the United States restrained them. In the immediate aftermath of the crisis the national sentiment was one of profound relief, and Kennedy's popularity rose.

President Kennedy and Secretary of Defense Robert McNamara at a National Security Council meeting at the climax of the Cuban missile crisis (JOHN F. KENNEDY LIBRARY)

Loosening of Alliances

While confronting one another over Cuba, the United States and the Soviet Union found themselves on the same side in a less serious and more remote crisis over India. The Chinese had launched surprise offensives along the Indian frontier. Already the Soviet Union was providing India with economic aid, and the United States now gave further assistance, ferrying weapons and other supplies in "flying boxcars" to the Himalayan front. Soon the Chinese agreed to negotiate their boundary dispute with India. The brief war had shown that, for the time being, Indo-American relations were close and cordial. It had also indicated that the Soviet Union and the People's Republic of China were drawing further apart.

As relations between the Communist powers were being strained, so were those between the United States and one of its NATO allies—France. In western Europe the Marshall Plan had helped stimulate a recovery so remarkable that by the 1960s some nations not only were more prosperous than ever before in their history but in percentage of annual growth were outstripping the United States. Their new economic power meant that, if they chose, they could either insist upon a more equal partnership or break loose to form a "third force" between the United States and the Soviet Union, such as some French leaders had long envisaged.

To strengthen western Europe against a possible Russian threat, the United States had encouraged the formation of the European Economic Community (or Common Market), in 1958. To give further encouragement Kennedy in 1962 obtained from Congress authority to lower tariffs on trade with the Common Market countries. But President Charles de Gaulle of France jolted Kennedy's hopes for closer economic and political cooperation with Europe. In 1963 de Gaulle vetoed the British application to join the Common Market and did so because of the close British ties with the United States. He also proclaimed his opposition to American plans for creating a multination nuclear force within NATO. He insisted upon creating a separate small nuclear force for France, in order to gain an independent voice in European policy. Later he recognized the People's Republic of China, thus asserting an independent position in Asian affairs as well.

In the summer of 1963, perhaps in part because of growing trouble with China, the Soviet Union, after years of negotiation, agreed to a treaty banning atmospheric (but not underground) tests of nuclear weapons. The treaty, the first definite step in the direction of international arms reduction since the onset of the cold war, was ratified by almost every important country except China (which was preparing to test its own nuclear bomb), France, and Cuba. A notable thaw in the cold war followed. President Kennedy announced that the United States would be willing to sell large quantities of surplus wheat to the Russians, who were suffering from a shortage.

By 1964 many Americans were thinking hopefully of the prospect of a détente with the Soviet Union. But these prospects soon dimmed as the United States became more and more deeply involved in an anti-Communist crusade far from home in Southeast Asia.

JOHNSON'S DILEMMAS

During the presidential campaign of 1964 the Republican candidate, Senator Goldwater, urged that the United States take a much more active part in the war then going on between Communist North Vietnam and non-Communist South Vietnam. But President Johnson specifically repudiated the Goldwater policy. "There are those that say you ought to go north and drop bombs, and try to wipe out the supply lines, and they think that would escalate the war," Johnson declaimed in a campaign speech. "We don't want our American boys to do the fighting for Asian boys. We don't want to get involved in a nation [China] with 700 million people and get tied down in a land war in Asia."

In fact, Johnson himself was already preparing to enlarge the American role in Vietnam, and soon he was ordering bombs dropped on the north and was sending American boys by the hundreds of thousands to fight in that faraway land. As a consequence, he lost all possibility of maintaining the "consensus" he had desired and of achieving the Great Society he had proclaimed. Never before had a President been elected by such a large popular majority, and never before had a President seen his popularity dwindle away so fast and so completely.

Dominican Intervention

While undertaking to prevent the spread of communism in distant Asia, President Johnson faced what seemed like a new Communist threat much closer to home, in the Caribbean. There appeared to be a danger that a Castro-type government might be imposed upon the Dominican Republic, thus making that country a second Cuba. Johnson acted quickly to forestall the supposed Communist coup. In doing so, he laid himself open to charges of fostering imperialism and right-wing dictatorship.

After the assassination of the dictator General Rafael Trujillo in 1961, the Dominican Republic was slowly and painfully emerging from three decades of economic exploitation and political repression. The government of the democratically elected president, Juan Bosch, who was leftist though not Communist, floundered. In 1963 a conservative military junta overthrew Bosch and, faring little better, became itself the target of unrest. There were rumors of Communist infiltration into the island. In the spring of 1965, when young military men sympathetic to Bosch rebelled against the junta, there was rioting, shooting, and looting in the streets of the capital, Santo Domingo.

Within the next few days, United States forces numbering 30,000 ashore and afloat helped restore order. In reply to criticisms that the United States had acted unilaterally, the President and Secretary of State Dean Rusk insisted that they had held preliminary consultations with other American states and that the need for sudden intervention to prevent loss of life arose too quickly for further reliance upon the Organization of American States (OAS).

The OAS did authorize the establishment of an Inter-American Peace Force. American troops, together with token forces from several other republics, donned blue and yellow OAS armbands, and served under the command of a Brazilian general. Bloody fighting continued for some days before order could be restored. More than a year later, on June 1, 1966, in a new presidential election, Bosch was defeated by a moderate candidate. The peace force was withdrawn in September 1966.

The United States achieved stabilization of the Dominican Republic only at the cost of much Latin American good will. In June 1965 a professor at the National University of Mexico wrote: "The way Juan Bosch has been treated and the clumsy invasion of the Dominican Republic have created more hatred toward the United States in Latin America than the combined anti-colonial propaganda of China and Russia."

Involvement in Vietnam

The involvement of the United States in Vietnam had developed so slowly that when it began spectacularly to grow, in 1964 and 1965, few Americans could remember how it had originated.

After the close of World War II, Vietnamese nationalists, seeking independence from France, rallied around Ho Chi Minh, a Communist who during the war had led the anti-Japanese resistance and had cooperated with the Americans. Ho issued a declaration of independence echoing the American Declaration of 1776 and began negotiations with France. When negotiations broke down, Ho and his followers resorted to arms. The American government was little concerned until the fall of Nationalist China and the outbreak of the Korean War. Then the Truman administration looked upon the French as manning a bastion to check the spread of communism in Southeast Asia and began to send substantial aid. The Eisenhower administration increased the economic assistance and, when the French forces faced disaster in 1954, considered sending large-scale military aid as well. Eisenhower held back, however, because of the opposition of Congress and because of the refusal of Great Britain to cooperate.

There followed the 1954 settlements at Geneva, establishing Laos and Cambodia, and temporarily splitting Vietnam into a Communist north and non-Communist south until free elections could be held to unify the new nation. The United States did not participate in the negotiations or sign the agreements. It promised not to use force to upset them but warned that "it would view any renewal of the aggression in violation of

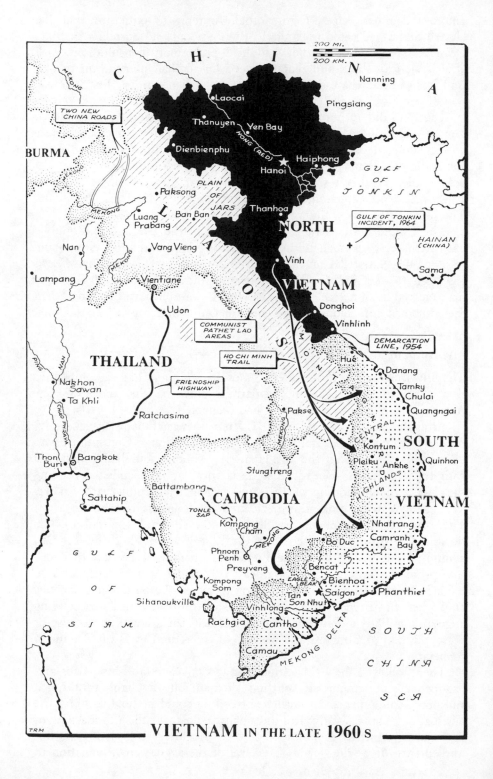

VIETNAM IN THE LATE 1960s

the . . . agreements with grave concern and as seriously threatening international peace and security." Subsequently, the State Department threw its influence against free elections, and they were never held.

The Eisenhower administration sought new arrangements to contain the Communists in Southeast Asia. Within two months of the Geneva agreements, Secretary Dulles succeeded in establishing the Southeast Asia Treaty Organization (SEATO), whose members agreed to consult one another regarding not only their own security but also the security of Laos, Cambodia, and South Vietnam. On October 23, 1954, President Eisenhower wrote to the premier of South Vietnam, promising aid in return for certain reforms and offering to "assist the Government of Viet-Nam in developing and maintaining a strong, viable state, capable of resisting attempted subversion or aggression through military means." The SEATO treaty and Eisenhower's letter were subsequently cited as the American commitments to assist South Vietnam—even though Dulles himself had told the Senate Foreign Relations Committee, when seeking its approval of SEATO, that if there should be a "revolutionary movement" in Vietnam, the SEATO members "would consult together as to what to do about it . . . but we have no undertaking to put it down; all we have is an undertaking to consult."

While the United States sought stabilization, it claimed that North Vietnam continued to seek through guerrilla activity the conquest of Laos and South Vietnam. Political turbulence and the economic dissatisfaction of many South Vietnamese made possible the successful growth of bands of Vietcong (short for Viet Communists), which by 1959 were receiving training and supplies from North Vietnam. At the end of 1960 the Vietcong established the "National Front for the Liberation of South Vietnam." Making its forays at night, murdering headmen and terrorizing villages, the Vietcong succeeded in controlling large parts of the countryside. The government of South Vietnam was confined to the cities and main lines of communication.

Gradually, the United States sent increasing aid to South Vietnam. Between 1954 and 1959, of $2.3 billion in aid, only two-fifths was military. American military advisers helped train the South Vietnam army. President Kennedy, inheriting the problem, tried to build more effective resistance in Vietnam, not only through military counterinsurgency but also through gaining the support of the peasants. Vice President Johnson, visiting Saigon in May 1961, recommended aid but warned against direct military involvement.

As political and military conditions in Vietnam continued to deteriorate, President Kennedy, despite his misgivings, added to the number of military advisers. By the time of his assassination in November 1963, the American personnel in that country had reached a total of 15,500. A new era of even greater instability began in the fall of 1963, when the South Vietnamese army seized control of the government from the aristocratic nationalist Ngo Dinh Diem.

United States military advisers train Vietnamese troops to combat Communist guerrillas (U.S. ARMY PHOTOGRAPH)

Escalating the War

Despite growing difficulties in Vietnam, in the summer of 1964 they were overshadowed by the political campaign in the United States. The number of military advisers was up to 20,000, and on its way to 25,000. Then, in August, there occurred an episode that was to give legal grounds for the reshaping of the war: American destroyers on patrol in international waters in the Gulf of Tonkin reported that they had been attacked by North Vietnamese torpedo boats. (In 1968 Senator Fulbright, chairman of the Foreign Relations Committee, held hearings and sharply inquired about what had happened in the Tonkin Gulf. He raised the question of whether there actually had been an attack.) In 1964 President Johnson and Congress were in a mood to take stern measures. Congress at the request of the President passed by a vote of 88 to 2 in the Senate and 416 to 0 in the House, a joint resolution authorizing the President to "take all necessary measures" to protect American forces and "prevent further aggression" in Southeast Asia. Subsequently, it served as legal authorization for the escalation of the conflict.

By the beginning of 1965 the Vietcong, aided not only by supplies but also by military units coming from North Vietnam along the jungle "Ho Chi Minh trail" through Laos, were in the ascendancy. The American "advisers" had gradually become combatants and were already suffering serious casualties. At this point the United States began a rapid build-up of troops in South Vietnam and the launching of regular bombing attacks upon supply depots, army camps, and transportation lines in North Vietnam. In 1965 United States armed forces in Vietnam grew from 23,000 to over 180,000; in 1966 the number was doubled; by the end of 1967 it was approaching an authorized half-million. Air sorties were intensified until the tonnage of bombs being dropped exceeded that in Europe during World War II. Casualties mounted. By every statistic the Vietnam War was becoming one of the most serious in United States history.

According to Johnson, the purpose of this enormous effort was to stop aggression and preserve the freedom of the South Vietnamese people. Yet the Johnson administration supported the military dictatorship of General Nguyen Van Thieu, who in 1965 seized control of the South Vietnamese government.

While the United States increased its economic and military aid to the Thieu regime, the Soviet Union and the People's Republic of China provided larger and larger shipments of arms and other supplies to the Ho Chi Minh government of North Vietnam, and the North Vietnamese stepped up their military action and their asistance to the Vietcong. The American intervention seemed to be bringing together the rival Communist superpowers, who had a mutual interest in preventing a Communist defeat in Vietnam. There appeared to be a danger that if the United States should press its intervention to the point of victory for Thieu, the Chinese might intervene with their own troops in Vietnam as they had done earlier in Korea.

On occasions, the United States limited or halted its bombings and other offensive actions in efforts to persuade the North Vietnamese to begin negotiations. Each time North Vietnam refused, for the most part adhering to the position that the United States must unconditionally and permanently end all bombing. At times a further stipulation was attached to this condition: all American forces were to leave Vietnam.

President Johnson and his advisers refused to end the bombing unconditionally and permanently. They pointed out that during each bombing halt at the time of a holiday truce the North Vietnamese rushed men and supplies southward or prepared for new attacks. American military leaders, following a policy of seeking out and destroying enemy forces, were confident at the beginning of 1968 that given sufficient men and matériel they could eventually triumph.

Deescalation Begins

In the United States, where television brought pictures of the cruelty and destruction of the war into every living room, the war became more and more unpopular. Liberals and university students participated vigorously in demonstrations, "teach-ins," and sit-ins. Some young men burned their draft cards. Senator Fulbright and a group of his colleagues became bitter critics of President Johnson and Secretary of State Rusk. Public-opinion polls indicated that a majority of Americans still endorsed the war, but it had become the transcendent issue in the nation.

The drain of enthusiasm accelerated rapidly in the early months of 1968. During a truce in the fighting to observe Tet—the Chinese New Year—the Vietcong suddenly struck in almost every city of South Vietnam. They were dislodged only after days of bitter fighting, great devastation, and heavy casualties. The single blow destroyed the homes of a half-million South Vietnamese. The Tet offensive intensified the opposition to the war on the part of a growing segment of the American voters.

In the fall of 1967 Senator Eugene McCarthy of Minnesota had begun what seemed to be a futile protest campaign for the presidency. He had behind him only a handful of liberals and a growing group of enthusiastic students. In the first of the primary campaigns in New Hampshire, some of the young men cut their long hair and shaved their beards before ringing doorbells for McCarthy. In the voting, McCarthy was startlingly strong against Johnson, winning almost all of the delegates to the convention. The next day, Senator Robert Kennedy of New York, also a critic of the Vietnam War, announced his candidacy. There were indications that the challenge to President Johnson would be so strong that he might not be able to win renomination.

For months Johnson had been considering a change in his course of action. On the evening of March 31, 1968, in a telecast to the nation, he suddenly announced that he was ordering a halt in the air attacks upon the populous areas of North Vietnam and was inviting the North Vietnamese to join him in a "series of mutual moves toward peace." At the close of his talk he made an announcement that removed any possibility that the de-escalation could be looked upon as a political gesture: "I shall not seek and I will not accept the nomination of my party for another term."

The North Vietnamese government accepted President Johnson's invitation, and in May 1968 lengthy, fruitless negotiations began in Paris.

ELECTION OF 1968

During 1967 and 1968, the issues of the Vietnam War and urban violence became the focus of the preconvention presidential campaigns. Significantly, the successful Republican contender, Richard Nixon, took no clear-cut stand on Vietnam. According to public-opinion polls, he was running so far ahead in the first of the primary campaigns in New Hampshire that his principal opponent, Governor George Romney of Michigan, withdrew before the balloting. Nixon easily fended off last-minute threats from Governor Ronald Reagan of California on the right, and Governor Nelson Rockefeller of New York on the left, to win nomination on the first ballot. He chose Spiro Agnew, governor of Maryland, as his running mate.

The Vietnam debate, by contrast, wracked the Democratic party. After Johnson made his announcement not to run for another term, only McCarthy and Robert Kennedy (holding much the same views on Vietnam and domestic problems) were left to battle each other in the Democratic primaries. In late April, too late to become embroiled in the primaries, Vice President Humphrey entered the campaign. So many Democratic leaders in states without primaries backed Humphrey that he became an immediate favorite to win the nomination. Public attention focused on the primary contests. Kennedy won Indiana, lost Oregon to McCarthy, and then, in the last primary in California, won again. At a Los Angeles hotel, on June 5, just after he had exhorted his cheering followers to seek victory with him at the Democratic convention, he was shot and killed by an assassin. National mourning for Kennedy brought a temporary cessation in the campaigning.

At the Democratic convention in Chicago, McCarthy (and some Kennedy followers backing Senator George McGovern of South Dakota) were unable to prevent the nomination of Humphrey on the first ballot. The critics of Humphrey, heir to administration policies, were bitter. Adding to their bitterness were the rough tactics of the Chicago police who shoved and harassed delegates and spectators to the convention and who, before television cameras, clubbed and manhandled demonstrators in the streets of Chicago. An investigating committee subsequently referred to the violent police reactions to the taunts and attacks by the demonstrators as a "police riot." Through the campaign, Humphrey (although he had been distinguished for his liberalism throughout his political career) received little support from those who had followed McCarthy and Kennedy.

The candidate who stirred the most enthusiastic responses and violent heckling wherever he spoke throughout the country was former Governor George Wallace of Alabama, running with General Curtis LeMay on the American Independent party ticket. "We are not talking about race," Wallace declared again and again, as he whipped up enthusiasm among audiences largely made up of white workers. General LeMay, who had been Chief of Staff of the Air Force, favored a hard line toward Vietnam. Public-opinion polls showed Wallace at one point to be the favorite of one-fifth of the voters; he hoped to throw the election into the House of Representatives. By Election Day his support had dropped substantially.

Neither of the major candidates evoked much enthusiasm. Nixon, campaigning methodically in almost computerized fashion, seemed far ahead from the outset. On the two main issues—law and order at home and the Vietnam War—Nixon favored conciliation from a position of strength. He declared in his acceptance address that he would heed "the voice of the great majority of Americans, the forgotten Americans, the non-shouters, the non-demonstrators, that are not racists or sick, that are not guilty of the crime that plagues the land." Regarding the Vietnam War, he pointed out that at every point he had been a critic of the administration, and Humphrey its defender; beyond that comment he made little commitment.

In contrast to Nixon's campaign, Humphrey's seemed lacking in both planning and finance. On Vietnam he and his opponent differed little, but on the problem of poverty he pledged federal aid for a massive "Marshall Plan for the cities" in contrast to Nixon's insistence that private capital must help the poor to help themselves. During the last weeks of the cam-

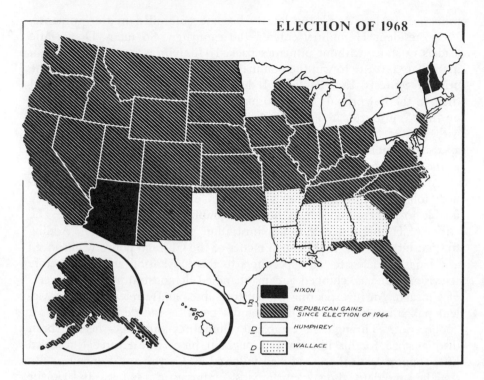

ELECTION OF 1968

NIXON

REPUBLICAN GAINS
SINCE ELECTION OF 1964

HUMPHREY

WALLACE

paign, Humphrey's standing in the public-opinion polls increased markedly, and the statements of both candidates became sharper. Yet, as the front runner, Nixon refused to debate on television. Both candidates were occupying middle positions, with Nixon to the right and Humphrey to the left of center.

By a fairly narrow margin of some 500,000 votes, out of more than 73 million cast, Nixon defeated Humphrey. The electoral vote was far more decisive, 302 for Nixon to 191 for Humphrey and 45 for Wallace. In his victory statement, Nixon returned to a theme he had frequently touched upon during the campaign and asserted that "the great objective of this Administration at the outset" would be "to bring the American people together."

twenty-seven
Nixon Seeks a New Balance

Even more than Presidents Kennedy and Johnson, President Nixon preoccupied himself with foreign affairs. In doing so he failed to "bring the American people together" and, instead, aroused increasing bitterness and division among them when he frustrated the hope for an early withdrawal from Vietnam. Nevertheless, he won widespread approval by finally withdrawing and by redirecting basic policy in such a way as to improve the prospects for moderating the cold war and for realizing what he hailed as a "generation of peace." Unfortunately, within a few months after he had left office, the collapse of the Vietnam settlement and fresh difficulties elsewhere gave indications of how precarious the new balance was.

THE NIXON-KISSINGER APPROACH

On the basis of his earlier experience as Vice President, Nixon considered himself something of an expert in diplomacy. During his first term as President, he depended on Secretary of State William P. Rogers, a New York corporation lawyer, to administer the State Department and to carry out certain diplomatic missions. He also turned frequently to Secretary of Defense Melvin R. Laird, a former Wisconsin congressman, for advice. But he relied mainly on his special assistant for national security affairs, Henry A. Kissinger, a Harvard professor of international politics, for aid in both the making and the execution of policy. For four years Kissinger's White House office overshadowed the Department of State. Then, after the inauguration of Nixon for a second term, the President put Kissinger at the head of the department. A refugee from Nazi Germany, Kissinger was the first German-born and the first Jewish Secretary of State (though a foreign-born Jew, Judah P. Benjamin, had been Secretary of State in the Confederacy during the Civil War).

Before his appointment as Nixon's security adviser, Kissinger in books and articles had criticized the assumptions on which American policy was based. To him, as well as to some other observers, it seemed that the developments of the 1960s had made obsolete the containment policy of the 1950s. The signs of growing antagonism between Communist China and Communist Russia belied the concept of a single, combined program of Communist aggression. No longer were there only two power centers, the United States and the Soviet Union; there were now at least three, with China, and potentially more than that, if western Europe and Japan were to be included. For this new "multipolar" world, Kissinger proposed a flexible, many-sided balance-of-power system to take the place of the rigid, two-sided system that had prevailed since the start of the cold war. In the new arrangement the United States would deal with Russia and China on the basis of practical interests rather than anti-Communist feelings.

Early in his first administration Nixon implied a change in policy when he put forth what he termed the Nixon Doctrine. The United States, he declared, would "participate in the defense and development of allies and friends" but would leave the "basic responsibility" to those friends themselves, especially when it came to actual fighting. In 1971 he clearly announced the new aim of a complex equilibrium: "It will be a safer world and a better world if we have a strong healthy United States, Europe, Soviet Union, China, Japan—each balancing the other, not playing one against the other, an even balance."

When Nixon decided to open relations with the Chinese People's Republic and to improve relations with the Soviet Union, his decision was in keeping with the new diplomacy that he and Kissinger had proposed. Meanwhile, Nixon continued the war in Vietnam, though Kissinger believed that American involvement had been based on "an outmoded foreign policy concept." Nixon undertook to "Vietnamize" the war—that is, to shift the burden of actual combat from Americans to the South Vietnamese, in accordance with the Nixon Doctrine—but the process was painfully slow.

VIETNAMIZATION: 1969–1972

Regarding Vietnam, Nixon said in May 1969 that he hoped to achieve "a peace we can live with and a peace to be proud of." He did not specify the kind of peace he had in mind, but presumably it would be one that kept in power the Thieu regime in Saigon. Whatever the details, his kind of peace, like Johnson's, remained unacceptable to Ho's government of Hanoi. In Paris the talks went on—among the representatives of the United States, South Vietnam, North Vietnam, and the National Liberation Front—but rumors of progress toward a settlement proved disappointing again and again. The demise of Ho, late in the summer, had no visible effect on either the Paris negotiations or the Vietnam bloodshed.

As the months passed and no end to the fighting appeared in sight, "Johnson's war" began to be looked upon as "Nixon's war," and its critics in Congress and throughout the country grew in numbers and determination. By the summer's end an opinion poll showed a clear majority of the American people believed the involvement in Vietnam was a mistake. Youthful peace advocates were planning a series of nationwide demonstrations until the United States was out of the war. Nixon turned opinion in favor of his Vietnam policy, however, by a televised speech on November 3, 1969. He said the "silent majority" agreed with him that a "precipitate withdrawal" would be "disastrous for the future of peace" in the world. Vice President Agnew afterward denounced the peace demonstrators as an "effete corps of impudent snobs" and reprimanded newspaper and television commentators for daring to question the Nixon policy.

Making a concession to the war's critics, Nixon had announced earlier the beginning of partial troop withdrawals, the first of which would reduce by 60,000 the United States force of about 540,000 men in Vietnam. These withdrawals, he explained, were steps toward the "Vietnamization" of the war. That is, the South Vietnamese themselves would be trained and equipped to take over the defense of their country as the American fighting men were gradually pulled out.

Nixon also sought to lessen opposition by reforming the draft, which because of its uncertainties and inequities added to the difficulty of justifying the sacrifice of American lives in a small and distant country. To its critics, the draft seemed all the worse because of the high-handed way in which it was administered. Its director persisted in advising local draft

Demonstrators at the Lincoln Memorial in Washington protesting against the Vietnam war (UPI)

boards to punish antiwar demonstrators by conscripting them, even after a federal court had held this to be illegal. Nixon recommended that the conscription law be changed so as to provide for a "draft lottery" that would take only nineteen-year-olds and would take them at random. Such a lottery went into effect in 1970. Going still further, Nixon urged the formation of an all-volunteer army, with improved pay and other incentives for enlistment. By 1973 Americans were no longer being drafted.

The Vietnamization plan was going so well, Nixon announced in April 1970, that he would bring home 150,000 additional men within a year or so. Suddenly, before the end of April, he broke the startling news that he had ordered American troops to cross into neutral Cambodia and, with their South Vietnamese allies, to seize military bases that the enemy had been using for operations in South Vietnam. He explained that "increased military aggression" by the Communists in Cambodia had begun to jeopardize the continuing success of the Vietnamization program.

Up to this point, Nixon said, it had been American policy "to scrupulously respect the neutrality" of Cambodia. What he did not tell the people was that the United States was already deliberately and systematically violating Cambodian neutrality. For more than a year he had personally authorized the secret bombing of suspected North Vietnamese bases on the Cambodian side of the border. For several years American ground forces had been carrying on clandestine operations in Cambodia and in Laos as well. If these facts had been made public at the time, the popular protest in the United States might have gone to even greater extremes than it actually went.

At the news of the Cambodian incursion, the languishing peace movement came to life with a more determined spirit than ever. On campuses all over this country, during May, youthful protesters demanded that the universities close down in a "strike" against the government's war policy. A radical minority resorted to violence, smashing windows and fire-bombing buildings. Policemen and National Guardsmen arrived to face rock-throwing mobs, which they tried to disperse with tear gas and, in a few instances, with gunfire. Four students (all white) were shot and killed at Kent State University in Ohio, and two (both black) at Jackson State University in Mississippi. A few months later a physicist died when antiwar protesters set off an explosion that wrecked several buildings at the University of Wisconsin in Madison.

After ending the invasion of Cambodia, in June 1970, Nixon launched an invasion of Laos, in February 1971. This time he sent no American ground troops (Congress in the Defense Appropriations Act of 1970 had prohibited their use in Laos) but gave American air support to the invading South Vietnamese army. "The South Vietnamese by themselves can hack it," he declared. This was a test of his Vietnamization program, and it proved a failure. Within a few weeks the badly mauled army scrambled back to the relative safety of South Vietnam.

American critics of "Nixon's war," like those of "Johnson's war," were appalled by the horrible sufferings it brought upon civilians, both South

Four students lay dead after Ohio National Guardsmen shot into a crowd of student demonstrators at Kent State University, May 1970 (UPI)

Vietnamese and North Vietnamese. Millions of them were deprived of life, health, shelter, or livelihood as a result of American action—napalm bombing, population transfer, village destruction, crop burning, and forest defoliation. Hundreds were shot or bayoneted by American soldiers, as in the My Lai massacre (March 16, 1968), for which Lieutenant William L. Calley, Jr., was convicted of premeditated murder in 1971.

Nixon had said the Calley case should be vigorously prosecuted, so that the incident would not "smear the decent men" who had gone to war in Vietnam. Continuing his troop withdrawals, he announced in January 1972 that the total of American troops in Vietnam would shortly be reduced to 69,000, the lowest figure in nearly seven years. As troops were withdrawn, American casualties in the war decreased, and so did the outcry at home. Yet, while taking out ground forces, Nixon was sending in more and more air and naval forces. Eventually, he authorized the dropping of a greater tonnage of bombs than Johnson had, and these bombs killed far more civilians than the 102 that Calley was charged with murdering at My Lai. Nixon ordered his greatest escalation of the war against the Vietnamese Communists after he had dramatically displayed his friendship with the Chinese and Russian Communists.

RAPPROCHEMENT WITH CHINA

Until 1949 the United States had sought to maintain the Open Door policy in China. Then, after the Communists under Mao Tse-tung and Chou

En-lai got control of the Chinese mainland, the doors were closed on both sides. The Peking government taught hatred of Americans and excluded them from the country. The Washington government prohibited trade between the United States and the Chinese mainland, refused to recognize the Mao regime, and opposed its being represented in the United Nations. Washington continued to treat Chiang Kai-shek, after his flight to the island of Taiwan, as an ally and as the rightful head of all China.

From 1949 to 1971 no American in national politics had opposed the recognition of the Peking government more resolutely than had Nixon. Eventually, making a complete turnabout, he reopened relations in a spectacular display of presidential diplomacy.

Recognition was long past due. China was the largest nation in the world, with about a quarter of all the world's people. It was one of the nuclear powers, having set off its first atomic bomb in 1964 and its first hydrogen bomb in 1967. By making friends with the Peking leaders, Nixon could hope to get their cooperation in ending the Vietnam War. He could also hope to use China as a counterbalance to the Soviet Union and thus as a means of inducing in the Russians a conciliatory mood and hastening a détente. The Chinese leaders, for their part, were eager to have the United States as a potentiality in their own balance-of-power arrangement against the Soviet Union. They feared that the Russians might attack China in an attempt to destroy the Chinese nuclear installations.

Early in 1971 Nixon hinted at a change in American policy when, in a public statement, he used the legitimate name "People's Republic of China" for what he and other American officials always had called simply Red China or Communist China. In July he made the startling announcement that he had received an invitation to visit the People's Republic (an invitation that Kissinger had arranged on a secret trip to Peking) and would make the visit within the next several months.

To succeed in his new China policy Nixon would have to approve the admission of the People's Republic to the United Nations. In the past the American delegates to the United Nations had repeatedly managed to prevent the seating of a Peking delegate, but the majorities on the American side had been growing smaller and smaller. Now the United States representative proposed giving a seat on the Security Council to the People's Republic while keeping a place for Nationalist China, that is, Taiwan. The Chinese Communists insisted, however, that the Chinese Nationalists must go. In October 1971 the United Nations admitted the People's Republic and expelled Nationalist China.

Nixon's China visit, when it finally came in February 1972, proved to be a theatrical success. For a whole week American television with Chinese cooperation followed the President and his entourage and explored various aspects of life in what had been to Americans a relatively unknown, mysterious land. Nixon was shown visiting the Great Wall and other tourist attractions, wining and dining with Communist dignitaries, exchanging pleasantries with party leader Mao Tse-tung and Premier Chou En-lai.

Never before had a summit meeting been so elaborately staged or so extensively viewed. One effect was to reduce, if not to reverse, the anti-Chinese feelings that had been instilled in the American people for a generation.

The summit meeting was also something of a diplomatic success. In Peking the leaders of the two countries agreed to scientific, cultural, journalistic, and other exchanges and to the development of trade. They did not agree to the immediate establishment of formal relations, with an exchange of ambassadors. The Communists, looking on Taiwan as part of their country, refused to accept an embassy from the United States so long as Taiwan had one. The United States must first break off diplomatic relations with Nationalist China. If the summit conferees arrived at any understanding in regard to the Vietnam War, they made no public announcement of the fact.

On subsequent journeys to Peking, Kissinger worked out details of

Upon President Nixon's arrival in Peking in February 1972, he reviewed an honor guard with Premier Chou En-lai (UPI)

trade arrangements and other matters and managed, as he put it, to "accelerate the normalization of relations." A year after the Nixon visit, the two countries agreed to set up "liaison offices" in each other's capitals. Except in name, these offices practically amounted to embassies. The United States was expected soon to remove some of the 9,000 American troops on Taiwan. By 1973 it appeared that relations with China were getting back to normal, after nearly a quarter-century of nonrecognition and estrangement.

DÉTENTE WITH THE SOVIET UNION

Nixon had been the first American President to make a trip, while in office, to China; he was the second to travel to the Soviet Union. His Russian visit, in May 1972, provided less drama, for there was less mystery about the Soviet Union, less to be revealed to the American public. Yet the summit conference in Moscow was even more important than the one in Peking, since the Soviet Union, like the United States, was a true superpower and China, as yet, was not.

From both the Russian and the American points of view, the time was ripe for a move toward a new understanding. The Soviet government, under the leadership of Communist party chief Leonid Brezhnev, looked to the United States for possible future support against China, for aid in overcoming Russia's technological lag, and for wheat and other foodstuffs to make up for her serious crop shortages. Having achieved something like nuclear parity with the United States, the Russians also were interested in the economies of slowing down the arms race. Nixon and his advisers shared the desire for a limitation of nuclear armaments, wished to promote American trade, and hoped for Soviet cooperation in ending the war in Vietnam and preventing war in other parts of the world, especially in the Middle East.

By 1972 the United States still led the Soviet Union in the number of long-range planes kept in readiness for delivering nuclear bombs. Moreover, this country had almost twice as many submarines equipped with nuclear missiles. But the Soviet Union had moved ahead in regard to land-based intercontinental ballistic missiles, or ICBMs, which could carry nuclear explosives all the way from the one country to the other.

The two superpowers were engaged in a "doomsday game" of competition in the development of more and more deadly weapons and delivery systems—a game that could conceivably lead to mutual annihilation. Each of the two was testing a multiple independently targeted reentry vehicle, or MIRV, a device that could be sent into orbit and then directed back into the earth's atmosphere above the enemy's territory, where it would drop separate nuclear warheads on widely scattered targets. Each nation was also planning an antiballistic-missile system, or ABM, which was intended to protect population centers or ICBM emplacements against missile attack. In the ABM system, nuclear "antimissile missiles" would be launched to intercept and explode approaching enemy missiles before these could reach their targets. The Nixon administration's ABM project aroused considerable opposition in the United States. Critics said the ABM would have little effect on ICBMs and still less on MIRVs but would endanger civilians in its vicinity and would intensify the arms race.

Already the United States and the Soviet Union had taken a small step toward the control of nuclear weapons, a step beyond the 1963 treaty banning atmospheric tests. In the "nonproliferation" treaty of 1968 the two powers agreed to discourage the spread of nuclear weapon technology to nations not yet possessing it. Great Britain was the only other nuclear power to sign the treaty, but France and China were producing their own hydrogen bombs, and Israel and India (among other countries) appeared to be capable of doing so. The treaty, then, did not prevent a widening of the arms race, nor did it lessen the competition between the two front runners.

The two took a step toward lessening this competition when, in 1969, American and Russian diplomats met in Helsinki to begin discussion of a strategic arms limitation treaty, or SALT. After continuing their talks, in Vienna, for two and one-half years, the negotiators arrived at a temporary agreement. This first-phase treaty, or SALT I, would limit each country to only two ABMs and the existing number of ICBMs. The compromise would leave the United States superior in numbers of warheads and the Soviet Union, with its warheads of greater size, superior in total megatonnage. The limitations were to last for five years. Applying only to quantity and not to quality, they would do nothing to prevent a continuing and even heightening contest for arms improvements in the meantime.

At their Moscow meeting in 1972, Nixon and Brezhnev signed SALT I and several other agreements. One of these promised a vast expansion of trade through American tariff reductions and credit extensions. A gigantic "wheat deal" led immediately to the sale of about one-fourth of the total American wheat supply at a bargain price, one well below the market price, and the American government was to make up the difference by means of subsidies to the American wheat sellers. The prospect of a reduction in arms spending, however, did not last long. After Nixon's return from Moscow, the administration asked Congress to approve the largest military budget ever except during a declared war.

In June 1973 Nixon welcomed Brezhnev to Washington for a round of partying and further negotiating. A series of new agreements confirmed and extended those of the previous year. The two countries pledged to abstain from nuclear war, to speed up the conclusion of SALT II for a permanent "freeze" on offensive nuclear arms, and to cooperate in various economic, scientific, and cultural fields. Toasting his Russian guest at a dinner, Nixon said: "The question is: Shall the world's two strongest nations constantly confront one another in areas which might lead to war, or shall we work together for peace?" The question remained to be answered, despite all the talk of détente.

EXIT FROM INDOCHINA

Nixon's China and Russia diplomacy gave him added strength in his conduct of the Vietnam War. Neither China nor Russia stopped sending military supplies to North Vietnam, but both powers indicated that there were limits to their aid. Apparently, each was somewhat reluctant to risk damaging its new relationship with the United States.

Between Nixon's China visit and his Russia visit, the fighting in Vietnam actually intensified, going in some respects to greater lengths than ever before. In March 1972 the North Vietnamese launched their heaviest attack since the Tet offensive of 1968. Well equipped with tanks and artillery, they crossed into South Vietnam and proceeded to overrun much of its territory. In April Nixon responded by sending B-52 bombers to strike near Hanoi and Haiphong, thus reversing Johnson's 1968 decision to de-escalate the air war in the north. On May 8—just before his scheduled trip to Peking—Nixon ordered the mining of Haiphong harbor and six other North Vietnamese ports, so as to prevent the delivery of war supplies by ship from China or the Soviet Union. Johnson had refrained from this extreme measure for fear it would provoke retaliation from one or both of those two countries. Now they confined themselves to comparatively mild protests.

In July 1972 the Paris peace negotiators (representing the two Vietnams, the Vietcong, and the United States) met for their 150th session, with no indication that, after four years, they were making any progress toward a settlement. It had recently come to light, however, that Kissinger and North Vietnamese Foreign Secretary Le Duc Tho were meeting separately and secretly, and it was rumored that they were nearing a cease-fire agreement. "Peace is at hand," Kissinger finally announced on October 26, just before the American presidential election. The North Vietnamese government was ready and eager to accept the terms that Kissinger and Tho had arrived at, but President Thieu of South Vietnam raised objectives, and Nixon refused to give his approval. On December 16, after Kissinger and Tho had broken off negotiations, Kissinger declared that the agreement was 99 percent complete, but he did not explain what the missing 1 percent consisted of.

The next day, December 17, without any announcement from the White House, American planes began to bomb North Vietnamese cities in the heaviest and most destructive raids of the entire war. The targets were docks, airfields, railyards, power plants, antiaircraft defenses, and the like, but these were located in or near residential areas, and homes, shops, schools, and even hospitals were hit. The destruction was achieved at considerable cost to the Americans. In the previous seven years of the Vietnam War, only one B-52 bomber had been lost in combat. Now, in two weeks of round-the-clock raiding, fifteen of the high-flying giant planes fell when struck by Russian-made surface-to-air missiles. On December 30 Nixon called off the bombing and announced that the North Vietnamese had consented to resuming the secret peace talks.

On January 27, 1973, representatives of the four parties (the United States and South Vietnam, North Vietnam and the "Provisional Revolutionary Government" of South Vietnam, that is, the Vietcong) signed an "agreement on ending the war and restoring peace in Vietnam." The main provisions of this agreement were the same as those of the October 1972 agreement, which Nixon had refused to approve. There was to be an immediate cease-fire, and within sixty days prisoners of war were to be returned and foreign military forces in South Vietnam were to be withdrawn. Contradictorily, both the South Vietnamese right of self-determination and the unity of all Vietnam, North and South, were recognized. Laos and Cambodia were to be evacuated, and their independence and neutrality were to be respected. An international commission was to supervise the cease-fire.

Nixon proclaimed that at last he had won a "peace with honor." In fact, he had gained two things in the peace arrangement. One was the return of several hundred American prisoners of war (whose numbers, incidentally, he had recently increased through the Christmas-season bombing and the exposure of downed B-52 crews to capture). The other gain for Nixon was to keep Thieu in power in South Vietnam for the time being. But Nixon had also yielded a lot in the truce terms. These included several references to the 1954 Geneva settlement, which the United States had never signed. They reconfirmed the Geneva principle of the ultimate reunification of Vietnam. That was what the North Vietnamese and the Vietcong had been fighting for, and at the time of the cease-fire they were in a strong position for achieving it, since they now occupied a large part of South Vietnam's territory.

Such were the inconclusive results of more than a decade of direct American military involvement in Vietnam, and they had been accomplished at a staggering cost. In money this exceeded $100 billion for the United States alone. In lives it was approximately 1 million Vietnamese Communists, 200,000 South Vietnamese, and 55,000 Americans. Some 300,000 Americans were wounded, half of them seriously, and many of these permanently maimed. A total of about 3 million Americans served in the war, most of them unwillingly. Perhaps as many as 70,000 evaded service by dodging the draft or deserting after enlistment. Thousands of deserters and draft dodgers remained in hiding at home or in refuge abroad, particularly in Canada and Sweden, as Nixon with the backing of a public majority vowed to grant no amnesty. The psychological cost to Americans, both veterans and nonveterans, was incalculable. Never since the Civil War had the people been so badly divided. Understandably, the announcement of peace, after the longest war in American history, provoked no such demonstrations of popular rejoicing as had followed World War I and World War II.

There was no peace in Vietnam. The international commission, set up to supervise the cease-fire, was powerless to keep the Communists and the non-Communists apart. During the first year after the cease-fire, the Vietnamese (both sides together) suffered more battle deaths than the Americans had suffered during the ten years before it. In Laos the fighting ended about a month after the cease-fire, when the Communists were left in control of more than half the country. In Cambodia the war continued, and American planes kept up and intensified their bombing in an effort to save the Lon Nol regime from its Communist enemies. Nixon refused to stop the bombing of Cambodia until Congress compelled him to do so.

Congress had been growing more and more critical of the President's assertion of warmaking powers without any congressional declaration of war, and both the Senate and the House had begun to consider proposals, mild at first, for holding him to constitutional limits. In 1969 the Senate advised the President that, in the future, he should get the approval of Congress before committing the United States to the use of armed forces abroad. In 1971 Congress repealed the 1964 Gulf of Tonkin resolution, which Johnson and Nixon had treated as the equivalent of a war declaration. Congress could have stopped the war by cutting off appropriations for it, but this would have been unpopular, since it would have looked like abandoning American soldiers in the field. Nixon maintained that, as commander in chief, he had the power to use the armed forces as he saw fit in order to protect the troops while he was withdrawing them under his Vietnamization plan.

After the signing of the cease-fire and the withdrawal of the troops, Nixon no longer had that justification for waging war as he and his advisers saw fit. When he persisted in bombing Cambodia, despite congressional protests, Congress set August 15, 1973, as a deadline for the cessation of all American military activity in Indochina, including the air warfare in Cambodia. Nixon discontinued the bombing only at the last minute.

Several months later Congress passed, over Nixon's veto, a measure intended to prevent a President from involving the country in future wars without congressional approval. Under this war-powers resolution of 1973, the President could order no troops into action without reporting to Congress, and he would have to halt the action immediately if Congress objected, or in ninety days if Congress failed to give its positive permission. The new law was a response to a growth in presidential power that Congresses as well as Presidents had been fostering for many years. Whether the measure was wise for the nuclear age, and whether it would work in any case, only time could tell.

OLD FRIENDSHIPS UNDER STRAIN

While relations with China and the Soviet Union were improving, relations with Japan, West Germany, Great Britain, and other allies were getting worse.

The American conduct of the Vietnam War antagonized many Europeans. Some felt the United States was neglecting western Europe while preoccupying itself with Southeast Asia. Some were outraged by the warfare upon Vietnamese civilians, especially by the 1972 Christmas-season bombing of North Vietnamese cities.

The switch in American policy toward China and the Soviet Union disturbed the leaders of Japan and the western European countries. Japan, which had looked to the United States for security against China, now worried about the prospect of being abandoned. West Germany, under Chancellor Willy Brandt, approved of détente and was furthering it by making treaties with the Soviet Union and its Polish and East German satellites. To offset the risks of his new diplomacy, however, Brandt counted upon all-out American assistance in case of a Russian threat, and he wondered if he could be sure of such support after Nixon's negotiations with Brezhnev. British officials suspected that, in the negotiations, Nixon had gained less than he had given up. In general, the allies were uneasy at the thought of the United States going over their heads and dealing directly with the Communist powers.

Both American and European spokesmen pledged their respective governments' continued devotion to the North Atlantic Alliance as the alliance approached the twenty-fifth year of its existence. The constant repetition of mutual reassurances, on the part of American and European leaders, was itself a sign that NATO was in serious trouble. American leaders had to pay some attention to the voice of the people, and more and more the American people were questioning the necessity of keeping United States troops in Europe (most of them, about 215,000, in West Germany). In response to popular demand, some of the Democrats in Congress were proposing to compel a reduction in the number of American troops abroad.

Nixon, along with Brandt and other western European leaders, opposed the withdrawal of American forces from western Europe unless there should be a corresponding withdrawal of Russian forces from eastern Europe. Nixon and Brezhnev, at their 1972 Moscow meeting, had agreed to the calling of a European security conference for the discussion of "mutual balanced force reductions" on both sides, and MBFR talks were getting under way in Vienna. Meanwhile, the American government disagreed with its European allies about the sharing of NATO costs. The Nixon administration insisted that the allies, now that they were financially strong, ought to make larger contributions than they had been making to the common defense.

Toward the European Economic Community (EEC), or the Common Market, the American government's attitude had become ambivalent by 1973. On the one hand, the United States still officially favored the strengthening of the EEC and approved its enlargement when Great Britain was finally admitted, along with Ireland and Denmark. On the other hand, the United States seemed to fear the economic competition of the EEC and complained that it was discriminating against American exports.

Already there was a crisis in trade and monetary relations between the

United States and both Japan and Europe. For years the American government and American citizens had been spending larger and larger quantities of dollars abroad, for tourist travel, foreign goods, capital investments, and economic and military aid. The expenditures on the Vietnam War, after its escalation in 1964, added greatly to the dollar outflow. All together, Americans spent far more in foreign countries than foreigners spent in the United States. Hence the balance of payments was upset, and the dollar tended to lose value in relation to foreign currencies.

By 1971 the Nixon administration felt compelled to take drastic steps. It put a temporary 10-percent surcharge on imports. Then it stopped giving up gold in return for the dollars that foreign governments held. This meant that the exchange rates were no longer controlled, and the dollar price of other currencies, especially the mark and the yen, began to rise. Finally, Nixon did what no President since Franklin D. Roosevelt had done—he officially devalued the dollar. He raised the official price of gold from $35 to $38 an ounce and thus reduced the gold content of the dollar from 1/35 to 1/38 of an ounce. In 1973 he further devalued the dollar, raising the gold price to $42.

Devaluation was intended to overcome the balance-of-payments deficit by causing Americans to buy less of foreign goods and services, and foreigners to buy more of American goods and services. But the deficit kept growing, and the dollar kept falling. By the summer of 1973 it was worth only a little more than half as many German marks as it formerly had been. To cut down imports the Nixon administration threatened to raise tariffs and to impose other trade controls, while the Japanese and the Europeans protested. By this time, exports had begun to increase, with large shipments abroad of American wheat and other crops. Now, to cut down on exports and prevent shortages at home, the administration put limits on the foreign sale of farm commodities and steel scrap, thus provoking new protests, especially on the part of Japan.

The international trade and monetary system of the preceding quarter-century appeared to have broken down, and economic conflicts between the United States and its allies were putting a serious strain on the alliances.

TROUBLE IN NONPOWER REGIONS

The Nixon-Kissinger theory of five power centers left a subordinate place for the nonpower regions of the world, the distinctly weaker countries of Latin America, Asia, and Africa. Yet clashes arising in these areas could jeopardize relations among the powerful, as the Vietnam War at times had seemed likely to do.

During Nixon's presidency, the relations of the United States with many of the Latin American countries deteriorated. At the outset his personal representative, Governor Nelson Rockefeller of New York, on a fact-finding tour, ran into popular hostility like that which Nixon himself had experienced when, as Vice President, he made a similar trip in 1958. Capitalizing upon the popular sentiment, new military governments in Peru and Bolivia seized the property of American corporations. The constitutionally elected government of the radical Salvador Allende did the same in Chile. In retaliation, Nixon undertook to block financial aid, from either American or international sources, to Chile and other countries that failed to compensate American property owners satisfactorily. It was revealed that the Central Intelligence Agency had helped subsidize those opposing Allende's election to the Chilean presidency. This revelation lent some credence to the charge, in 1973, after Allende's overthrow and death in a military coup, that the American government had connived with his opponents.

In Asia the Nixon administration reversed American policy toward India while reversing it toward China. Previous administrations had tried to encourage the development of India, the largest democracy in the world, as an offset to China, the largest Communist nation. They had also given arms aid to Pakistan, a military dictatorship, for defense against the Chinese. Pakistan had used its American equipment in clashes with India, however, and had become more and more friendly with China.

In 1971 the Pakistani ruler, Yahya Khan, ordered his armed forces to put down discontent in East Pakistan, and they attempted to do so by killing hundreds of thousands of civilians. Millions of East Pakistanis took refuge in India, where they constituted a grave burden for India's economy. India's Prime Minister, Indira Gandhi, turned to the Soviet Union for support, signed a friendship treaty with Brezhnev, and launched a war to detach East Pakistan from the rule of Yahya Khan. During this Indo-Pakistani war, Nixon wanted the United States to "tilt in favor of Pakistan," and he ordered an American fleet to the Bay of Bengal, thus giving Indians the impression that he was trying to intimidate them. India quickly won the war and proclaimed the independence of East Pakistan under the name of Bangladesh. The Nixon policy accomplished nothing except to reinforce the India-Russia alignment and lessen American influence on the Indian subcontinent.

The Middle East, the scene of continual fighting between Arabs and Israelis, presented a dilemma for the Nixon administration, as it had done for previous administrations. Israel (whose prime minister, Golda Meir, was a former Milwaukee schoolteacher) had many sympathizers, both Jewish and non-Jewish, within the United States. They could exert considerable pressure in American politics. The Arab countries could count upon no such American constituency, but they possessed two-thirds of the world's known oil reserves, and they occupied areas that were of strategic importance to the United States in its global conflict with the Soviet Union. So long as the United States backed the Israelis, it antagonized the Arabs and tended to throw them into the Russian embrace. If, however, the United States should discontinue its support, Israel might face destruction as an independent country.

Violence in the Middle East had been renewed in 1967, after a UN peace-keeping force had been withdrawn at the demand of Egypt. Expecting an attack from Egypt, which was well equipped with Russian arms, Israel struck and in the Six-Day War defeated Egypt, Jordan, and Syria and occupied parts of their territory. A 1967 UN resolution called upon Israel to withdraw her armed forces from the occupied territories but recognized the right of every nation in the area to "live in peace within secure and recognized boundaries." Israel refused to budge without guarantees of her security. After the 1967 war Israel rearmed with American aid, and Egypt and Syria with Russian aid. Intermittent shelling and raiding went on across the borders between Israel and her neighbors.

The Nixon administration, at first, attempted an "even-handed" policy in the Middle East. Nixon hoped for a compromise that would satisfy both sides and make it unnecessary for Egypt or Syria to depend on the Soviet Union. The Russians cooperated to the extent of agreeing to UN mediation, which resulted only in a brief truce, in 1970. Then Palestinian Arabs, living as refugees in Jordan, revolted against Jordan's King Hussein, who was trying to stay on good terms with Israel and the United States. While Hussein was putting down the rebellion, Nixon made a display of naval strength in the Mediterranean Sea, presumably as a warning to the Soviet Union against allowing Egypt to intervene in Jordan. Thereafter, the Soviet Union rapidly increased its naval force in the Mediterranean, and Russian ships soon outnumbered American vessels there.

After 1972 the détente between the United States and the Soviet Union could have been expected to defuse the explosive Middle Eastern situation. In October 1973, however, war again erupted, when on the Jewish holy day of Yom Kippur the Egyptians and the Syrians suddenly attacked. Both they and the Israelis quickly lost huge quantities of tanks, aircraft, and other equipment, and both the Russians and the Americans resorted to airlifts to make up for the losses. Only after the Israelis had gotten the upper hand did the Russians show any interest in ending the war. Then Kissinger and Brezhnev worked out and the UN Security Council adopted resolutions calling for an immediate cease-fire and for the beginning of peace negotiations on the basis of the 1967 resolution— which would presumably require Israel to give up most if not all of her 1967 conquests in return for some guarantee of her continued existence.

As the shooting died down, the American-Russian détente seemed belatedly to be having an effect in the Middle East. All at once Nixon made the startling announcement that he was putting American forces throughout the world on a stand-by alert. He was doing so, administration spokesmen said, because the Russians were increasing their already large naval force in the Mediterranean and were preparing to fly troops to the Middle East to enforce the cease-fire. The Russians sent no troops, and a new UN peace-keeping force began to arrive. Relaxing the alert, Nixon declared that the United States had just passed through its most dangerous war crisis since the Cuban missile crisis of 1962. "Without détente," he said, "we might have had a major confrontation in the Mideast."

While Egypt and Israel disputed over the details of the cease-fire and threatened to resume hostilities, the Arab countries announced plans to reduce oil production and to cut off petroleum sales to the United States. The Arabs intended, by withholding oil from Israel's friends, to pressure them into supporting a Middle Eastern settlement that would force Israel to leave the Arab territories she had conquered in 1967. Japan and western Europe, which had been getting respectively 82 percent and 72 percent of their petroleum from Arab sources, were much more vulnerable than was the United States, which had depended on those sources for only 11 percent of its supply. Understandably, Japan and the leading powers of western Europe were careful not to offend the Arabs. The United States seemed likely to become careful, too, as the American people increasingly felt the pinch of the oil embargo during the winter of 1973–1974.

Meanwhile the "Yom Kippur war" intensified the strains within the North Atlantic Alliance. None of the principal NATO allies had backed the United States in its support of Israel. During the airlift, several of them had forbidden American transport planes to refuel in their territories or even to fly over them. After the war the Nixon administration made its anger known to the allies. They, in turn, complained that the American government had disregarded their desperate need for Arab oil and had failed to consult them about its intentions, particularly about its intention to order a world-wide military alert. The alliance now appeared to be more badly shaken than at any time since 1956, when France and Great Britain had joined Israel in invading Egypt and the United States had sided with the Soviet Union in bringing about UN action against the invaders.

twenty-eight
The New Federalism

President Nixon took office in 1969 favoring what he called reform, which seemed to mean a reversal of the policies his immediate predecessors had sponsored under the slogans of "the New Frontier" and "the Great Society." He looked for a slogan of his own and came up with "the New Federalism." This implied that he would, in his words, "reverse the flow of power and resources from the states and communities to Washington and start power and resources flowing back . . . to the people all over America."

THE IMPERIAL PRESIDENCY

In fact, while reversing certain policies, Nixon did not stop the trend toward the centralization of power. Rather, he encouraged a development that had been accelerating since the presidency of Franklin D. Roosevelt. With respect to domestic as well as foreign affairs, Nixon undertook to concentrate more and more authority in the White House.

The cabinet had been losing influence on policy making ever since World War II, and it continued to do so under Nixon. His own cabinet was distinguished by little competence and still less continuity. He appointed few outstanding public figures to it, and during his first five years he made more changes in its membership than any other President had made during any length of time. For the most part the members merely administered their own departments, seldom if ever consulting with one another as a group or even individually with the President. An exception was John Mitchell, Nixons' former law partner, his 1968 campaign manager, and from 1969 to 1972 his Attorney General and chief adviser on politics. Mitchell had direct access to the White House.

Few other department heads, government officials of lesser rank, or congressmen or senators could approach the President directly. Almost all of them had to deal with him through his top White House aide, the "keeper of the gates," H. R. Haldeman, or through the chief of his domestic policy staff, John Ehrlichman. These two, old friends and veteran Nixon campaigners, now subject only to the President himself, ran the executive office with respect to domestic affairs from 1969 to 1973. The executive office was a large and rapidly swelling bureaucracy, whose numbers during that four-year period grew from 2,000 to more than 4,200.

By 1969 the domestic programs of the federal government and the agencies to administer them had become so numerous that they were difficult if not impossible for the President to control. As far back as the Truman and Eisenhower administrations a commission under former President Hoover had made proposals for reorganizing and streamlining the executive branch, but few of the proposals had been carried out. Now, on the advice of Roy Ash, a prominent businessman, Nixon proposed a new plan for bringing together the widely scattered threads of administration. The plan was to reorganize and enlarge the powers of the Bureau of the Budget, which had been set up during Harding's presidency to coordinate the requests of the various bureaus for appropriations from Congress. A new Office of Management and Budget, responsible to the President, was to oversee the financing and directing of all administrative agencies, including the formerly quasi-independent regulatory ones such as the Federal Power Commission. Congress approved the plan even though it meant that Congress would no longer be able to supervise the departments and commissions by negotiating directly with them in regard to their budget requests. These requests had to go through the Office of Management and Budget after it went into operation, in 1970.

Again acting on the advice of businessman Ash, Nixon proposed to reorganize and reduce the number of executive departments. When Congress failed to approve, the President in 1973 went ahead on his own, with a revised plan. By executive order he raised three of the department heads to the level of "presidential councillors" and directed that the others report to one of the three, who in turn would report to a presidential aide (Erhlichman). With the three councillors constituting a "super cabinet," the authority and prestige of the traditional cabinet would be still further reduced.

Nixon presented his reorganization measures as long overdue reforms that would bring businesslike efficiency to the government. They would, of course, enable the White House to manage more effectively the executive branch as a whole. But Nixon also claimed unprecedented authority for the presidential office in relation to the legislative branch, especially after his reelection in 1972. Asserting "executive privilege" seemingly without limit, he took the position that congressional committees could not question administrative officials without the President's consent. Implying that the President, not Congress, should have the power of the purse, he ordered administrative agencies not to spend appropriated money after Congress had overridden his vetoes of appropriation bills.

By the beginning of his second term, Nixon faced a congressional revolt. His critics in Congress—including some members of the Republican minority as well as the Democratic majority—talked of a constitutional crisis. For many years Congress had been allowing Presidents more and more discretion, particularly in foreign affairs (as seemed unavoidable in a nuclear age). Now Nixon, while stretching to the utmost his powers as commander in chief in Southeast Asia, was thought to be doing the same with his powers as chief executive at home. Unless Congress acted soon to regain its lost authority, some of the critics believed, the checks and balances of the Constitution would become meaningless in actual practice.

LAW AND ORDER

From the beginning of his first term, President Nixon hoped to alter the direction of the Supreme Court, which under Chief Justice Earl Warren had been actively enlarging the sphere of both personal liberty and civil rights. The Warren Court's decisions on civil rights had antagonized conservatives, particularly in the South, and the decisions on personal liberty had aroused advocates of "law and order" (one of Nixon's themes in the 1968 campaign) all over the country. Especially resented were the *Escobedo* and *Miranda* cases (1964, 1966), in which the judges had limited the power of local police to extract confessions from persons accused of crimes.

As Chief Justice Warren approached retirement, President Johnson had tried to replace him with Abe Fortas, whom Johnson earlier had appointed as an associate justice. Fortas, a liberal, could have been expected to keep the Court on essentially the same track it had been following under Warren. The Republicans in the Senate blocked the Fortas appointment and thus gave Nixon an opportunity to choose his own Chief Justice. Nixon—who insisted that it was "the job of the courts to interpret the law, not make the law"—chose a conservative strict constructionist who agreed with him. This was Warren Burger, who had served for thirteen years on the United States Court of Appeals for the District of Columbia and who had spoken out against what he considered the Supreme Court's protection of the rights of criminals. Burger's appointment received the prompt approval of the Senate.

Nixon soon had a chance to put another man of his choice on the Supreme Court, but this time he ran into difficulty and embarrassment. The opening occurred when Justice Fortas resigned after the revelation that he had received a salary payment from a foundation whose donor was under indictment for fraud. To take Fortas' place, Nixon named a federal circuit court judge from South Carolina, C. F. Haynsworth, who had the endorsement of the American Bar Association, but whose past decisions showed that he lagged considerably behind the Warren Court in his devotion to civil rights. Spokesmen for black organizations and for labor unions vociferously opposed the confirmation of Haynsworth. They were joined by others, including prominent members of Nixon's own party, when it was revealed that Haynsworth had sat on cases involving corporations in which he himself had a financial interest. His critics now said he was even more insensitive to possible conflicts of interest than Fortas had been. Eventually, the Senate rejected the Haynsworth nomination, and Nixon then named G. Harrold Carswell, a judge of the Florida federal appeals court, who lacked Haynsworth's legal eminence and who was shown to have made racist statements in the past. When the Senate turned down Carswell also, Nixon angrily charged the Senate majority with bias against the South. The Senate finally accepted the appointment of Harry A. Blackmun, who, like Chief Justice Burger, came from Minnesota and had a reputation as a conservative jurist.

Before Nixon had been in office three years, two more Supreme Court vacancies arose, and again he ran into trouble in trying to fill them. The American Bar Association refused to endorse his first two choices, one of whom was a woman. Nixon then nominated, and the Senate approved, Lewis F. Powell, Jr., a Virginian and a former head of the American Bar Association, and William H. Rehnquist, Assistant Attorney General in the Nixon administration and a Goldwater Republican from Arizona. "I shall continue to appoint judges," Nixon later said, "who share my philosophy that we must strengthen the peace forces against the criminal forces in America."

Through his four appointments to the Supreme Court, Nixon succeeded in changing its interpretations to some extent, at least in regard to criminal procedure. Usually his appointees voted together, and often Justice Byron White joined them to make a majority. With the cooperation of these five, the Court put new restrictions on the legal rights of defendants in criminal cases, even holding that a jury need no longer reach a unanimous verdict in order to convict. With White parting from the Nixon appointees, however, the Court in a 5-to-4 decision (*Furman* v. *Georgia*, 1972) banned capital punishment in states where juries could decide whether or not to impose it. With one or more of the new members concurring, the Court also diverged from Nixons' aims by giving some important decisions in favor of civil liberties and civil rights.

By 1969, a decade and a half after the Court's historic decision outlawing segregation, only about 20 percent of the black children in the South were attending mixed schools. Robert A. Finch—a civil rights advocate whom Nixon had put in charge of the Department of Health, Education, and Welfare (HEW)—expressed determination to make the most of the government's power to withhold federal aid from schools whose authorities permitted no more than token integration. Finch indicated that he would not be satisfied with "freedom of choice" plans, which required the black child or his parents to take the initiative in seeking entrance to a school attended by whites. Then, in September 1969, the Nixon administration suddenly pulled back, ceased to insist on immediate steps toward integration, and granted Mississippi an additional delay in eliminating its dual school system. Several weeks later the Court overruled the administration and demanded that Mississippi integrate its schools "at once." But Nixon prevented the HEW Department from cutting off funds from noncomplying districts and continued to delay the carrying out of its desegregation plans. Finch and a number of other HEW officials soon left the department.

In many areas the achievement of racial balance in schools (so as to eliminate all racially identifiable ones) would require the transporting of children from one neighborhood to another. Busing to segregated schools was a common practice, but busing to integrated schools was quite another matter in the opinion of most whites (and some blacks). When federal courts began to order such busing, Nixon spoke out with the many who denounced it as unthinkable if not unconstitutional. Nevertheless, the Supreme Court unanimously upheld it in a 1971 case involving Charlotte, North Carolina. The next year Nixon tried, unsuccessfully, to induce Congress to pass an antibusing law. Meanwhile, opponents of busing in northern cities violently resisted court-ordered busing, those in Denver, Colorado, and Pontiac, Michigan, resorting to the fire-bombing of school buses. In 1974 attention focused upon Boston opposition to busing. There was also resistance in the South, but on the whole desegregation proceeded faster there than in the North. Before the end of Nixon's first term—thanks to the federal courts—the proportion of Southern blacks in all-black schools had declined from about 80 to less than 20 percent.

Comparatively few blacks, North or South, approved of Nixon's policies in regard to schools or other matters. "For the first time since Woodrow Wilson," said an official of the National Association for the Advancement of Colored People, "we have a national administration that can be rightly characterized as anti-Negro." Nevertheless, during the first five years of Nixon's presidency, the country was spared the kind of racial violence that had been breaking out every summer for several years before 1969. The urban black communities had apparently come to the conclusion that rioting did them more harm than good.

The antiwar groups also calmed down after their campus eruptions at the time of the Cambodian invasion in 1970. Even the Christmas-season bombing of North Vietnam in 1972 provoked no riots. It was as if events had numbed the erstwhile protesters for peace.

But Indians resumed their demonstrations, sometimes with violence. At first, in 1969, the hopes of Indians had been raised when Nixon appointed a Mohawk-Sioux as Commissioner of Indian Affairs, and again in 1970 when Nixon promised Indians "self-determination without termination," that is, an increase in control over their own affairs and at the same time an increase in federal aid. The promises were not fulfilled, however, and among Indians anger and frustration took the place of hope. In November 1972 nearly a thousand protesters forcibly took over the Bureau of Indian Affairs building in Washington and, after six days, left it with damage to files and furniture that government officials estimated at $500,000 to $2 million. Later that winter members of the militant American Indian Movement occupied the hamlet of Wounded Knee on the Pine Ridge reservation in South Dakota, fortified the place (the site of a one-sided, bloody engagement between the United States cavalry and a group of Sioux in 1890), and held it for more than two months.

To deal with rioting and to put down "crime in the streets"—which were primarily state and local responsibilities—the Nixon administration gave millions of dollars to state and local law-enforcement agencies. Yet the number of crimes continued to rise, though at a decelerating rate. According to FBI statistics, there were more than 6 million serious crimes committed in 1972, as compared with 4.5 million in 1968. That meant an increase of fully one-third in three years under Nixon. Though under the supervision of the federal government, the city of Washington itself remained unsafe, its downtown streets almost deserted at night.

THE GENERAL WELFARE

In dealing with the problem of poverty, Nixon appeared to follow a zigzag course. At first he saw himself as a conservative reformer who, like Queen Victoria's great prime minister Benjamin Disraeli, would outdo his political opponents in his concern for the poor and thus would win broad popular support. Eventually, he went to the opposite extreme. At the beginning of his second term he announced his determination to put an end to what he called condescending policies of paternalism.

With rifles close at hand, an Indian demonstrator stands guard in a bunker during the occupation of Wounded Knee, South Dakota, March 1973 (UPI)

By 1969 the existing welfare system, which had remained essentially unchanged since the time of the New Deal, was in serious need of reform. During the 1960s, the number of persons receiving aid had doubled, from 1 to 2 million, and federal expenditures had increased from about $2 billion to nearly $18 billion. The welfare rolls had lengthened to the point where they included 6 percent of the population as a whole and a much higher proportion of the urban population, as high as 25 percent of the people of Newark, New Jersey. Approximately half of the recipients were black. Very few were employable men. Almost all were women or children or old, blind, or otherwise disabled persons. Among the worst faults of the existing program were the following: it denied benefits to families with able-bodied men, and so it induced husbands and fathers to desert; it denied benefits to the poor who were employed, and so it discouraged welfare recipients from accepting jobs.

In 1969 Nixon proposed a new Family Assistance Plan, which his special adviser on urban and poverty problems, Daniel P. Moynihan, had devised. Under the Moynihan plan every unemployed family of four would receive at least $1,600 a year. The working poor would get this minimum and would be allowed to keep part of their pay until their earned income reached $4,000, when the benefits would be discontinued. To be eligible for relief, the able-bodied (women as well as men) would be required to work. The plan would add about 6 million people to the welfare rolls, and it would increase federal spending by about $4 billion annually. In keeping with Nixon's principle of the New Federalism, the states would take over an increased share of the responsibility for administering the program.

The Moynihan plan had much to recommend it, but it provoked a bitter controversy, both in and out of Congress. Black militants, welfare recipients, and social workers opposed it as inadequate. Congress neither adopted it nor agreed on a substitute, and Nixon himself soon lost interest in the plan. He turned to recommending, instead, that welfare expenditures be cut and that payments to "ineligibles" be stopped.

Already Nixon had begun to undo the Johnson poverty program by closing more than half of the Job Corps training centers. He also reduced spending on other social welfare agencies, including the National Institute of Health. In his budget for 1973–1974 he proposed to abolish more than a hundred federal grant programs that were giving aid to the unemployed, the mentally ill, veterans, college students, small businessmen, and other groups. He also proposed to discontinue spending for urban renewal, to end assistance for hospital construction, and to reduce expenditures on lunches for schoolchildren. In 1973 he proceeded, without congressional approval, to break up the Office of Economic Opportunity, which had been the main agency of Johnson's war on poverty.

To replace many of the federal grants for specific purposes, Nixon had been urging that the federal government transfer funds to the states and cities, which would then be responsible for their own social programs. Such "revenue sharing" he viewed as the finest example of the New

Federalism in practice. Congress approved, and revenue sharing began in 1973, when the federal government turned about $5 billion over to state and local governments. Big-city mayors soon lost their enthusiasm for revenue sharing, since it promised them less money for dealing with urban problems than the specific grants, now being reduced or eliminated, had provided.

Nixon favored individual as well as local responsibility in overcoming poverty. To help blacks help themselves, he advocated the encouragement of "black capitalism" through both public and private assistance to black-owned business enterprises. Some progress was made along this line.

While economizing on aid to the poor, Nixon was generous to large corporations, especially those in the aircraft industry. He endorsed federal spending to subsidize an airplane manufacturer in the development of a supersonic transport (SST), a large plane that would carry passengers faster than the speed of sound and would compete with craft under construction by the Soviet Union and, cooperatively, by Great Britain and France. President Kennedy had put the government into the SST project, and by 1969 some $300 million of federal funds had already been contributed to it. President Nixon persuaded Congress to appropriate another $96 million for 1969–1970. Objections arose, however, on the grounds that the transport would never pay for itself and would damage the environment. Nixon suffered a personal defeat in 1971 when Congress killed the project by refusing to appropriate more money for it.

Many Americans had hoped that, once the United States was finally out of the Vietnam War, the government could cut its military spending and could afford to increase its domestic expenditures. Yet in his first postwar budget, the one for 1973–1974, Nixon not only demanded a reduction in domestic expenditures but also asked for an increase in military spending, from $74.8 billion to $79 billion. The extra money was to go largely for the development of new weapons and for pay raises to attract recruits to the all-volunteer armed forces.

THE NIXON ECONOMY

When Nixon talked of reducing expenditures on social programs, he justified it as a necessary means of controlling inflation and keeping prices within reason. He had inherited the inflation problem from his predecessor, Johnson, who had built up a tremendous inflationary pressure by increasing expenditures for both the Great Society and the Vietnam War. Nixon faced a dilemma, since rising prices could mean booming business, while deflationary policies might bring on widespread unemployment. In handling the problem he proved to be neither consistent nor successful.

At the outset, in 1969, Nixon announced a deflationary "game plan." He was going to maintain a balanced budget by spending less and taxing more, yet he signed a tax bill that enlarged exemptions and thus reduced revenue. He was also going to tighten bank credit and raise interest rates through the operations of the Federal Reserve System, and he succeeded in doing so. Nevertheless, prices continued to rise. At the same time, unemployment also rose. The country began to suffer from "stagflation," stagnation and inflation together.

The Economic Stabilization Act of 1970 authorized the President to impose direct controls on prices and also wages if and when he saw fit to do so. Nixon said: "I will not take this nation down the road of wage and price controls, however politically expedient that may seem." One year later, he put into effect a two-phase control system. In Phase I, to last for ninety days, nearly all wages and prices were frozen at their existing levels. In Phase II, to last indefinitely, most wage and price increases were kept within strict limits. Inflation now slowed down temporarily, but the business recession continued, and the unemployment rate rose to more than 6 percent of the labor force for 1971, as compared with less than 4 percent for 1969.

If these economic conditions had persisted, they might have threatened the reelection of Nixon in 1972. So, in 1971, he suddenly reversed his original game plan of tight credit and a balanced budget. He got from Congress a bill further reducing taxes. The Federal Reserve Board lowered interest rates and encouraged borrowing from banks. Government agencies began to spend at a rate of $1 billion a month more than had previously been planned. The Department of Agriculture increased its crop subsidies to farmers (for taking land out of production) from $3.1 billion to $4.1 billion a year. Altogether, the government paid out so much more than it took in that the deficit for 1972 was by far the largest for any year since World War II. By Election Day, incomes were up and unemployment was down. Politically, the combination of easy credit and deficit spending proved a great success.

The consequences, however, were disastrous for consumers. Foods and other raw materials were already becoming scarce throughout the world. Nixon's wheat deal with the Soviet Union made the food shortage worse than it would otherwise have been in the United States. The Russians took one-fourth of the entire American crop (at a price well below the market price, the difference being paid by American taxpayers through export subsidies to American grain dealers). Meanwhile, food production in the United States was declining as a result of Nixon's election-year farm policy. By pushing exports and restricting output, the administration was decreasing the available supply of foodstuffs within the country. By loosening credit and pouring out money, it was increasing the effective demand. Thus it was creating an explosive inflationary force. At this critical moment, early in 1973, Nixon chose to discontinue the strict wage-price controls of Phase II, which he replaced with the flexible, largely voluntary guidelines of what came to be called Phase III.

There followed the most rapid and extreme rise in the cost of living since the end of World War II. Prices of meat and grain products soared the highest. Housewives tried, with only partial and temporary success, to bring down prices by boycotting meat. Responding to consumer protests, the administration finally put a ceiling on the retail prices of meat and other foods but not on the prices of livestock or grain. This haphazard attempt at price fixing only worsened the food shortage. Squeezed between rising costs and fixed prices, some poultrymen killed baby chicks, and some packers and bakers went out of business.

Belatedly, the government took measures for stimulating instead of retarding farm output. The administration advised farmers to plant grain and soybeans on millions of acres they had left idle the previous year in order to qualify for subsidies, and it began to sell its own stocks of grain. It planned to abandon gradually the crop controls and price supports for wheat, feed grains, and cotton and to discontinue the purchase and storage of "surplus" crops. Thus it intended to change the basic agricultural policy that had prevailed ever since the New Deal. Presumably, the nation's farmers were to be left, for the most part, to make their own decisions about what and how much to produce, as they had done before the 1930s.

After his reelection in 1972 Nixon ended the government's spending spree and renewed his demands for economizing on social programs. He opposed a tax increase and argued that, if an increase should become necessary, Congress would be to blame because of its extravagance. In order to forestall a recession, he now wanted to moderate the business boom that had been under way in 1972 and that was to last through most of 1973.

The prospects for continued prosperity received a jolt in the fall of 1973, when the Arab nations cut back their oil production and put an embargo on petroleum shipments to the United States. There had already been, in this country, scattered shortages of fuel oil during the winter of 1972–1973 and gasoline during the summer of 1973. For the winter of 1973–1974 a much greater and more general shortage was anticipated, but experts differed as to how great it would actually prove to be. Natural gas and electric power (produced largely with petroleum) were also in short supply. To meet the "energy crisis" the federal and state governments took a variety of steps. These included an appeal to homeowners to lower their thermostats, allotments of fuel to airlines and a consequent elimination of many flights, allocation of fuel oil and gasoline to dealers, a reduction of highway speed limits to fifty-five miles an hour, a ban on Sunday sales of gasoline, and a contingency plan for gasoline rationing. Prices of gasoline and fuel oil started to take a steep rise. The shortage threatened to curtail production as well as transportation, since many industries depended directly or indirectly on petroleum for power, and others (such as those making or using plastics or synthetic fibers) depended on it also for raw material. By March 1974 the outlook was dim, with long lines of cars waiting for gas at service stations in many parts of the country. The next month the prospect brightened, at least temporarily, when the Arab oil ban was lifted.

A TRIUMPHANT REELECTION

According to a 1970 book, the "real majority" in the United States was "unyoung, unblack, and unpoor." The mature, white, well-off citizens were most concerned about things such as campus protests, school integration, street crimes, and welfare costs. If these worried people could be induced to vote for Nixon, his reelection would be assured. This prospect formed the basis for the campaign strategy that Nixon's Attorney General and political adviser, John Mitchell, adopted for 1972. In particular, Mitchell planned to attract to Nixon the voters who in 1968 had favored the American party candidate, George Wallace of Alabama. In addition to these Southern whites, the Republicans hoped to win over many Northern workers, especially the Catholics of immigrant background. Thus the Nixon forces might break up the already shaky Democratic coalition —which Franklin D. Roosevelt had put together in the 1930s—and replace it with a permanent Republican majority.

To Republican strategists it was hardly encouraging when, in 1970, Congress passed a bill to lower the voting age to eighteen. Nixon signed the bill, despite the widespread assumption that most of the young would vote Democratic. The Supreme Court ruled the new law constitutional for federal but not for state or local elections. The Twenty-sixth Amendment, ratified in time for the elections of 1972, made eighteen the minimum age for voters in state and local as well as federal contests.

For the Republicans the congressional elections of 1970 were also somewhat discouraging. Nixon put his own prestige at stake when he campaigned on behalf of Republican candidates, to denounce criminals and antiwar protesters, the "violent few." In San Jose, California, he taunted youthful demonstrators, who then threw stones and eggs at the presidential limousine. In Phoenix, Arizona, wildly gesticulating, he denounced the San Jose "terrorists." This performance was recorded and was nationally televised on election eve. It apparently did the Republicans little good. The next day they gained two seats in the Senate but lost nine in the House and also lost eleven state governorships.

Nixon's chances for reelection improved when, in May 1972, in a Maryland shopping center, a would-be assassin shot George Wallace, leaving him partially paralyzed and incapable of continuing his presidential campaign. Nixon's chances improved still further when, in July, the Democratic nominating convention met in Miami.

On the first ballot the convention chose McGovern, an opponent of the Vietnam War and an advocate of a $1,000 yearly grant from the government to every citizen. While still a relatively unknown senator from South Dakota, McGovern had begun openly to seek the presidency far in advance, in January 1971. In the primaries he outdid the early favorite, Senator Edmund Muskie of Maine, and the previous candidate, Senator Humphrey. At the convention, McGovern benefited from reforms he himself had helped to bring about. The "McGovern rules" were intended to

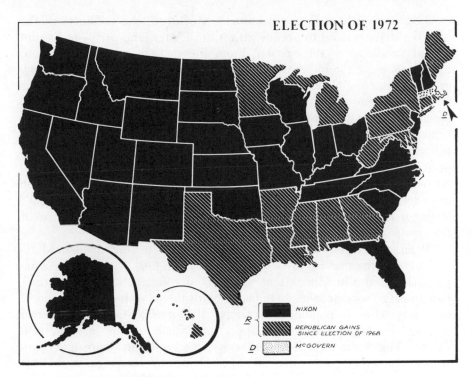

ELECTION OF 1972

R ■ NIXON

▨ REPUBLICAN GAINS
SINCE ELECTION OF 1968

D ░ McGOVERN

make the convention broadly representative of the party by requiring certain proportions of women, blacks, and youths among the delegates. But the rules antagonized old-line politicians and had a very divisive effect on the party, especially when the convention unseated a powerful boss, Mayor Richard J. Daley of Chicago.

Senator   George   McGovern
(TOMMY NOONAN)

The very qualities that had brought McGovern the nomination—the qualities that appealed to liberals within the Democratic party—made him a weak candidate in the election. From the make-up of the convention many voters got the impression that he was the candidate of hippies, aggressive women, and militant blacks. He offended many even among his adherents when—after the revelation that his vice-presidential choice, Senator Thomas Eagleton of Missouri, had undergone treatments for an emotional disturbance—he at first said he stood "1,000 percent" behind Eagleton and then suddenly removed him from the ticket. During the campaign, McGovern found it difficult to maintain his credibility when he compared Nixon to Hitler and charged that the administration was the most corrupt in history. George Meany, head of the AFL-CIO, the nation's largest labor union, opposed McGovern, and so did all but a very few of the newspapers throughout the country.

While McGovern campaigned strenuously with limited financial resources, which came mainly from small contributors, Nixon (after a renomination, also in Miami, that was more a coronation than a contest) had an easy "noncampaign." He had the advantage of more money, most of it from large corporations, than any other presidential candidate had ever had at his disposal. Seldom appearing, Nixon was an "invisible candidate." His choice for a second time as Vice President, Spiro Agnew, together with other government officials, carried the campaign burden for Nixon, never mentioning him by name but always referring to him as "the President." The President now had only to reap the benefits of his recent policies. By virtue of his China and Russia visits and the Vietnam negotiations he appeared to be a bringer of peace. Since business was finally booming, he could be credited with prosperity. As a foe of busing for racial balance in the schools, he had the gratitude of race-conscious whites. Through his "law-and-order" statements and his court appointments, he had made himself the apparent champion of peace at home as well as abroad.

Nixon won by one of the most decisive margins in history. He received the largest share of the popular vote (60.8 percent) of any candidate except Johnson (61.1 percent) in 1964. He received the largest proportion of the electoral vote (521 of 538) since Roosevelt (523 of 531) in 1936. McGovern carried only Massachusetts and the District of Columbia. He got little of the expected help from the newly enfranchised eighteen- to twenty-year-olds, as fewer than half of them bothered to go to the polls, and those who did divided their ballots almost evenly. He received a fairly solid black support, but scarcely more than half of the eligible blacks voted. He lost heavily among ethnic groups in the North and among whites generally in the South.

To judge by the presidential returns alone, it appeared that the Republicans had succeeded in their aim to replace the old Democratic coalition with a new one of their own. In the congressional elections, however, the Republicans had been deprived of two places in the Senate while gaining thirteen in the House, thus leaving the Democrats in control of the next Congress by margins of 57 to 43 and 243 to 192. So the returns as a whole hardly amounted to unqualified approval of the Republican party. Even the presidential victory, overwhelming though it was, probably meant less an endorsement of Nixon than a rejection of his opponent.

twenty-nine

America in the Bicentennial Years

As the United States in the 1970s celebrated the bicentennial of independence, the American people undertook a reappraisal of their life and institutions. As they had a hundred years earlier at the time of the centennial celebrations, they were full of pride over their technical advance and full of dismay over the failure of social developments to keep pace. Humanity needed inventions and achievements in society and government that would match those in science and technology.

THE TRIUMPHS OF TECHNOLOGY

Generation after generation, Americans had been preoccupied with material progress. Those of the late twentieth century saw technological achievements even more startling than those of earlier times. But people found it harder and harder to maintain the faith of their forefathers who had assumed that new inventions would almost automatically lead to a better life for everyone.

A future of increasing abundance for the American people seemed to be promised by the continuing development of technical innovations summed up in the term "automation." Yet automation, like earlier phases of technical change dating back to the eighteenth century, threatened to create unemployment and social upheaval. Continuous automatic production was older than the term "automation," which a Ford Motor Company executive coined in 1946 to describe a system Ford was installing for the automatic handling of parts.

Essential to automation as it developed after World War II were electronic controls and the development of computer systems. The first electronic computer went into operation in 1946. At first computers were large, cumbersome, and expensive, but the discovery that complicated electronic circuits, which had been assembled by hand, could be printed on cardboard or plastic and that compact durable transistors (invented in 1948) could replace fragile vacuum tubes made possible the rapid and spectacular advance in computer technology. By the end of the 1960s, computers were a hundred times faster, ten times smaller in their electronic components, and provided information in a thousandth the time of earlier ones.

Computers could give answers to innumerable informational problems previously so complex as to be unmanageable. They were helping industry control inventories to eliminate the periodic scarcity or glut that had contributed to irregularities in the business cycle. They could fly jet planes, guide rockets to the moon, or control almost any kind of machinery. They could, critics feared, through data storage on every individual, destroy privacy; through the tasks they could guide, they might create serious unemployment.

The bituminous coal industry was a spectacular example of what automation could mean. By the end of the 1940s, coal, being mined with some machinery, was being priced out of the market by cheaper petroleum and natural gas. In 1948 the United Mine Workers (UMW) gave the operators freedom to automate in exchange for a royalty of forty cents per ton to be paid into UMW welfare funds. The companies, investing $500 million in new machinery, automated the mines and laid off far more than half the workers. A quarter-million miners had lost their jobs; only 150,000 were kept at work.

Whether in the long run automation would mean chronic unemployment was not entirely clear. As production grew, the United States began to change from a have to a have-not nation in natural resources, but innovations postponed the danger of disastrous shortages in most resources except for petroleum. Between 1900 and 1950 the production of bituminous coal rose two and one-half times, of copper three times, of iron ore three and one-half times, and of crude oil thirty times. Although Gifford Pinchot, writing in the Progressive era, had feared that bituminous coal would soon be exhausted, exhaustion was still far off. As the rich iron deposits began to dwindle, steel companies developed processes to make use of lower-grade ore. New ore deposits were opened in Labrador. The United States became the largest importer of copper, lead, and zinc, leading to a flow of dollars overseas.

Already the United States was beginning to develop electric power from atomic energy, but nuclear power plants were costly to operate and often broke down.

Scientific Research

Applications of scientific knowledge, both civilian and military, were being developed at such a rapid pace that they created a sharp pressure for additional basic research. In 1957 a Department of Defense research officer declared: "We have been chewing up the findings of basic research since

World War II at a speed faster than they are being produced in the laboratories and ivory towers."

The chief agency for promotion of basic scientific research was the National Science Foundation. In 1945 Dr. Vannevar Bush, who had been wartime director of the Office of Scientific Research and Development, proposed the establishment of a peacetime government agency to promote basic research. The United States could no longer depend upon Europe, Bush warned. In 1950 Congress established the National Science Foundation but limited its annual appropriations to $15 million per year and appropriated less than that until the 1956 fiscal year. In the 1959 budget, after the sputnik crisis, President Eisenhower asked for $140 million for the National Science Foundation. Thereafter, its budget, and its impact upon scientific research, increased significantly.

Overall federal expenditures on research and development—no more than one-tenth of it for basic research—rose so spectacularly that by the end of the 1960s they totaled more than the entire federal budget before Pearl Harbor. These sums were so large that many universities were dependent upon them for a considerable portion of their budgets. Concentration of expenditures in a few universities (68 percent of federal research funds were going to twenty-five institutions) had important side effects.

Scientific and engineering work at Harvard and the Massachusetts Institute of Technology had helped attract science-based industry, especially in electronics, to Highway 128 ringing Boston; the University of California and Stanford had brought similar industry to the San Francisco Bay region. Understandably, there developed considerable pressure to allocate more scientific grants to the Midwest and other areas in the United States. The House Appropriations Committee forbade the granting of more than 10 percent of the National Science Foundation fellowships to the residents of any one state.

The most comprehensive and spectacular of basic research enterprises, in which the United States cooperated with sixty-two other countries including the Soviet Union, was the International Geophysical Year, from July 1, 1957, to the end of 1958. It involved exploring the globe from pole to pole and from ionosphere to core, and included the launching of satellites and the establishment of an American base at the South Pole. The research in Antarctica developed into a long-range scientific program, centering in a permanent base at McMurdo Sound, which supplied a number of outlying stations. By international treaty, national territorial holdings and armaments were barred from the continent; the United States, the Soviet Union, and a number of other nations carried on scientific work and shared information without friction.

In medical research the most important discovery was the development of an effective polio vaccine by Dr. Jonas Salk of the University of Pittsburgh. The vaccine was first used on a large scale in 1955, and within two years the polio rate in the United States dropped 80 percent. Many of the most spectacular innovations were made possible by electronic or atomic advances. The transplant of kidneys and even of a human heart were aided by chemical treatment and radiation to prevent rejection of the new organ. A number of mechanical and electronic inventions—among them artificial kidneys and miniature electronic generators to keep a heart beating at the right pace—helped to save lives. The laser beam, a ray of concentrated light, became a tool of eye surgery to repair damage to the retina.

Advances in medical research contributed to a lengthening life span. In 1900 life expectancy at birth had been forty-nine years; by 1955 it was seventy years. Most of the gain was in reducing the death rate among infants and children. Older people did not live much longer than before. In 1900 a sixty-four-year-old person had a remaining life span ahead of him that averaged about twelve years; in the 1960s it averaged fourteen years. Even if the two prime killers of the aged, heart disease and cancer, were to be eliminated, life expectancy would not be greatly increased.

The Space Race Begins

The American government had shown little interest in space exploration until October 1957, when the Soviet Union put its first satellite, Sputnik I, into orbit. Already the United States was carrying on a program of rocket research under the direction of Wernher von Braun, a German-born expert whose team had designed and built for the Hitler regime the V-2 rockets that devastated London during the final stages of World War II. As the Russians advanced into Germany in 1945, they captured a few of the top men and hundreds of the technicians engaged in the V-2 project. Braun and others turned themselves over to the United States army. In the early postwar years, however, the Americans were slower than the Russians in using German expertise to produce ballistic missiles and still slower in using it to develop space rockets.

"Our satellite program has never been conducted as a race with other nations," President Eisenhower declared as he congratulated the Soviet Union on the launching of Sputnik I. But most Americans, including prominent public figures, assumed that a race was indeed on, and the United States appeared to be lagging far behind. Sputnik II carried a dog into space in November 1957 while Braun and his co-workers were still trying to launch a tiny, three-pound sphere, which they did not succeed in orbiting until January 1958. In October of that year, twelve months after the appearance of Sputnik I, the American government set up the National Aeronautics and Space Administration (NASA) to coordinate the nation's space efforts but gave it only a small budget.

By 1961, when Kennedy took over the presidency from Eisenhower, the United States appeared to be making some gains. This country was ahead of the Soviet Union in the number of satellites put into orbit—thirty-three to nine. The total weight of the nine Soviet satellites, however, was more than twice as great as that of all thirty-three American ones, and the Russians were rumored to be testing a five-ton spaceship that could take a man into orbit. To the Russians, Kennedy said in his inaugural: "Let us explore the stars together." But the Russians showed little interest in that. In April 1961 they sent the world's first cosmonaut, Yuri Gagarin, once around the earth. After reentering the atmosphere and parachuting to safety, Gagarin issued the boastful challenge: "Now let the other countries try to catch us."

Eight days after Gagarin's flight (and just one day after the Bay of Pigs fiasco in Cuba), President Kennedy directed a memorandum to Vice President Johnson, whom he had named as chairman of an advisory Space Council. "Do we have a chance of beating the Soviets," Kennedy asked, "by putting a laboratory in space, or by a trip around the moon, or by a rocket to land on the moon, or by a rocket to go to the moon and back with a man?" The best the United States could do for the time being was to propel Alan Shepard into a suborbital flight that went some 100 miles up to the edge of space and some 300 miles out into the Atlantic Ocean. Three weeks later, May 25, 1961, Kennedy appealed to Congress: "I believe this nation should commit itself to achieving the goal, before the decade is out, of landing a man on the moon and returning him safely to earth." Congress soon responded by making the first of the necessary appropriations.

The moon program, Project Apollo, was expected to cost $20 billion, ten times as much as the development of the atom bomb (but less than the Vietnam War was to cost for a single year). Advocates of the program maintained that it would be well worth the price on account of its scientific and economic benefits as well as its enhancement of national prestige. One space official declared: "Each improvement in our ability to fly unmanned and manned spacecraft results in a corresponding improvement in our ability to solve nature's mysteries."

To the Moon and Beyond

Until 1965 the United States continued to trail the Soviet Union in the launching of manned spacecraft, though not in the firing of unmanned satellites. A Russian cosmonaut circled the globe seventeen times (August 1961) before the first American, John Glenn, was put into space (February 1962), to return to earth after making only three orbits. Another and yet another American went around in one-man Mercury capsules similar to Glenn's, but the Russians kept the lead in flight endurance and took the lead in orbiting two vehicles close together, in launching two-man and then three-man craft, and in releasing a man from one of the ships to float in nothingness. But the United States was putting up, all together, more than twice as many satellites as was the Soviet Union. Some of these were intended for scientific purposes—to study solar radiation, the earth's magnetic field, and weather phenomena. Others, such as Telstar, facilitated around-the-world communication by telephone and television. Still others, such as the "eye in the sky" satellites Samos and Midas, gave the military new means of observation or espionage. Meanwhile, from 1963 to 1965, the Americans discontinued manned flights and concentrated on the design and construction of improved space vehicles.

By 1965 the Americans were ready to achieve some firsts of their own with men in space. The new two-man Gemini, unlike the latest Soviet spaceships, was maneuverable; it was equipped with small rockets that could change its course in mid-orbit, as its pilots demonstrated on their first flight. On a second flight an astronaut stepped into space and, with a small oxygen-spitting gun, pulled the vehicle about on a tether. The third of the Geminis, orbiting for nearly 191 hours, broke the endurance record that the Russians had set. On a later launching, in 1966, a Gemini succeeded in overtaking an orbiting craft and joining up or "docking" with it—a maneuver essential for a moon trip. The United States now appeared to hold the lead in manned as well as unmanned flights.

The next stage involved the Apollo, a three-man spacecraft, which, with over 2 million parts, was far more complicated than the Gemini or the Mercury. The project was set back and the nation was stunned when, early in 1967, a fire killed the three astronauts while they were rehearsing for the first Apollo takeoff. While the craft was being redesigned and retested, a succession of Surveyors, unmanned, were being rocketed to the moon and were sending back tens of thousands of pictures of the lunar surface. One of the Surveyors landed on the moon and then took off from it, as a manned vehicle was scheduled to do eventually. In late 1968, after Apollo 7 had carried three men around the earth, Apollo 8 carried three

On the Apollo 15 mission of 1971, astronauts James Irwin and David Scott brought with them in their Lunar Module, Rover, *a small vehicle. They used it to explore the surface of the moon* (AERONAUTICS AND SPACE ADMINISTRATION)

others around the moon, the first men to leave the earth's gravitational field. During the next few months, Apollo 9 tested a lunar module (the landing craft that was to leave and rejoin the mother ship) in an earth orbit, and Apollo 10 tested one in a moon orbit.

At last, in July 1969, Apollo 11 was blasted off on its epochal flight to land men on the moon. Ahead of them streaked a Russian spacecraft, Luna 15, heading for lunar orbit, but Luna carried no crew. Its launching seemed to show dramatically that, in space enterprises, the Soviet Union was still competing rather than cooperating—and now competing at a decided disadvantage. Not that sovereignty over the moon was at stake: by a treaty signed in 1966 the two superpowers had agreed that the moon should be a no man's land open to exploration and use by all nations. At issue were national prestige and (to the extent that the space programs yielded new techniques of warfare) military advantage.

The flight of Apollo 11 was a beginning, not an ending. During the next three years, the United States launched a series of six additional Apollos, five of which succeeded in putting men on the moon and all of which returned safely to the earth. Meanwhile, both the United States and the Soviet Union sent space probes to Mars and Venus, and in 1973 the United States sent others to Jupiter and Mercury. Discontinuing lunar explorations for the time being, the Americans now concentrated their man-in-space efforts on experimental earth orbits. In 1973 they launched a two-story laboratory, Skylab, and three three-man crews in succession visited it to survey the earth's resources, test man's ability to live in space for long periods, and carry on other observations and experiments. At last, by an agreement of 1972, the Americans and the Russians were beginning to cooperate. They undertook a joint earth-orbiting mission in 1975.

"There is no question but that we will go to Mars and colonize the moon, probably sooner than we now think," a NASA official said in 1972. "I think it will also become a reality that we'll pick up communications from other intelligence in the universe."

CULTURE AND COUNTERCULTURE

After World War II the social and cultural life of Americans underwent noticeable changes. These, especially during the 1960s, seemed in some minds to portend the loss of moral values, the collapse of institutional authority, and the disintegration of society itself. Critics complained of a materialistic "consumer culture," a hedonistic "permissive society," and the "alienation" of children from parents and of individuals from the group. The changes, however, tended less in new and strange directions than in directions that already had long been set. Even the jeremiads were familiar. Complaints of the same tenor had been heard from time to time throughout the history of the American people and, indeed, the history of humanity.

The "Permissive" Society

World War I had been followed, during the "roaring twenties," by deviations from traditional manners and morals, especially on the part of "flaming youth." World War II did not have so pronounced an immediate aftermath, but during the 1960s, with the escalation of the Vietnam War, the deviations were even more spectacular. By the 1970s there were signs of a reaction away from some of the excesses.

"Togetherness" was a watchword of the 1950s, yet the family continued to lose its cohesion. By 1960 there was one annulment or divorce for every four marriages; by 1970, one for every three. Some attributed the rising divorce rate to the growing financial independence of women, more and more of whom were working outside the home. Yet the divorce rate, in 1970, was higher among the poor and the ill educated than among the better off and the better educated. It was higher for city dwellers than for rural folk, and much higher for nonwhites than for whites.

There was talk of a "sexual revolution" in the 1960s as sex relations outside of marriage appeared to become much more widespread than ever before. Presumably the oral contraceptive—"the pill"—encouraged extra marital intercourse by practically eliminating the risk of pregnancy. But studies by Dr. Alfred C. Kinsey and his Institute for Sex Research, at Indiana University, cast doubt on the idea of a revolution. Kinsey's *Sexual Behavior in the Human Male* (1948) showed that, among the preceding generation of Americans, sexual activity had been much more varied than laws or morals would have led anyone to believe. "People talk more freely about sex nowadays, and young people are far more tolerant and permissive regarding sex," Kinsey's successor observed in the 1960s. Yet, though premarital intercourse had increased, it had not risen suddenly or dramatically; "it has been on the rise ever since the turn of the century."

For some women, sexual freedom meant freedom from unwanted children, not only through contraception but, when necessary, through abortion. Advocates of abortion on demand asserted the right of a woman to control her own body. Opponents insisted on the right of the unborn to the enjoyment of life. A few states liberalized their laws so as to permit abortion under a wide range of conditions, but most of the states retained laws that made it difficult if not impossible—except for illegal and often dangerous practitioners. In 1973 the Supreme Court struck down those state laws that prohibited abortion during the first three months of pregnancy.

Freedom of sexual expression in words and pictures raised another constitutional issue, that of freedom of speech and the press. In 1957 the Supreme Court narrowed the legal definition of obscenity to include only those works that were morally offensive by prevailing national standards and were "utterly without redeeming social value." This decision put the burden of proof on local authorities in obscenity cases. It opened the way for an unprecedented flood of pornography. President Johnson appointed a Commission on Obscenity and Pornography to study the effects. The commission finally reported, in 1970, that "exposure to explicit sexual materials" apparently had little or nothing to do with causing emotional disorders, delinquency, or crime. The commission recommended the repeal of all laws forbidding the dissemination of such materials to consenting adults. Instead of acting on that recommendation, President Nixon denounced the report as "morally bankrupt," and the Senate condemned it by a vote of 60 to 5. The Supreme Court, instead of further relaxing its stand, soon practically reversed itself. In 1973 it held that works were obscene if they lacked "serious literary, artistic, political, or scientific value" and if they were offensive by the standards of the local community. The burden of proof was now on the defendant, and local authorities here and there began successfully to prosecute.

Clothes may not make the man or woman, but changing styles of clothing seemed to reflect a changing relationship between women and men. In 1947 fashion designers decreed the "new look" of ankle-length skirts, and women meekly obeyed. Thereafter, hemlines gradually rose until, in the late 1960s, they were much higher than they had been even during the 1920s. In 1971 the couturiers called for an end to "miniskirts" and to the even more abbreviated "hot pants" and for a return to long dresses, to mid-calf "midiskirts" or to full-length "maxiskirts." This time the women refused to heed. Instead, they turned to trousers and pant suits or to blue jeans, which were already the uniform of the young, male and female alike. With young men and women wearing their hair to their shoulders, it was often hard to tell boy and girl apart—until, perhaps, one of them turned around and revealed a beard. The day of "unisex" seemed at hand, as distinctions of appearance if not also of role, became increasingly blurred. In the spirit of the time, homosexuals and lesbians came forth as never before to avow themselves openly and even proudly.

A great many middle-class young people, though by no means all of them, rejected the values as well as the clothes of adults. People spoke of the "generation gap" as though it were something entirely new. It did take new forms. Fringe groups, the beatniks of the 1950s and the hippies of the 1960s, went to extremes of unconventional dress and behavior. Drug use spread as growing numbers of youth retreated from a world they disliked. They were "turning on" (or, more accurately, "turning off") by smoking marijuana, taking "mind-expanding" chemicals such as LSD, or injecting themselves with narcotics such as heroin. Blaring rock-and-roll music was a favorite with the young, along with ballads that, to a guitar accompaniment, protested against war, poverty, injustice, and the older generation, including everyone older than thirty. The youth movement reached a crescendo when, in August 1969, more than 300,000 gathered for a rock festival near Woodstock, New York, where most shed their inhibitions and many their clothing. The movement found a philosopher in Charles Reich, whose book *The Greening of America* (1970) praised "Consciousness III" as a new awareness, on the part of youth, of self as the only reality.

In the 1970s it appeared that young people were drawing away from their preoccupations of the previous decade. Some turned to religion of a traditional kind, the "Jesus freaks" singing, shouting, and clapping in the spirit of old-time revivalism. Others looked to even more unconventional cults.

The youth culture of the 1960s, in its various manifestations, had made so great an impression partly because young people were proportionally so numerous. With the aging of the population—with the disappearance of the youthful "bulge" in it—the influence of the young could be expected to decline.

Education and Religion

After World War II, critics of public education charged that the schools were neglecting things of the mind in favor of athletics, band contests, vocational training, and "life adjustment." When the Soviet Union launched the first artificial satellite, sputnik, in 1957, many Americans assumed that the Russians had proved the superiority of their education in science and technology. A demand arose for fewer "frills" and more intellectual rigor, and school officials, teachers, and pupils responded. So did Congress. In 1958 it passed the National Defense Education Act, which provided for the spending of nearly a billion dollars over a four-year period to encourage the study of science, mathematics, and foreign languages.

Nevertheless, the schools continued to be criticized for their performance. At the end of the 1960s it appeared that 10 to 15 of every 100 pupils entering the fourth grade could not read (in ghetto schools, 35 to 50 of every 100). About 25 million adults in the nation as a whole were functionally illiterate, unable to comprehend a newspaper or magazine article or to fill out an application form. Most of these people were school dropouts.

With the gaining momentum of the civil rights movement, the emphasis of school reformers had shifted from academic excellence to equality of educational opportunity. This presumably would help the poor to rise out of poverty. But Christopher Jencks and seven associates at Harvard University's Center for Educational Policy Research questioned the assumption in a 1972 report. "If we want economic equality in our society," Jencks wrote, "we will have to get it by changing our economic institutions, not by changing the schools."

In fact, educational equality was yet to be tried. Annual expenditures per pupil ranged from a few hundred dollars in some schools to several thousand in others, even within the same state. Schools depended mainly on local property taxes, and resources therefore varied tremendously as between the poorest and the wealthiest districts. In the early 1970s, after the supreme court of California had declared the reliance on local school taxes unconstitutional in that state, suits were brought against similar financing arrangements in more than thirty other states.

The swelling enrollments of the 1950s and 1960s necessitated costly programs of school construction. At first the voters responded willingly by approving the issue of construction bonds, but eventually they grew more and more reluctant. In 1960 they approved nearly 90 percent of the bond issues put to referendums; in 1970, less than 47 percent. Undoubtedly, the people were reacting against rising taxes, but they also seemed to be expressing a decline of confidence in the public schools.

During World War II, colleges and universities suffered from a loss of male students to the draft. The federal government helped many institutions by contracting with them to educate and train various kinds of specialists for the armed forces. After the war the government contributed to a sudden bulge in enrollments by paying the college expenses of veterans under the GI Bill of Rights. During the 1950s and 1960s, attendance continued to swell, and at a faster rate than the college-age population, for a larger and larger proportion of young people were going on to secondary and higher education. Graduate and professional schools were especially thriving, as the demand for university teachers and other professional workers grew. The federal government heavily subsidized many programs that were directly or indirectly related to the national defense. State universities multiplied as teachers' colleges were converted into general colleges and these were raised, at least in name, to university status. Large campuses grew larger still—there were thirty-nine with more than 20,000 students in 1969 as compared with only two in 1941.

By the early 1970s the quarter-century-long academic boom appeared to be at an end. Federal support had been curtailed. Enrollments were leveling off and, in many institutions, even falling, while unemployment rose among holders of Ph.D.'s and other advanced degrees. Private institutions, having had to raise tuition charges repeatedly in order to meet rising costs, had lagged far behind in the recruitment of students. Now many of the smaller and financially weaker private colleges faced the threat of extinction.

The first postwar generation of college students—especially the veterans, or GIs—seemed to be mainly interested in getting a degree in order to get ahead. A survey of members of the class of '49 concluded that they were "curiously old before their time" and were concentrating on the pursuit of economic security. Students of the 1950s also appeared to be looking ahead to jobs, especially corporation jobs. The prevailing campus spirit was quiet and conformist.

Then, in 1964, the campus of the University of California at Berkeley erupted, and during the next several years other large universities from coast to coast experienced a succession of student riots, with the rioters taking over and sometimes fire-bombing university buildings and "trashing" (vandalizing) business properties in the neighborhood. The rioters were giving expression to a variety of complaints—the impersonality of the gigantic and complex "multiversity," the irrelevance of its curriculum to their personal needs, its complicity in the Vietnam War (through war-related research and through the training of military officers in the ROTC), and its role as a bulwark of the socially unjust Establishment. Some of the rebels came from affluent families and were less preoccupied with upward striving than their successful fathers had been as college youths of the early postwar years. Other rebels, the blacks, were demanding the kind of college education that would enable them to rise in economic and social status and in self-esteem.

Colleges and universities responded to demands for "relevance" and personal involvement by relaxing requirements, adding courses in "black studies" and other contemporary concerns, and giving students some voice in administration. Some institutions, such as the City University of New York, adopted a policy of "open admissions," eliminating most entrance requirements.

During the postwar decade, church membership grew at about twice the rate of the population as a whole. This did not necessarily mean that Americans were becoming increasingly devout. When questioned, people generally identified themselves as Protestants, Catholics, or Jews, but relatively few expressed strong convictions. Many apparently referred to one faith or another as a means of indicating social background or of gaining, in an impersonal society, some sense of "belonging." Church attendance declined between 1958, when (according to a poll) 49 percent of the people were churchgoers, and 1972, when only 40 percent were.

Churchmen, both Protestant and Catholic, were divided among themselves in regard to the mission of the church. Among Protestants, the most famous preacher, Norman Vincent Peale, wrote of religion as a force for success in the world (much as Bruce Barton formerly had done). The most popular revivalist, Billy Graham, offered a conventional message of individual salvation and, as a personal friend of Presidents Eisenhower and Nixon, associated with the politically powerful. But a spokesman for the World Council of Churches declared: "The Church must identify itself much more radically with the interests of the poor, the 'losers,' the outcasts and the alienated."

Reflections in Literature

The most prestigious figures in American writing, during the quarter-century after World War II, were those who had made their reputations in earlier decades. Through the 1950s Ernest Hemingway and William Faulkner were two of the patriarchs of literature for the Western world as well as for the United States. Faulkner retained his master's touch in portraying the Deep South he knew so well and through it viewing the world. Hemingway at times seemed to be parodying his earlier, virile, trenchant style, but produced one work in these years, *The Old Man and the Sea* (1952), that seemed destined to endure. It was the brief tale of an aged Cuban striving heroically, and unsuccessfully, to protect from the forays of the sharks a huge fish he had caught. The poet Robert Frost seemed already a legendary figure before his death in 1963. After Eugene O'Neill's death in 1953, several of his previously unproduced plays ran for months on Broadway and on national tours.

By the 1960s all these individuals of great reputation were gone. A large new generation of vigorous writers was attracting attention, but it was too soon to be sure which if any of them would win enduring top reputations. Among the novelists, their work ranged from the realism of John O'Hara and James Gould Cozzens, portrayers of the upper middle class, whose work seemed old fashioned to younger critics, through a variety of newer styles and themes. The work of Robert Penn Warren, who won the Pulitzer Prize in both poetry and fiction, transcended Southern regionalism, but his most widely read novel, *All the King's Men* (1946), was a study of a political leader resembling Huey Long of Louisiana. In 1948 Norman Mailer produced the most acclaimed of the novels that came out of World War II, *The Naked and the Dead*, but in his subsequent work was more successful as a writer of nonfiction. J. D. Salinger through his account of the inward torture of an adolescent boy, *Catcher in the Rye* (1951), became the spokesman for the generation of the 1950s.

Through the writings of several of the novelists ran a theme of alienation from, or at least serious questioning of, their culture. Saul Bellow began his work in this vein with *Dangling Man* (1944) and continued it in a number of successful novels, including *The Adventures of Augie March* (1953) and *Herzog* (1964). Nelson Algren, no admirer of middle-class values, wrote with blunt clarity about the flotsam of society, the men and women who had never had a chance, in his stories and novels, most notably, *The Man with the Golden Arm* (1949). Several black writers fell within this pattern. The most famous was James Baldwin, perhaps at his best in works of nonfiction like *The Fire Next Time* (1963); the most bitter, the poet and playwright, LeRoi Jones, especially effective in his one-act plays; and the most distinguished, Ralph Ellison, for a single novel, *Invisible Man* (1952). When the New York *Herald Tribune Book Week* in 1965 queried some 200 critics, authors, and editors, their consensus was that the work of fiction of the previous two decades most memorable and most likely to endure was *Invisible Man*. It is the sweeping, at times fantastic, drama of a young black man's quest for identity. The novel that the critics listed second as most memorable was the polished social satire *Lolita* (1955) written by a Russian émigré, Vladimir Nabokov.

Among the novelists who emerged in the 1960s, perhaps the most notable were John Barth, Joseph Heller, Kurt Vonnegut, Jr., and Thomas Pynchon. Each dealt in his own way with what seemed to all of them like the cosmic absurdity of contemporary life. They were less interested in developing character or plot than in creating effects of intellectual ambiguity and emotional contradiction. In his mock-picaresque novel *The Sot-Weed Factor* (1961) Barth gave the impression that people could find no meaning in life except for the realization that they were merely acting their parts in a farce that had been written for them. In *Catch-22* (1964) Heller ridiculed the insanity and regimentation of war and, by implication, the insanity and regimentation of business society. In *Slaughterhouse-Five* (1969), his sixth novel, Vonnegut used his experience in World War II as a springboard for science fiction in which horror was mixed with humor. In his third novel, *Gravity's Rainbow* (1973), Pynchon made his central figure a German V-2 rocket of World War II. Baffling, jarring, full of complex symbolism, Pynchon's book gave an apocalyptic and paranoid vision of man's place in the universe. Some reviewers hailed it as the greatest American novel since *Moby Dick*.

Poetry, like painting, broke sharply with traditions after 1945. While poets like Robert Frost and Carl Sandburg enjoyed fame in their old age, the liberal activism that moved poets like Archibald MacLeish during the depression and war years subsided after 1945. The newer poets moved away from public causes, toward the psychological and mythological, as did Randall Jarrell, or toward the autobiographical or confessional, as did Robert Lowell. Through much of this poetry ran a distaste for the established order. One critic, M. L. Rosenthal, suggests:

> Behind it is the feeling, perhaps, that the humanistic way, which tradition-ally educated and romantic modern men still propose to protect, and indeed to project into a Utopian future, has already been defeated and is now no more than a ghost. It is that feeling which Robert Lowell in one of his poems calls, self-ironically, "our universal *Angst*"—a heart-heavy realization that remorseless brutality is a condition not only of the physi-cal universe but also of man himself.

Consumers of the Arts

Never had so many Americans shown so much interest in literature, art, and music as they did during the age of affluence that followed World War II. To some extent the federal and state governments encouraged cultural activity, the federal government establishing (1966) the Federal Arts and Humanities Endowments and a Federal Council on the Arts, and each of the states setting up its own arts council or commission. Some of the councils made financial grants, and private foundations provided more substantial sums. Most of the activity, however, was financed by individual spending.

The catering to cultural interests became a big business in itself, as statistics indicate. Between 1953 and 1960, expenditures on such interests rose by 130 percent, reaching an annual total of $3 billion. That was a larger sum than advertisers were spending on television commercials. In 1964 Americans paid the following amounts for certain cultural items: $1 billion for books, $600 million on musical instruments, $200 million on paintings or reproductions and art supplies, nearly $400 million to attend dramatic and musical performances, and $300 million to maintain art museums. By the end of the 1960s, total expenditures were approaching $7 billion a year. People were spending twice as much on the arts as on recreation in general and six times as much as on sports.

Nevertheless, the times were difficult for the performing arts, which suffered from rising costs, lagging attendance, and repeated deficits. A 1966 study showed that the nation was supporting only five full-time symphony orchestras, and the increase in attendance at concerts was somewhat slower than the increase in population. New York City accounted for nearly 40 percent of the receipts at musical performances and more than 50 percent of those at dramatic performances. The audiences represented only a very small and select portion of the people, consisting almost entirely of those with high incomes.

Of all stage performances, musical comedies generally had the widest appeal. They constituted the American equivalent of a popular opera. Every few years an extremely successful one made its appearance: *Oklahoma!* in 1943, *My Fair Lady* in 1956, *West Side Story* in 1957, *Camelot* in 1960, *Hello Dolly* in 1963, and *Fiddler on the Roof* in 1964. *My Fair Lady* set a record for the longest Broadway run of a musical comedy. *Hello Dolly* broke that record and then was surpassed by *Fiddler on the Roof*, which in 1973 was still going strong.

Classical and popular music was available on improved, inexpensive phonograph records, the sales of which rose astronomically. In the 1940s long-playing records of durable vinyl, turning at a speed of 45 or 33-⅓ revolutions per minute, began to replace the former short-playing, easily breakable 78 rpm disks. The quality of the reproduction was vastly improved, meanwhile, by the development of high-fidelity electronic recording and, during the 1950s, by the introduction of stereophonic sound. Together with television and both AM and FM radio, the improved phonographs provided good music to an audience vastly larger than that attending opera houses or concert halls.

The Role of Television

Television changed the leisure habits of the American people, made them better informed on the news and issues of the day, and even modified the patterns of American politics. In 1947 fewer than 10,000 people owned television sets with which they could view programs a few hours a day from a handful of stations. A decade later, over 40 million sets in homes, hotels, and bars were tuned in to 467 stations. Motion-picture attendance dropped from a wartime high of 90 million a week to about 40 million. Not until the 1960s did Hollywood begin to recuperate, by producing pictures that were better than before, or at least bolder. Professional sports, especially football and basketball, flourished as television brought them to millions of spectators at a time.

Television even more than radio meant mass communication to a nationwide audience. One musical show, telecast on 245 stations one night in March 1957 reached an estimated audience of 100 million— enough people to fill a Broadway theater every night for 165 years. Beginning with the 1952 campaign, television remade presidential elections as candidates began to make extensive and expensive use of the new medium. Radio was far from superseded, especially in the transistorized portable form that took over not only the United States but the entire world during these years.

Advertisers paid for the vast outpouring from commercial television and radio stations. They spent enormous sums to compete for the attention of the average television viewer, who, surveys indicated, sat in front of his set as much as six hours a day. The manufacturers of one headache remedy, for example, spent nearly $750,000 in one month in 1958; their two nearest competitors spent a combined total of nearly $1 million that same month. In consequence, programs were patterned to draw the largest number of viewers, and when surveys indicated that the sets were tuned in elsewhere, the programs were ruthlessly pruned. Television lost one of its biggest sources of income when the federal government banned cigarette commercials after January 1, 1971.

One critic, Richard Schickel, commented that, to literate people, television was "an unparalleled purveyor of trash." Nevertheless, "we sit there, eyes glued to the set, watching this explication of the obvious in hateful fascination." A Canadian scholar, Marshall McLuhan, won a large following by extolling in confusing but thought-provoking prose the new era of mass media. He wrote, in *The Medium Is the Massage* (1967): "The contained, the distinct, the separate—our western legacy— are being replaced by the flowing, the unified, the fused." The electronic medium of communication made its impressions all at once, he said, in contrast to the print medium, which made its impressions one after another. One reason for the generaton gap and the youth revolt, he suggested, was the influence of the new medium on the young, who for the first time had been exposed to it in their formative years.

Foundations and the federal government tried to further the positive role of television. The Carnegie and Ford foundations proposed that educational stations be encouraged to take advantage of television's educational and cultural potentialities. The Public Broadcasting Act of 1967 authorized, though it provided no financing for, a noncommercial television network. Soon university-affiliated and other stations from coast to coast were providing high-quality theater, musical performances, and lecture courses with the cooperation of the Public Broadcasting System.

Commercial stations received and transmitted a large share of their programs from one or another of three great networks, the American Broadcasting Company, the National Broadcasting Company, and the Columbia Broadcasting System. These sources provided not only entertainment but also news and opinion for their affiliated stations. Bringing world events, or chosen segments of them, visibly into the home, the network programs had a much greater emotional impact (as in reporting the Vietnam War) than did newspaper accounts. A comparatively small number of prestigious commentators, outstanding among them Walter Cronkite of CBS, dominated the presentation of TV news. Hence questions arose regarding the breadth and balance of the coverage.

Vice President Agnew and other spokesmen for the Nixon administration, as well as Nixon himself, objected strongly to what they considered hostile treatment by the news media, especially television. Agnew demanded that commentators be "made more responsible to the views of the nation." The director of the White House Office of Telecommunications Policy attacked TV newsmen as "so-called professionals who confuse sensation with sense and who dispense elitist gossip in the guise of news analysis." He proposed a law that would put the responsibility on local stations for assuring "fairness," and the administration threatened to revoke the licenses of stations that failed to meet its standards.

An independent study (1973) by the Twentieth Century Fund concluded, however, that "presidential television" gave the President a great advantage over his critics. "Presidential television means the ability to appear simultaneously on all national radio and television networks at prime, large-audience evening hours, virtually whenever and however he wishes." Nixon exploited this advantage even more than his predecessors, taking as much TV time during his first eighteen months in office as Eisenhower, Kennedy, and Johnson together had taken during theirs. Congress, the courts, the opposition party could not keep up with the President in his ability to command free time on the air. Television appeared to be one of the factors that had increased the power of the executive as against that of the other branches of government.

thirty_____
Watergate—
and the Ford Administration

The middle of the 1970s brought startling change for the American nation. There had never been such a dramatic overturn in administrations. First Vice President Agnew and then President Nixon were forced to resign over unrelated scandals, to be replaced by a new President, Gerald R. Ford, and Vice President, Nelson Rockefeller, who had been appointed rather than elected. No sooner had the new administration taken office than the nation, for world as well as internal causes, plunged into the most serious recession since the great depression of the 1930s. Within a few months parts of the international structure of the Nixon administration began also to crumble; the settlement in Vietnam started rapidly to collapse. Both the prosperity and peace that seemed so bright at the beginning of 1973 seemed to be slipping from grasp as the nation entered a new, uncertain era.

WATERGATE

As he began his second term, in January 1973, President Nixon stood at the height of his power and popularity. Soon his popularity, as measured by opinion polls, began to drop. It fell faster than that of any other President since such polls were first taken, in Franklin D. Roosevelt's time. Within a year, public confidence in Nixon was so low that serious doubts arose as to whether he should, or could, continue to lead the people. The reason for the sudden collapse of his prestige could be summed up in a word that became familiar to all newspaper readers and television viewers—"Watergate." That word designated a bewildering assortment of political scandals, the worst in American history.

The Watergate was a deluxe hotel-apartment-office complex in Washington. In it were located the headquarters of the Democratic National Committee. There, at about two o'clock in the morning of June 17, 1972,

President and Mrs. Ford and their family on Inauguration Day (UPI)

police arrested five men who had broken into the headquarters to "bug" them and to copy documents. Later two others were arrested, one of them the general counsel for Nixon's personal campaign organization, the Committee for the Re-election of the President (CREEP). Two months after the burglary, however, Nixon stated that "no one in the White House staff, no one in this Administration presently employed, was involved in this very bizarre incident." He added: "This kind of activity, as I have often indicated, has no place whatsoever in our political process." His opponent, McGovern, tried in vain to make a campaign issue out of the crime.

When, after the election, the captured burglars went on trial, all but one of them pleaded guilty, and that one refused to talk. The Justice Department prosecutors failed to implicate anyone higher up than those arrested, but Federal District Judge John J. Sirica suspected that the whole truth had not been told. While sentencing the defendants to long terms in prison, Sirica intimated that if they would cooperate in getting at the truth, he would reduce the sentences. One of the defendants, James W. McCord, Jr., a former CIA agent and a "security coordinator" for CREEP, now agreed to testify before a federal grand jury and a Senate investigating committee, which was headed by Senator Sam J. Ervin of North Carolina. McCord led a long parade of witnesses who appeared, voluntarily or under subpoena, before the grand jury and the Ervin committee. The committee hearings, televised, gave the public an opportunity to draw its own conclusions about the character and conduct of the people around the President. The testimony was so conflicting and confusing, however, that only with difficulty could the threads of the developing story be untangled.

Certain undisputed facts stood out. Nixon had been much concerned about the leaking of government secrets, especially the leaking of a Defense Department study of the Vietnam War, which *The New York Times* and other journals published as the Pentagon Papers in 1971. So, to plug the leaks he set up and put Ehrlichman in charge of a special group of White House employees, who called themselves the plumbers and who tapped the telephones of newsmen and members of Kissinger's staff. Nixon ordered the plumbers to investigate the background of Daniel Ellsberg, the man responsible for leaking the Pentagon Papers. Using White House funds, two of the plumbers led a team of burglars who broke into the Los Angeles office of Ellsberg's psychiatrist to search for Ellsberg's psychiatric files. Nixon was eager to prosecute and convict Ellsberg. While Ellsberg was on trial before a federal court, Nixon told Ehrlichman to approach the trial judge and find out if he would be interested in a promotion to the post of FBI director. The judge dismissed the case.

Four of the psychiatrist's office burglars, including the two leaders, took part, with CREEP financing, in the Watergate break-in. After the

Senator Sam J. Ervin, Chairman of the Senate Watergate Committee, swearing in a key witness, former White House Counsel, John W. Dean III (UPI)

arrests CREEP members and other government officials hastily destroyed a tremendous quantity of their records. Nixon told Haldeman and Ehrlichman to meet with top CIA officials, and the CIA director concluded that the White House was trying to "use" the agency as a means of slowing down an FBI probe and covering up CREEP activities. A White House attorney suggested to one of the Watergate defendants that he, the defendant, would get a presidential pardon after a short time in prison if he would keep silent about his superiors' involvement in the affair. Nixon's personal attorney and other White House staffers covertly passed more than $400,000, mostly from Nixon campaign contributions, to the defendants, their families, and their lawyers.

Besides the Watergate burglary, CREEP agents had perpetrated a variety of "dirty tricks" before and during the campaign, the worst of them having been intended to destroy the reputation of Nixon's strongest potential rival, Senator Muskie, and thereby prevent his getting the Democratic nomination. "I have often thought we had too much money," one of Nixon's campaign workers said afterward. Part of the money came from corporations that were making unlawful contributions, part of it from persons or groups who were receiving specific government favors. The Justice Department compromised an antitrust suit against the International Telephone and Telegraph (ITT) Company after ITT had agreed to contribute. The President raised price supports for milk after dairymen's organizations promised large payments. Attorney General Mitchell and Secretary of Commerce Maurice Stans interceded with the Securities and Exchange Commission on behalf of a disreputable financier who made a contribution. Mitchell and Stans were indicted but were eventually acquitted.

A PRESIDENT RESIGNS

Still others among Nixon's friends, advisers, and aides were indicted on, and some of them were convicted of, charges growing out of illegal campaign activities. The question became more and more insistent: Was Nixon himself guilty? Did he authorize any of the illegal activities or any of the attempts to cover them up? Did he have any knowledge of the misdeeds or the cover-up and fail to act on his knowledge, fail to stop what was going on and see that those responsible were punished? (Misprision of felony is itself a crime.) In a succession of statements Nixon altered and added to his original story, but he continued to maintain that he was innocent of any wrongdoing. "I am not a crook," he declared at one news conference. There was a possible way of testing, at certain points, his veracity as against that of his accusers. At his direction—as one of the very few who knew about it revealed in the midst of the Senate hearings—hidden tape recorders had been recording White House conversations. But Nixon refused to give up the relevant tapes until after Judge Sirica had ruled that he must, and then Nixon's spokesmen let it be known that two of the most important tapes were nonexistent and a third had a peculiar gap in it. A team of experts concluded that part of this tape had been deliberately erased.

To a growing number of Americans it seemed that, at the very least, Nixon had shown remarkably poor judgment in choosing some of his subordinates. It turned out that he had certainly been no judge of character when he twice endorsed Agnew for the vice presidency. Late in 1973 Agnew, the stern advocate of law and order, resigned as Vice President and pleaded nolo contendere (no contest) to a charge of income-tax evasion, the federal prosecutors agreeing in return to refrain from pressing charges of soliciting and accepting bribes. To replace Agnew, Nixon named the House Republican leader, Gerald Ford of Michigan. After a thorough investigation, Congress gave Ford its approval. He appeared to be, if not an imaginative or inspiring statesman, at least an honest politician.

With Ford as the prospective successor, old demands for the resignation or impeachment of Nixon were renewed. As 1974 began, Nixon still refused to resign. The Judiciary Committee of the House was busily gathering evidence for the decision whether or not to impeach. After requesting a number of the presidential tapes, the committee served the President with a subpoena when he refused to give them up. Finally, at the end of April, he responded, not by delivering the tapes, but by sending in and at the same time publishing 1,200 pages of selected and edited transcripts. He and other Republican spokesmen claimed that these told the whole story of his relation to the Watergate scandal and completely exonerated him. Others, especially Democrats, drew a quite different conclusion. By a partisan vote, the committee ruled that Nixon had not made an adequate response to the subpoena.

By the summer of 1974, nine men—in addition to the "Watergate seven," the burglars and their accomplices—had confessed to or been convicted of Watergate-related offenses. These nine were former members of CREEP or of the White House staff, the highest ranking of them being Erlichman. Several others, including Haldeman and Mitchell, had been indicted and were awaiting trial. Nixon himself had been named as an "unindicted co-conspirator" by a federal grand jury.

For use as evidence in these cases the special prosecutor for the Justice Department, Leon Jaworski, asked for tape recordings of sixty-four White House conversations. Nixon refused to give them up, claiming that "executive privilege" justified him in thus protecting the confidentiality of his office. In the case of *United States* v. *Richard M. Nixon* the Supreme Court decided unanimously against the President in July 1974.

A few days later, after several months of thorough inquiry, the House Judiciary Committee voted to recommend three articles of impeachment. These charged that Nixon had (1) obstructed justice by helping to cover up the Watergate crimes, (2) misused federal agencies so as to violate the rights of citizens, and (3) interfered with congressional powers by refusing to turn over tapes and other materials that the committee had subpoenaed.

Though Nixon continued to assert his innocence, more and more signs of his complicity were coming to light. Newly released tapes proved what he had always denied—that he had been aware of and indeed had directed the Watergate cover-up from the beginning. With impeachment and conviction finally looming as unavoidable, he did what no President had ever done before. He resigned.

THE FORD ADMINISTRATION

On the morning of August 9, 1974, as ex-President Nixon flew to California, Ford took his oath of office as President of the United States. "Our long national nightmare is over," he asserted. "Our Constitution works. Our great Republic is a government of laws and not of men." A relieved people acclaimed Ford as their new hero; they were delighted with his simple directness and his reputation for integrity.

Along with personal attractiveness, Ford brought to the White House a basic conservatism. During his twenty-five years in the House, nine of them spent as minority leader, he had been notable for his unwavering Republican regularity and, during the Nixon years, for his loyalty to the President. He used to describe himself as "a moderate in domestic affairs,

On Aug. 9, 1974 Gerald R. Ford and his wife Betty escorted President and Mrs. Nixon to an awaiting helicopter on the White House lawn. Later that morning Ford was sworn in as President (UPI)

a conservative in fiscal affairs, and a dyed-in-the-wool internationalist in foreign affairs." He had opposed most social welfare legislation and accepted civil rights measures only reluctantly, but he had emphatically supported the Vietnam War. These were the attitudes and actions that had caused Nixon to nominate him for Vice President. He was also adept in the arts of political accommodation, popular with members of Congress from both parties.

At first, President Ford worked largely through the White House staff and cabinet he had inherited from Nixon. It was reassuring in August 1974 that he kept Kissinger, highly popular at that time, as Secretary of State. He brought in several new staff members whom he had long known and trusted but did not let them gather as substantial power as their predecessors. As he slowly replaced part of the cabinet, he seemed to be trying to reclaim the middle ground in American politics and pull together the two wings of the Republican party. Two of his appointees, the new Attorney General Edward Levi and Secretary of Labor John Dunlop, had been university administrators and professors—unidentified with party politics. The Secretary of Transportation, William T. Coleman, was a black lawyer, and the Secretary of Housing and Urban Development, Carla A. Hills, a woman lawyer. Ford allowed these department heads to express their own views, even when they varied from White House policy.

Carla A. Hills being sworn in as Secretary of Housing and Urban Development
(DEPARTMENT OF HOUSING AND URBAN DEVELOPMENT)

*William T. Coleman, Secretary
of Transportation* (DEPARTMENT
OF TRANSPORTATION)

Toward the Congress, dominated by a majority decidedly more liberal than he, Ford was pleasant but engaged in continuing struggle. Again and again he made conservative recommendations, then either accepted defeat of them in measures enacted over his veto or modified them in order to obtain legislation.

Ford's early popularity took an abrupt dip from a Gallup poll rating of 72 percent to 50 percent only a month after he took office when he suddenly granted Nixon "a full, free, and absolute pardon . . . for all offenses against the United States" during his term of office. Ford asserted he was pardoning Nixon in part out of compassion and in part "to firmly shut and seal this book" of Watergate. Otherwise, litigation with its accompanying polarization of opinions, he said, might go on for years. Subsequently, Ford appeared voluntarily before a House Judiciary subcommittee and emphasized that he had made no deal with Nixon but had acted "out of my concern to serve the best interests of the country."

During the Watergate trial, controversy over the pardon of Nixon continued, and the absence of Nixon, who was too ill to appear as a witness, was conspicuous. Three of the defendants, former Attorney General Mitchell and the two former top White House advisers, Haldeman and Ehrlichman, were found guilty. Altogether in the Watergate trial and related trials and legal actions, twenty-seven former aides or agents of Nixon, including three former cabinet members, were either found guilty or pleaded guilty.

One immediate congressional response to the scandals was the enactment of the Federal Election Campaign Act Amendments of 1974, aimed at eliminating the influence of special-interest contributors from future presidential campaigns. It provided public financing of $20 million for each major party candidate in the general election and mixed public and private financing in primary races. The House defeated public financing for congressional candidates but set ceilings on expenditures in House and Senate races. No individual could contribute more than $1,000 to a federal candidate in a primary or general election or a total of more than $25,000 to federal candidates in an election year. Whether the law would be effective remained to be seen; in the aftermath of Watergate, corporations pleading guilty to huge illegal contributions received only nominal punishment.

The issue of immense wealth and power beset the Ford administration almost immediately when the new President nominated former Governor Nelson Rockefeller of New York to be Vice President. Ford, himself representing the right wing of his battered party, was seeking to strengthen it by choosing a most conspicuous liberal. In lengthy, and searching hearings, however, Congress explored the ramifications of Rockefeller's fortune and his uses of it before finally confirming him.

The onus not only of scandals but also of painful inflation and a growing recession burdened the Republican party in the congressional elections of 1974. The stock market was dropping, and unemployment was rising. Prices rose 12.2 percent in 1974, the worst increase in twenty-eight years, and the Labor Department announced that an urban family of four needed $14,300 to maintain a moderate living standard. President Ford acted rapidly to develop an economic program with which to back Republican candidates. In the early fall he held a conference with a number of leading economists, listened to their varying recommendations, then called upon Congress to participate in a new mobilization against inflation. "We must whip inflation now," he declared, wearing a button emblazoned "WIN" as a symbol of the campaign. But the ten-point program he proposed was cautious (including a one-year 5-percent tax increase) and Congress paid little attention to it.

Through the weeks before the election, Ford, citing Truman's campaign style as his model, stumped vigorously for Republican candidates against what he characterized as "a Congress stacked against fiscal responsibility." He warned that unless heavy spenders were defeated, two-party government would be in jeopardy. "We will have what amounts to a legislative dictatorship," he said, "—a Congress with no checks and no balance."

Democrats won substantial victories in both congressional and gubernatorial races, obtaining about 60 percent of the vote and gaining additional seats in both houses of Congress.

The make-up of the new Ninety-fourth Congress, which convened in January 1975, represented even more change than the statistics of heavy Democratic majorities would indicate. There were more new Democratic members of Congress than in many years, seventy-five in all, and eight new Democratic senators. Many of them, including some who replaced Southern conservatives, were firmly liberal. When Congress met, these liberal freshmen helped remove several elderly committee chairmen. The powerful conservative chairman of the House Ways and Means Committee, Wilbur Mills, who had virtually dictated tax policy, suffered a personal mishap and was replaced.

The Ninety-fourth Congress began to exercise such a counterweight to the White House that one British journalist suggested that the United States was in an era of parliamentary government. The new Congress enlarged staffs and increased committee operating funds by nearly 80 percent. It established a Congressional Budget Office to provide an overview of tax revenues and expenditures and appointed a woman economist, Alice Mitchell Rivlin, to head it.

By the time the new Congress met in January 1975, the recession had deepened into the worst since the 1930s. The decline in production in the first quarter of the year was more than 10 percent, and unemployment had already risen to 8 percent of the working force. As yet the economic decline was slight compared with that of the winter of 1932–1933, but distress was great among certain groups. More than a quarter of automobile workers were laid off, and by the spring of 1975 unemployment benefits were running out; at least one-fifth of construction workers and 40 percent or more of minority youths could not find jobs. Numbers of middle class, middle-aged persons with families to support and mortgage payments to meet, for the first time in their lives had no alternative but relief. There was spreading fear that the United States was approaching a depression if indeed, as George Meany of the AFL-CIO announced, it was not already in a depression. There was less concern over inflation, which seemed to be slackening somewhat, and more demand for bold programs comparable to those of the New Deal.

Responding to the pressure for economic stimulus, President Ford took what his press secretary called a 179-degree turn from his earlier request for a tax increase and proposed a modest tax cut. Although his proposals could lead to a peacetime deficit of unprecedented proportions, some economists felt they could scarcely compensate for the effects of inflation in increasing the income-tax bite on individual taxpayers, and the rapidly increasing state and local taxes. Congress sought a far larger tax cut unacceptable to the White House. In the spring of 1975 it enacted a compromise bill, reducing taxes nearly $23 billion and embodying a few reforms. It ended the oil depreciation allowance for large companies. Reluctantly, Ford signed the measure.

President Ford proved the critic wrong, and successfully set conservative economic policies. He vetoed nine measures on the grounds that they would increase the deficit. Eight times conservative Democrats joined Republicans to uphold his vetoes.

As the President and Congress tried to arrive at cautious policies that would stimulate production and reduce unemployment without fueling higher inflation, other industrial nations were undergoing similar economic crises. Their leadership was also responding conservatively.

In part the world economic crisis of the 1970s grew out of the quadrupling of oil prices in the aftermath of the 1973 Yom Kippur war the Arab states had waged against Israel. There had been an enormous outflow of currencies to the oil-producing nations, an outflow even more painful to Japan, the nations of western Europe, and countries not as wealthy as the United States. Some billions of so-called "petrodollars" returned to America to be invested or spent for industrial equipment. Ford continued the efforts of his predecessor to develop a program to make the United States less dependent upon outside energy sources, but the problem was highly complex and significant legislation was slow to emerge.

A further complication in the United States and the world was the critical shortage of food in 1974. This contributed to soaring prices within the United States and the threat of starvation in famine areas of the world. Experts warned that in the next few years population growth would outstrip expansion in food production. Nevertheless, by the spring of 1975, American farmers were worried by falling commodity prices, and Congress was preparing new price support legislation. Secretary of Agriculture Earl Butz, in a rare alliance with consumer groups, opposed the price supports. President Ford vetoed the price support bill and Congress did not override the veto.

Along with economic crises, critical changes in the world political balance contributed to pessimism in the United States. In the summer of 1974 American efforts to maintain a balance between Greeks and Turks on the island of Cyprus failed, and Greece and Turkey—both NATO powers—vented their displeasure against the United States. A further weakening of NATO, and of American influence, came from Portugal. The former right-wing dictatorship once friendly to the United States, gave way first to a liberal government and then to a military government leaning toward the Soviet Union.

A still more serious setback came in the Middle East. Secretary Kissinger's personal diplomacy, involving his shuttling back and forth between Egypt and Israel, seeking limited concessions toward a lasting settlement, broke down in the spring of 1975. Israelis were disheartened because there was no disposition in Congress to vote them as substantial arms aid as they wished. Despite much talk to the contrary, polls indicated that the American public had not abandoned its sympathy for Israel.

The major foreign shock came in the spring of 1975 when, almost simultaneously with the opening of the American bicentennial celebrations, Cambodia fell to the Khmer Rouge and South Vietnam to the North Vietnamese and the Vietcong. Years of intervention, involving the loss of 56,000 American lives and expenditures of more than $150 billion, had led only to failure.

The slow collapse of Cambodia, where Communist forces had long ringed the capital city of Phnom Penh, took place while Congress refused Ford's pleas for additional aid. The administration tried to place the onus on Congress; there were countersuggestions that the State Department had not sought to negotiate a settlement like that which had been achieved in Laos.

In South Vietnam, where serious fighting had continued despite the signing of the Paris agreements, the North Vietnamese forces slowly gained supremacy. Suddenly, in March 1975, President Thieu without consulting the United States, ordered troops to withdraw from several provinces to form a shorter defense perimeter. The withdrawal quickly turned into a rout.

Ford called upon Congress to vote $722 million in fresh military aid, but Congress refused to approve more than limited relief funds. Despite the bitter protests of Thieu, Ford abided by the congressional mandate of 1973 prohibiting further military intervention in Indochina. Allegedly, Thieu had received written assurances from President Nixon that the United States would give massive aid if the North Vietnamese engaged in major violation of the 1973 agreement. While the electorate was distressed over the agony of fleeing refugees, brought to them in excruciating detail by television, there was no disposition on the part of voters or Congress to dispatch armed forces back into Indochina. The assessment of blame would come later.

When President Ford met near Vladivostok with Soviet leaders in November 1974, they agreed on new limitations on strategic arms. Left to right: Ford, Brezhnev, Kissinger, and Gromyko (UPI)

Despite the many setbacks in American foreign policy, the limited détente with China and the Soviet Union seemed to continue. Late in 1974, Ford, after visiting Japan, went on to Vladivostok, Siberia, where he reached a new stage of agreement with Premier Brezhnev on strategic arms limitations.

In the summer of 1975 at a Hennsinki conference on European Security and Cooperation, President Ford signed the "final document," guaranteeing what the Soviet Union had sought since World War II—recognition of the national boundaries that had been created at the end of the war.

Under these inauspicious circumstances, both foreign and domestic, the United States reached the threshold of its third century. Amid both cheers and jeers, Ford participated in the commemoration of the Battles of Lexington and Concord. Speaking at the Old North Church, where lanterns had once signaled to Paul Revere, Ford declared:

> In the 200 years of our existence, it is not war and disillusionment which have triumphed. No, it is the American concept and fulfillment of liberty that have truly revolutionized the world. . . .
>
> The American dream is not dead. It simply has yet to be fulfilled. In the economy and energy and the environment . . . in housing and transportation . . . in education and communication . . . in social problems and social planning—America has yet to realize its greatest contribution to civilization. To do this, America needs new ideas and new efforts from our people.

Selected Readings

Titles followed by an asterisk(*) are available in paperback.

one

America Enters the Twentieth Century

GENERAL ACCOUNTS

R. H. Wiebe, *The Search for Order, 1877–1920* * (1967); S. P. Hays, *The Response to Industrialism, 1885–1914* * (1957); Ray Ginger, *The Age of Excess: The United States from 1877 to 1914* * (1965).

TECHNICAL ADVANCES

Sudhir Kakar, *Frederick Taylor* * (1970); Siegfried Giedion, *Mechanization Takes Command* (1948); Samuel Haber, *Efficiency and Uplift: Scientific Management in the Progressive Era, 1890–1920* (1964); M. J. Nadworny, *Scientific Management and the Unions, 1900–1932* (1955); H. G. J. Aitken, *Taylorism at Watertown Arsenal* (1960); Kendall Birr, *Pioneering in Industrial Research: The Story of the General Electric Research Laboratory* (1957).

BUSINESS AND GOVERNMENT

T. C. Cochran, *American Business in the Twentieth Century* (2nd ed., 1972); R. H. Wiebe, *Businessmen and Reform* (1962); Gabriel Kolko, *The Triumph of Conservatism* (1963); Mabel Newcomer, *The Big Business Executive* (1955); James Weinstein, *The Corporate Ideal in the Liberal State, 1900–1918* (1968); Milton Friedman and A. J. Schwartz, *A Monetary History of the United States, 1867–1960* * (1963); Vincent Carosso, *Investment Banking in America* (1970).

LABOR

Philip Taft, *The A. F. of L. in the Time of Gompers* (1957); S. B. Kaufman, *Samuel Gompers and the Origins of the American Federation of Labor* (1973); Bernard Mandel, *Samuel Gompers* (1963); Melvin Dubofsky, *We Shall Be All: A History of the Industrial Workers of the World* (1969); David Brody, *Steelworkers in America: The Nonunion Era* * (1960); W. R. Van Tine, *The Making of the Labor Bureaucrat, 1870–1920* (1973).

THE AUTOMOBILE AGE

J. B. Rae, *The American Automobile* (1965) and *The Road and the Car*

in American Life (1971); Anne Jardim, *The First Henry Ford* * (1970);
R. M. Wik, *Henry Ford and Grass-Roots America* (1972); N. T. Moline,
Mobility and the Small Town, 1900–1930 (1971); J. J. Flink, *America Adopts
the Automobile, 1895–1910* (1970).

LIVING STANDARDS

Albert Rees, *Real Wages in Manufacturing, 1890–1914* (1961); R. H. Bremner,
From the Depths: The Discovery of Poverty in the United States (1956).

two
The Progressive Movement

INTERPRETATIONS AND PROGRESSIVE THOUGHT

Richard Hofstadter, *The Age of Reform* * (1955); Eric Goldman, *Rendezvous
with Destiny* * (1952); Lewis L. Gould, ed., *The Progressive Era* (1974);
Charles Forcey, *The Crossroads of Liberalism: Croly, Weyl, Lippmann* *
(1961); Herbert Croly, *The Promise of American Life* * (1909); J. B. Quandt,
*From the Small Town to the Great Community: Social Thought of Progressive
Intellectuals* (1970).

PROGRESSIVE JOURNALISM

C. C. Regier, *The Era of the Muckrakers* (1932); Justin Kaplan, *Lincoln
Steffens* * (1974); Leon Harris, *Upton Sinclair* (1975); Harold S. Wilson,
McClure's Magazine and the Muckrakers (1970); Peter Lyon, *Success Story:
Life and Times of S. S. McClure* (1963); R. C. Bannister, *Ray Stannard
Baker* (1966); J. A. Semonche, *Ray Stannard Baker* (1969); Walter Johnson,
William Allen White's America (1947).

STATES

G. E. Mowry, *California Progressives* * (1951); R. S. Maxwell, *La Follette
and the Rise of Progressivism in Wisconsin* (1944); R. M. Abrams, *Conserva-
tism in a Progressive Era: Massachusetts* (1964); D. P. Thelen, *The New
Citizenship: Origins of Progressivism in Wisconsin, 1885–1900* (1972); Sheldon
Hackney, *Populism to Progressivism in Alabama* (1969); M. P. Rogin and
J. L. Shover, *Political Change in California: Critical Elections and Social
Movements, 1890–1966* (1970); R. S. La Forte, *Leaders of Reform: Progres-
sive Republicanism in Kansas, 1900–1916* (1974); C. H. Chrislock, *The
Progressive Era in Minnesota* (1971); H. L. Warner, *Progressivism in Ohio*
(1964).

CITIES

W. E. Bean, *Boss Ruef's San Francisco* * (1952); J. D. Buenker, *Urban
Liberalism and Progressive Reform* (1973); J. B. Crooks, *Politics and Progress:
Urban Progressivism in Baltimore* (1968); Z. L. Miller, *Boss Cox's Cincinnati*
(1968); W. D. Miller, *Memphis During the Progressive Era* (1965); J. A.
Tarr, *A Study in Boss Politics: William Lorimer of Chicago* (1971); J. M.
Allswang, *A House for All Peoples: Ethnic Politics in Chicago 1890–1936*
(1971); W. L. Riordan, *Plunkitt of Tammany Hall* * (1963 ed.).

PARTY POLITICS

H. S. and M. G. Merrill, *The Republican Command, 1897–1913* (1971);
R. B. Nye, *Midwestern Progressive Politics, 1870–1958* (1959 ed.); C. K.
Yearley, *The Money Machines: Breakdown and Reform of Governmental and
Party Finance in the North, 1860–1920* (1970); J. M. Kousser, *The Shaping
of Southern Politics: Suffrage Restriction and the Establishment of the One-
Party South, 1880–1910* (1974).

PROGRESSIVE ISSUES

A. F. Davis, *Spearheads of Reform: The Social Settlements and the Progressive Movement, 1890–1914* (1968); Roy Lubove, *The Progressives and the Slums: Tenement House Reform in New York City* (1962); S. P. Hays, *The Gospel of Efficiency: The Progressive Conservation Movement, 1890–1920* * (1959); E. R. Richardson, *The Politics of Conservation: Crusade and Controversies, 1897–1913* * (1962); O. E. Anderson, *The Health of a Nation: Harvey W. Wiley and the Fight for Pure Food* (1958); A. Martin, *Enterprise Denied: Origins of the Decline of the American Railroads, 1897–1917* (1971); Gabriel Kolko, *Railroads and Regulation: 1877–1916* (1965); S. P. Caine, *The Myth of a Progressive Reform: Railroad Regulation in Wisconsin, 1903–1910* (1970); W. I. Trattner, *Crusade for Children* (1970); D. M. Kennedy, *Birth Control in America: The Career of Margaret Sanger,* (1970); R. Alton Lee, *A History of Regulatory Taxation* (1973); C. R. Marchand, *The American Peace Movement and Social Reform* (1973); H. S. Tishler, *Self-Reliance and Social Security, 1870–1917* (1971); D. K. Pickens, *Eugenics and Progressives* (1968); J. H. Timberlake, *Prohibition and the Progressive Movement* (1963); W. L. O'Neill, *Divorce in the Progressive Era* (1967); Joseph Gusfield, *Symbolic Crusade: Status Politics and the Temperance Movement* (1963); S. B. Wood, *Constitutional Politics in the Progressive Era: Child Labor and the Law* (1968).

PROGRESSIVES AND CONSERVATIVES

Belle and Fola La Follette, *Robert M. La Follette* (2 vols., 1953); R. M. La Follette, *Autobiography* * (1913); Richard Lowitt, *George W. Norris: The Making of a Progressive, 1861–1912* (1963) and *The Persistence of a Progressive, 1913–1933* (1971); C. G. Bowers, *Beveridge and the Progressive Era* (1932); A. T. Mason, *Brandeis: A Free Man's Life* (1946); Melvin I. Urofsky, *A Mind of One Piece: Brandeis and American Reform* (1971); P. E. Coletta, *William Jennings Bryan* (3 vols., 1964–1969); L. W. Koenig, *Bryan* (1971); P. W. Glad, *The Trumpet Soundeth: Bryan, 1896–1912* (1960); C. A. Chambers, *P. U. Kellogg and the Survey* (1971); C. E. Larsen, *The Good Fight: Ben B. Lindsey* (1972); A. F. Davis, *American Heroine: Jane Addams* (1973); Daniel Levine, *Jane Addams* (1971); Fred Greenbaum, *Fighting Progressive: E. P. Costigan* (1971); W. H. Harbaugh, *Lawyer's Lawyer: John W. Davis* (1973); F. L. Allen, *The Great Pierpont Morgan* (1949); N. W. Stephenson, *Nelson W. Aldrich* (1920); Richard Leopold, *Elihu Root and the Conservative Tradition* * (1954).

SOCIALISTS AND UNIONS

Ray Ginger, *The Bending Cross: A Biography of Eugene Victor Debs* (1949); Ira Kipnis, *The American Socialist Movement, 1897–1912* (1952); D. A. Shannon, *The Socialist Party of America* (1955); Howard Quint, *Forging of American Socialism* (1953); R. E. Paulson, *Radicalism and Reform: Vrooman Family* (1968); S. M. Miller, *Victor Berger and the Promise of Constructive Socialism, 1910–1920* (1973); W. M. Dick, *Labor and Socialism in America: The Gompers Era* (1972); Marc Karson, *American Labor Unions and Politics, 1900–1918* (1958); R. J. Cornell, *The Anthracite Coal Strike of 1902* (1957); G. S. McGovern and L. F. Guttridge, *The Great Coalfield War* (1972).

WOMEN'S RIGHTS

A. S. Kraditor, *Ideas of the Woman Suffrage Movement, 1890–1920* (1965); June Sochen, *Movers and Shakers: American Women Thinkers and Activists, 1900–1970* (1973); R. E. Paulson, *Women's Suffrage and Prohibition: A*

Comparative Study (1973); W. L. O'Neill, *Everyone was Brave: The Rise and Fall of Feminism in America* (1969); David Morgan, *Suffragists and Democrats: Politics of Woman Suffrage* (1971).

INDIANS

R. W. Mardock, *Reformers and the American Indian* (1970); L. C. Kelly, *Navajo Indians and Federal Indian Policy, 1900–1935* (1968)); H. W. Hertzberg, *The Search for an American Indian Identity: Modern Pan-Indian Movements* (1971); D. W. Otis, *The Dawes Act and the Allotment of Indian Lands* (1973).

BLACKS

August Meier, *Negro Thought in America, 1880–1915* * (1963); C. V. Woodward, *The Strange Career of Jim Crow* * (1966 ed.); E. M. Rudwick, *W. E. B. DuBois* * (1960); R. S. Baker, *Following the Color Line* * (1908); E. S. Redkey, *Black Exodus: Black Nationalism and Back-to-Africa Movements, 1890–1910* * (1969); N. J. Weiss, *The National Urban League, 1910–1940* (1974); C. F. Kellogg, *History of the National Association for the Advancement of Colored People, 1909–1920* (1967); Gilbert Osofsky, *Harlem, 1890–1930* (1966); A. H. Spear, *Black Chicago, 1890–1920* (1967); R. B. Sherman, *The Republican Party and Black America, 1896–1933* (1973); Ira Katznelson, *Black Men, White Cities: Race, Politics, and Migration in the United States, 1900–30, and Britain, 1948–68* (1973); J. T. Kirby, *Darkness at the Dawning: Race and Reform in the Progressive South* (1972); Pete Daniel, *The Shadow of Slavery: Peonage in the South, 1901–1969* (1972); W. B. Weare, *Black Business in the New South: North Carolina Mutual Life Insurance Company* (1973).

three
Theodore Roosevelt: The Emergence of a Modern President

G. W. Chessman, *Theodore Roosevelt and Politics of Power* * (1969); G. E. Mowry, *The Era of Theodore Roosevelt* * (1958); H. F. Pringle, *Theodore Roosevelt* (1931); W. H. Harbaugh, *Power and Responsibility* * (1961); J. M. Blum, *The Republican Roosevelt* * (1954); J. A. Garraty, *Right Hand Man: The Life of George W. Perkins* (1960) [a leading Bull Mooser].

four
A Rift in Republican Ranks

P. E. Coletta, *Presidency of Taft* (1973); H. F. Pringle, *The Life and Times of William Howard Taft* (2 vols., 1939); Kenneth Hechler, *Insurgency: Personalities and Policies of the Taft Era* (1940); James Holt, *Congressional Insurgents and the Party System, 1909–1916* (1967); D. F. Anderson, *William Howard Taft: A Conservative's Conception of the Presidency* (1973); G. E. Mowry, *Theodore Roosevelt and the Progressive Movement* * (1946); S. P. Hays, *Conservation and the Gospel of Efficiency, 1890–1920* (1959); J. L. Penick, *Progressive Politics and Conservation: Ballinger-Pinchot Affair* (1968); E. R. Richardson, *Politics of Conservation, 1897–1913* * (1962); H. T. Pinkett, *Gifford Pinchot: Private and Public Forester* (1970).

five
The New Freedom Triumphs

A. S. Link, *Wilson and the Progressive Era, 1910–1917* * (1954); Link,

Wilson (vols. 1/5 1966/72); A. L. and J. L. George, Wilson and Colonel House: A Personality Study * (1956); J. M. Blum, Wilson and the Politics of Morality * (1956) and Tumulty and the Wilson Era (1951); L. H. Canfield, Presidency of Wilson (1966); G. B. Tindall, Emergence of New South, 1913–1945 (1967); J. J. Broesamle, William Gibbs McAdoo, 1863–1917 (1973).

six
Militant Progressivism
GENERAL

J. W. Pratt, Challenge and Rejection: United States and World Leadership, 1900–1921 (1967); H. K. Beale, Roosevelt and Rise of America to World Power (1956); D. H. Burton, Roosevelt: Confident Imperialist (1969); R. A. Esthus, Roosevelt and International Rivalries (1970); R. D. Challener, Admirals, Generals, and American Foreign Policy, 1898–1914 (1973); W. V. and M. V. Scholes, Foreign Policies of the Taft Administration (1970); R. F. Weston, Racism in U. S. Imperialism: Influence of Racial Assumptions on American Foreign Policy, 1893–1946 (1972).

EAST ASIAN POLICY

Akira Iriye, Pacific Estrangement: Japanese and American Expansion, 1897–1911 (1972); W. R. Braisted, United States Navy in the Pacific, 1897–1922 (2 vols., 1958–1971); Jerry Israel, Progressivism and the Open Door: America and China, 1905–1921 (1971); C. E. Neu, An Uncertain Friendship: Roosevelt and Japan, 1906–1909 (1967); R. A. Esthus, Roosevelt and Japan (1966); E. P. Trani, Treaty of Portsmouth (1969); J. A. White, Diplomacy of the Russo-Japanese War (1964); E. H. Zabriskie, American-Russian Rivalry in the Far East, 1895–1914 (1946); Charles Vevier, United States and China, 1906–1913: Finance and Diplomacy (1955); M. H. Hunt, Frontier Defense and the Open Door: Manchuria in Chinese-American Relations, 1895–1911 (1973).

CARIBBEAN POLICY

Dexter Perkins, The United States and the Caribbean (1947); D. G. Munro, Intervention and Dollar Diplomacy in the Caribbean, 1900–1921 (1964); W. H. Callcott, The Caribbean Policy of the United States, 1890–1920 (1942); Gerstle Mack, The Land Divided: A History of the Panama Canal and Other Canal Projects (1944); D. C. Miner, The Fight for the Panama Route (1940); L. O. Ealy, Yanqui Politics and the Isthmian Canal (1971); D. F. Healy, The United States in Cuba, 1898–1902 (1963); G. K. Lewis, Puerto Rico: Freedom and Power in the Caribbean * (1967); Hans Schmidt, United States Occupation of Haiti, 1915–1934 (1971).

MEXICAN RELATIONS

R. F. Smith, The United States and Revolutionary Nationalism in Mexico, 1916–1932 (1972); P. E. Haley, Revolution and Intervention: The Diplomacy of Taft and Wilson with Mexico, 1910–1917 (1970); L. D. Hill, Emissaries to a Revolution: Wilson's Executive Agents in Mexico (1973); D. M. Pletcher, Rails, Mines, and Progress: Seven American Promoters in Mexico, 1867–1911 (1959); C. C. Clendenen, The United States and Pancho Villa: A Study in Unconventional Diplomacy (1961); R. E. Quirk, An Affair of Honor: Woodrow Wilson and the Occupation of Vera Cruz (1962).

seven
The New Enlightenment
GENERAL

H. F. May, End of American Innocence (1959); Mark Sullivan, Our Times *

(6 vols., 1926–1935); H. U. Faulkner, *Quest for Social Justice* (1931).

PHILOSOPHY AND EDUCATION

R. J. Wilson, *In Quest of Community: Social Philosophy in the United States, 1860–1920* (1968); Morton White, *Social Thought in America* (1949); D. W. Marcell, *Progress and Pragmatism: James, Dewey, Beard and the American Idea of Progress* (1974); George Dykhuizen, *Life and Mind of John Dewey* (1973); L. A. Cremin, *The Transformation of the School, 1876–1957* * (1961); I. L. Kandel, *American Education in the Twentieth Century* (1957); David Riesman, *Thorstein Veblen: A Critical Interpretation* (1953); D. M. Fox, *The Discovery of Abundance: Simon N. Patten* (1968).

MEDICINE AND MEDICAL RESEARCH

Donald H. Fleming, *William H. Welch and the Rise of Modern Medicine* (1954); E. F. Dolan and H. T. Silver, *William Crawford Gorgas: Warrior in White* (1968); T. N. Bonner, *Medicine in Chicago, 1850–1950* (1958).

LITERATURE AND THE ARTS

Alfred Kazin, *On Native Grounds* * (1942); Van Wyck Brooks, *The Confident Years, 1885–1915* (1952); K. S. Lynn, *The Dream of Success* (1955); Maxwell Geismar, *Rebels and Ancestors: The Modern American Novel, 1890–1915* * (1953); Lloyd Goodrich and J. I. H. Baur, *American Art of Our Century* (1961); Barbara Rose, *American Art Since 1900* * (1967); John Burchard and Albert Bush-Brown, *The Architecture of America* * (Part 4, 1961); C. W. Condit, *Chicago, 1910–29: Building, Planning, and Urban Technology* (1973); Richard Schickel, *Movies: The History of an Art and an Institution* (1965); Robert Sklar, *Movie-Made America* (1975).

eight
Making the World Safe for Democracy

GOING TO WAR

E. R. May, *The World War and American Isolation, 1914–1917* * (1959); E. H. Buehrig, *Woodrow Wilson and the Balance of Power* (1955); Charles Seymour, *American Diplomacy During the World War* (1934) and *American Neutrality, 1914–1917* (1935); Walter Millis, *Road to War: America, 1914–1917* (1935); E. M. Borchard and W. P. Lage, *Neutrality for the United States* (1937); C. C. Tansill, *America Goes to War* (1938); Armin Rappaport, *The Navy League of the United States* (1962); R. H. Heindel, *The American Impact on Great Britain, 1898–1914* (1940); Bradford Perkins, *The Great Rapprochement: England and the United States, 1895–1914* (1968); C. P. Parrini, *Heir to Empire: United States Economic Diplomacy, 1916–1923* (1969); Ross Gregory, *The Origins of American Intervention in the First World War* (1971).

THE HOME FRONT

F. L. Paxson, *American Democracy and the World War* (3 vols., 1936–1948); S. W. Livermore, *Politics Is Adjourned: Woodrow Wilson and the War Congress, 1916–1918* (1966); D. R. Beaver, *Newton D. Baker and the American War Effort, 1917–1919* (1966); Margaret Coit, *Mr. Baruch* (1957); R. D. Cuff, *War Industries Board* (1973); Charles Gilbert, *American Financing of World War I* (1970); A. A. Godfrey, *Government Operation of the Railroads, 1918–1920* (1974); Charles Chatfield, *For Peace and Justice: Pacifism in America, 1914–1941* (1971); G. T. Blakey, *Historians on the Homefront: American Propagandists for the Great War* (1970); H. N. Scheiber, *The Wilson Administration and Civil Liberties, 1917–1921* (1960); H. C. Peterson and G. C. Fite, *Opponents of War, 1917–1918* (1957); J. R. Mock and Cedric Larson, *Words That Won the War* (1939); H. C. Peterson, *Propaganda for War* (1939); J. G. Clifford, *The Citizen Soldiers: The Plattsburg Training Camp Movement* (1972).

nine
Victory and Isolation
COMBAT

E. M. Coffman, *The War to End All Wars: The American Military Experience in World War I* (1969); H. A. De Weerd, *President Wilson Fights His War: World War I and the American Intervention* (1968); D. F. Trask, *The United States in the Supreme War Council: American War Aims and Inter-Allied Strategy, 1917–1918* (1961) and *Captains and Cabinets: Anglo-American Naval Relations, 1917–1918* (1972); A. E. Barbeau and Florette Henri, *The Unknown Soldiers: Black American Troops in World War I* (1974); Frank Freidel, *Over There: The Story of America's First Great Overseas Crusade* (1964) [a pictorial history]; E. E. Morison, *Admiral Sims and the Modern American Navy* (1942); J. J. Hudson, *Hostile Skies: A Combat History of the American Air Service in World War I* (1968).

WILSONIAN DIPLOMACY

Harley Notter, *The Origins of the Foreign Policy of Woodrow Wilson* (1937); A. S. Link, *Wilson the Diplomatist* * (1957); N. G. Levin, Jr., *Woodrow Wilson and World Politics: America's Response to War and Revolution* (1968); R. E. Osgood, *Ideals and Self-Interest in America's Foreign Relations* (1953); D. F. Smith, *Aftermath of War: Bainbridge Colby and Wilsonian Diplomacy, 1920–21* (1970).

PEACEMAKING

R. J. Bartlett, *The League to Enforce Peace* (1944); H. R. Rudin, *Armistice, 1918* (1944); L. E. Gelfand, *The Inquiry: American Preparations for Peace, 1917–1919* (1963); T. A. Bailey, *Woodrow Wilson and the Lost Peace* * (1944) and *Woodrow Wilson and the Great Betrayal* * (1945); L. W. Martin, *Peace Without Victory: Woodrow Wilson and the British Liberals* (1958); D. F. Fleming, *The United States and the League of Nations, 1918–1920* (1932); J. M. Keynes, *Economic Consequences of the Peace* (1919); Herbert Hoover, *The Ordeal of Woodrow Wilson* (1958); J. A. Garraty, *Henry Cabot Lodge* (1953); Ralph Stone, *The Irreconcilables: The Fight Against the League of Nations* (1970).

ten
The New Era
SURVEYS AND INTERPRETATIONS

J. D. Hicks, *Republican Ascendancy, 1921–1933* * (1960); W. E. Leuchtenberg, *The Perils of Prosperity, 1914–32* * (1958); George Soule, *Prosperity Decade: From War to Depression, 1917–1929* (1947); A. M. Schlesinger, Jr., *The Crisis of the Old Order* * (1957).

RADICALISM AND REACTION

Burl Noggle, *Into the Twenties: The U. S. from Armistice to Normalcy* (1974); William Preston, Jr., *Aliens and Dissenters: Federal Suppression of Radicals, 1903–1933* (1963); R. K. Murray, *The Red Scare* * (1955); Zechariah Chafee, Jr., *Free Speech in the United States* (1941); S. Coben, *A. Mitchell Palmer, Politician* (1963); G. L. Joughin and E. M. Morgan, *The Legacy of Sacco and*

Vanzetti * (1948); David Brody, *Labor in Crisis: The Steel Strike of 1919* * (1965); Irving Bernstein, *The Lean Years: A History of the American Worker, 1920–1933* * (1960); David Chalmers, *Hooded Americanism* * (1965) [on the Klan]; E. D. Cronon, *Black Moses: The Story of Marcus Garvey* * (1955); W. M. Tuttle, Jr., *Race Riot: Chicago in the Red Summer of 1919* * (1970); P. L. Murphy, *The Meaning of Freedom of Speech: First Amendment Freedoms from Wilson to FDR* (1972).

THE EIGHTEENTH AND NINETEENTH AMENDMENTS

J. H. Timberlake, *Prohibition and the Progressive Movement, 1900–1920* (1963); Andrew Sinclair, *Prohibition: The Era of Excess* * (1962); Charles Merz, *Dry Decade* (1931); Virginius Dabney, *Dry Messiah: The Life of Bishop Cannon* (1949); A. S. Kraditor, *The Ideas of the Woman Suffrage Movement, 1890–1920* (1965); David Morgan, *Suffragists and Democrats: The Politics of Woman Suffrage in America* (1972); J. S. Lemons, *The Woman Citizen: Social Feminism in the 1920's* (1973); A. F. Scott, *The Southern Lady: From Pedestal to Politics, 1830–1930* (1970); W. H. Chafe, *The American Woman: Her Changing Social, Economic, and Political Roles, 1920–1970* (1972).

THE HARDING ADMINISTRATION

R. K. Murray, *The Politics of Normalcy: Governmental Theory and Practice in the Harding-Coolidge Era* * (1973); Murray, *The Harding Era* (1969); R. C. Downes, *The Rise of Harding: 1865–1920* (1970); Andrew Sinclair, *The Available Man* * [Harding] (1965); D. L. Winters, *Henry Cantwell Wallace as Secretary of Agriculture, 1921–1924* (1970); R. H. Zieger, *Republicans and Labor: 1919–1929* (1969); Burl Noggle, *Teapot Dome* (1962); J. L. Bates, *Origins of Teapot Dome, 1909–1921* (1963).

FOREIGN AFFAIRS

L. E. Ellis, *Republican Foreign Policy, 1921–1933* (1968) and *Kellogg and American Foreign Relations, 1925–1929* (1961); Selig Adler, *The Uncertain Giant . . . 1921–1941* (1965); Betty Glad, *Hughes and the Illusions of Innocence* (1967); M. J. Pusey, *Charles Evans Hughes* (2 vols., 1963); Dexter Perkins, *Hughes and American Democratic Statesmanship* * (1956); T. H. Buckley, *The United States and the Washington Conference, 1921–1922* (1970); J. C. Vinson, *Parchment Peace* (1955); M. G. Fry, *Illusions of Security: North Atlantic Diplomacy, 1918–22* (1972); J. H. Wilson, *American Business and Foreign Policy, 1920–1933* (1968); Wilson, *Ideology and Economics: U. S. Relations with the Soviet Union, 1918–1933* (1974); R. J. Maddox, *Borah and American Foreign Policy* (1969); Joseph Brandes, *Hoover and Economic Diplomacy* (1962); G. E. Wheeler, *Prelude to Pearl Harbor: U. S. Navy and the Far East, 1921–1931* (1963); William Kamman, *A Search of Stability: U. S. Diplomacy toward Nicaragua, 1925–1933* (1968); J. S. Tulchin, *The Aftermath of War: World War I and U. S. Policy Toward Latin America* (1971).

eleven

A Precarious Prosperity

THE COOLIDGE ADMINISTRATION AND ISSUES

D. R. McCoy, *Calvin Coolidge: The Quiet President* (1967); Claude Fuess, *Calvin Coolidge* (1940); W. A. White, *Puritan in Babylon* * (1940); P. J. Hubbard, *Origins of the T.V.A.: The Muscle Shoals Controversy, 1920–1932*

(1961); J. H. Shideler, *Farm Crisis, 1919–1923* (1957); Theodore Saloutos and J. D. Hicks, *Agricultural Discontent in the Middle West, 1900–1939* (1951); Gilbert Fite, *George Peek and the Fight for Farm Parity* (1954); George Soule, *Prosperity Decade* (1974); Robert Sobel, *The Great Bull Market: Wall Street in the 1920's* * (1968); John Brooks, *Once in Golconda: A True Drama of Wall Street, 1920–1938* (1969).

POLITICAL OPPOSITION

K. C. Mackay, *The Progressive Movement of 1924* (1947); Richard Lowitt, *George W. Norris* (vol. 2, 1971); LeRoy Ashby, *Spearless Leader: Borah and the Progressive Movement in the 1920's* (1972); M. C. McKenna, *Borah* (1961); David Burner, *Politics of Provincialism: Democratic Party, 1918–1932* (1967); J. J. Huthmacher, *Massachusetts People and Politics, 1919–1933* * (1959); Frank Freidel, *Franklin D. Roosevelt* (vols. 2–3, 1954–56); W. H. Harbaugh, *Lawyer's Lawyer: John W. Davis* (1973).

ASPECTS OF LIFE

G. H. Knoles, *The Jazz Age Revisited* (1955); F. L. Allen, *Only Yesterday* * (1931); R. S. and H. M. Lind, *Middletown* * (1929); N. F. Furniss, *The Fundamentalist Controversy, 1918–1931* (1954); Ray Ginger, *Six Days or Forever?* * (1958) [about the Scopes trial]; Erik Barnouw, *A Tower in Babel: A History of Broadcasting in the United States*, vol. 1: to 1933 (1966); W. R. Ross, *The Last Hero: Charles A. Lindbergh* (1967); C. A. Chambers, *Seedtime of Reform: American Social Service and Social Action, 1918–1933* (1963); P. S. Boyer, *Purity in Print: The Vice Society Movement and Book Censorship in America* (1968); N. I. Huggins, *Harlem Renaissance* (1971); R. M. Crunden, *From Self to Society, 1919–1941* (1972); W. H. Wilson, *Coming of Age: Urban America, 1915–1945* (1974).

twelve
President Hoover and the Great Depression
GENERAL

Broadus Mitchell, *Depression Decade* (1947); Dixon Wecter, *Age of the Great Depression* (1948); R. F. Himmelberg, comp., *Great Depression and American Capitalism* (1968); M. N. Rothbard, *America's Great Depression* (1963); Charles P. Kindelberger, *The World in Depression, 1929–1939* * (1973); S. E. Kennedy, *The Banking Crisis of 1933* (1973).

THE 1928 ELECTION

Oscar Handlin, *Al Smith and His America* * (1958); Edmund Moore, *A Catholic Runs for President* (1956); R. C. Silva, *Rum, Religion, and Votes* (1962); David Burner, *Politics of Provincialism* (1967); Samuel Lubell, *Future of American Politics* * (1952).

THE HOOVER ADMINISTRATION

A. U. Romasco, *The Poverty of Abundance: Hoover, the Nation, the Depression* * (1965); H. G. Warren, *Hoover and the Great Depression* (1959); Herbert Hoover, *Memoirs* (vols. 2–3, 1952); J. H. Wilson, *Hoover: Forgotten Progressive* * (1975); E. E. Robinson and V. D. Bornet, *Hoover: President of the United States* (1975); J. J. Huthmacher and Warren Sussman, eds., *Hoover and the Crisis of American Capitalism* (1973); M. L. Fausold and G. T. Mazuzan, eds., *The Hoover Presidency: A Reappraisal* (1974); J. A. Schwarz, *Interregnum of Despair: Hoover, Congress, and the Depression* (1970); Craig Lloyd, *Aggressive Introvert: Hoover and Public Relations Management, 1912–1932* (1972); Roger Daniels, *The Bonus March* (1971); D. J.

Lisio, *The President and Protest: Hoover, Conspiracy, and the Bonus Riot* (1974).

DEPRESSION FOREIGN POLICY

R. H. Ferrell, *American Diplomacy in the Great Depression* (1957); E. E. Morison, *Turmoil and Tradition: Henry L. Stimson* (1960); R. N. Current, *Secretary Stimson* (1954); R. H. Ferrell, *Frank B. Kellogg—Henry L. Stimson* (1963); Armin Rappaport, *Stimson and Japan, 1931-33* (1963); Sara Smith, *The Manchurian Crisis, 1931-1932* (1948); Alexander De Conde, *Hoover's Latin American Policy* (1951); R. G. O'Connor, *Perilous Equilibrium: United States and the London Naval Conference of 1930* (1962); D. G. Munro, *United States and the Caribbean Republics, 1921-1933* (1974).

1932 ELECTION AND INTERREGNUM

Frank Freidel, *Roosevelt: The Triumph* (1956); and *Roosevelt: Launching the New Deal* * (1973); Raymond Moley and E. A. Rosen, *The First New Deal* (1966); R. G. Tugwell, *The Brains Trust* (1968); Hoover, *Memoirs* (vol. 3, 1952).

thirteen

Experimenting with a New Deal

GENERAL

W. E. Leuchtenburg, *Franklin D. Roosevelt and the New Deal, 1932-1940* * (1963); A. M. Schlesinger, Jr., *Age of Roosevelt: Coming of the New Deal* * (1959) and *Age of Roosevelt: Politics of Upheaval* * (1960); J. M. Burns, *Roosevelt: The Lion and the Fox* * (1956); E. E. Robinson, *The Roosevelt Leadership* (1959).

SPECIALIZED WORKS

Frank Freidel, *Roosevelt: Launching the New Deal* * (1973); Raymond Moley and E. A. Rosen, *The First New Deal* (1966); Herbert Feis, *1933: Characters in Crisis* (1966); E. W. Hawley, *The New Deal and the Problem of Monopoly* * (1966); Sidney Fine, *The Automobile Under the Blue Eagle* (1963); V. L. Perkins, *Crisis in Agriculture: The A.A.A. and the New Deal* * (1969); R. S. Kirkendall, *Social Scientists and Farm Politics in the Age of Roosevelt* (1966); D. E. Conrad, *The Forgotten Farmers: Sharecroppers in the New Deal* (1965); J. L. Shover, *Cornbelt Rebellion: Farmers' Holiday Association* (1965); J. M. Blum, *From the Morgenthau Diaries, 1928-1938* (1959); R. F. de Bedts, *The New Deal's SEC* (1964); Michael E. Parrish, *Securities Regulation and the New Deal* (1970); T. K. McCraw, *TVA and the Power Fight, 1933-1939* * (1971); S. F. Charles, *Minister of Relief: Harry Hopkins* (1963); J. A. Salmond, *The Civilian Conservation Corps* (1967); P. J. Funigiello, *Toward a National Power Policy: The New Deal and the Electric Utility Industry, 1933-1941* (1973).

SOME NEW DEALERS

Tamara Hareven, *Eleanor Roosevelt* (1968); J. J. Huthmacher, *Senator Robert Wagner and the Rise of Urban Liberalism* * (1968); O. L. Graham, *An Encore for Reform* * (1967); Frances Perkins, *The Roosevelt I Knew* * (1946); Raymond Moley, *After Seven Years* (1939); Bernard Sternsher, *Tugwell and the New Deal* (1964); F. L. Israel, *Nevada's Key Pittman* (1963); W. D. Rowley, *M. L. Wilson and the Campaign for the Domestic Allotment* (1970); T. E. Vadney, *The Wayward Liberal: Donald Richberg* (1970).

fourteen
The New Deal Shifts Toward Reform
PRESSURES FROM THE LEFT

T. H. Williams, *Huey Long* * (1969); D. H. Bennett, *Demagogues in the Depression* (1969); E. C. Blackorby, *Prairie Rebel: William Lemke* (1963); D. R. McCoy, *Angry Voices: Left of Center Politics in the New Deal Era* (1958); C. J. Tull, *Father Coughlin and the New Deal* (1965); Sheldon Marcus, *Father Coughlin* (1973); Abraham Holzman, *The Townsend Movement* (1963); F. A. Warren, *Liberals and Communism* (1966); Irving Howe and Lewis Coser, *The American Communist Party* * (1957); Earl Latham, *The Communist Controversy in Washington* (1966).

PRESSURES FROM THE RIGHT

D. R. McCoy, *Landon of Kansas* (1966); George Wolfskill, *Revolt of the Conservatives* (1962) [on Liberty League]; J. T. Patterson, *Congressional Conservatism and the New Deal* * (1967); Walter Goodman, *The Committee: House Committee on Un-American Activities* (1968).

REFORM PROGRAMS

Roy Lubove, *Struggle for Social Security, 1900–1935* (1968); E. E. Witte, *The Development of the Social Security Act* * (1962); A. J. Altmeyer, *The Formative Years of Social Security* (1966); J. L. Arnold, *The New Deal in the Suburbs: Greenbelt Town Program, 1935–1954* (1971); P. K. Conkin, *Tomorrow a New World: New Deal Community Program* (1959); D. S. Hirshfield, *The Lost Reform: The Campaign for Compulsory Health Insurance, 1932–1943* (1970); B. D. Karl, *Executive Reorganization and Reform in the New Deal, 1900–1939;* Richard Polenberg, *Reorganizing Roosevelt's Government* (1966); Sidney Baldwin, *Poverty and Politics: Farm Security Administration* (1968); D. H. Grubbs, *Cry from the Cotton: Southern Tenant Farmers' Union and the New Deal* (1971); T. A. Krueger, *And Promises to Keep: Southern Conference for Human Welfare, 1938–1948* (1968).

THE UNIONS

Irving Bernstein, *Turbulent Years: A History of the American Worker, 1933–1941* * (1970); Milton Derber et al., *Labor Under the New Deal* (1957); J. S. Auerbach, *Labor and Liberty: The La Follette Committee and the New Deal* (1966).

fifteen
The Limits of Reform
POLITICS

D. R. McCoy, *Landon of Kansas* (1966); George Wolfskill and J. A. Hudson, *All but the People: Roosevelt and His Critics, 1933–1939* (1969); J. T. Patterson, *The New Deal and the States* (1969) and *Congressional Conservatism* * (1967); Frank Freidel, *FDR and the South* * (1965); G. Q. Flynn, *American Catholics and the Roosevelt Presidency, 1932–1936* (1968); D. J. O'Brien, *American Catholics and Social Reform: The New Deal Years* (1968); G. B. Tindall, *Emergence of the New South* (1968); B. M. Stave, *The New Deal and the Last Hurrah: Pittsburgh Machine Politics* (1970).

THE SUPREME COURT

P. L. Murphy, *The Constitution in Crisis Times, 1918–1969* * (1972); A. T. Mason, *The Supeme Court from Taft to Warren* (1969 ed.); C. H. Pritchett, *The Roosevelt Court* (1948); Samuel Hendel, *Charles Evans Hughes and* *the Supreme Court* (1951); C. A. Leonard, *A Search for Judicial Philosophy: Mr. Justice Roberts and the Constitutional Revolution of 1937* (1971); A. T. Mason, *Harlan Fiske Stone* (1956); J. W. Howard, *Mr. Justice Murphy* (1968); H. S. Thomas, *Felix Frankfurter* (1960).

ASPECTS OF SOCIETY

F. L. Allen, *Since Yesterday* (1940); Wecter, *Age of the Great Depression* (1948); L. V. Armstrong, *We Too are the People* (1938); Dorothea Lange and P. S. Taylor, *An American Exodus* * (1969 ed.); R. S. and H. M. Lynd, *Middletown in Transition* * (1935).

BLACKS

Bernard Sternsher, ed., *The Negro in Depression and War* * (1969); Raymond Wolters, *Negroes and the Great Depression: The Problem of Economic Recovery* (1970); R. J. Bunche, *Political Status of the Negro in the Age of FDR* (1973); D. T. Carter, *Scottsboro* (1969); Gunnar Myrdal, *An American Dilemma* (2 vols., 1944).

IDEAS AND THE ARTS

R. H. Pells, *Radical Visions and American Dreams: Culture and Social Thought in the Depression Years* (1973); R. A. Lawson, *The Failure of Independent Liberalism, 1930–1941* (1971); J. D. Mathews, *The Federal Theatre, 1935–1939* * (1967); Jerre Mangione, *The Dream and the Deal: The Federal Writers Project* (1972); Maxwell Geismar, *Writers in Crisis* * (1947); Daniel Aaron, *Writers on the Left* * (1961); Edmund Wilson, *The American Earthquake* * (1958); R. D. McKinzie, *The New Deal for Artists* (1973); W. F. McDonald, *Federal Relief Administration and the Arts* (1969); Barbara Rose, *American Art Since 1900* * (1967); F. J. Hurley, *Portrait of a Decade: Roy Stryker and the Development of Documentary Photography in the Thirties* (1972); James Agee, *Let Us Now Praise Famous Men* * (1941).

sixteen
America Faces the World Crisis

BIOGRAPHICAL STUDIES

E. E. Morison, *Turmoil and Tradition: A Study of the Life and Times of Henry L. Stimson* (1960); R. N. Current, *Secretary Stimson: A Study of Statecraft* (1954); R. E. Sherwood, *Roosevelt and Hopkins* * (1948); J. W. Pratt, *Cordell Hull, 1933–44* (1964); W. S. Cole, *Senator Gerald P. Nye and American Foreign Relations* (1962); E. D. Cronon, *Josephus Daniels in Mexico* * (1960).

DEPRESSION DIPLOMACY

L. C. Gardner, *Economic Aspects of New Deal Diplomacy* (1964); Willard Range, *Franklin D. Roosevelt's World Order* (1959); J. P. Diggins, *Mussolini and Fascism: The View from America* (1972); Beatrice Farnsworth, *William C. Bullitt and the Soviet Union* (1967); David Green, *The Containment of Latin America: Myths and Realities of the Good Neighbor Policy* (1971); E. O. Guerrant, *Roosevelt's Good Neighbor Policy* (1950); Bryce Wood, *The Making of the Good Neighbor Policy* * (1961); A. W. Griswold, *The Far Eastern Policy of the United States* (1938); Dorothy Borg, *The United States and the Far Eastern Crisis of 1933–1938* (1964); R. P. Browder, *The Origins of Soviet-American Diplomacy* (1953); W. A. Williams, *American-Russian Relations, 1781–1947* (1952); R. P. Traina, *American Diplomacy and the Spanish Civil War* (1968); A. Guttmann, *The Wound in the Heart: America and the Spanish Civil War* (1962).

INTERVENTIONISTS VERSUS ISOLATIONISTS

Alexander De Conde, ed., *Isolation and Security: Ideas and Interests in Twentieth-Century American Foreign Policy* (1957); R. A. Divine, *The Illusion of Neutrality* (1962); M. L. Chadwin, *The Hawks of World War II* (1968); J. K. Nelson, *The Peace Prophets: American Pacifist Thought, 1919–1941* (1967); Manfred Jonas, *Isolationism in America, 1935–1941* * (1966); W. S. Cole, *America First* (1953); Walter Johnson, *Battle Against Isolation* (1944); Warren Moscow, *Roosevelt and Wilkie* (1968); B. F. Donahoe, *Private Plans and Public Dangers: F.D.R.'s Third Nomination* (1965); H. S. Parmet and M. B. Hecht, *Never Again: A President Runs for a Third Term* (1968); W. S. Cole, *Senator Gerald P. Nye and American Foreign Relations* (1962) and *Lindbergh and the Battle Against American Intervention in World War II* (1974); J. E. Wiltz, *In Search of Peace* (1963) [Nye Committee]; R. A. Divine, *Foreign Policy and U.S. Presidential Elections, 1940–1960* * (2 vols., 1974); L. V. Bell, *In Hitler's Shadow: American Nazism* (1973); S. A. Diamond, *Nazi Movement in the United States, 1924–1941* (1974).

REFUGEE PROBLEM

D. S. Wyman, *Paper Walls: America and the Refugee Crisis, 1938–1941* (1969); H. L. Feingold, *The Politics of Rescue: Roosevelt Administration and the Holocaust, 1938–1945* (1970).

STEPS TOWARD WAR

W. L. Langer and S. E. Gleason, *The Challenge to Isolation, 1937–1940* (1952) and *The Undeclared War, 1940–1941* (1953); C. A. Beard, *American Foreign Policy in the Making, 1932–1940* (1946) and *President Roosevelt and the Coming of the War, 1941* (1948); Basil Rauch, *Roosevelt from Munich to Pearl Harbor* (1950); D. F. Drummond, *The Passing of American Neutrality* (1955); R. A. Divine, *The Reluctant Belligerent: American Entry into World War II* * (1965); A. A. Offner, *American Appeasement: U. S. Foreign Policy and Germany, 1933–1938* (1969); Robert Dallek, *Democrat and Diplomat: William E. Dodd* (1968); P. A. Varg, *The Closing of the Door: Sino-American Relations, 1936–1946* (1973); S. E. Pelz, *Race to Pearl Harbor: Failure of the Second London Naval Conference and the Onset of World War II* (1974); Herbert Feis, *The Road to Pearl Harbor* * (1950); Roberta Wohlsetter, *Pearl Harbor: Warning and Decision* (1962); R. J. C. Butow, *Tojo and the Coming of the War* (1961); P. W. Schroeder, *The Axis Alliance and Japanese-American Relations, 1941* (1958); W. F. Kimball, *The Most Unsordid Act: Lend-Lease, 1939–1941* (1969).

seventeen

   Outproducing the Axis

GENERAL

Richard Polenberg, *War and Society: The United States, 1941–1945* (1972); and ed., *America at War: Home Front, 1941–1945* * (1968); Scott Hart, *Washington at War, 1941–1945* (1970).

WAR PRODUCTION

Bureau of Budget, *The United States at War* (1946); D. M. Nelson, *Arsenal of Democracy* (1946); Bruce Catton, *War Lords of Washington* (1946); Eliot Janeway, *The Struggle for Survival* (1951); H. M. Somers, *Presidential Agency: OWMR* (1950); L. R. Groves, *Now It Can Be Told* (1962) [on development of the A-bomb]; J. P. Baxter III, *Scientists Against Time* (1946);

W. W. Wilcox, *The Farmer in the Second World War* (1947); W. A. Nie-
lander, *Wartime Food Rationing in the United States* (1947).

WARTIME LIFE

Jack Goodman, ed., *While You Were Gone: A Report on Wartime Life in
the United States* (1946); W. F. Ogburn, ed., *American Society in Wartime*
(1943); R. Polenberg, *War and Society: The United States, 1941–1945* (1972);
Reuben Hill, *Families Under Stress* (1949); E. S. Corwin, *Total War and the
Constitution* (1947); Morton Grodzins, *Americans Betrayed: Politics and the
Japanese Evacuation* (1949); R. Daniels, *Concentration Camps, USA: Japanese
Americans and World War II* (1971); D. S. Myer, *Uprooted Americans: The
Japanese Americans and the War Relocation Authority* (1971); Audrie Girdner
and Anne Loftis, *The Great Betrayal: Evacuation of Japanese-Americans*
(1969); Louis Ruchames, *Race, Jobs, and Politics: FEPC* (1953); M. Q.
Sibley and P. E. Jacob, *Conscription of Conscience: The Conscientious
Objector, 1940–1947* (1952).

eighteen
Fighting a Global War
GENERAL

J. M. Burns, *Roosevelt: The Soldier of Freedom* * (1970); Robert Divine,
Roosevelt and World War II (1969); S. E. Morison, *Strategy and Compromise* * (1958).

MILITARY OPERATIONS

A. R. Buchanan, *The United States and World War II* * (2 vols., 1962);
Winston S. Churchill, *Second World War* (6 vols., 1948–1953); Fletcher
Pratt, *War for the World* (1950) [a brief account]; K. R. Greenfield, *American Strategy in World War II* (1963); M. S. Watson, *Chief of Staff: Prewar
Plans and Preparations* (1950); R. S. Cline, *Washington Command Post*
(1951); H. L. Stimson and McGeorge Bundy, *On Active Service in Peace and
War* (1948); Forest Pogue, *George C. Marshall* (3 vols., 1963); S. E. Am-
brose, *The Supreme Commander: Dwight D. Eisenhower* (1970); Eisen-
hower, *Crusade in Europe* * (1948); D. C. James, *The Years of MacArthur*
(2 vols., 1970); H. H. Arnold, *Global Mission* (1949); O. N. Bradley, *A
Soldier's Story* * (1951); S. E. Morison, *The Two Ocean War: A Short
History of the United States Navy in the Second World War* (1963); E. J.
King and W. M. Whitehill, *Fleet Admiral King* (1952); B. W. Tuchman,
Stilwell and the American Experience in China, 1911–1945 (1971).

WARTIME DIPLOMACY

J. L. Snell, *Illusion and Necessity: The Diplomacy of Global War, 1939–1945*
(1967); Gaddis Smith, *American Diplomacy During the Second World War,
1941–1945* (1965); R. G. O'Connor, *Diplomacy for Victory: FDR and Unconditional Surrender* (1971); Anne Armstrong, *Unconditional Surrender*
(1961); Robert Beitzell, *The Uneasy Alliance: America, Britain, and Russia,
1941–1943* (1972); R. D. Buhite, *Patrick J. Hurley and American Foreign
Policy* (1973); Herbert Feis, *Churchill, Roosevelt, Stalin* * (1957); W. S.
Schoenberger, *Decision of Destiny* (1969) [on use of atom bomb].

nineteen
Victory Without Peace
WARTIME CONFERENCES

Herbert Feis, *Churchill, Roosevelt, Stalin* * (1957), and *Between War and*

Peace: The Potsdam Conference * (1960), and *Contest Over Japan* (1967); Diane Shaver Clemens, *Yalta* (1970); J. L. Snell, ed., *The Meaning of Yalta* (1956); A. G. Theohairs, *The Yalta Myths: An Issue in U. S. Politics, 1945–1955* (1970); W. L. Neumann, *After Victory: Churchill, Roosevelt, Stalin and the Making of Peace* (1969).

ORIGINS OF COLD WAR

J. L. Gaddis, *The United States and the Origins of the Cold War, 1941–1947* (1972); G. C. Herring, Jr., *Aid to Russia, 1941–1946: Strategy, Diplomacy, the Origins of the Cold War* (1973).

THE UNITED NATIONS

R. A. Divine, *Second Chance: The Triumph of Internationalism in America During World War II* (1967); R. B. Russell, *A History of the United Nations Charter: The Role of the United States, 1940–1945* (1958).

twenty
The Menace of Cold War
THE COLD WAR

L. A. Rose, *After Yalta: America and the Origins of Cold War* (1973); J. L. Gaddis, *The United States and the Origins of the Cold War, 1941–1947* (1973); Herbert Feis, *From Trust to Terror: Onset of the Cold War, 1945–1950* (1970); D. F. Fleming, *Cold War and Its Origins, 1917–1960* (2 vols., 1961); N. A. Graebner, *Cold War Diplomacy, 1945–1960* * (1962); M. F. Herz, *Beginnings of the Cold War* (1966); G. F. Kennan, *Russia, the Atom, and the West* (1958); Walter LeFeber, *America, Russia, and the Cold War, 1945–1966* (1967); Joyce and Gabriel Kolko, *The Limits of Power: The World and United States Foreign Policy, 1945–1954* * (1972); T. G. Paterson, *Soviet-American Confrontation: Postwar Reconstruction and the Origins of the Cold War* (1973) and ed., *Cold War Critics: Alternatives to American Foreign Policy in the Truman Years* (1971); J. C. Campbell, *American Policy Toward Communist Eastern Europe* (1965); L. H. Miller and R. W. Pruessen, eds., *Reflections on the Cold War: A Quarter Century of American Foreign Policy* (1973); E. R. May, *"Lessons" of the Past: Use and Misuse of History in American Foreign Policy* (1973).

THE TRUMAN ADMINISTRATION

R. F. Haynes, *The Awesome Power: Truman as Commander in Chief* (1973); R. M. Freeland, *The Truman Doctrine and the Origins of McCarthyism* (1972); W. H. McNeill, *Greece: American Aid in Action, 1947–1956* (1957); Athan Theoharis, *Seeds of Repression: Truman and the Origins of McCarthyism* (1971); Hadley Arkes, *Bureaucracy, the Marshall Plan and National Interest* (1973); Robert Griffith and Athan Theoharis, eds., *The Specter: Original Essays on the Cold War and the Origins of McCarthyism* (1974); R. H. Ferrell, *George C. Marshall* (1966); Gaddis Smith, *Dean Acheson* (1972).

GERMANY

John Gimbel, *American Occupation of Germany, 1945–1949* (1968); Bruce Kuklick, *American Policy and the Division of Germany: Clash with Russia over Reparations* (1972); Walter Rundell, Jr., *Black Market Money* (1964); H. L. Coles and A. K. Weinberg, *Civil Affairs: Soldiers Become Governors* (1964); Eugene Davidson, *Death and Life of Germany: American Occupation* (1959) and *Trial of the Germans* (1966); W. J. Bosch, *Judgement on Nuremburg: American Attitudes* (1970); Manuel Gottlieb, *German Peace Settlement and the Berlin Crisis* (1960); J. E. Smith, *Defense of Berlin* (1963).

EAST ASIA

Akira Iriye, *The Cold War in Asia* (1974); E. O. Reischauer, *The United States and Japan* * (3rd ed., 1965); Herbert Feis, *Contest Over Japan* (1967); R. A. Fearey, *Occupation of Japan* (1950); B. C. Cohen, *Political Process and Foreign Policy: Japanese Peace Settlement* (1957); R. A. Smith, *Philippine Freedom, 1946–1958* (1958); J. K. Fairbank, *The United States and China* * (3rd ed., 1971); Herbert Feis, *China Tangle* (1953); Tang Tsou, *America's Failure in China, 1941–1950* (2 vols., 1963–1967); Akira Iriye, *Across the Pacific: American-East Asian Relations* (1967); E. R. May and J. C. Thomson, eds., *American-East Asian Relations: A Survey* (1972).

KOREAN WAR

Carl Berger, *The Korean Knot* (1957); David Rees, *Korea: The Limited War* (1957); G. D. Paige, *The Korean Decision, June 24–30, 1950* * (1968); Robert Leckie, *Conflict: The History of the Korean War* * (1962); J. W. Spanier, *The Truman-MacArthur Controversy and the Korean War* * (1959); R. J. Caridi, *The Korean War and American Politics: The Republican Party as a Case Study* (1969).

NUCLEAR POWER AND MILITARY POLICY

H. A. Kissinger, *Nuclear Weapons and Foreign Policy* (1957); H. L. Nieburg, *Nuclear Secrecy and Foreign Policy* (1964); R. G. Hewlett and Francis Duncan, *A History of the United States Atomic Energy Commission* (vols. 1–2, 1962–1969); A. A. Rogow, *James Forrestal* (1963); Kissinger, *Troubled Partnership: Atlantic Alliance* (1965); R. E. Osgood, *NATO* (1962); C. G. Lasby, *Project Paperclip: German Scientists and the Cold War* (1971).

twenty-one
The Truman Era

TRUMAN ADMINISTRATION

A. L. Hamby, *Beyond the New Deal: Truman and American Liberalism* (1973); Bert Cochran, *Truman and the Crisis Presidency* (1973); Cabell Phillips, *The Truman Presidency* * (1966); L. W. Koenig, ed., *The Truman Administration* (1956); B. J. Bernstein and A. J. Matusow, *The Truman Administration: A Documentary History* * (1966); M. S. Hartmann, *Truman and the Eightieth Congress* (1971); W. C. Berman, *The Politics of Civil Rights in the Truman Administration* (1970); D. R. McCoy and R. T. Ruetten, *Quest and Response: Minority Rights and the Truman Administration* (1973); Elmo Richardson, *Dams, Parks and Politics: Resource Development and Preservation in the Truman-Eisenhower Era* (1973); A. J. Matusow, *Farm Policies and Politics in the Truman Years* * (1967); R. O. Davies, *Housing Reform During the Truman Administration* (1966); S. K. Bailey, *Congress Makes a Law: Employment Act of 1946* * (1950); A. E. Holmans, *United States Fiscal Policy, 1945–1959: Its Contribution to Economic Stability* (1961); R. A. Lee, *Truman and Taft-Hartley* (1967).

POLITICS AND THE ELECTION OF 1948

R. A. Garson, *The Democratic Party and the Politics of Sectionalism, 1941–1948* (1974); Allen Yarnell, *Democrats and Progressives: The 1948 Presidential Election as a Test of Postwar Liberalism* (1974); N. D. Markowitz, *The Rise and Fall of the People's Century: Wallace and American Liberalism, 1941–1948* (1973); K. M. Schmidt, *Wallace: Quixotic Crusade* (1960); Irwin Ross, *The Lonliest Campaign: Truman Victory of 1948* (1968); Samuel

Lubell, *Future of American Politics* * (1952); J. T. Patterson, *Mr. Republican: Robert A. Taft* (1972).

THE LOYALTY ISSUE

Cedric Belfrage, *The American Inquisition, 1945–1960* (1973); Stefan Kanfer, *A Journal of the Plague Years* (1973); Richard Hofstadter, *Anti-Intellectualism in American Life* * (1963); Robert Griffith, *The Politics of Fear: Joseph R. McCarthy and the Senate* (1970); J. W. Caughey, *In Clear and Present Danger* (1958); A. D. Harper, *Politics of Loyalty: White House and the Communist Issue, 1946–1952* (1969); W. A. Jowitt, *Strange Case of Alger Hiss* (1953); R. M. Nixon, *Six Crises* * (1962); R. M. Freeland, *Truman Doctrine and Origins of McCarthyism* (1972); P. M. Stern, *The Oppenheimer Case* (1969); J. R. Starobin, *American Communism in Crisis, 1943–1957* (1972).

ELECTION OF 1952

P. T. David, Malcolm Moos, and R. M. Goldman, eds., *Presidential Nominating Politics in 1952* (5 vols., 1954); S. G. Brown, *Conscience in Politics: Stevenson* (1961); Samuel Lubell, *Revolt of the Moderates* (1956).

twenty-two
A Nuclear Balance of Terror

D. D. Eisenhower, *The White House Years* * (2 vols., 1963–1965); H. S. Parmet, *Eisenhower and the American Crusade* (1972); R. L. Branyan and L. H. Larsen, *Eisenhower Administration, 1953–1961: A Documentary History* (2 vols., 1972); Peter Lyon, *Eisenhower: Portrait of a Hero* (1974); M. A. Guhin, *John Foster Dulles* (1972); R. L. Gerson, *John Foster Dulles* (1967); Townsend Hoopes, *The Devil and John Foster Dulles* (1973); G. B. Noble, *Christian Herter* (1970); J. M. Schick, *The Berlin Crisis, 1958–1962* (1971); C. M. Green and Milton Lomask, *Vanguard: A History* * (1970); D. A. Baldwin, *Economic Development and American Foreign Policy, 1943–62* (1966); Mira Wilkins, *The Maturing of Multinational Enterprise: American Business Abroad from 1914 to 1970* (1974); M. S. Eisenhower, *The Wine is Bitter: United States and Latin America* (1963); David Wise and Thomas Ross, *The U-2 Affair* (1962); Melvin Gurtov, *The First Vietnam Crisis: Chinese Communist Strategy and United States Involvement, 1953–1954* (1967); Nadav Safran, *The United States and Israel* (1963); J. H. Kalicki, *The Pattern of Sino-American Crises: Political-Military Interactions in the 1950's* (1975).

twenty-three
Eisenhower Republicanism

In addition to the books on Eisenhower listed at the end of Chapter Twenty-two, see Sherman Adams, *First Hand Report* * (1961); E. T. Benson, *Crossfire* (1962); Richard Nixon, *Six Crises* * (1962); Aaron Wildavsky, *Dixon-Yates: A Study in Power Politics* (1962); Elmo Richardson, *Dams, Parks and Politics* (1973); J. A. Ferejohn, *Pork Barrel Politics: Rivers and Harbors Legislation, 1947–1968* (1974).

POLITICS AND ELECTION OF 1956

F. M. Shattuck, *The 1956 Presidential Campaign* (1960); J. B. Gorman, *Kefauver* (1971); G. B. Tindall, *The Disruption of the Solid South* (1972).

THE WARREN SUPREME COURT

P. L. Murphy, *The Constitution in Crisis Times, 1918–1969* (1972); G. T. Mitau, *Decade of Decision: The Supreme Court and the Constitutional Revolution, 1954–1964* (1967); A. M. Bickel, *Politics and the Warren Court* (1965); Archibald Cox, *The Warren Court: Constitutional Decision as an Instrument of Reform* (1968).

DESEGREGATION BEGINS

Anthony Lewis, *Portrait of a Decade: The Second American Revolution* * (1964); J. W. Anderson, *Eisenhower, Brownell, and the Congress: The Tangled Origins of the Civil Rights Bill of 1956–1957* (1964); D. M. Berman, *A Bill Becomes a Law: The Civil Rights Act of 1960* (1962); A. P. Blaustein and C. C. Ferguson, *Desegregation and the Law* * (1962); J. W. Peltason, *Fifty-eight Lonely Men: Southern Federal Judges and School Desegregation* (1961); N. R. McMillen, *The Citizens' Council: Organized Resistance to the Second Reconstruction, 1954–64* (1971); August Meier and Elliott Rudwick, *CORE: A Study in the Civil Rights Movement, 1942–1968* (1973).

twenty-four
A New Thrust Toward Reform

KENNEDY ADMINISTRATION

A. M. Schlesinger, Jr., *A Thousand Days: John F. Kennedy in the White House* * (1965); T. C. Sorensen, *Kennedy* * (1965); A. D. Donald, ed., *John F. Kennedy and the New Frontier* * (1966); T. H. White, *The Making of the President, 1960* * (1961); J. F. Heath, *Kennedy and the Business Community* (1969); V. S. Navasky, *Kennedy Justice* (1971); William Manchester, *Death of a President* * (1967).

JOHNSON ADMINISTRATION

Rowland Evans and Robert Novak, *Lyndon B. Johnson: The Exercise of Power* * (1966); Hugh Sidey, *A Very Personal Presidency* (1968); E. F. Goldman, *The Tragedy of Lyndon Johnson* * (1969); G. E. Reedy, *Twilight of the Presidency* (1970).

POLITICS AND ELECTION OF 1964

T. H. White, *The Making of the President, 1964* * (1965); Bernard Cosman and R. J. Huckshorn, *Republican Politics: The 1964 Campaign and Its Aftermath for the Party* (1968); J. H. Kessel, *The Goldwater Coalition: Republican Strategies in 1964* (1968); L. W. Huebner and T. E. Petri, eds., *The Ripon Papers, 1963–1968* (1969).

SUPREME COURT

R. G. McCloskey, *The Modern Supreme Court* (1972); Richard Claude, *The Supreme Court and the Electoral Process* (1970); R. C. Cortner, *The Apportionment Cases* (1970).

BLACK REVOLUTION

J. C. Harvey, *Black Civil Rights During the Johnson Administration* (1973); Benjamin Muse, *American Negro Revolution, 1963–1967* (1968); Stokely Carmichael and C. V. Hamilton, *Black Power: Politics of Liberation* (1967); R. C. Goldston, *Negro Revolution* (1968); Lee Rainwater and W. L. Yancey, *Moynihan Report and Politics of Controversy* (1967); A. I. Waskow, *From Race Riot to Sit-In, 1919 and 1960's* (1966); F. M. Wilhoit, *The Politics of Massive Resistance* (1973).

twenty-five
   The Quality of American Life
W. L. O'Neill, *Coming Apart: An Informal History of America in the 1960's* (1971).

POPULATION STUDIES

B. J. Wattenberg and R. M. Scammon, *This U.S.A.: An Unexpected Family Portrait . . . Drawn From the Census* (1965); Conrad and I. B. Taeuber, *The Changing Population of the United States* (1958); L. H. and A. T. Day, *Too Many Americans* (1965).

PROBLEMS OF THE CITIES

Charles Abrams, *The City Is the Frontier* * (1965); Martin Anderson, *The Federal Bulldozer: A Critical Analysis of Urban Renewal, 1949–1962* * (1965); Jane Jacobs, *The Economy of Cities* (1969); C. W. Condit, *Chicago, 1930–1970: Building, Planning, and Urban Technology* (1974); L. M. Friedman, *Government and Slum Housing: A Century of Frustration* (1968); S. B. Warner, *Planning for a Nation of Cities* * (1967); J. K. Hadden et al., *Metropolis in Crisis: Social and Political Perspectives* (1967); President's Commission on Law Enforcement and Administration of Justice, *The Challenge of Crime in a Free Society* (1967); Frank Graham, *Disaster by Default: Politics and Water Pollution* (1966).

TRANSPORTATION QUESTIONS

Wilfred Owen, *The Metropolitan Transportation Problem* * (rev. ed., 1966); J. R. Meyer et al., *The Urban Transportation Problem* (1966); Clairborne Pell, *Megalopolis Unbound: The Supercity and the Transportation of Tomorrow* (1966).

POVERTY

J. D. Donovan, *The Politics of Poverty* (1967); B. B. Seligman, *Permanent Poverty: An American Syndrome* (1968); Jeremy Larner and Irving Howe, eds., *Poverty: Views from the Left* (1969); D. R. Hunter, *The Slums: Challenge and Response* * (1968); D. P. Moynihan, *Maximum Feasible Misunderstanding: Community Action in the War on Poverty* (1969); H. M. Caudill, *Night Comes to the Cumberlands* (1963).

BLACKS

Talcott Parsons and K. B. Clark, eds., *The American Negro* * (1966); G. T. Marx, *Protest and Prejudice: A Study of Belief in the Black Community* (1968); M. L. King, *Where Do We Go From Here: Chaos or Community* * (1967); Alex Haley, ed., *The Autobiography of Malcolm X* * (1966); Julius Jacobson, ed., *The Negro and the American Labor Movement* * (1968); Herbert Hill, ed., *Anger and Beyond: The Negro Writer in the United States* (1966); Chandler Davidson, *Biracial Politics: Conflict and Coalition in the Metropolitan South* (1972).

INDIANS

E. S. Kahn, ed., *Our Brother's Keeper: The Indian in White America* * (1969); Stan Steiner, *The New Indians* * (1968); Vine Deloria, Jr., *Custer Died for Your Sins* * (1969); H. W. Hertzberg, *The Search for an Indian Identity* (1971); W. E. Washburn, *Red Man's Land/White Man's Law: A Study of the Past and Present Status of the American Indian* (1971); A. M. Josephy, ed., *Red Power* (1971).

SPANISH-SPEAKING MINORITIES

Wayne Moquin, ed., *A Documentary History of the Mexican-Americans* (1971); Stan Steiner, *La Raza* * (1970); M. S. Meier and F. Rivera, *The Chicanos: A*

History of Mexican Americans (1972); R. B. Craig, *The Bracero Program: Interest Groups and Foreign Policy* (1971); Julián Samora, *Los Mojados: The Wetback Story* (1971); Oscar Lewis, *La Vida: A Puerto Rican Family in the Culture of Poverty—San Juan and New York* * (1969).

WOMEN'S PLACE

W. H. Chafe, *The American Woman, 1920–1970* (1972); Judith Hole and Ellen Levine, eds., *Rebirth of Feminism* (1972); Elizabeth Janeway, *Man's World, Woman's Place: A Study in Social Mythology* (1971); Juliet Mitchell, *Women's Estate* (1972); Peggy Lamson, *Few are Chosen: American Women in Political Life Today* (1966); Katie Louchheim, *By the Political Sea* (1970); R. J. Lifton, ed., *The Woman in America* (1966); President's Commission on the Status of Women, *American Women* (1966).

twenty-six
Kennedy, Johnson, and Confrontation
In addition to books on Kennedy and Johnson already cited, see R. A. Divine, *Foreign Policy and U. S. Presidential Elections, 1940–1960* * (2 vols., 1974; R. J. Walton, *Cold War and Counterrevolution* * (1972); E. R. May, *"Lessons" of the Past* (1973); Seyom Brown, *The Faces of Power: Constancy and Change in United States Foreign Policy from Truman to Johnson* (1968); H. A. Kissinger, *American Foreign Policy* (1969); Gabriel Kolko, *The Roots of American Foreign Policy* (1969); Henry Brandon, *Retreat of American Power* (1973); Adam Yarmolinsky, *The Military Establishment: Its Impact on American Society* (1971); C. W. Pursell, Jr., *The Military Industrial Complex* * (1973); Melvin Gurtov, *The United States Against the Third World: Anti-nationalism and Intervention* (1974); Lloyd Jensen, *Return from the Nuclear Brink: National Interest and the Nuclear Nonproliferation Treaty* (1974); Stephen Weissman, *American Foreign Policy in the Congo, 1960–1964* (1974); Louise FitzSimons, *The Kennedy Doctrine* (1972); J. D. Donovan, *The Cold Warriors: A Policy-Making Elite* (1972); C. A. Murdock, *Defense Policy Formation: McNamara Era* (1974).

FOREIGN AID

M. K. O'Leary, *The Politics of American Foreign Aid* (1967); W. D. Rogers, *The Twilight Struggle: The Alliance for Progress and the Politics of Development in Latin America* (1967).

CUBA AND THE DOMINICAN REPUBLIC

H. B. Johnson, *The Bay of Pigs* (1964); G. T. Allison, *Essence of Decision: Explaining the Cuban Missile Crisis* (1971); Elie Abel, *The Missile Crisis* (1966); Abram Chayes, *The Cuban Missile Crisis: International Crises and the Role of Law* (1974); R. F. Kennedy, *Thirteen Days* (1969); Dan Kurzman, *Santo Domingo: Revolt of the Damned* (1966); J. B. Martin, *Overtaken by Events* (1966); Jerome Slater, *Intervention and Negotiation: The United States and the Dominican Revolution* (1970).

VIETNAM WAR

Alexander Kendrick, *The Wound Within: America in the Vietnam Years, 1945–1974* (1974); John Galloway, *The Gulf of Tonkin Resolution* (1970); H. F. Graff, *The Tuesday Cabinet: Deliberation and Decision on Peace and War under Johnson* (1970); Thomas Powers, *The War at Home: Vietnam and the American People, 1964–1968* (1973); David Halberstam, *The Best and the Brightest* * (1972); Neil Sheehan et al., *The Pentagon Papers* * (1971); Sandy Vogelsang, *The Long Dark Night of the Soul: The American*

Intellectual Left and the Vietnam War (1974); J. M. Moore, *Law and the Indo-China War* (1972); G. M. Kahin and J. W. Lewis, *The United States in Vietnam* (1967); Townsend Hoopes, *The Limits of Intervention . . . How the Johnson Policy of Escalation Was Reversed* (1969). For combat history, see U. S. Department of the Army, *Vietnam Studies* series.

LEFTWING MOVEMENTS

Irwin Unger, *The Movement: A History of the American New Left, 1959– 1972* (1974); Kirkpatrick Sale, *SDS* (1973).

ELECTION OF 1968

T. H. White, *The Making of the President, 1968* * (1969); Lewis Chester et al., *An American Melodrama* (1969); Marshall Frady, *Wallace* (1968); Ben Stavis, *We Were the Campaign: New Hampshire to Chicago for Mc-Carthy* (1969); William Boyarsky, *The Rise of Ronald Reagan* (1968); David Halberstam, *The Unfinished Odyssey of Robert Kennedy* (1969).

twenty-seven
Nixon Seeks a New Balance

In addition to books already cited, see R. E. Osgood et al., *America and the World* (vol. 2, *"Retreat from Empire? The First Nixon Administration"* 1973); A. M. Jones, Jr., ed., *U. S. Foreign Policy in a Changing World: The Nixon Administration, 1969–1973* (1973); Seyom Brown, *New Forces in World Politics* * (1974); W. R. Kintner and R. B. Foster, eds., *National Strategy in a Decade of Change: An Emerging U. S. Policy* (1973); Marvin and Bernard Kalb, *Kissinger* * (1974); W. R. Schilling et al., *American Arms and a Changing Europe* * (1973); J. A. Yager et al., *Energy and U. S. Foreign Policy* (1974); R. B. Mancke, *The Failure of U. S. Energy Policy* (1974); D. G. Johnson and J. A. Schnittker, eds., *U. S. Agriculture in a World Context* (1974); W. F. Monroe, *International Monetary Reconstruction: Problems and Issues* (1974); Roger Hilsman, *The Crouching Future: International Politics and U. S. Foreign Policy, A Forecast* (1975).

twenty-eight
The New Federalism

NIXON AND POLITICS

William Safire, *Before the Fall: An Inside View of the Pre-Watergate White House* (1975); Frank Mankiewicz, *Perfectly Clear: Nixon from Whittier to Watergate* (1973); Garry Wills, *Nixon Agonistes* (1970); Rowland Evans, Jr., and R. D. Novak, *Nixon in the White House: The Frustration of Power* (1971); R. J. Whalen, *Catch the Falling Flag* (1972); R. M. Scammon and B. J. Wattenberg, *The Real Majority* (1970); Samuel Lubell, *The Hidden Crisis in American Politics* * (1970); L. K. Howe, ed., *The White Majority* (1970); Walter DeVries and V. L. Tarrance, *The Ticket-Splitters* (1972); T. H. White, *The Making of the President, 1972* * (1973); R. S. Anson, *McGovern* (1972) [a campaign biography]; H. E. Alexander, *Money in Politics* (1972); L. Baritz, ed., *The American Left: Radical Political Thought in the Twentieth Century* (1972); J. P. Diggins, *The American Left in the Twientieth Century* * (1973); Robert Shogan, *A Question of Judgment: The Fortas Case and the Struggle for the Supreme Court* (1972).

ECONOMIC POLICIES

R. L. Miller, *The New Economics of Richard Nixon* (1972); Leonard Silk, *Nixonomics* (1972); F. F. Piven and R. A. Cloward, *Regulating the Poor:*

The Functions of Public Welfare (1971); D. P. Moynihan, *The Politics of a Guaranteed Income: The Nixon Administration and the Family Assistance Plan* (1973); Walter Hickel, *Who Owns America?* (1971); J. K. Galbraith, *The New Industrial State* * (1971); R. F. Buckthorn, *Nader, The People's Lawyer* (1972); J. C. Goulden, *Meany* (1972).

twenty-nine
America in the Bicentennial Years
SCIENCE AND TECHNOLOGY

D. K. Price, *The Scientific Estate* (1965); Gerald Holton, ed., *Science and Culture* * (1965); Herbert Simon, *The Shape of Automation* (1966); William Francios, *Automation: Industrialization Comes of Age* * (1964); H. H. Goldstine, *The Computer from Pascal to von Neumann* (1972).

TO THE MOON

Walter Sullivan, ed., *America's Race for the Moon* * (1962); Jay Holmes, *America on the Moon* (1962); Hugh Odishaw, ed., *The Challenges of Space* (1962); L. S. Swenson et al., *This New Ocean: A History of Project Mercury* (1966); R. L. Rosholt, *An Administrative History of NASA, 1958–1963* (1966).

AMERICAN SOCIETY

F. E. Armbruster and Doris Yokelson, *The Forgotten Americans: A Survey of the Values, Beliefs, and Concerns of the Majority* (1972); D. T. Bazelon, *Power in America* (1967); Alvin Toffler, *Future Shock* * (1970).

CULTURE

Ronald Berman, *America in the Sixties: An Intellectual History* (1968); Bernard Rosenberg and D. M. White, eds., *Mass Culture* (1957); K. S. Lynn, ed., *The Professions in America* * (1965); John Burchard and Albert Bush-Brown, *The Architecture of America* * (1961); W. J. Baumol and W. G. Bowen, *Performing Arts: The Economic Dilemma* (1966); Richard Kostelanetz, ed., *The New American Arts* * (1965); and *On Contemporary American Literature* * (1964); Stephen Stepanchev, *American Poetry Since 1945* * (1965); Charles Rembar, *The End of Obscenity* * (1968).

YOUTH AND EDUCATION

E. H. Erikson, *Identity: Youth and Crisis* (1968); Kenneth Keniston, *The Uncommitted: Alienated Youth in American Society* (1965); Christopher Jencks and David Riesman, *The Academic Revolution* (1968); S. M. Lipset and S. S. Wolin, eds., *The Berkeley Student Revolt: Facts and Interpretations* * (1965); J. B. Conant, *The American High School Today* * (1959) and *Slums and Suburbs* (1964).

thirty
Watergate—and the Ford Administration
WATERGATE

T. H. White, *Breach of Faith: The Fall of Richard Nixon* (1975); Frank Mankiewicz, *U. S. v. Richard M. Nixon: The Final Crisis* (1975); Carl Bernstein and Bob Woodward, *All the President's Men* * (1974); Dan Rather and G. P. Gates, *The Palace Guard* * (1974).

PRESIDENT FORD

Gerald Ter Horst, *Gerald Ford* (1975).

Index

Abortion, 427

Accidents, industrial: compensation for, 12, 28, 41, 55, 67; rate of, 11. *See also* Industrial safety

Acheson, Dean, 293, 310

Adams, Henry, 4

Adams, Sherman, 333, 340

Adamson Act, 67, 68

Addams, Jane, 23, 71

Aged, care for the, 343, 344

Agency for International Development, U.S. (AID), 373

Agnew,Spiro, 386, 391, 418, 435–6, 441

Agricultural Adjustment Act (1938), 198

Agricultural Adjustment Administration (AAA), 180, 193, 198

Agricultural Marketing Act (1929), 166

Agriculture: during Hoover's administration, 166; during 1920s, 149–50; during World War I, 105; extension work in education, 68; industrialization and, 4; mechanization of, 149, 182, 199; under F. D. Roosevelt, 180–2, 198–9; under J. F. Kennedy, 344

Air Commerce Act (1926), 147

Air Mail Act (1934), 188

Aircraft industry, during World War I, 106

Aircraft Production Board, U.S., 106

Alaska: boundary dispute, 74; coal lands in, 53

Aldrich, Nelson Wilmarth, 37, 52, 58, 63

Aldrich-Vreeland Act, 63

Algren, Nelson, 432

Allen, Hervey, 211

Allende, Salvador, 403

Alliance for Progress, 373

Allied Control Council, 282, 283

Amalgamated Clothing Workers, 196

Amendments, Constitutional: Fourteenth, 16, 41, 205, 337; Fifteenth, 16; Sixteenth, 62; Seventeenth, 30; Eighteenth, 130, 162; Nineteenth, 27, 130; Twentieth (Lame Duck), 173; Twenty-first, 168; Twenty-second, 338; Twenty-third, 349; Twenty-fourth, 349; Twenty-sixth, 416

America First Committee, 223

American Anti-Boycott Association, 65

American Bankers Association, 64, 189–90

American Bar Association, 408–9

American Broadcasting Company, 435

American Can Company, 333

American Economic Association, 166

American Expeditionary Force. *See* World War I

American Farm Bureau Federation, 68, 149, 150, 180, 243

American Federation of Labor, 145, 196–7; anti-trust action and, 65; boycott of Buck's Stove and Range Co., 41; growth, 39; merger with CIO, 333; opposes immigration, 12; Socialists in, 40

American Independent Party, 387. *See also* Election, presidential

American Indian Movement (AIM), 410

American Indians, 3, 14, 194, 365–6; civil rights of, 194, 365–6, 410–11. *See also* Minorities

American Legion, 132

American Liberty League, 190

American Medical Association, 212, 213, 307

American Plan, 41, 148

American Telephone & Telegraph Company, 66

Americans for Democratic Action (ADA), 305

Anderson, Clinton, 300

Anderson, Sherwood, 155

Anti-inflation Act (1942), 243

Anti-lynching legislation, 16, 194

Anti-poverty measures, 346, 353

Anti-Saloon League, 130

Anti-Semitism, 190

Anti-trust action, F. D. Roosevelt and, 200, 201; Justice, Dept. of and, 66, 201; organized labor and, 64–5; T. Roosevelt and, 38–9, 56; Taft and, 39; Wilson and, 64–6. *See also* Business, big

Anti-trust legislation. *See* Clayton Act; Sherman Anti-Trust Act

ANZUS Pact, 292

Architecture and architects, 90–1, 93, 156

Area Redevelopment Act (1962), 344

Arms control, 137–8, 171, 216, 285, 324; mutual balanced forced reductions

Democratic National Committee, 193, 437
Democratic Party, 19; progressivism and, 19–20, 57–60, 61, 62. *See also* Election, presidential
Denmark: World War II and, 220
Dennis v. United States, 348
Depew, Chauncey, 37, 38
Depression: of the 1890s, 19; of 1914, 66; of 1929, 163–5, 175–88; of 1974–75, 446. *See also* Economy; Recession
Dewey, John, 83–4, 159; progressive education and, 84–5
Dewey, Thomas E., 279, 280, 304
Dewson, Mary, 193
Diaz, Porfirio, 79
Disarmament. *See* Arms control
Disarmament conferences, 137, 138, 171, 216
Displaced Persons Act (1950), 307
Dixon-Yates syndicate, 334–5
Doheny, Edward L., 141, 145
Dolphin, U.S.S., 80
Dominican Republic: U.S. intervention in, 79, 138, 380–1
Dos Passos, John, 155
Dreiser, Theodore, 88–9, 155
Drug addiction, 428
Du Bois, William E. B., 31, 33
Dulles, John Foster, 292, 313, 314, 318, 320, 322, 324, 327, 330, 332, 383
Dumbarton Oaks conference, 277
Dunlop, John, 443
Dunne, Finley Peter, 38
Durkin, Martin P., 332

Eagleton, Thomas, 418
Eastman-Kodak Company, 8
Economic Cooperation Administration, U.S., (ECA), 287
Economic Opportunity Act, 366
Economic Opportunity, Office of, U.S. (OEO), 353, 412
Economic Stabilization Act (1970), 414
Economy: Arab oil embargo and the, 415; during World War I, 97–8, 103–7; *laissez-faire,* 47; pre-World War I, 19, 66; under Eisenhower, 333–6, 339–40; under Ford, 445, 446–7; under Johnson, 347–8; under Kennedy, 344–5; under Nixon, 413–15; under Truman, 300–3. *See also* Depression; Recession
Edison, Thomas Alva, 8
Education: agricultural extension, 68; of blacks, 337–8; federal aid to, 300, 304, 343, 344, 351–2; financial support for, 429–30; higher, 85, 430; in the 1920s,

152–3; in the 1930s, 212–14; medical, 86; pragmatism and progressive, 84–5; radio and television in, 435; vocational, 68, 212. *See also* Colleges and universities; Schools
Egypt: crisis of 1956, 322–4; Six-Day War (1967), 403–4; Yom Kippur War (1973), 404, 405
Ehrlichman, John, 407, 439, 440, 441, 444
E. I. DuPont de Nemours and Company, 8
Einstein, Albert, 86, 237
Eisenhower, Dwight D., 341, 342, 350, 351, 373; cabinet, 315, 332–3; charges of corruption in administration, 340; China and, 315–19; civil rights and, 337–8; commanding general, European Theater, 263; communist challenge in Indochina, 315–19; Cuba and, 374; desegregation issue, 337–8; economic policy, 333–6, 340; elected president, 310–11; election of 1948 and, 305; election of 1958 and, 339–40; as Far Eastern expert, 253; farewell address, 371, 372; foreign policy, 313–31; illnesses of, 339; Khrushchev's visit to U.S., 327; Korean War and, 313–14; Latin-American policy, 328–31; McCarthy and, 336; Middle East crisis, 322–4, 339; missile development, 324–6; NATO and, 290; nuclear test suspension, 325; re-elected president, 338–9; road-building program, 335; U-2 incident, 328; Vietnam and, 381, 383; welfare program, 335
Eisenhower Doctrine, 323
Election, presidential: of 1904, 42–3; of 1908, 49–51; of 1912, 54–8; of 1916, 101–2; of 1920, 134–6; of 1924, 144–6; of 1928, 161–3, 168; of 1932, 172–3; of 1936, 202–3; of 1940, 221–5; of 1944, 278–81; of 1948, 304–6; of 1952, 310–13; of 1956, 338–9; of 1960, 341–3; of 1964, 350–1; of 1968, 386–8; of 1972, 416–19
Election campaign reform, 445
Electric power, 6, 44, 185–6, 200
Electronic computers, 420
Elementary and Secondary Education Act (1965), 352
Eliot, Charles W., 41
Eliot, T. S., 155
Ellison, Ralph, 432
Ellsburg, Daniel J., 439
Emergency Banking Act (1933), 177, 178
Emergency Fleet Corporation, 109
Energy. *See* Power

ABOUT THE AUTHOR

Frank Freidel is Charles Warren Professor of History at Harvard University. He is writing a six-volume biography of Franklin D. Roosevelt, four volumes of which have been published. Among his other books are: *Our Country's Presidents*; *F.D.R. and the South*; and *American History: A Survey*, co-authored by Richard N. Current and T. Harry Williams. He is co-editor of the 1974 edition of the *Harvard Guide to American History*, and President of the Organization of American Historians. He is also a former president of the New England Historical Society.

A NOTE ON THE TYPE

This book was set on the Linotype in Electra, designed by W. A. Dwiggins. The Electra face is a simple and suitable for printing books by present-day processes. It is not based on any historical model, and hence does not echo any particular time or fashion.

Typography and binding design: Meryl Sussman Levavi